The HipHop Nation:
Willie Lynch's Newest Slave
Written by Philip A. Muhammad

Brought to you by

The People's Language Media Group

**For Information visit:
www.thepeopleslanguage.com**

The HipHop Nation:
Willie Lynch's Newest Slave

Written by Philip A. Muhammad

Copyright 2009, by TPL Media Group

Los Angeles, California 2009

All rights reserved. No part of this book may be reproduced or transmitted in any form by any means, electronic or mechanical, including photocopying, recording or any information storage or retrieval system without written permission from the author, except for the inclusion of brief quotations in a review.

Special rates apply to those who wish to purchase a copy of this book with intent to send it to a man or woman that is presently confined within the various state and federal correctional facilities with the United States and its surrounding territories. Those of you who desire to do so may contact us at: TPLMediaGroup@gmail.com or www.thepeopleslanguage.com

ISBN 978-0-578-03224-5

Contents

ACKNOWLEDGEMENTS	III
A SPECIAL RECOGNITION	IV
DISCLAIMER	V
DEDICATION	VII
NOTE	VIII
AUTHOR'S NOTE	XXIV
WILLIE LYNCH	1
LET'S MAKE A SLAVE	2
AMERICA'S NEW POP (ULAR) MUSIC	11
HIPHOP TAKES A BITE	26
THE TAKE OVER	29
CRUMBS FROM THE MASTER'S TABLE	31
THE PLANTATION	46
THE TENTACLES OF INFLUENCE	48
LET'S EXAMINE A FEW HISTORICAL FACTS	61
THE POLITICS OF EXPRESSION	67
THE SLAVE TRADER	70
EDGAR BRONFMAN: HIPHOP'S MOST POWERFUL SLAVE MASTER	73
THE PROFITS OF DIVISION	78
PRO BLACK – STILL A SLAVE	81
THE SLAVES TURN GANGSTER	88
HIPHOP STARTED IN THE WEST	90
DR. DRE AND ICE CUBE	104
REALITY MEANS NOTHING… IMAGE IS EVERYTHING!	108
WILL THE REAL GANGSTER PLEASE STAND UP!	114
DRE'S SLAVE MASTER	124
THE LEVIATHANS	129
THE TENTACLES OF INFLUENCE II	137
RUPERT MURDOCH—CORPORATE NEWS	141
THE SCRIBES	143
MISERY'S PROFIT	146

FROM IRON CHAINS TO GOLD CHAINS	150
CECIL JOHN RHODES—SOUTH AFRICAN DIAMOND THIEF	153
DE BEERS	155
THE OPPENHEIMERS	157
THE DECEPTION BACK TO THE FED	163
THE REAL STORY OF THE MONEY-CONTROL OVER AMERICA	164
THE AMERICAN PIMP MEETS THE HIPHOP WHORE	176
THE REAL SMUT PEDDLERS	179
RAPPERS PUSH POISON!	185
WORDS OF AN UNCLE TOM!	195
MICHAEL AND TOMMY	221
AIPAC—AMERICAN ISRAEL PUBLIC AFFAIRS COMMITTEE	229
SO-CALLED JEWS OF THE BUSH ADMINISTRATION	234
CHASING DOLLARS	245
ARE YOU A SLAVE?	248
A NATION OF SLAVES	255
CLOSING WORDS!	258
SPECIAL MESSAGE TO THE SO-CALLED CONSCIOUS RAPPERS	261
REFERENCES	264
AN INTERVIEW WITH PHILIP A. MUHAMMAD	266

ACKNOWLEDGEMENTS

My world is filled with those that I wish to acknowledge and thank for their contribution to the person that I presently am; regardless if it is a writer, son, brother, father or what not, I appreciate those that have helped to shape me into my present form. For it is from this present form that I will continue to grow; and with the grace of GOD, manifest into the MAN that ALLAH (GOD) ultimately desires me to be!

Along the path of my life I have rejected some, embraced others... perhaps I should have embraced some of those that I rejected; and rejected some of those that I embraced... Never the less, everything happens for a reason, and I am certainly grateful for everything and everyone that has given me a reason and motivation to go forward.

I would like to send a special thank you to my mother, sisters, nieces and the four Mary's within my life; you all know who you are! A man cannot be a MAN without the presence of a particular caliber of woman in his life... thank you, and keep the faith!

I would also like to thank my pops... the HNIC (lol); my brothers both blood and spirit... and my little nephew(s)... a special thank you to my main man, and business partner; K.O... lets knock'em OUT bruh; Muhammad said so!!

I would like to thank GOD (ALLAH) for my beautiful children, for it is their presence and future presence that gives me the strength and conviction of spirit to do what I do, the way that I do it. I pray that in time Allah (GOD) will allow them to understand their father, and the mathematical thinking that generates my movements!

Finally, I would like to acknowledge The Honorable Minister Louis Farrakhan for his guidance and example of what a REAL MAN and Teacher is. I thank Allah (GOD) for the strength of the MINISTER and the LOVE for his people; a love that allows him to stand up and tell the truth in a world that has been conditioned to prefer a LIE.

Oh yeah, I almost forgot... I would like to acknowledge all the haters and self and institutionalized propelled obstacles that are found along the path to success and my meeting with the Lord of the Worlds; keep up the good work, your work allows Allah (GOD) to do HIS..... PEACE!

—A Special Recognition—

As I present this writing to those who may see value in it, I do so realizing that it is just a mere link in a chain of mathematical actions and reactions that have been initiated by the Lord of the Worlds himself. Although I am proud of the outcome of this document, I certainly understand and accept the responsibility that comes with the presenting of a truth that I myself am not the author of—for without a doubt, I am neither the conveyor nor concealer of any original thought that exists within the vastness of the universe. With this in mind I thank Allah (God) for any success or positive significance that this work may achieve; and will always hold in my heart these words spoken by The Honorable Minister Louis Farrakhan:

"One of the Great lessons that The Honorable Elijah Muhammad taught us—was the lesson of humility. That no ONE man can rise above the condition of his people; and no matter how much learning any ONE of us may acquire, how much fame or fortune any ONE of us may acquire—it is not until WE as a people, acquire Knowledge, Wisdom, Understanding that WE as a people can better life for ourselves, and for others—that we can say, that WE have truly achieved.

The achievements of individuals mark individual struggle against odds; but that individual who achieves after struggling, MUST submit his achievement to his people—to help his people to achieve. And it is by submitting what we know to the feet of those who MAY not know, not from pride or arrogance—or a feeling of superiority; but truly recognizing the natural principle that nature is not concerned with individuals, but rather with the preservation of a species.

And if I become individually great—and my people are collectively nothing, then I as an individual am also nothing. But if WE as a people become collectively great, then all of us as individuals tied to that collective greatness—share in that greatness."

Minister Louis Farrakhan—April 16, 1982

Disclaimer

Although I am a Muslim student of The Honorable Minister Louis Farrakhan and the Nation of Islam, this book is written by an independent writer under the auspices of a man that has done the due diligence and research that renders this particular fruit.

This book is the express opinion and perspective of the writer unless otherwise stated. This book is not written to endorse nor represent the official position of the Nation of Islam—nor is it an official document of the Nation of Islam or The Honorable Minister Louis Farrakhan. Any attempt to claim it as such is in violation of the author and publisher's intent; therefore making it no more than another trick of the enemy to alter the truth and make faulty indictments!

Does every book written by a Christian author instantly become an official document of the Pope of Rome, or the Roman Catholic Church? Alright then, don't make this one anything more or less than what it is.

AND ALSO:

To my fellow students and followers of The Most Honorable Elijah Muhammad and The Honorable Minister Louis Farrakhan, this book is a working attempt to contribute to the mission, function, and purpose of the coming and presence of Master Fard Muhammad. As students and potential servants of Allah (God), we were all given our marching orders within the following words found within our **Original Instuctions**: *Big fields are awaiting for the wide Awake man to work out. Arise the Dead by the thousands! The dead Nation must arise— for the Time is at hand. Look in your Poison Book. Work cheerfully and fear not! You are the Righteous, the Best and the Powerful.*

Within the context of this instruction I have attempted to simply participate in a process that is far greater in scope than any follower or student, including myself, could possibly ever fully comprehend. This disclaimer is to assure my fellow students and laborers in the CAUSE of truth that I hold The Honorable Minister Louis Farrakhan as the divine criterion and standard by which we measure any so-called student or laborer in terms of the Mission divinely given to The Most Honorable Elijah Muhammad. Without pause or inconsistency I will continue to know and bear witness that The Honorable Minister Farrakhan has been divinely placed in the seat of The Most Honorable Elijah Muhammad; and from this position, The Minister is fulfilling the functional purpose of the Head of The Nation of Islam. Neither this book, nor anyother works that I have done or will do in the future by the grace, inspiration, or permission of Allah is intended to suggest anything other than this most indelible fact. It is my prayer that my intended works and subsequent achievements will be seen in the spirit that they are intended and not manipulated by the enemies of truth and righteousness into any indication contrary to the above stated.

As Allah (God) continues to grow all of The Most Honorable Elijah Muhammad's students into positions awaiting them, I pray that we will all be motivated by the words that Sister Latonja Muhammad wrote within the Introduction of the book entitled **Closing the Gap:** *Inner Views of the Heart, Mind & Soul of The Honorable Minister Louis Farrakhan, by Jabril Muhammad.*

She Wrote:

"Every student's dream is to be close to his or her teacher. So close that he or she is considered the favorite; and even closer, that one day, the student hopes to be "like" or "equal" to the one teaching.

Any good student yearns for the day when his teacher calls upon him; because he takes pleasure in showing the teacher he got his lesson. He takes pleasure in being pleasing in the teacher's sight.

Not only is it the student's desire, to be "like" the teacher, or to one day become a teacher, it is the aim and purpose of the teacher, that the student one day equals and even surpasses him. This is what fuels any good teacher. It is his driving force, it is also what gives him patience with the student, for he sees and knows the power that is active in the teacher lays dormant in the student. So it is the teacher's aim to ignite the energy that is potential and turn it to kinetic"—**Kinetic is defined as: Ki*net"ic (?), q. [Gr. , from to move.] (Physics) Moving or causing motion; motory; active, as opposed to latent. Kinetic energy.**

Based upon the above words that are found within one of the most profound books ever written and produced by the Nation of Islam, we should see that one of the most vital aspects of the Minister's purpose or function as the "HEAD" in our midst is for him to provide an example for us through his words, deeds, and lifestyle. We should realize that his words and instructions are not meant to be worshiped—his words and instructions are to be followed, examined, and studied, for he is in fact the EXAMPLE that The Messenger has given to us.

As we all move forward by the grace and permission of Allah (God) into our roles and purpose for being created, let's dedicate our talents and efforts to the service of the GOD that gave us our functional purpose for being created into His Universe. As we journey along the road to become a Servant of Allah (God), lets try with all our might to resist the impediments to this reality by staying focused on the goal and remaining committed to the process.

Now with that being said—let's get started!

Dedication

This book is dedicated to all those who desire to learn the truth; and all those who ain't scared to SPEAK IT, once they've LEARNED IT!

Remember! ONE voice can make a difference- But SEVERAL voices can CAUSE a REVOLUTION!

To let YOUR voice be HEARD join US at...

www.thepeopleslanguage.com

NOTE

Within the context of this writing I have confronted the corporate and negative influences of HipHop; through making an overall point, I do not want to lose sight of those HipHop artists that are trying to have a positive effect on the black nation and the oppressed peoples of the world. I extend a special thank you and appreciation to the following artist...

JERU THE DAMAJA	Paris
Wise Intelligent	Mos Def
Immortal Technique	Talib Kweli
Professor Griff	DA SMART
West coast KAM	Black ICE
NYOIL	Common
Lord Jamar	KRS-ONE
Dead Prez	The Roots
Poor Righteous Teachers	The Coup
Public Enemy	Nas
X-Clan	Chuck D
The Conscious Daughters	Planet Asia
Uno the Prophet	Sellassie

Certainly there are others; if I failed to mention your name, believe me when I say that your work has not gone unnoticed! Continue to fight the good fight!!

* Be sure to see the **"Special Message to the so-called Conscious Rappers"** located in the back of this book.

** In an attempt to make and establish a much broader point, I ask the reader to understand that when I use the term HipHop...I am referring to the entire culture, lifestyle, and music as presently seen and recognized as such. As a lover of the culture and music, I write this book being fully aware of the many nuances that exist, and being aware that what is presently being seen is NOT the HipHop that many have fallen in love with! I use the sweeping indictment of what is commonly referred to as HipHop so not to be mired down in a rhetorical discussion of the difference of what WAS vs. what IS! I respect the true defenders of the REAL HipHop, and their attempts to save and preserve their culture and music. I simply hope that everyone takes the journey with me through these pages, so that at its conclusion my points will be understood. I am not asking for everyone to agree with me, what I am asking, is that all of us consider what is being said... and think on its many points! May we be blessed with understanding and the necessary spirit to make a difference! Before I begin, please allow me to share the special words of two of HipHop's finest. Although these brothers are not generating the huge dollars as the HipHop imposters, it is certain that their efforts and dedication will extend way beyond record sells and chart toppers.

In hopes of defending and preserving what they love...Both Hakim Green of Channel Live notoriety, as well as NYOIL, the former Kool Kim of UMC fame...have evolved and emerged into the necessary soldiers that will prevent the death of a HipHop that many of the youth of today simply fail to understand! To this end, please take time to consider their words, because they are certainly backing those words with action in a very real way...and like previously said, may we all be blessed with understanding!

Words from My Man...Hakim Green

Let me first acknowledge the supreme creative force of the universe. All manifestations of this divine spark is the beginning, of which HIP HOP is another expression.

HIP HOP, in its perfect state, is an idea. A shared idea, which those in HIP HOP instinctively respond to as HIP HOP.

If we break up the component parts of The WORD we call HIP HOP we get

HIP: "Means to know it's a form of intelligence to be Hip means to be update and relevant". This goes back to HIP HOP being an idea. A shared idea that we, who are HIP HOP, KNOW.

HOP: "is a form of movement. You can't just observe a hop; you gotta hop up and do it." This speaks to the expression of HIP HOP.

KNOWLEDGE/EXPRESSION.......

Knowledge and Expression are the fundamental keys to experiencing HIP HOP. I like to say, "If it's not intelligent or not moving us any where it's not HIP HOP"...

WE, as a people called Hiphoppas, carry a legacy that is ancient. Rap or expression of the spoken word has always been with us. We can look at the African Griot on down to the Last Poets to evidence the power of the Spoken Word in the form of Rap/emceeing.

We have always had those who could use the spoken word in a way to reach the community. The word was used to inspire all kinds of emotions. Some pleasant and peaceful, like Lauren Hill's "Sweetest Thing". Other works in history are more violent and militant like Francis Scott Key's "A star spangled banner". And some deal with relationships like Sheakspear's "A Taming of the Shrew"..

All are expressions of the Spoken Word but only "Sweetest Thing" is

HIP HOP. This is because HIP HOP is not measured by what you do but how you do it.

This not only speaks to expression of the spoken word called Rap but equally to the other basic elements of HIP HOP. Much too often we stay focused on Rap exclusively as HIP HOP when only the hip hop expression of Rap is a component part of HIP HOP (note small h for adj and capital H for noun/idea).

The complete list of the basic elements of HIP HOP are:

Rap/emceeing

DJaying

Break Dancing

Grafitti Arts

Knowledge

The Knowledge element I have listed as last but we could easily consider this first.

The Amen Ra of HIP HOP aka Africa Bamabatta came into the Knowledge of HIP HOP after a trip to South Africa where he was inspired by a Zulu Chief to create a movement powerful enough to unify our people. At this time the divisiveness of gang culture was ravaging the South Bronx much like every major city at that time. Through Bam's work back at home in The Bronx New York, HIP HOP was given texture by unifying all the cultural expressions our community had to offer. But the Knowledge or IDEA of something better than what was being offered to our people is what spurned Africa Bambatta to move or HOP to create what is HIP.

"Street Knowledge is the accumulation of HIP HOP's cultural self awareness." KRS ONE's Gospel of HIPHOP pg122

Self Awareness is what enables the Hiphoppa to see themselves as HIP HOP. To see themselves as something uniquely and distinctly different from others. HIP HOP seeks to incorporate unlimited understanding and expression in order for HIP HOP to grow and move..

I received an education regarding what was HIP HOP and what was not HIP HOP in 1995 while on the road in Cleveland, Ohio looking for a "HIP HOP" party. I was told that we could go to a "gangsta" party or go to a "HIP HOP" party. That is when I first realized that HIP HOP was distinctly different than Gangsta culture. Though there has been a merger of the two, "Gangsta" as a culture is not HIP HOP. The knowledge and expression of gangsterism can be delivered in a HIP HOP form but the two are not synonymous. To reiterate, HIP HOP is not what you do but how you do it.

HIP HOP is how we as hiphoppas were able to live life during the last 30-40 years... All Praises Due to the CREATOR for allowing us to tap into The Great HE/SHE. This tapping in is what gives us access to HIP HOP... This is what is meant by the current slang term "going in"... To go into ones self to release the god force energy in its form called HIP HOP.

HIP HOP, as it is expressed, equates to what the 5% Nation of Gods and Earth's call Culture Freedom. Culture Freedom is what occurs when a people are able to independently create. When they have the ability to freely express the god force from within. Conversely, since 1990/91 most of what has been sold as HIP HOP is not.

It is the corporate package, the" Rapping". It is RAP music. This RAP music is the cover on a book and you know you are never supposed to judge a book by its cover.

The Recorded Music Industry is and has always been in the business of selling NOTHING. Record Labels sell plastic. This plastic has no functional use whatsoever. It adds nothing to society. The music recorded on the plastic is there to promote the product.

The music is "intellectual property" the value of which is determined by "publishing rights" and not the mechanical sale/distribution of the record itself. You don't need the plastic in order to sing the song. This is clearly understood by studying the fall of the major Record Labels due to the digital revolution. The sale of recorded music is predicated on Marketing and Promotions or what can be called brain washing.

More money is spent on marketing and promotion budgets than on Artist Development, which for the most part is a lost art form.

In this type of paradigm mediocrity is elevated because it is cheap to create thus having more resources to grease relationships at the

MEDIA outlets. The masses or" market" can only support that which it is aware of. Music or art that can possibly educate the market is filtered or blocked from mainstream access.

The messages we are getting from the Corporate Rap Music business are meant to perpetuate and reinforce the value/moral structure of the group that controls these corporate instruments. These individuals are not Hip Hop. They are not from the neighborhoods that create HIP HOP and surely do not work for the best interest of HIP HOP or its community.

The corporate institution's #1 and only focus is profit and greater profit with the least amount of investment is ideal. The profits that come from CAPITALIZING off of the community do not get recycled back into that COMMUNITY.

The power of RAP music, as a tool for our oppression, lies in the manipulation of beat and rhythm. Having simple phrases repeated over and over on top of monotonous drum loops assist in hypnotizing the masses. Thus, "The 85%" are dancers to a beat not of their own drum. We, as an uneducated market, are being manipulated and lead to our own demise. The tools of our enslavement look sound and act so familiar that it makes identifying the source of our oppression much more difficult. We become slave catcher, task master, overseer and whip cracker but never plantation owner and definitely not freedom fighter. The system will never free its slaves. When the slaves decide to revolt we look to our oppressor for consent. Since this is a war for your mind, The Revolution is one of reclaiming ones own mind then possibly we can reclaim HIP HOP.

Verse from "Crack and the Electric Chair"

I move through a cypher let me demonstrate, God starts at 7 then we make an 8.

To build what is righteous the devil knows his fate, at 9 we born again so the cypher elevates.

The key is the knowledge it's wise to go to college but understanding is the best part and why we pay homage thru the culture of HIP HOP we remain free to express ourselves with power and share equality.

God starts at 7 then we make an 8

To build what is righteous the devil knows his fate

At 9 we born again so the so the cypher elevates. Pardon self if this too much to contemplate.

It's all simple math not the kind you learn in class

Cash don't make the man, the man makes the cash.

It's just a little jewel my OG used to drop

'Bout the time I found out Jewish people owned my block....

In addition to the above please consider the following lyrics of Hakim's "Drop a Jewel":

Since niggas like jewels I'm gon' drop a jewel

Jews make the money

Niggas make like fools

The blind lead the blind, we all blinded by the shine

Badboys die like Biggie to live life Shyne.

I aint gotta dis 50, 50 dissed himself,

Supportin George Bush like he aint got knowledge of himself.

Knowledge is wealth so I keep that thing upon the shelf.

Jacob makes ya freeze but the FED's make ya melt.

Everybody want the belt, who wants the crown in New York?

Too many Puff Daddy niggas that's why the world is clowning New York.

They call me Negus The Most High, my Niggas be The Most High

We stay burnin' Bush like Mt. Sinai.

Soldiers don't cry and Gangsta don't die

But when rappers get killed they go to the place where people lie.

85 uncivilized, 10% capitalize, 5 others realize HIP HOP is in disguise.

Part hustler, part drag queen the way we pimp the black Queen

The rap game full of bitches like a King Magazine.

Clips and magazines will make ya Caddy lean

That shit your father sniff will make ya Daddy lean.

Katrina's act of God left niggas out to rob

Aint it deep how Willie Lynch be rollin' like the mob.

Time to get up out that fog and put down that blunt.

You gotta protect what is yours and take what you want.

Now a day's people don't want the real HIP HOP.

They rather hear that shit meant to kill HIPHOP.

Who deal around the clock? Who's ill will the glock? 10 years done past and you still on the block??

You still selling rock, servin fiends' non stop?? You worst than a snitch, you deal for the cops!!! Niggas lay traps then scream trap or die, like all we got is that or we can stay black and die.

Or you can relax it wit the lie but the facts won't lie.

Another rapper die everybody ask why..

Take some chump change, get yourself a chump chain, go juice some little crew and have'em pump Kane.

Or you can G off with the Rap but you gotta master that.

Don't try to drop no science you better of pumping Crack..

Hakim Green is a HipHop soldier, please follow him and support his music and efforts…you can contact him by following the links found on the website www.thepeopleslanguage.com

AND now... the powerful and enlightened words of My brother NYOIL!

NYOIL: On the Moment!

It is flawed thinking... for us, any of us in a moment to have the expectation that this moment will achieve that which is assigned to us to accomplish. Hip Hop is really just a word or term used to describe a moment, a moment when the genetic history of a people lost found its way back into the world.

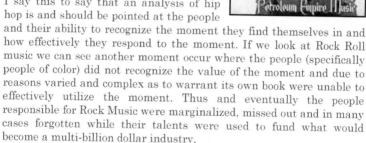

When ancient traditions dance and customs find themselves remixed in the body of today's Hip Hopper—Traditions that most would have no historical context or connection with and yet act out as if possessed by. But the responsibility of both understanding the moment and effectively utilizing the moment cannot be placed on the moment. The moment is not sentient and therefore has no control over how it is interpreted or utilized, the moment just is.

I say this to say that an analysis of hip hop is and should be pointed at the people and their ability to recognize the moment they find themselves in and how effectively they respond to the moment. If we look at Rock Roll music we can see another moment occur where the people (specifically people of color) did not recognize the value of the moment and due to reasons varied and complex as to warrant its own book were unable to effectively utilize the moment. Thus and eventually the people responsible for Rock Music were marginalized, missed out and in many cases forgotten while their talents were used to fund what would become a multi-billion dollar industry.

In the case of hip hop this moment not only represents a billion dollar industry (the likes of which have never been seen by the record and associated industries) but it also and more nefariously represents the most direct and, sans Slavery, effective means of controlling and culturally influencing the people.

This is why identifying Hip Hop as a moment is so vitally important! Recognizing a moment doesn't require emotional connection or favor; however, it does require a Keen eye and the ability to see historical patterns. It requires the ability to create and initiate strategy based on raw fact.

This is the task set before us as members of the HipHop community experiencing this moment and even more so the elders who've experienced their own moments and understand what moments lost mean to the perpetuation and cultural growth of our people. We will need the 20/20 vision that Hindsight provides, the innovation of youthful minds to harness this moment and create new institutions and initiatives that can benefit the people in the long run.

This is Hip Hop to me.. a moment in time. The real question will be "Where were YOU during that moment in time?"

My name is NYOIL and I approve this message

--
NYOIL
the ideal

Consider the Lyrics of NYOIL:

Un-Conscious
This go out to all u fake revolutionaries arm chair activist talking all that backward shit
the fact is this it's just another click on some silly shit dilly shit talking bout things u don't really get
I know a tree by the fruit that it bares I checked the branches boughs and roots and nothing was there
I spent time on your comities NY is HERE and worked with your organization and went nowhere
y'all ain't committed to doing jack but talking bout the problems facing black and I'll be damned if u ever act
pontificating considering contemplating and overly complicating our conditions and situations
y'all love analyzing and while your analyzing kids are dying and mothers is crying while your theorizing

Just cause u a teacher don't make u no black leader cause u a preacher don't make u no black leader great speaker don't make u no black leader and

politics certainly don't make u one either
There ain't no discipline no unity the leadership is wack that's why the kids ain't coming and parents don't come back
Y'all cats is feeling ya'self more than u feel like revealing the help that get community to healing and health
y'all the illuminati y'all the new world order y'all the ones leading your people to slaughter
you got your people chasing windmills analyzing dollar bills tryna find a secret society that they never will
And all you new world order pricks get off Alex Jones dick Farrakhan been saying that shit since 86

Brothers love marching and singing after they been played I guess it's true mufuggas love a parade
and a conference I gotta have a conference to keep my lack of progress off my conscious make a profit off a concert
and the people that follow that swallow that hollow crap is more sheep than the peeps y'all be laughing at
y'all don't want to change nuffin you talk all that revolutionary shit really it's just bluffing
them words we need verbs we need men with back bones and nerves we need women that wanna do more than serve or observe and I've heard how they only want u for your curves how absurd
People really strived for this bled and died for this for y'all to tell lies bout they lives and shit!
Follow and get connected with my man NYOIL...at NYOIL.com!

INTRODUCTION

In the year 2006, although life seemed good for the reigning king of HipHop the infamous Curtis "50 cent" Jackson; life in Black America had become more and more bleak. Hurricane Katrina and its shameful and perhaps purposeful governmental response have all but wiped New Orleans off the face of the map. Although young Curtis "50 cent" Jackson was the most popular commodity in the *"HipHop Nation"*, the southern region of the United States was and is its reigning Kingdom. Notable personalities such as Lil Jon, Lil Wayne, Ludacris, T.I, Mike Jones (WHO?), Paul Wall, and others are completely dominating radio and video airplay. A music and lifestyle that was at one time viewed as "rebellious and revolutionary" has been accepted into the commercial mainstream, and adopted as the *"New American Pop Music"*.

Lost, is Kris "KRS-ONE" Parker, the controversial, politically motivated, self-pro-claimed "The Teacha"; found, is Christopher (Ludacris) Bridges, the also controversial; yet money and bling - bling motivated, self-proclaimed *"Disturber of the Peace"*. A movement of expression that was previously defined as a sub-culture that reveled in being a separate and unequal entity of the American mainstream, has merged and coalesced into the dominate culture, with its only remnants being the misused and abused "HipHop" moniker.

Once identifying itself as a *"Nation"* with its own rules, by-laws, and traditions, the HipHop community has forfeited their sovereignty and adopted the ways and actions of the very culture that it previously railed against.

As an example, take the case of Stanley *"M.C. Hammer"* Burrell. M.C. Hammer was considered by the average 90's HipHop Nation's citizen as a mainstream rapper. His radio and video dominance over the airwaves was perceived by many as sell-out achievements, and not a real representation of the music or the HipHop culture. Due to commercial success and a flamboyant lifestyle, M.C. Hammer received ridicule and scorn from a culture that at that time prided itself in its purity and strict adherence to the rule of *"No Sell-outs"*. The majority of the rappers viewed Hammer's lyrics as weak, and absent of any relevant social content.

Fast forward to 2008 and we see the glaring difference between then and now. HipHop is presently defined by record sells, and video exposure. Those who are to be considered as successful are the most flamboyant and commercially accepted of their peers... and the rule of "No Sell-outs", has been replaced with "Only Sell-outs". The once ridiculed, blasted, and hated behaviors of M.C. Hammer have now become the accepted, embraced, and defining aspects of a true "HipHop Giant".

By today's HipHop standard, Stanley (M.C Hammer) Burrell should be considered the true father, pioneer, and innovator of what is today considered as the "HipHop Nation". Curtis "50 Cent" Jackson, Shawn "Diddy" Combs, Sean "Jay Z" Carter, Jermaine Dupree, and many others should pay homage in their songs to the father of their style and contribution to the "HipHop Nation", Stanley "M.C. Hammer" Burrell. For despite argument, M.C. Hammer is in fact the pioneering agent from which today's mega HipHop star is made.

The earlier proponents of HipHop, the early citizens of the HipHop Nation, and its protectors and defenders viewed M.C. Hammer as a HipHop imposter. Not accepted as a "true" HipHop representative, but merely a talented entertainer that took catchy beats and production and injected them into the stream of American acceptance; Hammer was ridiculed, bashed, and openly confronted as an opponent of what was at that time considered "real" HipHop. With that being the case, what would those same individuals say of the present state of HipHop and its representatives?

Of course rappers such as 50 Cent, Jay Z, P Diddy, Jermaine Dupree, Snoop, Nelly, Lil Jon, T.I, Game, among others will have a hard time giving credit to Hammer as the father of today's HipHop; but their reluctance means nothing in the face of the facts. Hammer was scorned, mocked, and attacked by early hip-hoppers for squandering over 30 million dollars on foolish and flamboyant purchases of helicopters, horses, and gold gates for his over 12 million dollar home. He was clowned and accused of being a sell-out for doing Pepsi commercials and being financially backed by corporate America. Hammer's music was seen as anti HipHop for his continuous use of samples of pop hits, and the rhetorical use of the same "ole lyrics".

Does this sound familiar, of course it does! Today's HipHop is honey-combed with the same realities that Hammer was continually maligned for. Backed by corporate America, and sponsored by financial entities the likes of Chevy, Reebok, Seagram's, Taco Bell, McDonalds, St. Ides, Burger King, and many more, today's HipHop stars have financial deals that would put Hammer's to shame. In addition, today's HipHop rapper continues to not only recycle the same lyrics, but the same concepts, and gimmicks as well. The remake of entire songs, not merely the samples are the blueprint foundation for today's HipHop hit!

I am not writing this book to attack any certain rapper or entertainer; that is not the purpose of its writing. This book is intended as a sweeping indictment of the current state of what is commonly referred to as the "HipHop Nation" and the role it is currently playing within the global ambitions of the rich and powerful. Although I confront this present music and cultural genre generally, I additionally criticize and ridicule the American Corporate Government and culture at large. The systematic implementation of a slave state of mind has been used to destroy not only black people here in the United States, but people of color all over the planet earth. By dumbing down the masses, and financially assisting those artists that exploit filth and degeneracy, Corporate and Governmental powers have been able to control nearly one hundred percent of the total global resources.

In my attempt to shed light on this reality, it is necessary that in certain instances I, like Kurupt said, "Call Out Names". Although there will be those who will get upset because of this, I would hope that the entirety of the argument be considered and the relevance of the truth be applied…so in any case of criticism, like P.E. said, "Bring the Noise"!

I am an admitted fan of HipHop and its culture, and I grew up listening to it and thoroughly embracing it in almost a religious sense. My most recent purchases have been Scarface, Jay Z, Common, Kanye West, Wise Intelligent, NYOIL, T.I. and a used copy of Public Enemy's "Apocalypse 91…The Enemy Strikes Black" (to replace the one that was stolen) I play them often, not due to research, but because they bump, and I like them. Each one is a quality release, in terms of, production and talent. I also keep within my personal rotation, Nas, 2 Pac, Paris, Snoop, Jada, Game, WestCoast Kam, Immortal Technique, Glasses Malone, Crooked I, Rass Kass, and a personal friend named the "Dirty Birdy"; never the less, this book is not based on the playability of today's rappers or their level of talent, that is already a known and accepted fact. This book is to explore the causes of today's HipHop expression and its effect on future generations. Although I can certainly nod my head to today's music, I most definitely understand that poison is often masked within a **pretty container** and a **flavorful taste**.

The title of this book is derived from a Letter Penned by **Willie Lynch** in the year 1712, and a speech reportedly delivered by him in the same year on the banks of the James River in the Colony of Virginia. Following this letter is a document entitled "The Making of a Slave". Willie Lynch, from which the term "lynching" was derived, was a slave owner from the West Indies. He was reportedly invited by American slave owners to teach them on the making of a slave. From his systematic methods came the docile slave and a mentality that he boasted would last for at least 300 years.

I have posted the letter and speech in its entirety in chapter one, and from this initial chapter will flow the premise of this writing. I hold on to the conviction that the present state of HipHop is nothing more than a slave to a master that has comprised a deliberate plan to dumb down the global population in hopes of totally controlling the world and its resources.

As a representative of a "freedom" that is being marketed throughout the world, HipHop and its agents are being used to sell democracy under the guise of the obtaining of wealth, status and power. Although "Money, Power and Respect" have been portrayed as the "Keys to Life", the reality of the communities from which these salesmen/women have been plucked or drafted, is that its young people don't get rich, but certainly die trying! This is an unacceptable reality; and those that understand it as such, should make the appropriate adjustments or be deemed as the 2008 versions of the "Uncle Tom".

What is worse is that the global image, while selling the "American Dream" in terms of opportunity (if the niggers can make it, anyone can), the self inflicted and then exploited image of the so-called Negro Rapper is painting a less than flattering image of black people in general. Marketing strategies deliberately exploit black stereo types and are creating new ones, and the so-called Negro rappers seem to be at best, ignorant of this fact; or at worse, knowing and accepting whores to the fact...neither is acceptable, and both need to be confronted openly, deliberately, unapologetically, without pause or inconsistency.

In a culture that seems to be following the money; in fact chasing the money, the HipHop Nation has represented its women as bitches and whores, and has represented their men as dope dealers, killers, hustlers, pimps and sex crazed maniacs that only care about money, jewelry, cars, big rims and pussy! This reality has been displayed to the entire world via the internet, MTV, B.E.T., and other forms of the controlled media. So-called Negro rappers and producers are selling out while the image of black people is being assaulted on a global scale. This can be seen by the increase of HipHop record sells internationally, and the increase in sells within the suburban United States to white children and young adults. It is clear that the global population is buying wholesale into the marketed image of black people, but what is even worse; that due to a lack of black-folk outrage, we as black people in America have seemingly bought into it as well, or simply don't give a damn. Filthy minds are purchasing filthy music.

After reading the articles of Willie Lynch, I am sure that we will see the correlation between his desire, and the reality of today's so-called Negro rapper. The HipHop Nation is a plantation (Record Company) based entity focused on size and status, and is a cultural collective sectioned and sub-sectioned based on region, style, coasts, and affiliations. All of these characteristics and the exploitation and manipulation of these characteristics go into the making of a slave. Understanding the depth of the science utilized by Willie Lynch, we recognize that today's so-called Negro rapper and the HipHop Nation is a direct result of a mentality shaped and formed over 300 years prior to its genesis, and is in fact a fruit of the Willie Lynch Science itself.

Just as historically there has been the concept of the "house Niggas" and the "field Niggas" within the realm of the American Slave Legacy, today's so-called Negro rapper might view themselves as field Niggas, when in fact they have allowed themselves to be positioned as the "house nigger". They are the best dressed, fed, and housed, and they eat based on the open damage they do to their fellow slaves. They talk like rebels, but their acts of rebellion fit squarely within the plan outlined within the doctrines or Mr. Lynch. The rebellion of the house nigger is only seen within the context of how they treat and abuse their fellow slaves. The rebellion of the house nigger is never directed to the slave master, because it is the slave master that assigns the house nigger his lofty position in relation to his fellow, but not so "fortunate", brothers and sisters. Corporate Hip-Hoppers view themselves as MEGA-stars; not realizing it is the slave master that has put them in that position because their words are sanctioned by the colonial powers and their corporate sponsors!

These slaves do the bidding of their master by the continuation and glorification of behaviors and practices designed and instituted directly to make and continue the existence of the slave. These so-called Negro rappers pride themselves as the voices of the masses, or voices of their community, while they simultaneously boast and brag on their wealthy reality in contrast to the "hood" and its members left behind. This braggadocios behavior then separates the rich slave from the poor slave thereby facilitating and perpetuating the science of good 'ole' Willie.

What is then left within the heart of a poor slave is the suicidal mentality perpetuated by the so-called Negro rapper that the way out of slavery is to "get rich, or die trying", when the true rallying cry should be, "GET FREE, OR DIE TRYING". The so-called Negro rapper is the shiny and tempting bait that is being used to entice the poor slaves into ways and actions that are leading them to death. The message to the "field nigger" from the "house nigger" is "You too can become a house nigger if you work hard enough and kiss the appropriate ass!" In this and all instances, the "appropriate ass" is attached squarely upon the backsides of Corporate and Governmental America.

By keeping this in mind, we recognize that the state of HipHop today should help people of color in general, and black people here in America in particular to see Willie Lynch and his affect; thereby allowing us to formulate and accept a method to alter that affect. Although some truths are painfully acknowledged and accepted, we understand that we (black people) are all victims, and none of our people should be thrown away. It is only after the non-emotional embracing of the truth and the acknowledgement of error is made, that we can re-build and restore our people to the proper place. Only after this attempt is made, and the enemies of this restoration process identified, should we thoughtfully consider the elimination of those who are to be defined as traitors and sell-outs of the people. In other words, this writing will allow those that are being used as a tool and also a slave for government and corporate America to make a choice, either ride with your own people on the bases of truth and justice, or be seen as an open enemy to the black man and woman's complete liberation.

We should always understand the hands (sometime hidden), that have a play in our condition and global positioning. HipHop is a multi-billion dollar a year giant, and those who participate in our demise are the same ones that benefit from it. This book would be derelict in its purpose and duty if it did not mention a relative few of those that directly and indirectly benefit from destroying the positive fabrics of our (Black People) community.

To this end, I realize that this book can in fact be three separate books in one; **one dealing strictly with Willie Lynch and his psychological control of the modern slave**. The second being **one dedicated to the emergence and significance of the HipHop culture and its present cultural dominance**; and the third being **a book completely unearthing the truth and reality of governmental and corporate America and the slave master role they play on a global scale**.

Understanding the individual significance of each reality, I have attempted to paint a broad picture of a significant correlation of circumstances that will support the premise of this book. The foundation upon which this books rest can be seen as the following:

- **Willie Lynch's strategy was based upon the proliferation of a slave mentality.**

- **The Willie Lynch mentality allows members of the HipHop Nation, as well as black people in general, to fall victim to the slave master.**

- **Due to Willie Lynch and the slave mentality, the HipHop Nation allows itself to be pimped and manipulated by outsiders that play the role of financial and moral blood suckers.**

- **Corporate and Governmental America is the Slave Master that has sifted, the HipHop Nation like wheat, and continues to manipulate the HipHop artist toward their social, political, educational, and spiritual global agenda.**

Lastly, I hope and pray that the HipHop community would embrace the concept of this book and look at itself with an eye of self-correction. Black people find righteousness at our base, but we cannot allow our enemies to use our desire for wealth and riches to destroy the entirety of our race and people. We must confront wickedness at all levels, and we must eliminate any weeds that would affect the beauty and purity of our garden. If the so-called Negro rapper refuses to meet and adapt, he must be identified, isolated, and destroyed.

Author's Note

A Special Message for You Know Who!

This book is controversial in nature; ***controversy*** in the Webster's dictionary is defined as follows:

Pronunciation: 'kän-tr&-"v&r-sE, *Brit also* k&n-'trä-v&r-sE
Function: *noun*
Inflected Form(s): *plural* **-sies**
Etymology: Middle English *controversie*, from Anglo-French, from Latin *controversia*, from *controversus* disputable, literally, turned against, from *contro-* (akin to *contra-*) + *versus*, past participle of *vertere* to turn -- more at <u>WORTH</u>
1 : a discussion marked especially by the expression of opposing views : **<u>DISPUTE</u>**

2 : <u>QUARREL, STRIFE</u>

It will be shown within the context of this writing that the news, media, and entertainment world are all controlled by a certain group of individuals that share the same basic political, social, economic, and religious ideologies. These ***ideologies*** are brought into reality by a strategic implementation of mergers, coalitions, and personnel transfers and reassignments that are governed by mutual interest and a particular agenda.

What, is at a superficial glance, perceived as competition is in reality an allusion that is created by diverse elements of the same plan, ambition, and agenda. The world politic has been created by several thousand years of mathematical calculations of individuals and groups that desire to control and dominate the world. The masses; or those that are viewed as expendable, have for centuries been used and abused in order to maintain and sustain the lifestyles and ideas of a certain few whose unity and wicked machinations have placed them on the thrown of power.

We must come to understand that America was founded as a **Corporate State**, and it has not changed, it has simply evolved. It acquired land from the Native Americans by deceit, shady dealing, false contracts, and outright force. America's first commodity was human beings; and Corporate America placed stolen people on stolen land in order to secure and develop a financial structure that today controls the entire globe.

For over three hundred years America was able to use free labor as well as free land to institute systems of growth and development that would support their ultimate agenda. This agenda was centered on the idea of white supremacy and the desire to control the entire earth and its resources. All people, especially people of color, will have to face this truth head on in the very near future. Our reaction to America's global Imperialism will be determined by what side of the proverbial line that we stand.

The financial center of America was at its conception the state of New York, and this stands true even today. With Wall Street as its financial backdrop, New York's rich history is built on its participation in the African Slave Trade. Though we may tend to associate the southern portion of the United States with slavery; New York, prior to the American Revolution was second only to Charleston, South Carolina in the owning of slaves. One out of every five New Yorkers was slaves, 40 percent of all colonial New York's households owned slaves.

Between the years 1600 to 1827, the African Slave Trade played the most vital role in building New York into America's wealthiest state and the financial capital of the world. The slave trade, the labor of enslaved people, and slavery's integration into everyday commerce shaped the global destiny and blue print of what is today recognized as Corporate America.

As the largest forced migration in human history—Corporate America, under the auspices of the King of England and later the mega-conglomeration of the thirteen original colonies, over saw and were the Chief-Executive Officers (CEO's) of hundreds of slave-ships that transported an average of 80 people per day for several hundred years. The enormous profits from this *trade* of human *stock* financed the industrial revolution of England, all of Europe, and later the United States.

Because of its geographical location and its proximity to the other American colonial territories (corporate offices), as well as its valuable inland waterways, the state of New York was seen as the most important asset of the corporate agenda of the King of England and the founding fathers of his corporate flagship, America.

Wall Street, as a narrow street in lower Manhattan that runs downhill to the East River, is considered the financial heart of the global monster that is known as Corporate America. As the center of the financial district, Wall Street was the first permanent home of the **New York Stock Exchange (NYSE)**. Logical deduction causes us to understand that the Slave Trade was the primary driving force of **Wall Street** and its financial market. All business and commerce was built on the back of the institutional slave trade. For this reason, we can understand that the initial **"STOCK"** that was traded was in fact black people!

The enslavement enterprise was comprised of a myriad of activities, including the buying and selling of African Human Beings; harvesting, processing, packing of foodstuffs for the slave trade, and using slave labor within the financially prosperous craft workshops. It also required the formation of companies that got rich by supplying slave plantations in the West Indies and North America with grains, tools, and manufactured foods.

Economic strength was secured by companies that built and maintained the ships used for the slave trade. In addition, financial institutions such as banks and insurance companies waxed rich by borrowing, lending, and insuring the slave vessels. The government itself secured riches by the taxing of these hugely profitable seeds of modern America. The number one producer of revenue for the early newspapers of America was the paid notices or advertisements of reward to anyone who secured the re-capture of runaway slaves. Advertisements of slaves for purchase were a major source of revenue for the 18th century newspapers of New York.

In addition to the above, almost everything was produced by free slave labor—including cheese, tobacco, rum, sugar, cloth, butter, and clothes. All profits were associated with the free slave labor of Africans and the managerial abilities of the slave master that managed his goods and the slaves that produced them. Wall Street was the financial scale upon which the economic prosperity of slavery was weighed and maximized.

The slave trade was enormously profitable for the traders, ship-builders, bankers, and insurers who made it possible. At its peak the margin of profit soared just above 369 percent. At its ebb the profit margin was still a whopping 94 percent. For example, in 1675, a slave could be purchased in Africa for today's equivalent of $355 dollars and later sold in New York for $3,793 dollars.

As for Wall Street itself, it was physically made to be a stockade that protected and identified the New Amsterdam settlement that was later renamed and incorporated as New York City. The physical "Wall" from which Wall Street receives it name, was built by African slaves that were owned and controlled by the *West India Company* and its CEO, a Mr. Peter Stuyvesant.

As the Dutch Director General of the colony of New Netherlands, Mr. Stuyvesant ordered the construction of the "Wall" of Wall Street, and the canal which became "Broad Street" and "Broadway". As the director of the *West India Company,* a company that was comprised of Dutch Merchants that were granted a charter for a trade monopoly in the West Indies by the *Republic of the Seven United Netherlands* and given jurisdiction over the African Slave Trade of Brazil, the Caribbean, and North America; Mr. Stuyvesant made his fortune and name from the selling of African human beings.

In 1991, while constructing a New York City skyscraper, an African Slave burial ground was discovered. Located in the heart of the New York financial district, the burial ground was the final resting place of over 419 African human beings, mostly women and children. The burial grounds extended from Broadway southward under City Hall, and almost to the site of the former World Trade Center, in close proximity to the Wall Street financial center.

Why is this information important and from what standpoint would it be viewed as controversial? The controversy stems from the ignorance of many that refuse to accept or recognize the diabolical and inhumane national traditions of America. The root word of tradition is *trade,* and the trade that vaulted America into the world scene and into its present dominance is no other than the African Slave Trade. **Slavery is America's prime Tradition!**

This book is designed to confront the ignorance of a social class of individual minds that are commonly referred to as the HipHop Nation. By pointing the reader's attention to certain facts and undeniable truths, I hope to stimulate the minds of those that are presently in a hypnotic trance under the influence of a social degenerating and filth based tool of the American Corporate structure, into raising their individual and collective standards of decency and responsibility.

Being reduced to a culture of slaves, the HipHop Nation has allowed itself to be the poster boys and girls of Corporate America. The Music, the videos, the ways and actions of these HipHop slaves can be recognized as nothing more than running commercials that sale the various products of the corporate slave master. These products include but are not limited to: cars, jewelry, alcohol, clothes, drugs, sex, and the white man's idea of morality and societal priorities.

Is it not interesting that the birth place of the American Corporate monster, New York City, is the same place of origin of the culture of what is commonly referred to as HipHop? Is it further interesting that the nickname of the state of New York is no other than the "Empire State"? Let's define the word Empire so that we can make sure that we are all on the same page:

EMPIRE

Pronunciation: 'em-"pI(-&)r
Function: *noun*
Etymology: Middle English, from Anglo-French *empire, empirie,* from Latin *imperium* absolute authority, empire, from *imperare* to command -- more at <u>EMPEROR</u>

1 a (1) : a major political unit having a territory of great extent or a number of territories or peoples under a single sovereign authority; *especially* : one having an emperor as chief of state (2) : the territory of such a political unit **b** : something resembling a political empire; *especially* : an extensive territory or enterprise under single domination or control

2 : imperial sovereignty, rule, or dominion

Although the HipHop Nation is presently viewed as a single unit divided among its own citizens based on coasts, regions, cliques, gangs, and affiliations; HipHop would be more accurately described as a single "EMPIRE" governed and controlled by a certain group of likeminded slave masters. These individuals are hell-bent on manipulating and exploiting the existing differences that make up the "PLANTATION" presently referred to as the HipHop Nation.

It would be very easy to send this book out on a confrontational tangent, engaging the corporate world and its rulers in a way that allows them to shake its criticism and keep on moving in the direction that the ruling nature of themselves have historically dictated, however, that has been done before and with little result.

To this end I have made the calculated assumption that only by penetrating the minds of the youth, the minds that are so thoroughly indulged in HipHop and its culture, could we finally make progress. You see, greed fuels the imperialistic mind, and power motivates it. These two inherent qualities of man and mankind, if not checked will bring about the destruction of those that continue to feed on it and its by-products. Therefore, it is my desire to allow the greed of the walking beasts and their desire for power to consume them without consuming those that are victimized by those beasts. In this instance "BEASTS" are defined as those that ravage the earth and devour those that would stand in its way.

All revolution has started within the heart and actions of the youth, it is for this reason that those who are in power desire to keep the masses of young people completely dumb and impotent in regards to the true and complete dynamics of the social, political, religious, and economic politic. Though the rulers of Corporate America (which includes government and so-called private industry) desire to keep the youth ignorant, they spend huge sums of money to insure that their personal offspring will benefit from social, political, educational, religious, and economic circles that will train them up into the roles of the master and not the slave.

It does not matter if we believe it or not; even if we refuse to accept what is so evidently clear, the plans of Corporate America is moving swiftly in the direction that it has historically dictated. They have chosen the music and culture of HipHop as their primary tool to keep the young blind, deaf, and dumb to what is truly taking place right before their eyes. This reality allows the youth to be used as a tool and also a slave.

The Empire desires to spread its idea by using material possessions and the desire for them to make the world's youth population sell-out the aspirations of true freedom and liberation in exchange for big wheels, naked women, gold and diamond teeth, and fancy cars. **This book is controversial because I and others have decided not to let that happen, it is as simple and as complex as that!**

I am certain that there will emerge the "YES, but…" arguments of all social and intellectual cowards. I'm speaking of those people that will acknowledge the truth of a statement, the facts of a statement, the historical evidence of a statement; yet will say, "BUT" it's really not that bad, or "the natural results of the truth of what you have stated is exaggerated or unproven". These people will probably die with their noses shoved deep into the corporate backsides (asses) of their open enemies. Therefore their ignorance bears a witness and supports the entire premise of this book.

There will also be an even more powerful and organized cry against this book and its truths, this cry will emerge from the mouths of so-called Jewish organizations that will claim that what I have written is anti-Semitic, and that I hate the Jewish people. This cry and tactic is **GARBAGE**, and I have written this note specifically to destroy this argument before it even takes place.

During the course of this writing it will become more and more evident who is in control of the HipHop Nation and its product and branding. It will also become clear to the reader that there is a specific group of people that are profiting from the depleting moral condition of black people. One can choose to argue if that one has not the intelligence nor courage to acknowledge the obvious; but the facts reveal that many, if not most who garnish millions of dollars and translated power from the exploitation of the HipHop world are in fact those whom consider themselves as Jews.

As we move forward recognize these following organizational names:

- **Anti-Defamation League**- founded by B'nai B'rith- Headquartered in **New York City**
- **The Independent Order of B'nai B'rith**- founded by Henry Jones and 11 others- Headquartered in New York City
- **Jewish Defense League**- founded by Rabbi Meir Kahane- Headquartered in **New York City**
- **Jewish Defense Organization**- founded by Mordechai Levy- Headquartered in **New York City**
- **Jewish Task Force**- ran by Chaim Ben Pesach- Headquartered in **New York State**.
- **The World Jewish Congress**- ran by Edgar M. Bronfman- Headquartered in **New York City**.

Though there are certainly others, the above organizations have an established track record of labeling black people and those who dare to speak the truth as anti-Semitic—and although I understand that there are many anti-Semitic people in the world, I am not one of them. The above organizations have alliances with many of the mainstream news sources that will print faulty reports and editorials labeling as anti-Semitic those that dare to criticize or confront the so-called Jewish actions and agendas. Since the American public have been effectively dumb-downed, the tactics of the above groups and organizations have been proven effective.

Let's define *anti*:

Pronunciation: 'an-"tI, 'an-tE
Function: *noun*
Inflected Form(s): *plural* **antis**
Etymology: *anti-*
: one that is opposed

Now, let's define **Semitic**:

Pronunciation: s&-'mi-tik *also* -'me-
Function: *adjective*
Etymology: German *semitisch*, from *Semit, Semite* Semite, probably from New Latin *Semita*, from Late Latin *Semitic* Shem
1: of, relating to, or constituting a subfamily of the Afro-Asiatic language family that includes Hebrew, Aramaic, Arabic, and Amharic

2: of, relating to, or characteristic of the Semites

I am certainly not anti-Semitic within the actual definition of the word, but it seems that the two words *anti* and *Semitic* has been merged into a meaning of "Jew Hater" by those that receive an economic and social benefit by redefining the term.

If I was to criticize the terrorist activities of a certain group of so-called Muslims would I be considered anti-Islamic? In addition, if these particular Muslims were of Arab decent, would I then become anti-Arab? But—the real question would be, since by definition the Arabs are *of* the Semitic peoples of the earth, would all those that criticize the actions of so-called Muslims that happen to be Arabs, be considered as anti-Semitic? If so, all of the above listed groups and many others are in fact the very thing that they accuse others of.

No I am not anti-Semitic; I am "ANTI" lie and deception. I am against those that receive special favor and recognition because they associate themselves with the faith of Judaism, and then abandon the moral brilliance of its doctrine in order to secure riches, wealth, and the earth's resources—resources that belong to us all.

I believe there are many so-called Jews that *claim* the faith of Judaism yet have attempted to alter that faith. I also believe it is these people that have effectively taken the very real horrors of the Holocaust, and traditional ill feelings levied against the Jewish faith and developed a superior unity of those that practice true Judaism, only to then place themselves atop of the faith so that they can systematically incorporate their form of false Judaism.

I refer to these particular Jew claimers as so-called Jews because they are not true Jews, they are imposters that worship money, power, wealth, and seek global domination. They use the faith of Judaism to shield their true actions and intentions. They do not seek the establishment of God's kingdom, they seek the establishment of their own empire, and they will step upon any man, woman, and child to fulfill their desires.

Please understand that I do not suggest that there are not so-called Muslims, Christians, and other faiths; those that misrepresent the true values of their faith and adopt ways and actions that lead people into a false understanding of what their faith actually represents and believes. However, this writing shows how those of the so-called Jewish faith have developed control of the world of news and entertainment and utilized its profits to secure riches for themselves while at the same time promoting filth and moral degeneracy through its product.

I move forward with this writing on the backs of many truth tellers that have went before me, and I stand upon the works of the spiritual and intellectual soldiers of history that have attempted to free the enslaved masses from the tyrannical clutches of ignorance and the proliferation of a global slave state. I realize that the majority of the readers of this book have been systematically conditioned to reject the truth when they hear it. I understand that radio, television, newspapers, and textbooks cry out against the reality of what I desire to paint a clear picture; but that is why this book must be written and read.

The State of New York has historically been the seat of financial power and control; this power and control is designed to grow as it merges with the governmental and military might that proceeds from the hollow halls of Washington D.C. This unholy alliance, Corporate America and Governmental America has taken the marriage vows of a husband and wife that share a mutual goal yet play distinct roles. No role is more important or more powerful than the other, their ambitions are the same, and their global perception is singular.

It is an allusion set forth by this unholy couple to have the American public and the world's public believe that there is no conspiracy of desire and agenda where the corporate and government America is concerned. However, the reader must at some point come to accept the nature of power, a power that most of us can't even imagine, not to mention experience.

When two individuals share the same ambition, the same desire, these two people become competitors. When these same two individuals desire world dominance, an inventory of liabilities and assets must be made. In the process of this inventory, these wise individuals have to acknowledge the flaws and inadequacies of their individual plans and agendas, and then move out on forming alliances that will subsidize their individual flaws and power inadequacies. A mutual dependency of two competitors forces them to become partners. As time moves on, these partners realize that their individual power is so connected and depended on the other that their power becomes singular, and their weakness become singular. This is because though they at one time enjoyed separate power, a power that was not strong enough to bring about their ultimate plan or goal, that power grew only by the alliance of those that would otherwise be seen as competitors

A conspiracy took place based on mutual desires and dependency, not on the emotional basis of friendship and loyalty. At this point it is no longer a conspiracy, it is a single idea and agenda, different elements of the same plan. There is no difference between corporate

America and governmental America; they are two sides of the same coin. If we continue to speak of this as a conspiracy we fail to understand the nature of the threat. If there was a conspiracy at this stage of the game, then perhaps we could break it up by isolating the individual conspirators into turning on the other, but because they have merged out of a conspiracy into a singular power structure, if one turned on the other, they simultaneously turn on themselves. The first law of nature is said to be "self preservation".

When I speak of the government of America, I am also speaking of the so-called Jews. When I speak about the so-called Jews, I am speaking of the government; why, because identity is based on ideology, not physical characteristics. Wickedly wise power brokers spend billions of dollars to get people to continue to focus on physical characteristics. This is the purpose of news and entertainment, which is their business, to sell images and get people to buy into them. However, the real person, the real absolute, is the idea that the person carries underneath a dove like exterior... even Adam wore a fig-leaf.

Individuals continue to argue over Israel and the United States; regardless of what position you hold, unless you view Israel "AS" the United States, and the United States "AS" Israel, your arguments are fundamentally flawed. People argue over Democrat or Republican; again, two sides of the same coin, an allusion. Republicans and Democrats are sustained and maintained by the same forces and desires, they have superficial differences on tactics, yet they have the same goal and agenda. It boils down to if they kiss you while fucking you, or slap you while fucking you; the bottom line is you get fucked!

I would ask you to excuse my language, but I don't want you to. Most of us get caught up on meaningless aspects of speaking yet totally abandon the undeniable truths that you hear. All you self righteous individuals, sit down, all the individuals that desire to confront the beast standup and let's go to work! I will point out just a couple more facts, and we will then move on.

For those that choose to be ignorant and choked by the paralyzing effects of intellectual cowardice, please understand that history bears an account of those that have chosen to use the good name of the biblical Moses to shield an idea and agenda that Moses himself did not conceive nor approve. When we witness the present world we live, can we accept that its politic is all centered on the Jewish question, the Israeli and Palestinian conflict, Iran and Iraq, the Saudi's and the American refusal to address their concerns where Israel is involved?

In addition to the above global politic that is centered on Israel and the Zionist agenda; are not Americans concerned about their national and individual financial situation. Do we ignore that the Federal Reserve is an institution that was created and has been sustained by the so-called Jews? Is our fear of being labeled as anti-Semitic causing us to be cowards within the face of actual facts? Can we accept the fact and its consequence that every single chairmen of the Federal Reserve has been so-called Jewish—including the last two, Alan Greenspan and its present Mr. Ben Shalom Bernanke (Yes, that's his real middle name)?

The HipHop Nation in particular and the global community in general, must at some point come to recognize the role of America and the so-called Jewish reality in order to free themselves from a slavery that is true to form, and devastating to the future condition of us all.

Though I certainly don't endorse the entirety of the philosophical stance of the following individuals, I never the less, elucidate their words concerning the so-called Jew in order to show the similar perception of those with various political, social, religious and national backgrounds. In many cases the same people have voiced negative words concerning black people, and I can and will bring those philosophical assumptions to task in future works. It should be understood that I neither endorse nor put a stamp of approval upon their comments or suggestions; I simply bring them to the reader's attention as a tool of information that will assist you in the assessment of this book's value and accuracy.

CICERO (Marcus Tullius Cicero).

First century B.C. Roman statesman and writer

"Softly! Softly! I want none but the judges to hear me. The Jews have already gotten me into a fine mess, as they have many other gentlemen. I have no desire to furnish further grist for their mills"

"The Jews belong to a dark and repulsive force. One knows how numerous this cliques is, how they stick together and what power they exercise through their unions. They are a nation of rascals and deceivers."

DIODORUS SICULUS. First century Greek historian

"Usury" is the practice of lending money at excessive interest rates. This has for centuries caused great misery and poverty for Gentiles. It has brought strong condemnation of the Jews!"

BERNARDINO OF FELTRO 15th century Italian priest

"Jewish usurers bleed the poor to death and grow fat on their substance, and I who live on alms, who feed on the bread of the poor, shall I then be mute before outraged charity? Dogs bark to protect those who feed them, and I, who am fed by the poor, shall I see them robbed of what belongs to them and keep silent?" (E. Flornoy, Le Bienbeureux Bernardin the Feltre)

HILAIRE BELLOC, in the book THE JEWS, page 9

"There is already something like a Jewish monopoly in high finance . . . There is the same element of Jewish monopoly in the silver trade, and in the control of various other metals, notably lead, nickel, quicksilver. What is most disquieting of all, this tendency to monopoly is spreading like a disease."

H. H. BEAMISH, in New York Speech, October 30, 1937

"The Boer War occurred 37 years ago. Boer means farmer. Many criticized a great power like Britain for trying to wipe out the Boers. Upon making inquiry, I found all the gold and diamond mines of South Africa were owned by Jews; that

Rothschild controlled gold; Samuels controlled silver, Baum controlled other mining, and Moses controlled base metals. Anything these people touch they inevitably pollute."

MARTIN LUTHER, Table Talk of Martin Luther, translated by William Hazlet, page 43

"But the Jews are so hardened that they listen to nothing; though overcome by testimonies they yield not an inch. It is a pernicious race, oppressing all men by their usury and rapine. If they give a prince or magistrate a thousand florins, they extort twenty thousand from the subjects in payment. We must ever keep on guard against them."

BEAMISH, HENRY H. 20th century British publisher "There is no need to be delicate on this Jewish question. You must face them in this country. The Jew should be satisfied here. I was here forty-seven years ago; your doors were thrown open and you were then free. Now he has got you absolutely by the throat -- that is their reward." (New York speech, October 30, 1937)

HARRINGTON, LORD. 19th century British statesman

"They are the great moneylenders and loan contractors of the world... The consequence is that the nations of the world are groaning under heavy systems of taxation and national debt. They have ever been the greatest enemies of freedom. (Speech in the House of Lords, July 12, 1858)

WALTER CRICK, British Manufacturer, in the NORTHAMPTON DAILY ECHO, March 19, 1925)

"Jews can destroy by means of finance. Jews are International. Control of credits in this country is not in the hands of the English, but of Jews. It has become the biggest danger the British Empire ever had to face."

WORLD FAMOUS MEN of the past accused the Jews of founding Communism. This charge is well founded. The Communist philosophy was drawn up by Karl Marx who descended from a long line of Rabbis. His ideology of anti-Christian and Socialist thought is outlined in the Jewish "TALMUD" which is the "bible" of the Jews. Of the four political groups which overthrew the Christian Czar of Russia two were 100percent Jewish. They were the Mensheviks and The Jewish Bund. The other two were the Socialist Revolutionary Party and the Bolsheviks. Both were headed by Jews but had some Gentile members. Today we now know that Lenin was Jewish and all of the leaders of his first government were Jews. They were Trotsky, Zinoviev, Kamenev and Sverdlow. The wealthiest Jewish banker in the world at that time, Jacob Schiff of Kuhn, Loeb investment bank of New York City, gave Trotsky and Lenin $20 million to overthrow the Czar and establish the Soviet tyranny (according to the "NEW YORK JOURNAL-

AMERICAN" of February 3, 1949.)

CHURCHILL, WINSTON. 20th century British politician

"In violent opposition to this entire sphere of Jewish efforts rise the schemes of the International Jews. The adherents of this sinister confederacy are mostly men reared up among the unhappy populations of countries where Jews are persecuted on account of their race. Most, if not all, of them have forsaken the faith of their forefathers, and divorced from their minds all spiritual hopes of the next world. This movement among the Jews is not new. From the days of Spartacus-Weishaupt to those of Karl Marx, and down to Trotsky (Russia), Bela Kun (Hungary), Rosa Luxemburg (Germany), and Emma Goldman (United States), this world-wide revolutionary conspiracy for the overthrow of civilization and for the reconstitution of society on the basis of arrested development, of envious malevolence, and impossible equality, has been steadily growing. It played, as a modern writer, Mrs. Webster has ably shown, a definite recognizable part in the tragedy of the French Revolution. It has been the mainspring of every subversive movement during the Nineteenth Century; and now at last this band of extraordinary personalities from the underworlds of the great cities of Europe and America have gripped the Russian people by the hair of their heads and have become practically the undisputed masters of the enormous empire. There is no need to exaggerate the part played in the creating of Bolshevism and in the actual bringing about of the Russian Revolution by these international and for the most part atheistic Jews. It is certainly the very great one; it probably outweighs all others. With the notable exception of Lenin, the majority of the leading figures are Jews. Moreover, the principal inspiration and driving power comes from the Jewish leaders . . . In the Soviet institutions the predominance of Jews is even more astounding. And the prominent if not the principal part in the system of terrorism applied by the extraordinary Commissions for combating Counter Revolution has been take by Jews, and in some notable cases by Jewesses. The same evil prominence was obtained by Jews in the brief period of terror during which Bela Kun ruled in Hungary. The same phenomenon has been presented in Germany (especially Bavaria), so far as this madness has been allowed to prey upon the temporary prostration of the German people. Although in all these countries there are many non-Jews, every bit as bad as the worst of the Jewish revolutionaries, the part played by the latter in proportion to their numbers in the population is astonishing. ("Zionism versus Bolshevism: A Struggle for the Soul of the Jewish People." ILLUSTRATED SUNDAY HERALD, London, February 8, 1920.)

WILHELM II. German Kaiser.

"A Jew cannot be a true patriot. He is something different, like a bad insect. He must be kept apart, out of a place where he can do mischief - even by pogroms, if necessary. The Jews are responsible for Bolshevism in Russia, and Germany too. I was far too indulgent with them during my reign, and I bitterly regret the favors I showed the prominent Jewish bankers." (CHICAGO TRIBUNE, July 2, 1922)

ADRIEN ARCAND, New York speech, October 30, 1937

"When it came to Mexico, the promoters of Communism were the Jews Calles, Hubermann and Aaron Saenz; in Spain we saw Azaa and Rosenberg; in Hungary we saw Bela Kun, Szamuelly, Agoston and dozen other Jews; in Bavaria, we saw Kurt Eisner and a host of other Jews; in Belgium Marxian Socialism brought to power Vadervelde alias Epstein, and Paul Hymans, two Jews; in France, Marxian Socialism brought forth the Jews Leon Blum (who showed so well his Jewish instincts in his filthy book Du Mariarge), Mandel, Zyromsky, Danain and a whole tribe of them; in Italy we had seen the Jews Nathan and Claudio Treves. Everywhere, Marxism brings Jews on the top -- And this is no hazard."

HILAIRE BELLOC, renowned historian in G. K.'s WEEKLY, February 4, 1937

"The propaganda of Communism throughout the world, in organization and direction is in the hands of Jewish agents. As for anyone who does not know that the Bolshevist movement in Russia is Jewish, I can only say that he must be a man who is taken in by the suppression of our deplorable press."

A. HOMER writes in Judaism and Bolshevism, page 7

"History shows that the Jew has always been, by nature, a revolutionary and that, since the dispersion of his race in the second century, he has either initiated or assisted revolutionary movements in religion, politics and finance, which weakened the power of the States wherein he dwelt. On the other hand, a few far-seeing members of that race have always been at hand to reap financial and political advantage coincident with such upheavals."

MRS. CLARE SHERIDAN, Traveler, Lecturer in NEW YORK WORLD, December 15, 1923

"The Communists are Jews, and Russia is being entirely administered by them. They are in every government office, bureau and newspaper. They are driving out the Russians and are responsible for the anti-Semitic feeling which is increasing."

MAJOR ROBERT H. WILLIAMS, in Fecp and the Minority Machine, page 10

"B'nai B'rith, the secret Jewish fraternity, was organized in 1843, awakening world Jewish aspirations, or Zionism, and its name, meaning "Sons of the Covenant," suggests that the 12 men who organized the fraternity aimed at bringing about the fulfillment of "the Covenant," or the supposed Messianic promise of ruler ship over all peoples. To rule all peoples, it is first necessary to bring them together in a world federation or world government -- which is the avowed aim of both Communists and Zionists."

JOSEPH STALIN in a reply given on January 12, 1931 to an enquiry made by the Jewish Telegraphic Agency of America (Stars and Sand, page 316)

"Anti-Semitism is dangerous for the toilers, for it is a false track which diverts them from the proper road and leads them into the jungle. Hence, Communists, as consistent internationalists, cannot but be irreconcilable and bitter enemies of anti-Semitism. In the U.S.S.R., anti-Semitism is strictly prosecuted as a phenomenon hostile to the Soviet system. According to the laws of the U.S.S.R. active anti-Semites are punished with death."

VLADIMIR, LENIN, Founder of Bolshevik Communist (From an article in Northern Pravda, October-December 1913, quoted in Lenin on the Jewish Question, page 10)

"There the great universally progressive features of Jewish culture have made themselves clearly felt: its internationalism, its responsiveness of the advanced movements of our times (the percentage of Jews in democratic and proletarian movements is everywhere higher than the percentage of Jews in the general population.) . . . Those Jewish Marxists who join up in the international Marxist organizations with the Russian, Lithuanian, Ukrainian and other workers, adding their might (both in Russian and in Jewish) to the creation of an international culture of the working class movement, are continuing the best traditions of Jewry."

A. N. FIELD, in Today's Greatest Problem

"Once the Jewishness of Bolshevism is understood, its otherwise puzzling features become understandable. Hatred of Christianity, for instance, is not a Russian characteristic; it is a Jewish one."

FATHER DENIS FAHEY; in his book The Rulers of Russia, page 25

"The real forces behind Bolshevism in Russia are Jewish forces, and Bolshevism is really an instrument in the hands of the Jews for the establishment of their future Messianic kingdom."

A. N. FIELD, The Truth About the Slump, page 208

"The World today, however provides a spectacle of a great concentration of Jewish power. In New York there is a concentration of Jewish financial power dominating the entire world in its material affairs, and side by side with it is the greatest physical concentration of the Jews ever recorded. On the other side of the globe, there has taken place in Russia the greatest concentration of the Jewish revolutionary activity in all history . . . The enormously significant thing in the world today is that both this power of the purse

(Theodor Herzl's "terrible (Jewish) power of the purse") and revolutionary activity are working in the direction of destroying the entire existing order of things, and not only are they working in a common direction, but there is a mass of evidence that they are working in unison."

H. H. BEAMISH, N.Y. speech, 1937

"Communism is Judaism. The Jewish Revolution in Russia was in 1918."

HILARY COTTER, author of Cardinal Minszenty, The Truth About His Real "Crime," page 6

"Communism and Judaism are one and the same."

ADRIEN ARCAND, Canadian political leader in New York Speech, October 30, 1937

"There is nothing else in Communism -- a Jewish conspiracy to grab the whole world in their clutches; and no intelligent man in the world can find anything else, except the Jews, who rightly call it for themselves a "paradise on earth."

"Jews are eager to bring Communism, because they know what it is and what it means. It is because Communism has not been fought for what it really is -- a Jewish scheme invented by Jews -- that it has progressed against all opposition to it. We have fought the smoke-screen presented by Jewish dialecticians and publicists, refusing to fight the inventor, profiteer and string-puller. Because Christians and Gentiles have come to fear the Jews, fear the truth, and they are paralyzed by the paradoxical slogans shouted by the Jews."

REV. KENNETH GOFF, in STILL 'TIS OUR ANCIENT FOE, page 99

"The Frankenstein of Communism is the product of the Jewish mind, and was turned loose upon the world by the son of a Rabbi, Karl Marx, in the hopes of destroying Christian civilization -- as well as others. The testimony given before the Senate of the United States which is taken from the many pages of the Overman Report reveals beyond a shadow of a doubt that Jewish bankers financed the Russian Revolution."

GRANT, ULYSSES S. 19th century American general, politician

"I have long since believed that in spite of all the vigilance that can be infused into post commanders, the special regulations of the Treasury Department have been violated and that mostly by Jews and other unprincipled traders. So well satisfied have I been of this that I instructed the commanding officers at Columbus to refuse all permits to Jews to come South, and I have frequently had them expelled from the department, but they come in with their carpet-sacks in spite of all that can be done to prevent it. The Jews seem to be a privileged class that can travel anywhere. They will land at any wood yard on the river and make their way through the country. If not permitted to buy cotton themselves, they will act as agents for someone else, who will be at military post with a Treasury permit to receive cotton and pay for it in Treasury notes which the Jew will buy up at an agreed rate, paying gold. (Letters to C. P. Wolcott, assistant secretary of war, Washington, December 17, 1862)

1). The Jews, as a class, violating every regulation of trade established by the Treasury Department, and also Department orders, are hereby expelled from the Department.

2). Within twenty-four hours from the receipt of this order by Post Commanders, they will see that all of this class of people are furnished with passes and required to leave, and anyone returning after such notification, will be arrested and held in confinement until an opportunity occurs of sending them out as prisoners, unless furnished with permits from these headquarters.

3). No permits will be given these people to visit headquarters for the purpose of making personal application for trade permits. By order of Major Gen. Grant Jno A. Rawlings, Assistant Adjutant General (General Order Number 11, December 17, 1862)

The expulsion order was immediately countermanded by the general-in-chief, H. W. Halleck, in Washington. Apparently the expelled Jews had immediately contacted their kinsmen there and had pressure brought to bear.

HERMAN, WILLIAM T. 19th century American soldier

"I found so many Jews and speculators here trading in cotton, and secessionists had become so open in refusing anything but gold, that I have felt myself bound to stop it. The gold can have but one use -- the purchase of arms and ammunition . . . Of course, I have

Respected all permits by yourself or the Secretary of the Treasury, but in these new cases (swarms of Jews), I have stopped it." (The Sherman Letters)

ROSS, L. F. 19th century American military man

"The cotton speculators are quite clamorous for aid in the getting their cotton away from Middleburg, Hickory Valley, etc., and offer to pay liberally for the service. I think I can bring it away with safety, and make it pay to the Government. As some of the Jew owners have as good as stolen the cotton from the planters, I have no conscientious scruples in making them pay liberally to take it away."

OLMSTED, GREDERICK LAW. 19th century American architect, historian

"A swarm of Jews has, within the last ten years, settled in every Southern town, many of them men of no character, opening cheap clothing and trinket shops, ruining or driving out of business many of the old retailers, and engaging in an unlawful trade with the simple Negroes, which is found very profitable. (The Cotton Kingdom For other views on Jewish involvement in exploiting the South, see ULYSSES S. GRANT and MARK TWAIN.)

TWAIN MARK (S. L. Clemens). 19th century American writer

"In the U.S. cotton states, after the war . . . the Jew came down in force, set up shop on the plantation, supplied all the Negroes' wants on credit, and at the end of the season was the proprietor of the Negro's share of the present crop and part of the next one. Before long, the whites detested the Jew.

1). The Jew is being legislated out of Russia. The reason is not concealed. The movement was instituted because the Christian peasant stood no chance against his commercial abilities. The Jew was always ready to lend on a crop. When settlement day came, he owned the crop; the next year he owned the farm -- like Joseph.

2). In the England of John's time everybody got into debt to the Jew. He gathered all lucrative enterprises into his hands. He was the King of Commerce. He had to be banished from the realm. For like reasons, Spain had to banish him 400 years ago, and Austria a couple of centuries later. In all ages Christian Europe has been obliged to curtail his activities. If he entered upon a trade, the Christian had to retire from it. If he set up as a doctor, he took the business. If he exploited agriculture, the other farmers had to get at something else. The law had to step in to save the Christian from the poor-house. Still, almost bereft of employments, he found ways to make money. Even to get rich. This history has a most sordid and practical commercial look. Religious prejudices may account for one part of it, but not for the other nine. Protestants have persecuted Catholics -- but they did not take their livelihoods away from them. Catholics have persecuted Protestants -- but they never closed agriculture and the handicrafts against them. I feel convinced that the Crucifixion has not much to do with the world's attitude toward the Jew; that the reasons for it are much older than that event . . . I am convinced that the persecution of the Jew is not in any large degree due to religious prejudice. No, the Jew is a money-getter. He made it the end and aim of his life. He was at it in Rome. He has been at it ever since. His success has made the whole human race his enemy. You will say that the Jew is everywhere numerically feeble. When I read in the Cyclopedia Britannica that the Jewish population in the United States was 250,000 I wrote the editor and explained to him that I was personally acquainted with more Jews than that, and that his figures were without doubt a misprint for 25,000,000. People told me that they had reasons to suspect that for business reasons, many Jews did not report themselves as Jews. It looks plausible. I am strongly of the opinion that we have an immense Jewish population in America. I am assured by men competent to speak that the Jews are exceedingly active in politics. ("Concerning the Jews," Harper's Monthly Magazine, September 1899)

GOLDWIN SMITH, Professor of Modern History at Oxford, wrote in Nineteenth Century, October 1881

"The Jew alone regard his race as superior to humanity, and looks forward not to its ultimate union with other races, but to its triumph over them all and to its final ascendancy under the leadership of a tribal Messiah."

SOMBART, WERNER. 20th century German economist

"Capitalism was born from the money loan. Money lending contains the root idea of capitalism. Turn to the pages of the TALMUD and you will find that the Jews made an art of lending money. They were taught early to look for their chief happiness in the possession of money. They fathomed all the secrets that lay hid in money. They became Lords of Money and Lords of the World . . ."

FITZGERALD, F. SCOTT 20th century American novelist

"Down a tall busy street he read a dozen Jewish names on a line of stores; in the door of each stood a dark little man watching the passers from intent eyes -- eyes gleaming with suspicion, with pride, with clarity, with cupidity, with comprehension. New York -- he

could not dissociate it from the slow, upward creep of this people -- the little stores, growing, expanding, consolidating, moving, watched over with hawks' eyes and a bee's attention to detail - they [were Jews.]

EMERSON, RALPH WALDO. 19th century American philosopher, poet

"The sufferance which is the badge of the Jew has made him, in these days, the ruler of the rulers of the earth. (Fate an essay)

DREISER, THEODORE. 20th century American writer

"New York to me is a scream -- a Kyke's dream of a ghetto. The Lost Tribe has taken the island. (Letter to H. L. Mencken, November 5, 1922) "

"Liberalism, in the case of the Jew, means internationalism. If you listen to Jews discuss Jews, you will find they are money-minded, very sharp in practice. The Jews lack the fine integrity which at last is endorsed, and to a certain degree followed, by lawyers of other nationalities. The Jew has been in Germany for a thousand years, and he is still a Jew. He has been in America for all of 200 years, and he has not faded into a pure American by any means -- and he will not. (Letter to Hutchins Hapgood, The Nation magazine, April 17, 1935)"

WELLS, H. G. 20th century British writer

"The Jews looked for a special savior, a messiah, who was to redeem mankind by the agreeable process of restoring the fabulous glories of David and Solomon, and bringing the whole world at last under the firm but benevolent Jewish heel." (The Outline of History)

"Zionism is an expression of Jewish refusal to assimilate. If the Jews have suffered, it is because they have regarded themselves as a chosen people." (The Anatomy of Frustration)

"A careful study of anti-Semitism prejudice and accusations might be of great value to many Jews, who do not adequately realize the irritations they inflict." (Letter of November 11, 1933)

Wells was in the habit of referring to KARL MARX as "a shallow third-rate Jew," and "a lousy Jew" in private correspondence. (Norman MacKenzie, H. G. Wells)

LINDBERGH, CHARLES. 20th century American aviator, writer Wednesday, August 23, 1939

"We are disturbed about the effect of the Jewish influence in our press, radio and motion pictures. It may become very serious. [Fulton] Lewis told us of one instance where the Jewish advertising firms threatened to remove all their advertising from the Mutual system if a certain feature were permitted to go on the air. The threat was powerful enough to have the feature removed."

Thursday, May 1, 1941 "The pressure for war is high and mounting. The people are opposed to it, but the Administration seems to have 'the bit in its teeth' and is hell-bent on its way to war. Most of the Jewish interests in the country are behind war, and they control a huge part of our press and radio and most of our motion pictures. There are the 'intellectuals' and the 'Anglophiles,' and the British agents who are allowed free rein, the international financial interests, and many others." (The Wartime Journals)

GENERAL GEORGE VAN HORN MOSELY, in the New York Tribune, March 29, 1939

"The war now proposed is for the purpose of establishing Jewish influence throughout the world."

HERDER, JOHANN GOTTFRIED. 18th century German philosopher

"The Jewish people is and remains in Europe an Asiatic people alien to our part of the world, bound to that old law which it received in a distant climate, and which, according to its confession, it cannot do away with . . . How many of this alien people can be tolerated without injury to the true citizen? A ministry in which a Jew is supreme, a household in which a Jew has the key of the wardrobe and the management of the finances, a department or commissariat in which Jews do the principal business, are Pontine Marshes which cannot be drained. (Bekehrung der Juden) For thousands of years, since their emergence on the stage of history, the Jews were a parasitic growth on the stem of other nations, a race of cunning brokers all over the earth. They have cause great evil to many ill-organized states, by retarding the free and natural economic development of their indigenous population. ("Hebraer," in Ideen)

BONAPARTE, NAPOLEON. French statesman, general

"The Jews provided troops for my campaign in Poland, but they ought to reimburse me: I soon found that they are no good for anything but selling old clothes . . ." "Legislating must be put in effect everywhere that the general well-being is in danger. The government cannot look with indifference on the way a despicable nation takes possession of all the provinces of France. The Jews are the master robbers of the modern age; they are the carrion birds of humanity . . . "They must be treated with political justice, not with civil justice. They are surely not real citizens."

"The Jews have practiced usury since the time of Moses, and oppressed the other peoples. Meanwhile, the Christians were only rarely usurers, falling into disgrace when they did so. We ought to ban the Jews from commerce because they abuse it . . . The evils of the Jews do not stem from individuals but from the fundamental nature of this people." Excerpt from Napoleon's Reflections and from speeches before the Council of State on April 30, and May 7, 1806.

"Nothing more contemptible could be done than the reception of the Jews by you. I decided to improve the Jews. But I do not want more of them in my kingdom. Indeed, I have done all to prove my scorn of the most vile nation in the world." (Letter to his brother Jerome, King of Westphalia, March 6, 1808)

1). Every big and small Jew in the peddling trade must renew his license every year.

2). Checks and other obligations are only redeemable if the Jew can prove that he has obtained the money without cheating. (Ordinance of March 17, 1808. The Napoleonic Code

DE GAULLE, CHARLES. 20th century French politician

"The Jews remain what they have been at all times: an elite people, self-confident and domineering."

SAND, GEORGE (Amantine Dupin Dudevant). 19th century French novelist

"I saw in 'the wandering Jew' the personification of the Jewish people, exiled in the Middle Ages. Nevertheless, they are once again extremely rich, owing to their unfailing rude greediness and their indefatigable activity. With their hardheartedness that they extend toward people of other faiths and races they are at the point of making themselves kings of the world. This people can thank its obstinacy that France will be Judized within fifty years. Already some wise Jews prophesy this frankly." (Letter to Victor Lorie, 1857)

COMMUNITY OF STRASBOURG, FRANCE

"Everyone knew the inherent bad character of the Jews and no one doubted they were foreigners . . . Let the 'enlighteners' stop defaming the Gentiles by blaming them for what is wrong with the Jews. Their conduct is their own fault. Perhaps the Jews might eventually give up every aspect of their separation and all the characteristics of their nature. Let us sit and wait until that happens; we might them judge them to be worthy of equality. (Tres Humble Adresse qui Presente la Commune de la Ville Strasbourg)

ROBERTS, STEPHEN H. 20th century Australian historian

"It is useless to deny that grave Jewish problems existed in Germany. The nation was in the unfortunate geographical position of being the first stage in the perennial push westward of the Polish Jews. Unless forced on, they tended to stop in Berlin and Hamburg, where they obtained an unduly share of good professional positions. In Berlin, for example, when the Nazi came to power, 50.2 percent of the lawyers were Jews. In medicine, 48 percent of the doctors were Jews, and it was said that they systematically seized the principal hospital posts. The Jews owned the largest and most important Berlin newspapers, and they had made great inroads on the educational system."

FRANCO, FRANCISCO. 20th century Spanish statesman

"Let us be under no illusion. The Jewish spirit, which was responsible for the alliance of large-scale capital with Marxism and was the driving force behind so many anti-Spanish revolutionary agreements, will not be got rid of in a day."

H. H. BEAMISH, in a New York address, October 30 - November 1, 1937

"In 1848 the word "anti-Semitic" was invented by the Jews to prevent the use of the word "Jew." The right word for them is "Jew" . . . "I implore all of you to be accurate -- call them Jews. There is no need to be delicate on this Jewish question. You must face them in this country. The Jew should be satisfied here. I was here forty-seven years ago; your doors were thrown open to the Jews and they were free. Now he has got you absolutely by the throat—that is your reward."

CHRISTEA, PATRIARCH. 20th century Romanian prelate

"The Jews have caused an epidemic of corruption and social unrest. They monopolize the press, which, with foreign help, flays all the spiritual treasures of the Romanians. To defend ourselves is a national and patriotic duty -- not anti-Semitism. Lack of measures to get rid of the plague would indicate that we are lazy cowards who let ourselves be carried alive to our graves. Why should we not get rid of these parasites that suck Romanian and Christian blood? It is logical and holy to react against them." (New York Herald Tribune, August 17, 1937)

ADRIEN ARCAND, Canadian political leader of the 1930s

"Through their (Jew's) international news agencies, they mold your mind and have you see, the world not as it is but as they want you to see it. Through their cinema, they are the educators of our youth -- and with just one film in two hours, can wipe out of a child's brain what he has learned in six months in the home, the church or the school."

NESTA WEBSTER, in her book Germany and England

"England is no longer controlled by Britons. We are under the invisible Jewish dictatorship -- a dictatorship that can be felt in every sphere of life."

ENRY WALLACE, Secretary of Commerce, under President Harry Truman, wrote in his dairy that in 1946

"Truman was "exasperated" over Jewish pressure that he support Zionist rule over Palestine. Wallace added "Pres. Truman expressed himself as being very much 'put out' with the Jews. He said that 'Jesus Christ couldn't please them when he was here on Earth, so how could anyone expect that I would have any luck?' Pres. Truman said he had no use for them and didn't care what happened to them."

WILLIAM JENNINGS BRYANT, three times the Democratic Party candidate for President

"New York is the city of privilege. Here is the seat of the Invisible Power represented by the allied forces of finance and industry. This Invisible Government is reactionary, sinister, unscrupulous, mercenary, and sordid. It is wanting in national ideals and devoid of conscience . . . This kind of government must be scourged and destroyed."

HENRY ADAMS (Descendant of President John Adams),

"The Jewish question is really the most serious of our problems."

SPRING-RICE, SIR CECIL 20th century British politician

"One by one, the Jews are capturing the principal newspapers of America. (Letter of November 1914, to Sir Edward Grey, foreign secretary Letters and Friendships)

CAPOTE, TRUMAN. 20th century American writer

In an interview, he assailed "the Zionist mafia" monopolizing publishing today, and protested a tendency to suppress things that do not meet with Jewish approval. (Playboy magazine, March 1968)

VOLTAIRE (Francois Marie Arouet) 18th century French philosopher, writer

"Why are the Jews hated? It is the inevitable result of their laws; they either have to conquer everybody or be hated by the whole human race . . ." "The Jewish nation dares to display an irreconcilable hatred toward all nations, and revolts against all masters; always superstitious, always greedy for the well-being enjoyed by others, always barbarous -- cringing in misfortune and insolent in prosperity." (Essai sur le Moeurs)

You seem to me to be the maddest of the lot. The Kaffirs, the Hottentots, and the Negroes of Guinea are much more reasonable and more honest people than your ancestors, the Jews. You have surpassed all nations in impertinent fables in bad conduct and in barbarism. You deserve to be punished, for this is your destiny."

"You will only find in the Jews an ignorant and barbarous people, who for a long time have joined the most sordid avarice to the most detestable superstition and to the most invincible hatred of all peoples which tolerate and enrich them." ("Juif," Dictionnaire Philosophique)

"I know that there are some Jews in the English colonies. These Marranos go wherever there is money to be made . . . But whether these circumcised who sell old clothes claim that they are of the tribe of Naphtali or Issachar is not of the slightest importance. They are, simply, the biggest scoundrels who have ever dirtied the face of the earth." (Letter to Jean-Baptiste Nicolas de Lisle de Sales, December 15, 1773, Correspondence. 86:166)

"They are, all of them, born with raging fanaticism in their hearts, just as the Bretons and the Germans are born with blond hair. I would not be in the least bit surprised if these people would not someday become deadly to the human race." (Lettres de Memmius a Ciceron, 1771)

HENRY FORD in (The Dearborn Independent, 12-19 February 1921

"Jews have always controlled the business . . . The motion picture influence of the United States and Canada . . . is exclusively under the control, moral and financial, of the Jewish manipulators of the public mind."

WASHINGTON, GEORGE, in Maxims of George Washington by A. A. Appleton & Co.

"They (the Jews) work more effectively against us, than the enemy's armies. They are a hundred times more dangerous to our liberties and the great cause we are engaged in... It is much to be lamented that each state, long ago, has not hunted them down as pest to society and the greatest enemies we have to the happiness of America."

This prophecy, by **Benjamin Franklin**, was made in a "CHIT CHAT AROUND THE TABLE DURING INTERMISSION," at the Philadelphia Constitutional Convention of 1787. This statement was recorded in the dairy of Charles Cotesworth Pinckney, a delegate from South Carolina.

"I fully agree with General Washington, that we must protect this young nation from an insidious influence and impenetration. The menace, gentlemen, is the Jews. In whatever country Jews have settled in any great number, they have lowered its moral tone; depreciated its commercial integrity; have segregated themselves and have not been assimilated; have sneered at and tried to undermine the Christian religion upon which that nation is founded, by objecting to its restrictions; have built up a state within the state; and when opposed have tried to strangle that country to death financially, as in the case of Spain and Portugal. For over 1,700 years, the Jews have been bewailing their sad fate in that they have been exiled from their homeland, as they call Palestine. But gentlemen, did the world give it to them in fee simple, they would at once find some reason for not returning. Why? Because they are vampires, and vampires do not live on vampires. They cannot live only among themselves. They must subsist on Christians and other people not of their race. If you do not exclude them from these United States, in their Constitution, in less than 200 years they will have swarmed here in such great numbers that they will dominate and devour the land and change our form of government, for which we Americans have shed our blood, given our lives our substance and jeopardized our liberty. If you do not exclude them, in less than 200 years our descendants will be working in the fields to furnish them substance, while they will be in the counting houses rubbing their hands. I warn you, gentlemen, if you do not exclude Jews for all time, your children will curse you in your graves. Jews, gentlemen are Asiatic, let them be born where they will. Nor how many generations they are away from Asia, they will never be otherwise. Their ideas do not conform to an American's, and will not even thou they live among us ten generations. A leopard cannot change its spots. Jews are Asiatic, are a menace to this country if permitted entrance, and should be excluded by this Constitutional Convention.

JEFFERSON, THOMAS. 18th century American statesman

"Dispersed as the Jews are, they still form one nation, foreign to the land they live in." (D. Boorstin, THE AMERICANS)

"Those who labor in the earth are the Chosen People of God, if ever he had a chosen people." (NOTES ON VIRGINIA)

As we close this special note and move on with this book's message, I challenge the so-called black preachers, the so-called black Christians, the so-called follower's and students of Jesus to consider his words as he has a conversation with the so-called Jew:

John 8.31 - 8.59

31 Jesus then said to the Jews who had believed in him, "If you continue in my word, you are truly my disciples,
32 and you will know the truth, and the truth will make you free."
33 They answered him, "We are descendants of Abraham, and have never been in bondage to anyone. How is it that you say, 'You will be made free'?"
34 Jesus answered them, "Truly, truly, I say to you, everyone who commits sin is a slave to sin.
35 The slave does not continue in the house for ever; the son continues for ever.
36 So if the Son makes you free, you will be free indeed.
37 I know that you are descendants of Abraham; yet you seek to kill me, because my word finds no place in you.
38 I speak of what I have seen with my Father, and you do what you have heard from your father."
39 They answered him, "Abraham is our father." Jesus said to them, "If you were Abraham's children, you would do what Abraham did,
40 but now you seek to kill me, a man who has told you the truth which I heard from God; this is not what Abraham did.
41 You do what your father did." They said to him, "We were not born of fornication; we have one Father, even God."
42 Jesus said to them, "If God were your Father, you would love me, for I proceeded and came forth from God; I came not of my own accord, but he sent me.
43 Why do you not understand what I say? It is because you cannot bear to hear my word.
44 You are of your father the devil, and your will is to do your father's desires. He was a murderer from the beginning, and has nothing to do with the truth, because there is no truth in him. When he lies, he speaks according to his own nature, for he is a liar and the father of lies.
45 But, because I tell the truth, you do not believe me.
46 Which of you convicts me of sin? If I tell the truth, why do you not believe me?
47 He who is of God hears the words of God; the reason why you do not hear them is that you are not of God."

48 The Jews answered him, "Are we not right in saying that you are a Samaritan and have a demon?"
49 Jesus answered, "I have not a demon; but I honor my Father, and you dishonor me.
50 Yet I do not seek my own glory; there is One who seeks it and he will be the judge.
51 Truly, truly, I say to you, if any one keeps my word, he will never see death."
52 The Jews said to him, "Now we know that you have a demon. Abraham died, as did the prophets; and you say, 'If any one keeps my word, he will never taste death.'
53 Are you greater than our father Abraham, who died? And the prophets died! Who do you claim to be?"
54 Jesus answered, "If I glorify myself, my glory is nothing; it is my Father who glorifies me, of whom you say that he is your God.
55 But you have not known him; I know him. If I said, I do not know him, I should be a liar like you; but I do know him and I keep his word.
56 Your father Abraham rejoiced that he was to see my day; he saw it and was glad."
57 The Jews then said to him, "You are not yet fifty years old, and have you seen Abraham?"
58 Jesus said to them, "Truly, truly, I say to you, before Abraham was, I am."
59 So they took up stones to throw at him; but Jesus hid himself, and went out of the temple.

Revelation 2:9-10, 3:9.

I know thy works, and tribulation, and poverty, (but thou art rich) and *I know* **the blasphemy of them which say they are Jews, and are not, but** *are* **the synagogue of Satan**. Fear none of those things which thou shalt suffer . . . be thou faithful unto death, and I will give thee a crown of life. . . . Behold, I will make them of the **synagogue of Satan**, which say they are Jews, and are not, but do lie; behold, I will make them to come and worship before thy feet, and to know that I have loved thee.

Matthew 23:27-33.

Woe unto you, scribes and Pharisees, hypocrites! for ye are like unto whited sepulchres, which indeed appear beautiful outward, but are within full of dead *men's* bones, and of all uncleanness. Even so ye also outwardly appear righteous unto men, but within **ye are full of hypocrisy and iniquity**. Woe unto you, scribes and Pharisees, hypocrites! Because ye build the tombs of the prophets, and garnish the sepulchres of the righteous, and say, if we had been in the days of our fathers, we would not have been partakers with them in the blood of the prophets. Wherefore ye are witnesses unto yourselves, that ye are the children of them which killed the prophets. Fill ye up then the measure of your fathers. **Ye serpents,** *ye* **generation of vipers, how can ye escape the damnation of hell?**

WILLIE LYNCH
The Letter

Greetings,

Gentlemen, I greet you here on the bank of the James River in the year of our Lord one thousand seven hundred and twelve. First, I shall thank you, the gentlemen of the Colony of Virginia, for bringing me here. I am here to help you solve some of your problems with slaves. Your invitation reached me on my modest plantation in the West Indies, where I have experimented with some of the newest, and still the oldest, methods for control of slaves. Ancient Rome would envy us if my program is implemented.

As our boat sailed south on the James River, named for our illustrious King, whose version of the Bible we cherish, I saw enough to know that your problem is not unique. While Rome used cords of wood as crosses for standing human bodies along its highways in great numbers, you are here using the tree and the rope on occasions. I caught the whiff of a dead slave hanging from a tree, a couple miles back. You are not only losing valuable stock by hangings, you are having uprisings, and slaves are running away, your crops are sometimes left in the fields too long for maximum profit, you suffer occasional fires, and your animals are killed. Gentlemen, you know what your problems are; I do not need to elaborate. I am not here to enumerate your problems; I am here to introduce you to a method of solving them.

In my bag here, **I HAVE A FULL PROOF METHOD FOR CONTROLLING YOUR BLACK SLAVES**. I guarantee every one of you that, if installed correctly, **IT WILL CONTROL THE SLAVES FOR AT LEAST 300 HUNDREDS YEARS**. My method is simple. Any member of your family or your overseer can use it. **I HAVE OUTLINED A NUMBER OF DIFFERENCES AMONG THE SLAVES; AND I TAKE THESE DIFFERENCES AND MAKE THEM BIGGER. I USE FEAR, DISTRUST AND ENVY FOR CONTROL PURPOSES**. These methods have worked on my modest plantation in the West Indies and it will work throughout the South. Take this simple little list of differences and think about them. On top of my list is "AGE," but it's there only because it starts with an "a." The second is "COLOR" or shade. There is **INTELLIGENCE, SIZE, SEX, SIZES OF PLANTATIONS, STATUS** on plantations, **ATTITUDE** of owners, whether the slaves live in the valley, on a hill, East, West, North, South, have fine hair, course hair, or is tall or short.

Now that you have a list of differences, I shall give you an outline of action, but before that, I shall assure you that **DISTRUST IS STRONGER THAN TRUST AND ENVY STRONGER THAN ADULATION, RESPECT OR ADMIRATION**. The Black slaves after receiving this indoctrination shall carry on and will become self-refueling and self-generating for **HUNDREDS** of years, maybe **THOUSANDS**. Don't forget, you must pitch the **OLD** black male vs. the **YOUNG** black male, and the **YOUNG** black male against the **OLD** black male. You must use the **DARK** skin slaves vs. the **LIGHT** skin slaves, and the **LIGHT** skin slaves vs. the **DARK** skin slaves. You must use the **FEMALE** vs. the **MALE**, and the **MALE** vs. the **FEMALE**. You must also have white servants and overseers [who] distrust all Blacks. But it is **NECESSARY THAT YOUR SLAVES TRUST AND DEPEND ON US. THEY MUST LOVE, RESPECT AND TRUST ONLY US.**

Gentlemen, these kits are your keys to control. Use them. Have your wives and children use them, never miss an opportunity, **IF USED INTENSELY FOR ONE YEAR, THE SLAVES THEMSELVES WILL REMAIN PERPETUALLY DISTRUSTFUL.**

Thank you gentlemen

LET'S MAKE A SLAVE

It was the interest and business of slave holders to study human nature, and the slave nature in particular, with a view to practical results. I and many of them attained astonishing proficiency in this direction. They had to deal not with earth, wood and stone, but with men and, by every regard, they had for their own safety and prosperity they needed to know the material on which they were to work, conscious of the injustice and wrong they were every hour perpetuating and knowing what they themselves would do. Were they the victims of such wrongs? They were constantly looking for the first signs of the dreaded retribution. They watched therefore with skilled and practiced eyes, and learned to read with great accuracy, the state of mind and heart of the slave, through his sable face. Unusual sobriety, apparent abstractions, sullenness and indifference indeed, any mood out of the common was afforded ground for suspicion and inquiry. Frederick Douglas LET'S MAKE A SLAVE is a study of the scientific process of man-breaking and slave-making. It describes the rationale and results of the Anglo Saxons' ideas and methods of insuring the master/slave relationship. **LET'S MAKE A SLAVE** "The Original and Development of a Social Being Called **'The Negro.'**" Let us make a slave. What do we need? First of all, we need a black nigger man, a pregnant nigger woman and her baby nigger boy. Second, we will use the same basic principle that we use in breaking a horse, combined with some more sustaining factors. What we do with horses is that we break them from one form of life to another; that is, we reduce them from their natural state in nature. Whereas nature provides them with the natural capacity to take care of their offspring, we break that natural string of independence from them and thereby create a dependency status, so that we may be able to get from them useful production for our business and pleasure.

CARDINAL PRINCIPLES FOR MAKING A NEGRO

For fear that our future generations may not understand the principles of breaking both of the beasts together, the nigger and the horse. We understand that short range planning economics results in periodic economic chaos; so that to avoid turmoil in the economy, it requires us to have breadth and depth in long range comprehensive planning, articulating both skill sharp perceptions.

We lay down the following principles for long range comprehensive economic planning. Both horse and niggers [are] no good to the economy in the wild or natural state. Both must be **BROKEN** and **TIED** together for orderly production. For orderly future, special and particular attention must be paid to the **FEMALE** and the **YOUNGEST** offspring. Both must be **CROSSBRED** to produce a variety and division of labor. Both must be taught to respond to a peculiar new **LANGUAGE**. Psychological and physical instruction of **CONTAINMENT** must be created for both.

We hold the six cardinal principles as truth to be self-evident, based upon following the discourse concerning the economics of breaking and tying the horse and the nigger together, all inclusive of the six principles laid down above.

NOTE: Neither principle alone will suffice for good economics. All principles must be employed for orderly good of the nation. Accordingly, both a wild horse and a wild or natural nigger is dangerous even if captured, for they will have the tendency to seek their customary freedom and, in doing so, might kill you in your sleep. You cannot rest. They sleep while you are awake, and are awake while you are asleep.

They are **DANGEROUS** near the family house and it requires too much labor to watch them away from the house. Above all, you cannot get them to work in this natural state. Hence, both the horse and the nigger must be broken; that is breaking them from one form of mental life to another. **KEEP THE BODY, TAKE THE MIND!**

In other words, break the will to resist. Now the breaking process is the same for both the horse and the nigger, only slightly varying in degrees. But, as we said before, there is an art in long range economic planning. **YOU MUST KEEP YOUR EYE AND THOUGHTS ON THE FEMALE and the OFFSPRING** of the horse and the nigger. A brief discourse in offspring development will shed light on the key to sound economic principles. Pay little attention to the generation of original breaking, but **CONCENTRATE ON FUTURE GENERATION**. Therefore, if you break the

FEMALE mother, she will **BREAK** the offspring in its early years of development; and when the offspring is old enough to work, she will deliver it up to you, for her normal female protective tendencies will have been lost in the original breaking process.

For example, take the case of the wild stud horse, a female horse and an already infant horse and compare the breaking process with two captured nigger males in their natural state, a pregnant nigger woman with her infant offspring. Take the stud horse, break him for limited containment. Completely break the female horse until she becomes very gentle, whereas you or anybody can ride her in her comfort. Breed the mare and the stud until you have the desired offspring. Then, you can turn the stud to freedom until you need him again. Train the female horse whereby she will eat out of your hand, and she will in turn train the infant horse to eat out of your hand, also.

When it comes to breaking the uncivilized nigger, use the same process, but vary the degree and step up the pressure, so as to do a complete reversal of the mind. Take the meanest and most restless nigger, strip him of his clothes in front of the remaining male niggers, the female, and the nigger infant, tar and feather him, tie each leg to a different horse faced in opposite directions, set him afire and beat both horses to pull him apart in front of the remaining niggers. The next step is to take a bullwhip and beat the remaining nigger males to the point of death, in front of the female and the infant. Don't kill him, but **PUT THE FEAR OF GOD IN HIM**, for he can be useful for future breeding.

THE BREAKING PROCESS OF THE AFRICAN WOMAN

Take the female and run a series of tests on her to see if she will submit to your desires willingly. Test her in every way, because she is the most important factor for good economics. If she shows any sign of resistance in submitting completely to your will, do not hesitate to use the bullwhip on her to extract that last bit of [b----] out of her. Take care not to kill her, for in doing so, you spoil good economics.

When in complete submission, she will train her offspring's in the early years to submit to labor when they become of age. Understanding is the best thing. Therefore, we shall go deeper into this area of the subject matter concerning what we have produced here in this breaking process of the female nigger. We have reversed the relationship; in her natural uncivilized state, she would have a strong dependency on the uncivilized nigger male, and she would have a limited protective tendency toward her independent male offspring and would raise male offspring's to be dependent like her.

Nature had provided for this type of balance. We reversed nature by burning and pulling a civilized nigger apart and bullwhipping the other to the point of death, all in her presence. By her being left alone, unprotected, with the **MALE IMAGE DESTROYED**, the ordeal caused her to move from her psychologically dependent state to a frozen, independent state. In this frozen, psychological state of independence, she will raise her **MALE** and female offspring in reversed roles.

For **FEAR** of the young male's life, she will psychologically train him to be **MENTALLY WEAK** and **DEPENDENT**, but **PHYSICALLY STRONG**. Because she has become psychologically independent, she will train her **FEMALE** offspring's to be psychologically independent. What have you got? You've got the nigger **WOMAN OUT FRONT AND THE** nigger **MAN BEHIND AND SCARED**. This is a perfect situation of sound sleep and economics.

Before the breaking process, we had to be alertly on guard at all times. Now, we can sleep soundly, for out of frozen fear his woman stands guard for us. He cannot get past her early slave-molding process. He is a good tool, now ready to be tied to the horse at a tender age. By the time a nigger boy reaches the age of sixteen, he is soundly broken in and ready for a long life of sound and efficient work and the reproduction of a unit of good labor force.

Continually through the breaking of uncivilized savage niggers, by throwing the nigger female savage into a frozen psychological state of independence, by killing the protective male image, and by creating a submissive dependent mind of the nigger male slave, we have created an orbiting cycle that turns on its own axis forever, unless a phenomenon occurs and re-shifts the position of the male and female slaves. We show what we mean by example. Take the case of the two economic slave units and examine them close.

THE NEGRO MARRIAGE

We breed two nigger males with two nigger females. Then, we take the nigger male away from them and keep them moving and working. Say one nigger female bears a nigger female and the other bears a nigger male; both nigger females—being without influence of the nigger male image, frozen with an independent psychology—will raise their offspring into reverse positions. The one with the female offspring will teach her to be like herself, independent and negotiable (we negotiate with her, through her, by her, negotiates her at will).

The one with the nigger male offspring, she being frozen subconscious fear for his life, will raise him to be mentally dependent and weak, but physically strong; in other words, body over mind. Now, in a few years when these two offspring's become fertile for early reproduction, we will mate and breed them and continue the cycle. That is good, sound and long range comprehensive planning.

WARNING: POSSIBLE INTERLOPING NEGATIVES

Earlier, we talked about the non-economic good of the horse and the nigger in their wild or natural state; we talked out the principle of breaking and tying them together for orderly production. Furthermore, we talked about paying particular attention to the female savage and her offspring for orderly future planning, and then more recently we stated that, by reversing the positions of the male and female savages, we created an orbiting cycle that turns on its own axis forever unless a phenomenon occurred and re-shifts positions of the male and female savages.

Our experts warned us about the possibility of this phenomenon occurring, for they say that the mind has a strong drive to correct and re-correct itself over a period of time if it can touch some substantial original historical base; and they advised us that the best way to deal with the phenomenon is to shave off the brute's mental history and create a multiplicity of phenomena of illusions, so that each illusion will twirl in its own orbit, something similar to floating balls in a vacuum.

This creation of multiplicity of phenomena of illusions entails the principle of crossbreeding the nigger and the horse as we stated above, the purpose of which is to create a diversified division of labor; thereby creating different levels of labor and different values of illusion at each connecting level of labor. The results of which is the severance of the points of original beginnings for each sphere illusion.

Since we feel that the subject matter may get more complicated as we proceed in laying down our economic plan concerning the purpose, reason and effect of crossbreeding horses and niggers, we shall lay down the following definition terms for future generations.

Orbiting cycle means a thing turning in a given path.

Axis means upon which or around which a body turns.

Phenomenon means something beyond ordinary conception and inspires awe and wonder.

Multiplicity means a great number.

Sphere means a globe.

Crossbreeding a horse means taking a horse and breeding it with an ass and you get a dumb, backward ass, long-headed mule that is not reproductive or productive by itself.

Crossbreeding niggers mean taking so many drops of good white blood and putting them into as many nigger women as possible, varying the drops by the various tones that you want, and then letting them breed with each other until another circle of color appears as you desire.

What this means is this: Put the niggers and the horse in a breeding pot, mix some asses and some good white blood and what do you get? You got a multiplicity of colors of ass backward, unusual niggers, running, tied to backward ass long-headed mules, the one productive of itself, the other sterile. (The one constant, the other dying, we keep the nigger constant for we may replace the mules for another tool) both mule and nigger tied to each other, neither knowing where the other came from and neither productive for itself, nor without each other.

CONTROLLED LANGUAGE

Crossbreeding completed, for further severance from their original beginning, **WE MUST COMPLETELY ANNIHILATE THE MOTHER TONGUE** of both the new nigger and the new mule and institute a new language that involves the new life's work of both. You know language is a peculiar institution. It leads to the heart of a people.

The more a foreigner knows about the language of another country the more he is able to move through all levels of that society. Therefore, if the foreigner is an enemy of the country, to the extent that he knows the body of the language, to that extent is the country vulnerable to attack or invasion of a foreign culture.

For example, if you take a slave, if you teach him all about your language, he will know all your secrets, and he is then no more a slave, for you can't fool him any longer, and **BEING A FOOL IS ONE OF THE BASIC INGREDIENTS OF ANY INCIDENTS TO THE MAINTENANCE OF THE SLAVERY SYSTEM**.

For example, if you told a slave that he must perform in getting out **"our crops"** and he knows the language well, he would know that **"our crops"** didn't mean **"our crops"** and the slavery system would break down, for he would relate on the basis of what **"our crops"** really meant. So you have to be careful in setting up the new language; for the slaves would soon be in your house, talking to you as **"man to man"** and that is death to our economic system.

In addition, the definitions of words or terms are only a minute part of the process. Values are created and transported by communication through the **body of the language**. A total society has many interconnected value systems. All the values in the society have bridges of language to connect them for orderly working in the society. But for these language bridges, these many value systems would sharply clash and cause internal strife or civil war, the degree of the conflict being determined by the magnitude of the issues or relative opposing strength in whatever form.

For example, if you put a slave in a hog pen and train him to live there and incorporate in him to value it as a way of life completely, the biggest problem you would have out of him is that he would worry you about provisions to keep the hog pen clean, or the same hog pen and make a slip and incorporate something in his language whereby he comes to value a house more than he does his hog pen, you got a problem. He will soon be in your house.

Many argue over the source of the above document; in fact, many claim that it is a made up concoction, and that the slave owner Willie Lynch never existed. This book's position is not to further any aspect of that particular argument, it is designed to elucidate a perpetuated condition of a people that has and continues to manifest the deviant traits that are referenced in the letter as the *"Keys to control"*. The fact is black people remain slaves in 2006, and the fact further remains that the HipHop Nation has been high-jacked by the mentality of Mr. Willie Lynch.

The HipHop Nation is presently divided on the basis of record companies (plantations), regional affiliation, state and area code identifying elements, type of HipHop i.e. . . . . Dirty South, Gangster, Under-Ground and mainstream rap! These competing elements that divide the HipHop Nation, help splinter the overall black collective, and those that hold HipHop as more than just a form of music.

The black man and woman of America have been systematically divided along the lines outlined within the Willie Lynch letter and program. An already splintered and divided people cannot afford further division on the basis of music and artistic expression. In a world that is controlled by the Caucasian white male, the unity of the black man and woman, as well as all people of color within the global context, is quite literally our only chance for survival.

After reading this letter and considering its content—whether authentic in terms of authorship or not, no one can deny that the black nation in general, and the "HipHop Nation" in particular is marginalized and fractured along the lines highlighted within the letter. This reality trumps the argument against its authenticity, and expands the argument into, is it *"REAL"*?!

This book's contention is that the letter is in fact *"REAL"* in the truest sense of the HipHop word; therefore, the solution must be real and applied regardless of the pain and emotional outbreak it may cause. If the HipHop Nation refuses to accept forthright criticism and a subsequent over-haul, it should be first exposed, and then dealt with as what it has been made to be, *"an agent of the state"*. If the HipHop Nation refuses to correct itself, it should be viewed as an enemy of black people, and a tool to spread a demonic system of rule, power, and influence throughout the world. By using young black youth to further the *American Imperialistic Ambition*, the perception of the freedom loving, spiritually minded, do the right thing, consciousness that was spread globally during the sixties has been fatally compromised by the emergence of a universal apathy in regards to our current condition.

As black people died on the roof-tops of New Orleans, and White-American "rescue" helicopters flew over the heads of dying black folk to rescue their white brethren; the whole world watched seemingly not giving a damn. Of course there will be those that point to the many dollars collected by the Red Cross and F.E.M.A as an answer to the apathy argument, but dollars sent, and tears shed is a pathetic answer to the horrible condition that black people were forced to go through for no other reason than their black skin. Again, there will be arguments to the contrary, but I am not concerned with those who disagree, I am attempting to reach out and appeal to those that agree, pointing to the fact that public representation and public presentation affects how the global collective views us, and subsequently reacts to any injustice that confronts us. We should not for one minute believe that the manipulating powers that be aren't aware of this fact.

In terms of the money sent, and supposedly spent, to correct the horrors of Hurricane Katrina, we should contrastingly view the monies given annually to causes such as save the whales, pro-life, pro-choice, gubernatorial and presidential campaigns and various other profit yielding institutions designed to further an agenda or idea. Money given, in some instances, help to publicize a cause, but recognition of a problem, acceptance of that problem, and unrelenting action applied to the problem is the only way to elevate the problem and correct the effects of the said problem. Because of this, we as black people cannot afford to sit and wait for a benevolent white group (democrat or republican etc...) or individual to change our condition and representation. We must change it ourselves, and as our chief voice to the world, the HipHop Nation must abandon their present ways and actions, and adopt new ones that confront the Willie Lynch Syndrome in order to free the minds of the masses...failure to do so, justifies the claims of treason thrown at the head of the Negro rapper.

Ode to a Black Man and Brother called "George"

The following letter was written to the Jewish owner of an African Black Man called "George." It exemplifies the courage, spirit and dignity of the Black Man as he fought his Jewish oppressor.

Reading, March 2, 1772
Mr. Bernard Gratz, Merchant in Philadelphia

Sir: I took your negroe George, some time ago, home, thinking I might be the better able to sell him, who, after being with me a night, behaved himself in such an insolent manner I immediately remanded back to the jail. About a week since, I put him up for sale at Christopher Witman's tavern, where there was a number of persons who inclined to purchase him. But he protested publickly that he would not be sold, and if anyone should purchase him, he would be the death of him, and words to the like purpose, which deterred the people from bidding. I then sent him back again with directions to the jailer to keep him at hard labour, which he refuses to do, and goes on in such an insolent manner that it is impossible to get a master for him here. I therefore request you'll send for him on sight hereof, or send me a line by Drinkhouse, or the first opportunity, what I shall do with him. He's now almost naked, and if not furnished soon with some clothes, I fear he'll perish. Pray let me hear from [you] and, in the mean time, I remain, with great regard, sir, your humble servant, George Nagel.

P.S. He's now chained and handcuffed on account of his threats.

www.blacksandjews.com

****

AMERICA'S NEW POP (ULAR) MUSIC

Webster's dictionary defines the word popular the following way, "1: of, relating to, or coming from the whole body of people (*popular* government) (*popular* opinion) 2: suitable to the majority: as a: easy to understand (*popular* science) b: suited to the means of the majority: INEXPENSIVE (*popular* prices) 3: having general currency: PREVALENT (*popular* opinion) 4: commonly liked or approved (voted the most *popular* girl in the class).

In the latter part of the 90's, HipHop replaced Country Music as the biggest selling genre of music in America. When this took place, many mainstream or popular publications in the United States wrote articles articulating the significance and magnitude of such an accomplishment. HipHop had been officially ushered in as an enormous cash cow for all those who desired to exploit it. The bandwagon was rolling, and many people who opposed it in its earlier years *"jumped on it"*.

To the average HipHop citizen, it was nice to finally hear radio stations that had traditionally shunned the music, begin to play it in a consistent rotation. To the average rapper, it seemed as if their art form and expression was finally accepted, recognized, and validated by endorsements and more lucrative recording deals. Everybody was on the *"jock"* of HipHop, including Bugs Bunny, Fred Flintstone, Ronald McDonald, and little old white ladies. Based on the above definition, HipHop was truly crowned as America's new pop music.

But how did this happen, how did a music that at one time prided itself on rebellion, creativity, truth to power speaking, and racial and cultural identifying and qualifying elements, become America's most powerful and influential musical instrument? The answer lies within the **Willie Lynch Letter!**

Let us continue…. In the early 80's, HipHop dominated the East Coast, although who started and how it started has been argued time and time again, that is not my concern; simple research can answer that question. What is interesting is that HipHop had the hearts and minds of an entire region of black youth. During that time, and even in the 70's, the party rhymes and braggadocio lyrics of the young rappers dominated the regional HipHop scene. Though they made the listener dance and chuckle, the early HipHop lyrics lacked any real, powerful, thought provoking significance. Of course, there were exceptions, and we'll look at them later, but for the most part; the only revolutionary qualities offered by early HipHop were the style and creation of the music itself.

During the time that America was representing itself as a boot wearing, shit kicking, straw chewing, twang speaking, cattle wrestling, good ole American cowboy, two independent and radically different sub-cultures were brewing behind the scenes. Although Country music was experiencing record breaking sells and exposure, HipHop and Heavy Metal music was beginning to expose, what was viewed by the American public at large, its ugly head. Unlike heavy metal, however, HipHop did not have the exposure of MTV and other forms of media to give it dollars and credibility. For this reason, HipHop was allowed to incubate and develop seemingly undetected by the American masses.

Prior to 1986 the only black artists that were receiving considerable video play were Rick James and Michael Jackson. I'm sure that we all remember the time when MTV was totally dominated by white artist. While the white American youth *"wanted their MTV"*, black America rejected MTV completely and viewed it as a entertainment outlet for heavy metal and white acts. It was in 1983 that Rick James spoke against MTV on a Nightline program for not airing black videos. Subsequently; five years later, in August of 1988 two white men by the name of **Ted Demme** and **Peter Dougherty** introduced a program by the name of *"Yo! MTV Raps"*—this program aired between the years of 1988 and 1995. Although it had considerable commercial success, the program's ratings fell when they pulled rap group Public Enemy's video *"By The Time I get To Arizona"* claiming that it was too violent. We must remember that this particular video was the group's (Public Enemy) answer to the refusal of the states of New Hampshire and Arizona to recognize the birth date of Martin Luther King Jr. as an official state holiday. **Check out the following lyrics:**

Artist: Public Enemy
Album: Apocalypse 91
Song: By the Time I Get to Arizona

I'm countin' down to the day deservin'
Fittin' for a king
I'm waitin' for the time when I can
Get to Arizona
'Cause my money's spent on
The goddamn rent
Neither party is mine not the
Jackass or the elephant
20.000 nig niggy niggas in the corner
Of the cell block but they come
From California
Population none in the desert and sun
Wit' a gun cracker

Runnin' things under his thumb
Starin' hard at the postcards
Isn't it odd and unique?
Seein' people smile wild in the heat
120 degree
'Cause I wanna be free
What's a smilin' fact
When the whole state's racist
Why want a holiday F--k it 'cause I wanna
So what if I celebrate it standin' on a corner
I ain't drinkin' no 40
I B thinkin' time wit' a nine
Until we get some land
Call me the trigger man
Looki lookin' for the governor
Huh he ain't lovin' ya
But here to trouble ya
He's rubbin' ya wrong
Get the point come along

An he can get to the joint
I urinated on the state
While I was kickin' this song
Yeah, he appear to be fair
The cracker over there
He try to keep it yesteryear
The good ol' days
The same ol' ways
That kept us dyin'
Yes, you me myself and I'ndeed
What he need is a nosebleed
Read between the lines
Then you see the lie
Politically planned
But understand that's all she wrote
When we see the real side
That hide behind the vote
They can't understand why he the man
I'm singin' 'bout a king
They don't like it
When I decide to mike it
Wait I'm waitin' for the date
For the man who demands respect
'Cause he was great c'mon
I'm on the one mission

To get a politician
To honor or he's a gonner
By the time I get to Arizona

I got 25 days to do it
If a wall in the sky
Just watch me go thru it
'Cause I gotta do what I gotta do
PE number one
Gets the job done
When it's done and over
Was because I drove'er
Thru all the static
Not stick but automatic
That's the way it is
He gotta get his
Talin' MLK
Gonna find a way
Make the state pay
Lookin' for the day
Hard as it seems
This ain't no damn dream
Gotta know what I mean
It's team against team
Catch the light beam
So I pray
I pray everyday
I do and praise jah the maker
Lookin' for culture
I got but not here
From jah maker
Pushin' and shakin' the structure
Bringin' down the babylon
Hearin' the sucker
That make it hard for the brown
The hard Boulova
I need now
More than ever now
Who's sittin' on my freedah'
Opressor people beater
Piece of the pick
We picked a piece
Of land that we deservin' now
Reparation a piece of the nation
And damn he got the nerve

Another niga they say and classify
We want too much
My peep plus the whole nine is mine
Don't think I even double dutch
Here's a brother my attitude hit 'em
Hang 'em high
Blowin' up the 90s started tickin' 86
When the blind get a mind
Better start and earn while we sing it
Now
There will be the day we know those down and who will go

During the time that white children were choosing to where lipstick and pink hair, black youth and the HipHop movement was evolving into a conscious, synchronized expression of black struggle, black thought, and black reality. Black people were wearing African Fezzes and red, black, and green medallions—with the help of HipHop groups such as the Poor Righteous Teachers, Public Enemey, and X Clan, the black youth were on the "Black Watch". Due to a marginalized reality determined by social, economic, political and religious factors, the urban black youth saw themselves outside of the **"popular culture"**. White America had not bought into the black urban dynamic, and refused to invest the time or energy to evaluate the economic potential of those that were systematically and historically isolated from what was considered by the white collective as the **"American Dream"**.

Within the framework of a system that was dedicated to the establishment and maintenance of the white cultural expression, black people were considered a sub-culture that was deplete of any profitable qualities within the economic paradigm that existed at that time. The walk of the black youth at that time was diametrically opposed to the reality that the American White male and political power brokers were marketing throughout the world. In fact, the rhythmic chants of freedom, justice, and equality that came from the lips of those that were trapped within the oppressed class of America reminded the world that America was far from the moral example that America marketed herself to be. **In short, the** *Niggas in America* **were a thorn in the side of an aspiring giant that had ambitions of global rule.**

Check Out what HipHop was saying in the late 80's and early 90's:

Artist: Poor Righteous Teachers
Album: Holy Intellect
Song: So Many Teachers

Verse 1
[Wise]
So many teachers, yet so little men are being seen
Everybody's ruling, yet nobody's being king.
[Culture Freedom]
Word iz life 'G'
[Wise]
But Culture Free how could this be?
Our people need some leaders and some positivity.
[Culture Freedom]
Like Farrakhan 'G'
[Wise]
Or like that brother Malcolm X
Who turn the hands of time when giving knowledge of himself
[Culture Freedom & Wise]
It's sort ta simple see
[Wise]
The Father Shah upon the techniques
Weak... nobody in me possee
[Culture Freedom]
T'cha, T'cha! Please teach the untaught one
[Wise]
Strictly I be ghetto so you know it's from the heart
Strike for peace for peace which rightfully be mine
Disagree?
Then let the teacher take ya back in time
Once upon a time upon the earth
Many say we're cursed
But those who are black are that of first
Ever to exist upon the planet
Let me speak more candid
I'm here to give a greater understanding
Peace was the flow of the universe
So shut your bible stop tellin' lies that you were first
[Culture Freedom]
T'cha, T'cha! What about these students lackin' lessons
[Wise]
There's oh so many teachers, yet a lack of manifestin'
Teachers oughtta teach if they be teachers
Educate the weaker
Poor Righteous Teachers teachin' cuzz we feel
So many teachers grab the mic and just be talkin'
So many lackin' cuzz these teachers ought'ta build.

Verse 2
[Wise]
I am a teacher
some what symbolic to a king
Some disagree when I state this
I where a crown
Which represents the knowledge of the teacher
Weaker speak of the snake
Which try to take this
Wisdom
Wise words being spoken
The purified ways in which I manifest
I'm never sested
Because the knowledge stimulates me
And brain cells are to great for havin' this
[Culture Freedom]
Well come again 'G'
[Wise]
Within an automatic second
I manifest thoughts that I accumulate
[Culture Freedom]
To demonstrate 'G'
[Wise]
Mainfest weight.
Weight of the insight
[Culture Freedom]
Light!
[Wise]
Right!... Some positivity
Why can't we
The black communities
Come together to conquer thee opponent
Cuzz if we show just a small sense of unity
Everything the eye see before me
We'd own it.
Truth be the wise words spoken
The I swings the sword
The Lord of all worlds being born
Word bond to the lost and the found
I down any clown
And on my crown that is sworn
Yes, the set consist of many teachers
Time for I to question what these teachers say they're teachin'
Who am I to question what another man is stating?
[Culture Freedom]

To whom are you relating?
[Wise]
To you if you know not of what you're speaking.

Verse 3
[Wise Intelligent]
So many teachers they taught me
I say they taught me well
They taught me to be self wise of one self.
I study what they teach me
No one could teach me how to
So you know I'm not takin' anything on face value.
[Culture Freedom]
Observation
[Wise Intelligent]
Mandatory... Whenever present
To study what is spoken by teacher manifested
[Culture Freedom]
Perception
[Wise Intelligent]
I say perceiving of a thought
Conceiving be delivering the weight of what one's taught.
It's sort'ta simple, some would say it's somewhat complicated
But LIFE IS OFTEN BALANCED BY THE WAY IN WHICH YA TAKE IT!
Me fake it?!
Never 'G', The truth reveals itself
My understanding's understood
And mine will come from no one else
Make knowledge born the duty of the civilized
'G' not satisfied
till the dark prince rise
[Culture Freedom]
Peace Wise, peace Wise
[Wise Intelligent]
But I'm not signing off yet
These teachers don't reveal so it's time to manifest

And ALSO...check out what X CLAN was saying:

Artist: X-Clan
Album: To the East, Blackwards
Song: Verbs of Power

Verbs of Power - now here's the sum of another drum
Now mortals aware, now prepare for illogical son
My Verbs of Power are the spiritual spank
My deep, deep Blackness, your mind gets dank
Revelation to Genesis, something you cannot dismiss
Keys to Crossroad, come to abyss!
And find a verb-stick swingin' while I'm livin', giving the rhythm
Heed the word, and the bass-drop given!
A funk down, super sound, lyrical, visual
Illogical wisdom, forever continual
You're living simplistically, yet speak of reality
Your science, elementary - Dare speak? You can't get with me
Look at the wax, it's hieroglyphic, it's actual fact
I'm not reading and striving to wanna be Black
Here's the move 'cause I see none
I never boast, I never brag, I get the job done
I'm not the [?Buckley?] political, nor am I the physical
The rhythmical spiritual, the mystical magical
Movement is circle, never 90 degrees of a square
I'm the gorilla - robotics will run in a scare
Just to find that the zero's the ground
Come into my temple, have a seat at the round, feel the power

[Professor X]
Brother, Brother, Brother, how you make 'em get down?
[Brother J]
Professor Overseer, I've got pimp in my crown
It was the pimp that drove the mountainous elephant
It was ignorance that made this irrelevant
I'm not the pasta boy, I'm the African, call me by name
I'm the original, I taught you to set up this game
You silly mortal, keep on playing the Trump
I think they're gonna have to get me,
from stompin' and kickin' your rump
Once again, now it comes in the trend
I said "Free South Africa!" - you went to Berlin
Now there's the problem, I stand firm, beating my chest
You think a silly polar bear could ever put this to rest?
And yet they still will apologize, while I will epitomize
Embrace my children, show them Creator's eyes
Onto the path of the mystical teaching the math
No more to suffer - it's time for the wrath
Feel the power

On to the throne, the throne I come forth
Weapon of our rule, the verbs of great Thoth
Look at the sundial, look at the child of man
Where's the faith in the Spirit, the master plan?
Opportunity - the spoils of religion of God-man
Hero to rescue the drum jam
Fire, water, air and earth, I AM the fool
Teaching power that I never could learn in school
I am the teacher from the far and beyond
Turn an apple to a lotus, turn a rib to a wand
To compare me or dare me is foolish, it's more than a job
No entertainment - illogical odd god
Has come - straight from Amon-Tet with the herb dish
Come with the Verb Stick, the bag of the new tricks
Stronger than ever, my intent of the universe
Coming of immortals is the strength of the verse
That's the power

And then there was KRS-ONE:

Artist: Boogie Down Productions
Album: Ghetto Music - The Blueprint of Hip-Hop
Song: Why is That?

Verse One

The day begins, with a grin
And a prayer to excuse my sins
I can walk anywhere I choose
Cause everybody listens to the B.D.P. crew
We're not here for glamour or fashion
But here's the question I'm askin
Why is it young black kids taught {flashin?}
They're only taught how to read, write, and act
It's like teachin a dog to be a cat
You don't teach white kids to be black
Why is that? Is it because we're the minority?
Well black kids follow me
Genesis chapter eleven verse ten
Explains the geneology of Chem
Chem was a black man, in Africa
If you repeat this fact they can't laugh at ya
Genesis fourteen verse thirteen
Abraham steps on the scene

Being a descendent of Chem which is a fact
Means, Abraham too was black
Abraham born in the city of a black man
Called Nimrod grandson of Kam
Kam had four sons, one was named Canaan
Here, let me do some explaining
Abraham was the father of Isaac
Isaac was the father of Jacob
Jacob had twelve sons, for real
And these, were the children of Isreal
According to Genesis chapter ten
Egyptains descended from {Hahm,Kam}
Six hundred years later, my brother, read up
Moses was born in Egypt
In this era black Egyptians weren't right
They enslaved black Isrealites
Moses had to be of the black race
Because he spent fourty years in Pharoah's place
He passed as the Pharoah's grandson
So he had to look just like him
Yes my brothers and sisters take this here song
Yo, correct the wrong
The information we get today is just wack
But ask yourself, why is that?

Verse Two

The age of the ignorant rapper is done
Knowledge Reigns Supreme Over Nearly Everyone
The stereotype must be lost
That love and peace and knowledge is soft
Do away with that and understand one fact
For love, peace must attack
And attack real strong, stronger than war
To conquer it and its law
Mental pictures, stereotypes and fake history
Reinforces mystery
And when mystery is reinforced
That only means that knowledge has been lost
When you know who you really are
Peace and knowledge shines like a star
I'm only showin you a simple fact
It Takes A Nation of MILLIONS to Hold Us people Back
Which is wack, but we can correct that
Teach and learn what it is to be black

Cause they're teachin birds to be a cat
But ask yourself homeboy, why is that?

But don't forget about Kam:

Artist: Kam
Album: Neva Again
Song: Neva Again

[Kam]
Lift every voice and sing
Yeah, but we gon' lift every fist and swing
So save the negro spiritual
It's 1992 and niggaz need a miracle
And no more song and dance
like we shall overcome, and ain't got a chance
Y'all stuck on "I have a dream"
Need to put the picket sign down and get on the team
Stand up and do somethin
Stop beggin for a meal, cause everything is real
Nigga look at yourself, you in hell
Claimin wel-fare, or should I say fare-well
Mr. Christian, you was too spooky
Now Bush wanna slave, and Russia wanna nuke me
And the most you can tell me is love thy enemy?
Stay off the Hennesey
Pops I want freedom, so hand me the nine
You can pray for yours, but I'ma go get mine
Now how long has it been?
For a hundred and thirty-seven years, but neva again

[Kam]
God bless America.. but for what?
How bout God damn America, the slut (yeah)
Now I can name that tune
Cause the land of the free is sellin negroes at noon
But how soon we forget
Mention the holocaust, niggaz have a fit
Sorry ISRAEL but I'm fresh out of tears
Cause lynch that nigga's still ringin in my ears
I want freedom, justice, equality, Islam
So it's hard to keep calm
when I'm accused of bein racist for lovin my people first
Now they wanna put me in a hearse

but black people never made white slaves
And we was too lovin to put Jews in a oven
But the pilgrims wasn't so friendly then
And by the way, I never ate a Indian
So who's the real savage?
Six feet tall on the average
Count the number of the God damn beast
To the East my brother to the East say neva again

[Kam]
Oh say can y'all see?
It's the home of the slave, land of the never free
America me, the so called negro
with another verse, so here we go
As long as y'all been givin me hell
No wonder there's a crack in the Liberty Bell
to tell on America the Beautiful
The bitch need a facelift, for this race myth
And now for you to pull a caper, kidnap rape her
The penalty is DEATH
Cause we ain't forgave or forgot
blacks bein murdered, tortured and shot
Six hundred million, one-eighty-sevens
It's bringin wrath down from the heavens
So let my people go Pharoahe, the arrow
is point at your dome, and if we don't make it home
Cancel Christmas
Like EPMD we got some "Unfinished Business"
From way back, payback for your sin
So paleskin, tell a friend, neva again

The conflict between what America was claiming, and what America was in reality, created a political dilemma on a global scale for the power brokers of a culture that had a specific marketing plan attached. The black youth of America through their rap, informed the world that the opportunity that the American white Male was selling was a farce. It informed the global population that the American Dream was in fact a nightmare to a huge segment of America.

At this stage of HipHop's evolution, its citizens did not buy into the *"American Dream"*, because at that time it was not being marketed to black folk; and if it was, we simply could not afford it in terms of not merely finance, but the cost that would be demanded of our souls. An America that had not shown any level of interest for black people outside of sport and entertainment had not seen the potentiality of HipHop in terms of finance and influence. Therefore, out of the spirit of rejection from the American slave Master, the HipHop Nation beat the hell out of her (America) and forced her to recognize its (HipHop) presence.

We must recognize that America did not, nor does she now have love or respect for black people and their cultural expression. The overall aspirations of America are now, and have always been global control and dominance. With this in mind, we understand that America's embracing of HipHop was a political move that furthers her global aspirations. Since the reality of her Negro slaves were being made known through the music of HipHop, and this reality was contradicting her claim of moral excellence and financial opportunity—the wise power brokers were forced to change the song that sprang from the lips of these slaves.

Since black folks knew that they were marginalized and secluded from the dominant culture; in order to change the song, white folks had to change the level of inclusion where this sub-culture was concerned. A realization took place, *"in order for white folks to gain the world, they had to give up some of their Apple Pie."* By giving up some of their pie, perhaps the rappers would fill their pie-holes (mouths) with the trinkets and bobbles offered up by the slave masters, thereby shutting their mouths to the hard truths that were exposing America to the world. HipHop silenced itself as soon as corporate America gave them some goodies.

I must mention that the American agenda is a summation of a Caucasian thought, a thought that is centered on an idea that what is white is right... not just based on a political, social, and economic reality, but within the divine context as well. The American reality for black people continues to this day to reek of slavery. The so-called abolition of slavery was really the evolution of slavery. From one form into another, slavery has adjusted to time and circumstance, and has demonstrated itself within the political structure of not only America, but the entire global system of politics, economics, education, and religion. The slavery based system of governance as demonstrated by the Caucasian race, a race that is not limited or confined to national, religious, or social allegiances, does not make social adjustments based on what's right or morally correct, it makes its adjustments based on what's profitable. Regardless if it is a white American, Britain, Russian or Jew, history proves that white folks make decisions based not on what is morally correct, but what is best in terms of their political, social, and economic profit.

In terms of pop music, that which is considered popular is the music or culture that presently tends to dominate, dictate, and inspire the prevalent social trends of a society. As the "new pop music", HipHop has become that dominant cultural force that is seen within, and significantly impacts—a huge segment of not only America, but the world. What is commercially recognized today as HipHop has been grown into a premier advertisement agency for not only the prevalent American lifestyle, but has been sanctioned and funded by corporate outsiders that have gained controlling interest of a musical and cultural force that they did not create. In this manner, and under the auspices of powerful cultural manipulators, HipHop has become pseudomonas with pop music, or pop culture. But the question remains—*who* are these manipulators, and what agenda do they serve? Hopefully by book's end these questions and more will be answered....so lets continue!

HIPHOP TAKES A BITE

"I HAVE A FULL PROOF METHOD FOR CONTROLLING YOUR BLACK SLAVES. I guarantee every one of you that, if installed correctly, IT WILL CONTROL THE SLAVES FOR AT LEAST 300 HUNDREDS YEARS."

The HipHop of the early days was marked by struggle, and the expression of that struggle. For the most part, the only rich people that black people had to offer were those that were accepted into the mainstream of American society. These isolated cases of success were generally situated on a backdrop of buffoonery, and comprised of social neuters in terms of the black struggle. By offering the so-called Negro a token offering, a proverbial crumb from the master's table, the so-called Negro entertainer, sports figure, and business puppet was allowed to utilize that "crumb" to buy into a world that they previously could not afford.

Even though the so-called Negro purchased a place in the house, they do not realize that what they have purchased is a small "broom closet" that does not afford them the opportunity to explore and utilize the whole house. The slave master uses their *"puppets"* as *"tools"*—when needed they are allowed out the *"closet"*; but when not needed, they are locked squarely within. Like all brooms, they are used out of necessity to sweep up a mess that the master has made. In this case the American image was being compromised by a society of poor black folk that lacked a political, social, and economic voice. Out comes the so-called *"Negro success stories"* to give the appearance that not only the times, but white folks have changed…nothing could be further from the truth!

Let's examine this a little more closely… prior to the year 1984, HipHop's expression was limited primarily to local east coast clubs, street corners, and a small but surprisingly effective underground mix-tape circuit. In 1984, however, a black man by the name of Russell Simmons partnered up with a so-called Jewish graduate of NYU with notable contacts with MTV to formulate the now famous Def-Jam recording label. The partners name was Rick Rubin. Mr. Rubin had the responsibility of marketing HipHop to the world. For the first time a legitimate power broker of white folks and their global ambition had made contact with a so-called common Negro (Russell Simmons) to market the HipHop element of the black culture not only to America, but to the world. Rick Rubin's primary objective was to sell HipHop and its artist to the world, and this had to be done in a clever way that would not offend white people, but to invite them in.

The product was young black youth, and the package was the music. A superficial approach to this subject may have us believing that wealthy white America is concerned with the music of HipHop and its various expressions i.e.... clothing, jewelry, cars, and the potential dollars associated with it. However, a deeper insight will reveal that the real product is the black youth themselves, the HipHop citizens that have tapped into the psyche of the global youth population. If one can control what comes from the mouths of these children, then these children can be used to further the global objective of the Slave Master! It should be considered that white power brokers already have money, wealth and riches, what they desire are the *"souls"* of all the peoples of the planet earth.

Acting as a liaison between the urban youth and the wealthy power brokers, Rick Rubin was not necessarily concerned with selling the notion of riches to his white colleagues; his primary concern was to sell the ideal of global influence and manipulation. His sales pitch was basic, "if we (white folk) would sacrifice a few dollars, we would not only control these Negroes and the words that they speak, but we will control the global population and the world in which they live".

Russell Simmons who merely had a desire to see the culture grow, and to gain the financial rewards that accompanied such growth, penned his contracts seemingly with the best motives at heart; never the less, he was dealing with a person that had allegiances to a society of men that had other motivating factors. Russell Simmons being ignorant of the nature of the powerful beast, bought into a plan that I hope, had he been aware, he would have rejected.

In 1984, after formulating Def Jam Records, Russell and Rick dropped their first record, it was "I Need a Beat" by L.L. Cool J, and it was relatively successful and was utilized in the formulation of a distribution contract between Def Jam and Columbia / CBS records. L.L. Cool J's album "Radio" was the first full length album released by Def Jam. This early success assisted the label to become the premier HipHop label of that time. Def Jam was able to contract pioneering artist such as Run DMC, Public Enemy, EPMD, Slick Rick, and Eric B. and Rakim.

The success of Def Jam penetrated the Music business to its core, and created a political restructuring that was never before seen in any form of media at any time or place in history. The slave represented a new product, and the growth potential of that product was seen as unlimited. With this in mind, the power brokers scrambled to prepare their plantations to make way for their new commodity. Wicked minds in high places were beset by a new method of reaching society's core and the minds that stimulate economic, social, and political activity and behaviors. The New American gold rush was on and the ignorant slaves had no idea what was happening, or what was about to take place.

In terms of Rick Rubin, I do not want to suggest that the friendship between him and Russell Simmons was not sincere, nor do I wish to suggest that Rick Rubin intended to help handover HipHop to the white power brokers knowingly or without conscious. What I will be attempting to show the reader is that just as the black collective suffers from an induced slavery mentality, white people in general, and those white folks with considerable amounts of political, economical, religious, social, and economic clout in particular, suffer from a slave-master's mentality. This mentality would create the actions that would support the group in which an individual resides... in the case of Rick Rubin, a mentality that is drastically different from the societal induced slavery mentality of Russell Simmons will cause certain results for Rick Rubin, and different results for Russell Simmons--regardless of friendships or business relationships, a slave is a slave, and a slave master is a slave master.

Born Frederick Jay Rubin on March 10, 1963 in Long Island New York, "Rick" Rubin was raised in a so-called Jewish household, and was a product of New York University. After assisting Russell Simmons with the formation and development of Def Jam Records, Rick Rubin became the unfortunate victim of a power struggle between himself and fellow so-called Jew Lyor Cohen—after getting replaced in the offices of Def Jam, Rick has continued his career as a viable power broker of the so-called Jewish dominated record industry.

Parent (Company) Plantation: Universal Music Group

Founded: 1984

Founders: Russell Simmons, Rick Rubin

Distributing Plantation (label): The Island Def Jam Music Group (US), Mercury Music Group (UK)

Location: New York City

THE TAKE OVER

"DISTRUST IS STRONGER THAN TRUST AND ENVY STRONGER THAN ADULATION, RESPECT OR ADMIRATION."

Def Jam had become a political, social, and economic power broker...NOT Russell Simmons, but Def Jam!, the Def Jam that was signed over to white folk the minute Rick Rubin came on board. Rick took Def Jam into places that the American Negro was not, and is still not allowed to go. Russell could look, but he certainly could not touch. He was given trinkets of appreciation that when measured against the reality of "white wealth" is seen as pathetically weak. The soul was not "stolen", in this case it was "sold".

In 1988, after winning a "power struggle" over Rick Rubin, a new and more developed Jew by the name of Lyor Cohen became president of Def Jam. This streamlined Jew and power broker of those who desire global domination, is affectionately referred to within the realm of the music industry as "LANSKY" after the Polish, so-called Jewish immigrant "Myer Lansky" who was instrumental in forming the "American Mafia".

After the two so-called Jewish men, Mr. Cohen and Mr. Ruben, battled over rights to their Negro slaves, the spoils of war were handed over to a man whose first move within the offices of Def Jam was to de-emphasize the name and logo of Def Jam, and introduce into the HipHop community the acronym, or term "RAL". Within the office spaces of Def Jam, "RAL" was seen to mean "Russell and Lyor"; but was officially to mean "Rush Associated Labels". Remember, the gold "RUSH" was on, and if Lyor Cohen had no business sympathy for his "Jewish" brethren Rick Ruben, what would be the outcome for a Negro slave by the name of Russell that Cohen had no political, social, religious, and financial loyalty to. In regards to the name change of Def Jam, the slave master always changes the name of his slave in order to denote ownership.

HipHop was emerging as big business, and based on the newly envisioned plan of Lyor "Lansky" Cohen, it will be a battle over sub-unit record companies that would act as stilts to the more monumental beasts of the record industry. These companies would move about swallowing minor, often time, black-owned companies, growing fat by the talents and ambitions of a slave. By throwing huge amounts of dollars into the faces of the products of the ghetto, those who are slaves, those that had a limited knowledge of their enemy forfeited their sovereignty (though limited) in the quest for cash and the American scheme—excuse me, I mean DREAM!

Cohen is the CEO of Recorded Music at Warner Music Group, the entertainment giant controlled by Edgar Bronfman, Jr. He's better known, though, as the former president of Def Jam and partner of Russell Simmons. Due to his ways and actions in terms of business and personal relationships he is known as "LANSKY", after the so-called Jewish gangster MEYER LANSKY.

Maier Suchowljansky, better known as Meyer Lansky—is a so-called Jew from Grodno, Poland. He is known to truly have had the last word of crime in terms of the so-called Mafia and the underground crime Syndicates. Although Lucky Luciano and Frank Costello were known by many as the ruthless arms associated with the so-called Mafia, all the mobsters and gangsters knew that the true "BRAINS" behind the infamous crime syndicates was Meyer Lansky—this is what they referred to him as...the BRAINS!

Wow... won't we all be so surprised and enlightened once all the hidden truths and connections come forth? Its here, and it's not difficult at all to see if we choose to look! Will we look?

CRUMBS FROM THE MASTER'S TABLE
"But it is NECESSARY THAT YOUR SLAVES TRUST AND DEPEND ON US. THEY MUST LOVE, RESPECT AND TRUST ONLY US."

The political backdrop of the 80's consisted of a former actor turn president, Ronald Reagan. From 1981 through 1989, Reagan instituted macroeconomic policies and procedures that were dubbed as *Reaganomics*. This particular brand of economics was popularized by individuals such as Jude Wanniski, Robert Mundell, and Arthur Laffer in the early 1970s. Its base concepts were that if you allowed government to shrink and business to expand, the increased revenues that were stockpiled at the top would trickle down to the bottom. This particular economic ideology falls squarely within a *"crumbs from the master's table"* doctrine that contains the crucial elements of a slave, and slave master relationship.

During the time of Mr. Reagan's presidency, big business grew bigger, richer and more powerful. Unrestrained by huge tax-cuts and governmental assistance (welfare), big business took root in the social, political, economic, and moral dirt of American globalization and imperialism. The cold war ended and the Berlin Wall crumbled, America was positioned as the only superpower left. Within this political climate American Imperialism thrived, and its power brokers felt the delicious spoils of an economic, social, and political war that had been fought ever since the Western World had been established. The war was over global dominance, and the culture that would be born of it.

The mathematical realities of Reaganomics assured that the rich would get richer and the poor would get poorer. The argument from the Reagan supporters stemmed in their twisted interpretation of the nature of a *fat beast*. These supporters claimed that if the beast was allowed to get fatter, this beast would then begin to trickle down anything that was left over. This claim is trumped however by the nature of the beast, a nature based upon and comprised of sheer greed and gluttony. The only thing that the beast would willingly give up to those underneath them is that which would assist the beast in getting fatter. Those who were permitted access to a certain level of monetary gain were allowed so simply to promote the idea of that particular economic system and thought. Because some of those at the bottom obtained their economic growth from the crumbs of others, an appearance of growth was shown based on the lower half's ability to now purchase *new things*, but no real economic ground was made in relationship to the slave and slave master.

On December 1, 1981, the first case of AIDS was recognized… since then it has emerged as an monstrous pandemic that has murdered over 25 million people worldwide, most of which are black people. There is ever increasing evidence that this biological killer was manufactured in American controlled laboratories with the specific intent of reducing the global population of black people. Also in the 1980's, crack

cocaine boomed into the ghettos of America and left in its wake a plague of crack babies, crack whores, birth defects, gang murders, senseless killings, armed robberies, and severely over packed prison and jail cells. While the 80's marked tremendous growth for white people and their political and economic systems, the 80's offered death and destruction to the masses of people of color throughout the world, particularly the black man and woman of America.

With these two seemingly unattached realities as its backdrop, the HipHop nation began to boom in the 80's, record sells grew and ghetto children got famous. These children that had never had anything of great monetary value in life, found themselves with fine cars, jewelry, and homes. The slave master began to lavish his slaves with gifts of money and illusionary elements of power. These so-called Negro rappers that had never experienced wealth or power in its truest sense developed a false sense of security based on their faulty perception of true power. White businessmen that have traditionally understood and accepted the connection between business and war, marched into a field of ignorance and staked their claim. So-called Negro neophytes comprised of street-smart dope dealers, corner claiming gang bangers, and nickel and dime hustlers did nothing; nor could they do anything, to withstand the wicked machinations of the mother of all criminals, the American white business man.

As the power brokers of western domination moved in, their wealth and influence grew. This reality made it nothing for those who actually control the distribution of wealth and resources to increase their bounties of appreciation to their loyal slaves. Contracts grew fatter, money was distributed at a larger and faster rate, and the so-called Negro rapper was wooed to sleep by crooked deceivers that stole their cultural expression right from underneath them.

The 1980's marked the beginning of a new era for black people. The 50's was marked by Jim Crow and the southern cracka that outlawed the colored folk's use of white only toilets. The 60's was marked by the civil rebellions of so-called Black Muslims, Black Panthers, and white Hippies. The 70's was known for Afro's, Negroes dancing in discos, and rolling on skates... but in the 1980's, a little over 200 years after America declared its independence; white folks began their latest and greatest attack on black people and their future generations.

By unleashing crack-cocaine, the government of the United States and their wicked agents began to stimulate the ghetto economy. Never before had there been a monetary movement within the urban centers (cities) of America such as what came with the implementation of crack cocaine. The American CIA, under the guise of the Iran-Contra affair; permitted, and in many cases was directly involved in the trafficking of what has been proven to be the deadliest narcotic in the history of the planet.

In order to get a clear understanding of this period of time, and its affect on the HipHop Nation we must deal with this subject from a particular angle... Since crack-cocaine has created an entire generation of crack-babies, crack-whores, crack-wars, and crack-murders; do we believe for one moment that it's unleashing into the urban centers of America was an accident or coincidence, if not, where is the collective black outrage!!

Consider the following...

In 1986 the Iran-Contra Affair was revealed; if the reader is unaware of this historical reality I suggest you begin researching this particular political scandal NOW!! Without going into every single detail, I will touch it in a way that will get you to see a certain point that I am trying to make.

Ronald Reagan was the President of the United States; this president permitted the sale of weapons to Iran in order to secure the release of American hostages. Now, this is the catch... On September 22, 1980, Iraq had invaded Iran at the behest and support of the American government. Iraq was a friend of America, and so was Saddam Hussein. The Iran-Iraq war lasted for eight years.

Supposedly seeking the release of six U.S. hostages, a deal was brokered by the National Security Agency (NSA) to provide weapons to the so-called moderate elements of the Iranian military. According to the National Security Agency, the weapons were sold in order to give the Iranian moderates a chance to destabilize the official government of Iran; the destabilization never took place, nor was it ever attempted! These so-called "Iranian Moderates" would be considered terrorists in today's media lexicon.

America was a friend of Iraq; yet, it was supplying arms to Iran. But how did this take place? Since America was a so-called friend of Iraq, and Iran was the apparent enemy, America could never openly sale weapons to Iran. So, what did they do... they got Israel to sell the weapons to Iran. Remember, Israel got its weapons from America; therefore, Israel sold its weapons to Iran, and America then gave Israel weapons to replace the ones they sold to Iran. The money that Iran gave to Israel was then given to America.

This, my people is called MONEY LAUNDERING and ILLEGAL ARMS DEALING, the government of America officiated the selling of weapons to their apparent enemy, by using the government of Israel. The question is raised... If America was doing this for the exchange of hostages, why didn't they just make a straight trade... weapons for hostages? Why did they need money? After America got its financial kickback from Israel, the CIA (Central Intelligence Agency) then gave the money to the Contras of Nicaragua in order to help them to fight the Sandinistas, or communist elements of Nicaragua.

Why! Is this relevant to the HipHop Nation... simple, in addition to gaining financial support from the American government, the Contras was permitted to, and in many cases assisted in supplying cocaine to American cities. This major flow of cocaine under the auspices of the CIA, created a Crack epidemic that allowed for the formation of urban gangs and crime families that ravaged the black and brown communities.

As Corporate America waxed rich by the economic policies of Ronald Reagan, so did the Negroes that chose to sell the poison to their people? Just as the money from the illegal sale of weapons to Iran found its way to the Contra rebels of Nicaragua, and the flow of drugs into the American cities, the money from the selling of those drugs went a long way in developing major record labels and their talented rosters of Negro rappers. What is consistent in all of this is the presence of the American government and the often times hidden hand of the so-called Jew... America's partner in crime!

Consider the following:

THE CIA-CONTRA-CRACK COCAINE CONTROVERSY: A REVIEW OF THE JUSTICE DEPARTMENT'S INVESTIGATIONS AND PROSECUTIONS

A. The San Jose Mercury News Articles

On August 18, 1996, the San Jose Mercury News published the first installment of a three-part series of articles concerning crack cocaine, the Central Intelligence Agency (CIA), and the Nicaraguan Contra army. The introduction to the first installment of the series read:

For the better part of a decade, a San Francisco Bay Area drug ring sold tons of cocaine to the Crips and Bloods street gangs of Los Angeles and funneled millions in drug profits to a Latin American guerrilla army run by the U.S. Central Intelligence Agency, a Mercury News investigation has found.

This drug network opened the first pipeline between Colombia's cocaine cartels and the black neighborhoods of Los Angeles, a city now known as the "crack" capital of the world. The cocaine that flooded in helped spark a crack explosion in urban America ... and provided the cash and connections needed for L.A.'s gangs to buy automatic weapons.

The three-day series of articles, entitled "Dark Alliance: The Story Behind the Crack Explosion," told the story of a Los Angeles drug operation run by Ricky Donnell Ross, described sympathetically as "a disillusioned 19-year-old . . . who, at the dawn of the 1980s, found himself adrift on the streets of South-Central Los Angeles." The Dark Alliance series recounted how Ross began peddling small quantities of cocaine in the early 1980s and rapidly grew into one of the largest cocaine dealers in southern California until he was convicted of federal drug trafficking charges in March 1996. The series claimed that Ross' rise in the drug world was made possible by Oscar Danilo Blandon and Norwin Meneses, two individuals with ties to the Fuerza Democratica Nicaraguense (FDN), one group comprising the Nicaraguan Contras. Blandon and Meneses reportedly sold tons of cocaine to Ross, who in turn converted it to crack and sold it in the black communities of South Central Los Angeles. Blandon and Meneses were said to have used their drug trafficking profits to help fund the Contra army's war effort.

Stories had previously been written about the Contras' alleged ties to drug trafficking. For example, on December 20, 1985, an Associated Press article claimed that three Contra groups "engaged in cocaine trafficking, in part to help finance their war against Nicaragua." Rumors about illicit activities on the part of the Contras had also been probed in Senate hearings in the late 1980s. However, the Mercury News series contained -- or at least many readers interpreted it to contain -- a new sensational claim: that the CIA and other agencies of the United States government were responsible for the crack epidemic that ravaged black communities across the country. The newspaper articles suggested that the United States government had protected Blandon and Meneses from prosecution and either knowingly permitted them to peddle massive quantities of cocaine to the black residents of South Central Los Angeles or turned a blind eye to such activity.

The Mercury News later proclaimed that the article did not make these allegations. However, notwithstanding the Mercury News' proclamations, involvement by the CIA and the United States government in the crack crisis was implied through oblique references and the juxtaposition of certain images and phrases in the Dark Alliance articles: the Contras, who purportedly received drug money from Blandon and Meneses, were referred to as the "CIA's army" and links between the CIA and the leadership of the Contra movement were repeatedly emphasized throughout the articles; the stories reported how investigations into Blandon's cocaine operation conducted by the Drug Enforcement Administration (DEA) were allegedly dropped without cause or shunted aside for unexplained reasons; the articles told how United States prosecutors invoked the Classified Information Procedures Act (CIPA) to prevent certain testimony concerning Blandon from being presented to a jury in the interest of national security during Ross' federal trial; and, from August 1996 until October 1996, the image of a crack smoker silhouetted against the emblem of the CIA was emblazoned on the Mercury News web page carrying the Dark Alliance stories.

The news media picked up on the Mercury News series' insinuation and made it explicit in coverage of the series. On August 20, 1996, the headline of the first article to cover the Mercury News series, published by the Associated Press, stated,

"Newspaper Alleges that CIA Helped Spark Crack Cocaine Plague." It was followed by other articles and editorials declaring that the crack cocaine crisis had been created by the CIA and/or agents of the United States government: "CIA's War Against America," (Palm Beach Post, September 14, 1996); "The U.S. Government Was the First Big Crack Pusher," (Boston Globe, September 11, 1996); "Thanks to the U.S. Government, Oscar Blandon Reyes is Free and Prosperous Today; One Man is Behind L.A. Tide of Crack," (Pittsburgh Post Gazette, September 16, 1996).

Critics and commentators would later debate whether the Mercury News articles in fact accused the United States government of being responsible for the nation's crack cocaine epidemic. In an October 2, 1996, Washington Post article, Gary Webb, the reporter who wrote the Dark Alliance series, asserted that the article had not claimed that the CIA knew about Blandon's drug trafficking. The Washington Post article quoted Webb as saying, "We've never pretended otherwise . . . This doesn't prove the CIA targeted black communities. It doesn't say this was ordered by the CIA. . . . Essentially, our trail stopped at the door of the CIA. They wouldn't return my phone calls." Webb would say as late as June 22, 1997, in an interview with The Revolutionary Worker, "We had The Washington Post claim that the stories were insinuating that the CIA had targeted Black America. It's been a very subtle disinformation campaign to try to tell people that these stories don't say what they say. Or that they say something else, other than what we said. So people can say, well, there's no evidence of this, you know . . . You say, well, this story doesn't prove that top CIA officials knew about it. Well, since the stories never said they did, of course they don't."

According to The Washington Post, Mercury News editor Jerry Ceppos stated that he was troubled by the interpretive leap many people made about the article's claims of CIA involvement in the growth of crack cocaine. Ceppos was quoted as saying, "Certainly talk radio in a lot of cities has made the leap. We've tried to correct it wherever we could . . . People [have been] repeating the error again and again and again." Approximately a month and a half after the Dark Alliance series was posted on the Mercury News website, the newspaper changed the introduction to the articles, in apparent recognition that certain wording had contributed to the misunderstanding. Rather than stating:

For the better part of a decade, a Bay Area drug ring sold tons of cocaine to the Crips and Bloods street gangs of Los Angeles and funneled millions in drug profits to a Latin American guerilla army run by the U.S. Central Intelligence Agency . . .

the Dark Alliance website introduction was altered to read:

The Mercury News published a three-part series in late August that detailed how a San Francisco Bay Area drug ring sold tons of cocaine to the street gangs of South-Central Los Angeles in the 1980s, sending some of the millions in profits to the Contras. The series never reported direct CIA involvement, although many readers drew that conclusion.

Regardless of the intent of the Mercury News, the accusation of government involvement in the crack epidemic had taken root. This dramatic interpretation of the series continued to build with ferocious velocity, especially in black communities, as the Mercury News story attracted the attention of newspapers across the country.

Throughout September 1996, the Dark Alliance series was published in one newspaper after another: the Raleigh News and Observer ran the articles on September 1, 1996; the Denver Post published them on September 13, 1996; the Pittsburgh Post Gazette ran them on September 15, 1996; and so on. While many other newspapers did not publish the Dark Alliance series, they carried stories about the sensation created by the series' claims. The story garnered further exposure from television and radio talk show appearances by Gary Webb. Ricky Ross' attorney, Alan Fenster, also made several appearances on television shows to assert that the government, not his client, was responsible for cocaine dealing in South Central Los Angeles.

Many African-American leaders were particularly troubled by the articles, mindful of the frequency with which young black men were being incarcerated for drug offenses. If the Mercury News was right, it appeared that the same government that was arresting so many black men had played a role in creating the drug crisis that precipitated their arrest. This point was emphasized by the Mercury News' Dark Alliance series, which included articles entitled, "War on drugs has unequal impact on black Americans; Contras case illustrates the discrepancy: Nicaraguan goes free; L.A. dealer faces life"; and "Flawed sentencing the main reason for race disparity; In 1993, crack smokers got 3 years; coke snorters got 3 months." The president of the Los Angeles chapter of the NAACP issued the following statement in response to the Dark Alliance series: "We believe it is time for the government, the CIA, to come forward and accept responsibility for destroying human lives." In a letter dated August 30, 1996, Representative Maxine Waters (D-Calif.) requested that the Department of Justice (DOJ) and the House Judiciary Committee conduct investigations of the allegations. The Congressional Black Caucus and many leaders in the black community also insisted upon an investigation into the charges raised by the Mercury News.

B. The Contra Story

As noted above, the Mercury News series was not only a story about the United States government and crack cocaine. It also revisited allegations concerning the Contras and drug trafficking that has been reported upon and investigated for many years. In 1987, the Subcommittee on Terrorism, Narcotics, and International Operations of the Senate Committee on Foreign Relations began an investigation focusing on allegations received by the subcommittee chairman, Senator John Kerry, concerning illegal gun-running and narcotics trafficking associated with the Contras. A two-year investigation produced a 1,166-page report in 1989 analyzing the involvement of Contra groups and supporters in drug trafficking, and the role of United States government officials in these activities. Allegations of cocaine trafficking by Contras also arose during the investigation conducted by Independent Counsel Lawrence Walsh into the Iran-Contra affair. Drug trafficking allegations, however, were not the focus of that inquiry and the Walsh report included no findings on these allegations.

The issue of drug trafficking by the Nicaraguan Contras has also been the subject of books: e.g., On Bended Knee: The Press and the Reagan Presidency, by Mark Hertsgaard, 1989; Cocaine Politics: Drugs, Armies, and the CIA in Central America, by Peter Dale Scott and Jonathan Marshall, 1991. It was also reported upon in the news media. Following the December 1985 piece mentioned above from the Associated Press, the San Francisco Examiner ran stories in 1986 about Norwin Meneses, Carlos Cabezas (an individual with links to Contra organizations who was convicted in the mid-1980s of drug charges), and drug trafficking by the Contras.

It is undisputed that individuals like Meneses and Blandon, who had ties to the Contras or were Contra sympathizers, were convicted of drug trafficking, either in the United States or Central America. There is also undeniable evidence that certain groups associated with the Contras engaged in drug trafficking. The pervasiveness of such activities within the Contra movement and the United States government's knowledge of those activities, however, are still the subject of debate, and it is beyond the scope of the OIG's investigation, which we describe below. Yet it is noteworthy that, as interesting as the story of Contras and illicit drug deals may be, it was not the catalyst for the public's or the media's interest in the Dark Alliance series. Investigations into the alleged connection between Contras and cocaine dealing were conducted and articles were printed in the late 1980s, at a time when interest in the Iran-Contra story was cresting. Neither those investigations nor the published articles tracking the allegations sparked a firestorm of outrage comparable to that created by the Dark Alliance series. The furor over the Mercury News series was driven by the allegations of the government's complicity in cocaine deals within black communities. If the Dark Alliance series had been limited to reporting on Contras, it seems unlikely that the groundswell of press and public attention would have occurred.

C. Reaction from the Journalism Community

Notwithstanding the Mercury News' explosive allegations, the series did not receive extensive coverage from major newspapers in either August or September 1996. The Los Angeles Times briefly discussed the Mercury News series in several articles in August and September 1996 that covered Ross' postponed sentencing and other events in the Ross trial. Similarly, the Dark Alliance series did not initially receive much television coverage. With the exception of CNN, which ran several pieces on the story in September, and the NBC Nightly News, which ran a piece about the allegations on September 27, 1996, the story received little national television news coverage. By early October 1996, however, that changed.

The Washington Post weighed in first on October 2, 1996, with a short analysis -- "Running with the CIA Story: Reporter Says Series Didn't Go as Far as Readers Took It" -- noting that the allegation of CIA involvement in drug trafficking in the United States had not actually been made in the article. The Washington Post followed-up two days later, on October 4, 1996, with a story entitled, "The CIA and

Crack: Evidence Is Lacking of Alleged Plot." The Washington Post piece concluded that "available information does not support the conclusion that the CIA-backed Contras -- or Nicaraguans in general -- played a major role in the emergence of crack as a narcotic in widespread use across the United States." The Washington Post article mainly addressed the Mercury News series' claims about Ross' and Blandon's roles in the growth of crack cocaine. It did not, for the most part, wrestle with the series' claims about drug dealing by the Contras. The Washington Post noted that the series had been selective in its use of Blandon's testimony to support its claims:

The Mercury News uses testimony from Blandon in establishing that Nicaraguans selling drugs in California sent profits to the Contras. But if the whole of Blandon's testimony is to be believed, then the connection is not made between Contras and African American drug dealers because Blandon said he had stopped sending money to the contras by [the time he began selling to Ross].

And if Blandon is to be believed, there is no connection between Contras and the cause of the crack epidemic because Blandon said Ross was already a well-established dealer with several ready sources of supply by the time he started buying cocaine from Blandon.

The Washington Post piece also emphasized apparent contradictions between Ross' and Blandon's accounts. For example, while Blandon claimed to have been a used car salesman in 1982 who on the side sold two kilograms of cocaine for Meneses, Ross said Blandon was instead handling bulk sales of 100 kilograms of cocaine for Meneses at the time. The article did not seek to resolve these issues and merely noted the conflicts.

The Washington Post piece was followed on October 20 and 21, 1996, by two New York Times articles that also found fault with the Mercury News series. One article, "Though Evidence Thin, Tale of CIA and Drugs Has Life of Its Own," primarily reported on the reactions within the black community to the series. The other article, "Pivotal Figure of Newspaper Series May Be Only Bit Player," noted problems with the series' portrayal of Blandon and Meneses. It concluded, after conducting interviews of various unnamed sources:

[W]hile there are indications in American intelligence files and elsewhere that Mr. Meneses and Mr. Blandon may indeed have provided modest support for the rebels, including perhaps some weapons, there is no evidence that either man was a rebel official or had anything to do with the C.I.A. Nor is there proof that the relatively small amounts of cocaine they sometimes claimed to have brokered on behalf of the insurgents had a remotely significant role in the explosion of crack that began around the same time.

After reportedly assigning three editors and fourteen reporters to the story, the Los Angeles Times published its own three-part analysis of the Mercury News piece, which ran from October 20 to October 22, 1996. The Los Angeles Times concentrated on three claims raised by the Mercury News series: 1) that a drug ring related to the CIA had sent millions of dollars to the Contras; 2) that the same drug ring had created a cocaine epidemic in South Central Los Angeles and other United States cities, and 3) that the CIA had approved a plan for the ring to raise money for the Contras through drug trafficking or had deliberately turned a blind eye to the drug ring's activities. The Los Angeles Times found that "the available evidence, based on an extensive review of court documents and more than 100 interviews in San Francisco, Los Angeles, Washington and Managua, fails to support any of those allegations."

The first installment of the Los Angeles Times series was devoted to a discussion of the origins of crack cocaine. It found that crack cocaine existed in Los Angeles long before Ross began selling it. In response to the claim that Ross had played a principal role in bringing cocaine to South Central Los Angeles, it identified several drug dealers from South Central Los Angeles who were contemporaries of Ross and were reputed to have sold similar quantities of cocaine.

The second installment of the Los Angeles Times series explored whether there was in fact a CIA-sanctioned operation that funneled millions of dollars into the Contras. It found no proof that Blandon and Meneses had given millions of dollars to the Contra party and could confirm only that Blandon had given about $50,000. Indeed, the Los Angeles Times article concluded that the Mercury News had arrived at its million-dollar estimate of Meneses' and Blandon's donations based on its own calculations derived from "the volume of cocaine that they were selling, and Blandon's statement that what he sold, he gave to the Contras."[2] Rejecting the Dark Alliance assertion that Blandon had sent profits to the Contras from 1981 to 1986, the Los Angeles Times found, based upon Blandon's testimony, that he had sent profits to the Contras in only one year. The second installment of the Los Angeles Times series also suggested, based on interviews with various CIA officials and former government officials, that CIA involvement in such a scheme was improbable. But the article quoted the chief investigator for Senator Kerry's subcommittee investigation, Jack Blum, as saying that, while the CIA did not have agents selling drugs to fund the Contras, the United States government may have opened channels that helped drug dealers bring drugs into the United States and protected them from law enforcement.

The last installment of the Los Angeles Times series examined the reaction in black communities to the series, particularly the proliferation of conspiracy theories.

The Los Angeles Times, New York Times, and Washington Post articles were criticized by some who believed that the mainstream press was attempting to minimize a story that it had failed to cover. Some accused the papers of erecting strawmen by accusing the Mercury News of making allegations that it had not in fact made: e.g., that the CIA "targeted" communities into which crack cocaine was distributed. Others stated that the major papers had committed the same mistakes it criticized the Mercury News of making: e.g., selectively picking from among available information to support their conclusions, crediting information provided by suspicious sources, and failing to evaluate contradictory evidence.[3]

Despite the major newspapers' mounting criticism of the Dark Alliance series, the Mercury News continued to defend its story. However, in the meantime the paper launched its own investigation of the claims made by the Dark Alliance series. On May 11, 1997, Jerry Ceppos, the Executive Editor of the Mercury News, published the results of the newspaper's analysis of its own series. Ceppos wrote that the story had four short-comings: 1) it presented only one side of "complicated, sometimes-conflicting pieces of evidence"; 2) it failed to identify the estimate of Blandon's financial contributions to the Contra movement as an "estimate"; 3) it "oversimplified the complex issue of how the crack epidemic in America grew," and 4) it contained imprecise language and graphics that fostered the misinterpretation concerning the CIA and crack dealing. Ceppos attributed some of these problems to the newspaper's failure to present conflicting evidence that challenged its conclusions. The column also revealed that the same debate over the correct interpretation of the Mercury News' conclusions found in the press also existed in the Mercury News newsroom:

The drug ring we wrote about inflicted terrible damage on inner-city Los Angeles, and that horror was indeed spread to many other places by L.A. gangs. Webb believes that is what our series said. I believe that we implied much more, that the ring was the pivotal force in the crack epidemic in the United States. Because the national crack epidemic was a complex phenomenon that had more than one origin, our discussion of this issue needed to be clearer.

Some of the reporting on Ceppos' column by the major newspapers failed to recognize that it was not intended as a repudiation of the entire Dark Alliance series. Rather, it was a limited admission that portions of the story had been misleading and should have been subjected to more rigorous editing. Ceppos specifically did not disclaim what he believed were the articles' central allegation -- that a drug ring "associated with the Contras sold large quantities of cocaine in inner-city Los Angeles in the 1980s at the time of the crack explosion there" and that "some of the profits went to the Contras." It is noteworthy, however, that the facets of the article about which Ceppos had the greatest reservations were the articles' most sensational claims -- the way crack cocaine spread in the United States, and the ties between the CIA and the spread of crack.

D. What Did the San Jose Mercury News Articles Allege?

It is difficult to discern which allegations the Mercury News intended to make, in large part because the series is replete with innuendo and implication that verge on making assertions that are in fact never made. Many readers interpreted the series to assert that the CIA and other agencies of the United States government had intentionally funneled crack cocaine into black communities by either permitting or endorsing cocaine trafficking by Blandon and Meneses. Others interpreted the Dark Alliance series to charge that the spread of crack cocaine was the unintended -- but proximate -- result of actions taken by the United States government to promote the Contra war effort. While the series does not allege that there was a deliberate plan to target black communities by the CIA or other agencies of the United States government mentioned in the article (e.g., DEA, U.S. Attorney's Offices, and the Immigration and Naturalization Service (INS), the articles strongly imply such a plot.

First, the title of the series, "Dark Alliance," is itself ambiguous, since the series fails to identify the parties to the purported "alliance." One interpretation is that it refers to the link between Blandon and Ross. However, another interpretation, bolstered by the repeated mention of the CIA throughout the series, is that the title refers to an agreement between the CIA and drug-trafficking Contras. The web page bearing the "Dark Alliance" title and the image of a crack smoker silhouetted against the CIA emblem strengthened the insinuation. The Dark Alliance story also included leaps of logic that suggested direct CIA involvement in Blandon's trafficking activities. For example, the article notes: "The most Blandon would say in court about who called the shots when he sold cocaine for the FDN was that 'we received orders from the -- from other people.'" An explanation of how the CIA created the FDN from various anti-communist factions immediately follows the quote. The writer's implication is patent: the CIA was giving "orders" to the FDN about cocaine deals.

One oft-quoted portion of the articles relates to a meeting that allegedly occurred in Honduras among Meneses, Blandon, and Enrique Bermudez, a leader of the FDN's military effort. The preceding paragraph in the article recounted how cocaine "has spread across the country . . . turning entire blocks of major cities into occasional war zones." The paragraph that immediately followed reads:

"There is a saying that the ends justify the means," former FDN leader and drug dealer Oscar Danilo Blandon Reyes testified during a recent cocaine trafficking trial in San Diego. "And that's what Mr. Bermudez (the CIA agent who commanded the FDN) told us in Honduras, OK? So we started raising money for the Contra revolution."

The implication of this paragraph, made through its juxtaposition to the discussion of black communities ravaged by cocaine, is that a "CIA agent" decided to raise money for the Contras by any means, including by selling cocaine in black communities. It is noteworthy that the parenthetical reference to Bermudez as a "CIA agent who commanded the FDN" was added by the Mercury News and was not a statement actually made by Blandon. The parenthetical underscores reputed ties between Bermudez and the CIA.

The specter of a government-wide plan to target black communities is raised throughout the article in other ways, but mostly through innuendo. The subtext of the article seems to be: If there was no government plot, why else would an Assistant U.S. Attorney prevent evidence relating to Blandon's drug trafficking from being raised in open court under the claim of protecting classified information during a 1990 federal trial?; how else would Blandon have escaped more vigorous prosecution by the Department of Justice or other prosecutor's offices for drug trafficking?; why else would federal agents descend upon the Los Angeles Sheriff's Department to claim evidence obtained in a search of Blandon's home in 1986?; and how else would Meneses escape arrest and prosecution in the United States or be allowed by the INS to freely enter and exit the country? While the allegation of a deliberate government plan was not explicitly made, the drumbeat of questions insinuated a multi-agency, government scheme designed to protect Blandon's illegal activities, which "opened the first pipeline between Colombia's cocaine cartels and the black neighborhoods of Los Angeles."

The Mercury News stated repeatedly that the series was not intended to allege a deliberate government scheme to use cocaine dealing in black communities to finance the Contra effort, notwithstanding the logical inference that could be drawn from the series' substance. But while it is true that the articles did not explicitly allege a government conspiracy, the path charted by the Dark Alliance series' trail of implications led to that conclusion. In fact, a prophetic editorial that appeared in the Mercury News on August 21, 1996, the day after the Dark Alliance series finished running in the paper, made just that point. It read:

[T]he CIA-Contra story can only feed longstanding rumors in black communities that the U.S. government "created" the crack cocaine epidemic to kill and imprison African-Americans and otherwise wreak havoc in inner cities.

At times, the Mercury News sent conflicting messages that confounded attempts to correct misconceptions about the article. While the newspaper was disavowing allegations of CIA involvement in the spread of crack, the articles' author was making public comments to the contrary. In an article entitled, "The CIA-crack connection: The story nobody wants to hear: Your worst fears are true -- the CIA did help to smuggle drugs into American ghettos, says an investigative reporter," Webb was asked whether his story had confirmed the suspicion within the black community "that the crack cocaine epidemic might be part of a government conspiracy." He replied:

It confirms the suspicion that government agents were involved. Clearly, when you're talking about drug dealers meeting with CIA agents it does go a long way toward validating this suspicion. There's a grain of truth to any conspiracy theory and it turns out there are a lot of grains of truth to this one. If you want to stretch it to its logical conclusion, the government was involved in starting the crack epidemic, because it was this pipeline that did it. Now we know what we didn't know in the '80's -- which is where they were selling the stuff. We were able to close the circle and show how this affected American citizens, whereas before it was some sort of nebulous foreign policy story. Now we can see the damage. Whether or not these guys were part of our government or just contract agents is unclear.

Further, the newspaper itself was sending mixed messages. An August 21, 1996, Mercury News editorial supported claims of CIA or United States government involvement. The editorial, entitled "Another CIA disgrace: Helping the crack flow," stated:

It's impossible to believe that the Central Intelligence Agency didn't know about the Contras' fund-raising activities in Los Angeles, considering that the agency was bankrolling, recruiting and essentially running the Contra operation. The CIA has a long history of embarrassing the country it is supposed to work for, from the Bay of

Pigs in Cuba to the jungles of Vietnam. But no action that we know of can compare to the agency's complicity, however tacit, in the drug trade that devastated whole communities in our own country.

1. In contrast, Webb has made other statements all but stating that the Dark Alliance series did demonstrate CIA involvement in the spread of crack in America. In September 1996, in the immediate wake of the Dark Alliance series, Webb reportedly posted the following comment on the Mercury News electronic bulletin board: "One thing I did want to respond to directly is the writer who claimed there wasn't any 'proof ' of CIA involvement in this thing. That's like saying there's no proof of General Motors involvement in making Chevrolets. I also heard a great line while I was doing a radio show in Florida yesterday: 'Now we know what CIA really stands for: Crack in America.'"

2. In a response to a May/June 1997 Columbia Journalism Review article analyzing the Mercury News series, Webb more specifically explained how he arrived at a figure, which he believed to be between $12 million and $18 million: "My stories were about the drug money [Blandon] admitted delivering to Meneses for the FDN. When you look at that cash, the sums are obvious. Blandon told a federal grand jury in 1994 that he sold between 200 and 300 kilos of cocaine for Meneses in L.A. In court, Blandon swore that all the profits from that cocaine went to the contras, and said he was selling it for $60,000 a kilo ... Some might call it an extrapolation to describe $12 million to $18 million as 'millions.' I call it math."

As the general public formulates opinions and critiques concerning the so-called war on drugs, and those who deal them, most people are completely ignorant of the ties that bind government, politics, and economics to the so-called gang bangers and urban dope dealers. The HipHop Nation with the senseless braggadocios mentality concerning crack and drugs, has allowed themselves to be played within the vices of a conspiracy that they don't know shit about! And if for some reason they do understand… should not they be found utilizing their talents exposing the real realities associated with the present day holocaust that is attacking the uban-centers of AMERICA?! In all fairness, it should be stated that there are a relatively small few that attempt to do just that. Please find time to listen and track the lyrics of rappers such as Immortal Technique, Rass Kass, Nyoil, Nas, and Wise Intelligent of Poor Righteous Teachers' fame; especially his song Globe Holders, whose video can be seen and heard on the website www.thepeopleslanguage.com.

An August, 1996, series in the <u>San Jose Mercury News</u> by reporter Gary Webb linked the origins of crack cocaine in California to the contras, a guerrilla force backed by the Reagan administration that attacked Nicaragua's Sandinista government during the 1980s. Webb's series, "The Dark Alliance," has been the subject of <u>intense media debate</u>, and has focused attention on a foreign policy drug scandal that leaves many questions unanswered.

This electronic briefing book is compiled from declassified documents obtained by the National Security Archive, including the notebooks kept by NSC aide and Iran-contra figure Oliver North, electronic mail messages written by high-ranking Reagan administration officials, memos detailing the contra war effort, and FBI and DEA reports. The documents demonstrate official knowledge of drug operations, and collaboration with and protection of known drug traffickers. Court and hearing transcripts are also included.

Special thanks to the Arca Foundation, the Ruth Mott Fund, the Samuel Rubin Foundation, and the Fund for Constitutional Government for their support.

http://www.gwu.edu/~nsarchiv/NSAEBB/NSAEBB2/nsaebb2.htm

The National Security Archive obtained the hand-written notebooks of Oliver North, the National Security Council aide who helped run the contra war and other Reagan administration covert operations, through a Freedom of Information Act lawsuit filed in 1989. The notebooks, as well as declassified memos sent to North, record that North was repeatedly informed of contra ties to drug trafficking.

We will return to this subject later… but for now let us move on; keeping in mind what we have just learned, as we continue…

THE PLANTATION

"There is INTELLIGENCE, SIZE, SEX, SIZES OF PLANTATIONS, STATUS on plantations, ATTITUDE of owners, whether the slaves live in the valley, on a hill, East, West, North, South, have fine hair, course hair, or is tall or short."

As we return to Def Jam; we do so not to single out this particular record company (plantation) as the only plantation that exists, but because of its early pioneering elements. We point to Def Jam as a case study that supports the premise of this entire writing. Black owned record labels, and their so-called Negro rappers, singers, and entertainers fall within the category of a slave as supported by this book's context, and have been completely subjugated by those that exhort control over the record industry.

From 1990 through 1999, Lyor Cohen's power and influence grew. In a ten year period as president of Def Jam (RAL) records, Lyor Cohen's personal value rose so much, that when Def Jam was sold to Universal Music Group (UMG), he personally earned over 100 million dollars from the acquisition. This level of earnings from the sell of a company that he did not start nor create, begs for the question, "What exactly was it about Lyor Cohen and his role of president of Def Jam records that allowed him to earn a personal pay (off) out of over 100 million dollars when it was sold?"

The answer to the above question resides in the obvious... Russell Simmons is the figure head of a company that is not controlled by him. He had an idea to express elements of the black culture, but due to business impotence and a lack of access into the entertainment and media network comprised of American so-called Jews and white people, his dream could not be realized without their help and influence. Within this reality came the formulation of a relationship based on necessity and dependence. When Russell was unable to take HipHop and its expression to the next level, support was offered by a so-called Jewish graduate of NYU. Rick Rubin then garnished deals through his privileged access that allowed for the expression of something that this particular so-called Jew did not create or spiritually connect too. Rick saw an opportunity that he could exploit, and his slave needed his help! Consider the obvious... **Rick Rubin is a so-called Jewish educated man from New York, he is not black, nor was he a product of the black community or circumstance. This means that he was drawn into the black experience by a source that was, and is foreign to his natural circumstance and condition. Are we to believe that Rick was drawn into the black experience because he chose to wear the pain of the struggle that comes with being associated with the black experience... or, do we understand that the black** experience offered an opportunity for an alien of that experience to capitalize or exploit that experience... we should think on this!

In the mind of Rick Rubin, it was never about the culture or the people from which the culture was born... it was and still is about power and influence. The fight between Rick and Lyor was not over the music or the money; the fight was over the so-called Negro slaves that gave them access to the minds of the global masses of the people that felt the struggle, condition and plight of the American rejected class. Proof resides in the operational tendencies of those who desire to have the influence.

After facilitating a deal that sold Def Jam to Universal Music Group (UMG), Lyor Cohen was named president of a UMG subsidiary called *"Island Def Jam"*. Island records was a sub-unit of UMG, and the fact that they chose to have the name *Def Jam* associated with *Island* shows that these clever business minds recognized the power of the concept of the early Def Jam brand and its psychological attachments to the HipHop Nation. This marketing move was designed to sift the true elements of the early Def Jam years, and leave only a grafted and altered name as a mocking reminder.

When Def Jam was originally formulated, it was given avenues of expression by Rick Rubin and the contacts that he had. Rick Rubin's connections that had a lot to do with his being a so-called Jew and his skin color, was then maximized to allow Def Jam the opportunity to gain exposure. HipHop was then exposed on a larger scale to a broader audience. This exposure allowed the wise American power brokers to see HipHop as not only a supplier of revenue, but as a road of influence through the lips of the black urban youth. The vision of the American power broker was then facilitated by the transfer of power, and the replacement of Rick Rubin with a more sophisticated, business developed so-called Jewish man by the name of Lyor Cohen.

Mr. Cohen then proceeded to maximize the influence that came with having control of the most powerful HipHop record label of that time. Nevertheless, the question remains... how did Russell Simmons allow a power struggle between Lyor and Rubin to take place? It would seem that the power struggle could have been avoided by a simple decision by Russell Simmons... he wanted either Rick or Lyor. If Russell chose Lyor, we would assume that a payout or buy out would be given to Rubin and that would seemingly be that. Nevertheless, there was a struggle between two so-called Jews over a company that was not theirs, or was it? Why didn't Russell make the decision? Perhaps it was because his decision did not matter, and he had no say so in the overall direction of the company.

The record industry is a huge plantation, those that are not "masters" are slaves, and it will be proven very shortly who the masters are, and who the slaves are.

THE TENTACLES OF INFLUENCE

"Gentlemen, these kits are your keys to control. Use them. Have your wives and children use them, never miss an opportunity. IF USED INTENSELY FOR ONE YEAR, THE SLAVES THEMSELVES WILL REMAIN PERPETUALLY DISTRUSTFUL."

The American so-called Jew yields huge doses of social, political, and economic power and influence. This influential juice stems from their control of media and entertainment. Several individuals would like to label my telling this truth as evidence of my being some sort of anti-Semite. My response would be three fold... first, I would define the word Semite in relationship to the reality of the national and racial reality of those that claim themselves to be Jews but or not. Second, I would show that based on biblical terminology, spirituality, and lineage of both the old and New Testament they are not Jews. Third, I would show that based on their understanding of what "anti" means, it is clear that they are anti-black, anti-right and proper, and certainly anti-God... and I would probably add that, "whatever they claim I am, I simply don't give a damn, the truth stands as an adequate defender of my words!"

The so-called Jewish tentacles of influence stretch from the east to the west coast. Their primary residence of choice is New York, the reigning kingdom of the news, media, and financial world; and Hollywood, California, the Mecca of the entertainment world. One would simply have to look briefly into the who's who of entertainment and media to come to the conclusion that individuals that find themselves as major power brokers in the realm of business and finance, media and entertainment are in fact so-called Jewish people. This fact is not to be ignored no more than the fact that NBA team rosters are primarily comprised of so-called African-American players. The influence of so-called Jewish Americans on media and entertainment is unparalleled and disproportionate in comparison to their relatively small American and global population.

Those that consider themselves as Jews have embarked on dominating all avenues leading to the control and manipulation of the global politic; a politic that consists of governmental, financial, educational, social, and religious institutions. This small group of individuals clearly and unarguably exhorts a disproportionate amount of power and influence.

The following is a list of some of the most powerful so-called Jews in the world of media:

GAIL BERMAN, president of Fox Entertainment

WOLF BLITZER, host of CNN's Late Edition

LLOYD BRAUN, Chair, ABC Entertainment

PHIL BRONSTEIN, Executive Editor, San Francisco Chronicle,

PETER CHERNIN, second in-command at Rupert Murdoch's News Corp., owner of Fox TV

RICHARD COHEN, syndicated columnist for the Washington Post

BARRY DILLER, chair of USA Interactive, former owner of Universal Entertainment

MICHAEL EISNER, major owner of Walt Disney, Capitol Cities, ABC

STEPHEN EMERSON, every media outlet's first choice as an expert on domestic terrorism

JEFF FAGER, Exec. Director, 60 Minutes II CBS

HOWARD FINEMAN, Chief Political Columnist, Newsweek

ARIE FLEISCHER, President Bush's press secretary.

TOM FRIEDMAN, syndicated columnist for the NYT.

JEFF GASPIN, Executive Vice-President, Programming, NBC

DAVID GEFFEN, co-owner of DreamWorks

MARK GOLIN, VP and Creative Director, AO

BRIAN GRADEN, president of MTV entertainment

DONALD GRAHAM, Chair and CEO of Newsweek and Washington Post

SANDY GRUSHOW, chair of Fox Entertainment

HENRICK HERTZBERG, Talk of the Town editor, The New Yorker

DON HEWITT, Exec. Director, 60 Minutes, CBS

JEFF JACOBY, syndicated columnist for the Boston Globe

PETER R KANN, CEO, Wall Street Journal, Barron's

MEL KARMAZIN, president of CBS

JEFFREY KATZENBERG, co-owner of DreamWorks

LARRY KING, host of Larry King Live

LAWRENCE KIRSHBAUM, CEO, AOL-Time Warner Book Group

JOEL KLEIN, chair and CEO of Bertelsmann's American operations

DAVID KOHAN, co-executive producer of NBC's "Good Morning Miami"

ANDREA KOPPEL, CNN Reporter

TED KOPPEL, host of ABC's Nightline

CHARLES KRAUTHAMMER, syndicated columnist for the Washington Post. Honored by Honest Reporting.com, website monitoring "anti-Israel media"

WILLIAM KRISTOL, Editor, Weekly Standard, Exec. Director Project for a New American Century (PNAC)

ANDREW LACK, president of NBC

SHERRY LANSING, President of Paramount Communications and Chairman of Paramount Pictures' Motion Picture Group.

MICHAEL LEDEEN, editor of National Review

DENNIS LEIBOWITZ, head of Act II Partners, a media hedge fund

RICHARD LEIBNER runs the N.S. Bienstock talent agency, which represents 600 news personalities such as Dan Rather, Dianne Sawyer and Bill O'Reilly

NICHOLAS LEHMANN, writer, the New Yorker

JORDAN LEVIN, president of Warner Bros. Entertainment

WARREN LIEBERFORD, Pres., Warner Bros. Home Video Div. of AOL- Time Warner

MICHAEL MEDVED, Talk Show Host, on 124 AM stations

DANIEL MENAKER, Executive Director, Harper Collins

BARRY MEYER, chair, Warner Bros

CATHERINE GRAHAM MEYER, former owner of the Washington Post

ATHAN MILLER, chair and CEO of AOL division of AOL-Time-Warner

JON LESLIE MOONVES, president of CBS television, great-nephew of David Ben-Gurion, and co-chair with Norman Ornstein of the Advisory Committee on Public Interest Obligation of Digital TV Producers, appointed by Clinton.

RUPERT MURDOCH, Owner Fox TV, New York Post, London Times, News of the World (Jewish mother)

MAX MUTCHNICK, co-executive producer of NBC's "Good Morning Miami"

JACK MYERS, NBC, chief. NYT 5.14.2

SAMUEL NEWHOUSE JR. and **DONALD NEWHOUSE** own Newhouse Publications, includes 26 newspapers in 22 cities; the Conde Nast magazine group, includes The New Yorker; Parade, the Sunday newspaper supplement; American City Business Journals, business newspapers published in more than 30 major cities in America; and interests in cable television programming and cable systems serving 1 million homes.

DONALD NEWHOUSE, chairman of the board of directors, Associated Press.

BRUCE NUSSBAUM, editorial page editor, Business Week

NORMAN ORNSTEIN, American Enterprise Inst., regular columnist for USA Today, news analyst for CBS, and co-chair with Leslie Moonves of the Advisory Committee on Public Interest Obligation of Digital TV Producers, appointed by Clinton

RON OWENS, Talk Show Host, KGO (ABC-Capitol Cities, San Francisco

AMY PASCAL, chair of Columbia Picture

MARTY PERETZ, owner and publisher of the New Republic, which openly identifies itself as pro-Israel

KENNETH POLLACK, for CIA analysts, director of Saban Center for Middle East Policy, writes op-eds in NY Times, New Yorker

DAVID POLTRACK, Executive Vice-President, Research and Planning, CBS

DENNIS PRAGER, Talk Show Host, nationally syndicated from LA
SUMNER REDSTONE, CEO of Viacom, "world's biggest media giant" (Economist, 11/23/2) owns Viacom cable, CBS and MTVs all over the world, Blockbuster video rentals and Black Entertainment TV.

DAVID REMNICK, Editor, The New Yorker

RALPH J. & BRIAN ROBERTS, Owners, Comcast-ATT Cable TV

RON ROSENTHAL, Managing Editor, San Francisco Chronicle

KENNETH ROTH, Executive Director of Human Rights Watch

JOHN ROTHMAN, Talk Show Host, KGO (ABC-Capitol Cities, San Francisco)

WILLIAM SAFIRE, syndicated columnist for the NYT

MICHAEL SAVAGE, Talk Show Host, KFSO (ABC-Capitol Cities, San Francisco) Syndicated in 100 markets

DAVID SCHNEIDERMAN, owner of the Village Voice and the New Times network of "alternative weeklies."

IVAN SEIDENBERG, CEO of Verizon Communications

TERRY SEMEL, CEO, Yahoo, former chair, Warner Bros.

NEIL SHAPIRO, president of NBC News

BRAD SIEGEL., President, Turner Entertainment.

ROBERT SILLERMAN, founder of Clear Channel Communications

STEPHEN SPIELBERG, co-owner of DreamWorks

HOWARD STRINGER, chief of Sony Corp. of America

ARTHUR O. SULZBERGER, JR., publisher of the NY Times, the Boston Globe and other publications.

MIKE WALLACE, Host of CBS, 60 Minutes

BARBARA WALTERS, Host, ABC's 20-20

BEN WATTENBERG, Moderator, PBS Think Tank.

HARVEY WEINSTEIN, CEO. Miramax Films
DAVID WESTIN, president of ABC News

PAULA ZAHN, CNN Host

JEFFREY ZUCKER, President of NBC Entertainment

MORTIMER ZUCKERMAN, owner of NY Daily News, US News & World Report and chair of the Conference of Presidents of Major Jewish American Organizations, one of the largest pro-Israel lobbying groups.

The fact that these individuals are so-called Jews and are successful is not in question; and certainly they all posses some positive traits and characteristics that any person could use within their individual quest for professional success. The purpose for this listing is to show high profiled so-called Jewish presence in a field of endeavor that is becoming increasingly more controversial in terms of the political, social, economic reality of the global population.

If the list of these particular media giants seems vast, understand that all are not listed, and some of those not listed will be mentioned in more detail within later chapters.

However, for now examine this list of so-called Jewish actors and actresses, and then ask yourself if Hollywood, based on its level of so-called Jewish entertainment executives and its number of actors and actresses is dominated and controlled by those that refer to themselves as Jews:

Bette Midler
Paul Reiser
Sid Caesar
Gary Schandling
Estelle Getty
Harry Houdini
Elliot Gould
Dinah Shore
Hal Linden
Matthew Broderick
Neil Diamond
Maury Povich
John Rubenstein
Monty Hall
Dustin Hoffman
Pauly Shore
William Shatner
Barbra Steisand
Fred Savage
Ann Landers
Leonard Nimoy
Madeline Kahn
Adam Sandler
Lauren Bacall
Jerry Seinfeld

Howard Stern
Jamie Lee Curtis
Ed Asner
Melissa Manchester
Billy Crystal
Walter Matthau
Jason Alexander
Jeff Goldblum
Jerry Springer
Steven Spielberg
Paul Simon
All of the Marx brothers
Shelly Winters
Bebe Neuwirt
Jack Klugman
Bob Dylan
Fran Drescher
M. C. Escher
David Duchovny
Embeth Davidtz
Jerry Stiller
Natalie Portman
Edward G. Robinson
John Garfield

Debbie Friendman-songwriter/singer

Leonard Bernstein -composer, West Side Story and others

Marcel Marceau -A mime

Isaac Asimov - science fiction writer

Scott Simon - host on National Public Radio

Mara Wilson - actress in Miracle on 34th Street, Mrs. Doubtfire

Don Black - wrote lyrics for Sunset Boulevard

Rick Moranis - Ghostbusters, Spaceballs, many others

Rhea Perlman - waitress on Cheers

Judy Blume - children's author

Alain Boublil - wrote lyrics for Miss Saigon

Randy Newman - composer of Toy Story music

Kent Brockman - TV Anchor

Elie Weisel - Holocost survivor, writer of Night and others

Elizabeth Taylor - converted

Scott Wolf - Party of Five

Bob Einstein - aka. Super Dave Osborne

Mel Blanc - was voice of Bugs Bunny and many others

Peter Himmelman - Musician, son in law to Bob Dylan

Lorne Michaels - created Saturday Night Live

Harry Shearer- voices on The Simpsons, Comedian

Haim Topol - Actor in Fiddler on the Roof

Emma Lazarus - wrote inscription on Statue of Liberty

Claude-Michel Schonberg - composer of Les Miserables

Billy Wilder - Director

Saul Hudson - aka. Slash in Guns and Roses

Brett Spiner - Data in Star Trek TNG

John Stossel - from 20/20

Maeve Kinkead - Guiding Light

Kim Greist - Homeward Bound actress

Patricia Richardson - Home Improvement

Laurin Sydney - Showbiz Today on CNN

Judd Hirsh - Actor on Taxi

Harrison Ford - Jewish Mother

Adam Horwitz - Beastie Boys

Jon Lovitz - Actor, the Critic

Jennifer Grey - Dirty Dancing

Matt Stoner - co-creator of South Park

Ben Stein - Ben Stein's Money

Jon Stewart - The Daily Show

If that is not enough, maybe you will recognize some of these names:

Bowzer of Sha Na Na

Aaron Spelling	Bill Macy	Red Buttons
David Copperfield	Albert Brooks	Gene Simmons
Gary Lewis	Paul Newman	Larry David
Jennifer Gray	David Brenner	Richard Simmons
Joey Bishop	Joan Lundin	David Schwimmer
Mel Brooks	Paul Stanley	

Jack Lemmon	Eydie Gorme	Jud Hirsch
Vicki Lawrence	Barbara Bach	Lawrence Harvey
Sarah Michelle Gellar	Michelle Lee	Andy Kaufman
Michael Weiss	Kenny G	Jeff Chandler
Gilbert Gottfried	Phil Ramone	Rhea Perlman
Paul Glaser	Janis Ian	Vic Morrow
Carol Leifer	Ed Ames	Goldie Hawn
Julia Dreyfus	Don Rickles	Joan Collins
Carol King	Phil Harris	George Siegel
David Lee Roth	Jackie Mason	Jon Stewart
Carly Simon	Jack Carter	Lorne Greene
Yasmin Bleeth	Jesse Raphael	Lenny Kravitz
Ricki Lake	Ross Martin	Katie Seigal
Henry Winkler	Roseanne	Jerry Stiller
Michael Landers	Morey Amsterdam	Sheldon Leonard
Freddie Prinze	Sarah Gilbert	Ben Stiller
Tina Louise	Carl Reiner	Stuart Margolin
Milton Berl	TraceyPollan	Ben Savage
Bess Myerson Jeff Goldblum	Rob Reiner	Howie Mandel
Peter Green	Jane Seymour	
Marissa Tome	Joana Cassidy	
Linda Mcartney	Adam Sandler	

Why is this list relevant to the overall message of this writing... simple, the number of so-called Jewish actors and actresses are extremely large in comparison to their total population. How can an estimated few be so numerous in one particular profession, and not be connected to a specific purpose or desire?

Are we to believe that the numerical presence of the so-called Jewish actor and actresses are a coincidence? If we do believe that, then do we also believe that the numbers of so-called Jewish media and entertainment power brokers is likewise a coincidence, and that one has absolutely nothing to do with the other? I truly pray that we are not that naive.

Though I have listed some of these power brokers and actors, it is virtually impossible to name all of those that are of the so-called Jewish class, or those that share the minds of those such classed. In a profession that is known for its stage names and its identity alterations, a great many so-called Jews have chosen to abandon their so-called Jewish identifiers for names that are less characterizing. Please consider the following:

Rodney Dangerfield (actor, comedian) - Jacob Cohen

Sylvia Porter (columnist) - Sylvia Feldman

Larry King (CNN) - Lawrence Harvey Zeiger

Kirk Douglas (actor) - Issur Danielovitch Demsky

Mel Brooks (actor) - Melvin Kaminsky

Al Jolson (actor, comedian) – Asa Yoelson

Cary Grant (actor) - Archibald Alexander Leach

Michael Landon (actor) – Eugene Maurice Orowitz

Robert Downey Sr. (actor) – Robert John Elias Jr.

Artie Shaw (bandleader) – Arthur Arshawsky

Alan King (comedian) – Irwin Alan Kniber

Abigain Van Buren (newspaper columnist) – Pauline Friedman

Judith Crist (film and drama critic) – Judith Klein

Betty Friedan (author, feminist leader) – Betty Naomi Goldstein

Ann Landers (columnist) – Esther Friedman

Woody Allen (actor, writer, director) – Allen Stuart Konigsberg

Jerry Lewis (actor, comedian) – Joseph Levitch

Judy Holiday (actress) – Judith Turin

Tony Randall (actor) – Leonard Rosenberg

Joey Bishop (comedian) – Joseph Gottlieb

Jackie Mason (comedian) – Yaakov Moshe Maze

Leo Rosten (author) – Leonard Q. Ross

Shelly winters (actress) – Shirley Schrift

Mama Cass Elliot (rock singer) – Ellen Naomi Cohen

Barbara Walters (talk-show host) – Barbara Volters

Bob Dylan (singer, songwriter) – Robert Zimmerman

Jill St. John (actress) – Jill Openheim

Gene Wilder (actor, producer, screenwriter) – Jerome Silberman

Tony Curtis (author) – Bernard Schwartz

Ayn Rand (author) – Alissa Rosenbaum

Joan Rivers (actress, comedian, talk-show host) – Joan Molinsky

Pee-Wee Herman (actor) – Paul Rubens

George Burns (actor, comedian) -Nathan Birnbaum

Andrew Dice Clay (comedian) – Andrew Silverberg

All three stooges (Jerome Lester Horwitz = **Curly**, Moses Horwitz = **Moe**, Louis Feinberg = **Larry**, Shemp Horwitz=**Shemp**)

Jack Benny - Benjamin Kubelsky

All of these; as well as others, have changed their names.

Murray Rothstein: Born as "SUMNER REDSTONE" is majority owner and Chairman of the Board of the National Amusements theater chain. Through National Amusements, Sumner Redstone and his family are majority owners of CBS Corporation, Viacom, and MTV Networks, BET, and movie production and distribution Paramount Pictures and DreamWorks movie studios, and are equal partners in MovieTickets.com.

Edgar Miles Bronfman, Jr. (born May 16, 1955), formerly CEO of Seagram and vice-chairman of Vivendi Universal, has been CEO of Warner Music Group since 2004. He is the son of Edgar Miles Bronfman and the grandson of Samuel Bronfman, one of the wealthiest and most influential so-called Jewish families in Canada. The Bronfman family has garnished huge wealth from the sell and distribution of alcohol such as Hennessey and Gin, the HipHop drink of choice.

In 2005, **Jeff Zucker** was promoted by NBC, to Chief Executive Officer of NBC Universal Television Group. Zucker was responsible for all programming across the company's television properties, including network, news, cable, and Sports and Olympics. His responsibilities also included the company's studio operations and global distribution efforts. Zucker was promoted on February 6, 2007, to the position of president & CEO of the entire NBC Universal, replacing Bob Wright, who held the position at NBC Universal, and before that, at NBC, for 21 years.

In September, 1984, **Michael Eisner** left Paramount to become Chairman and Chief Executive Officer of The Walt Disney Company. Since the death of Walt Disney in 1966, the studio had continued to enjoy periodic box office successes, and to earn profits from its theme parks and merchandising, but many in the industry felt the company was suffering from a lack of direction. Within a few years, Eisner transformed the company into the industry leader.

Peter Chernin born May 29, 1951, President and Chief Operating Officer of News Corporation, and Chairman and CEO of Fox Entertainment Group. He is also a Corporate Director for American Express. Fox News is known to have a conservative news slant. Owner Rupert Murdoch is a staucnh supporter of so-called Jewish causes, including the Zionist movement.

Mortimer Benjamin "Mort" Zuckerman is a so-called Jew that is a Canadian-born magazine editor, publisher, and real estate billionaire. He is a naturalized citizen of the United States. In 2008, Zuckerman was the 147th wealthiest American, and in 2007, he was the 188th as per *Forbes*. In 2006, he was ranked 382. The increase was related to the sale in 2007 of 5 times square and 280 Park Avenue in New York, which together realized US $2.5 billion, for his company, Boston Properties, Inc.

He has been the publisher/owner of the *New York Daily News* since 1993 and, as of 2007, is the current Editor-in-Chief of *U.S. News & World Report*. He co-founded Boston Properties, Inc. in 1970. He is chairman of the board, and director.

Donald E. Graham was elected to the board of The Washington Post Company in September 1974 and was made executive vice president and general manager of the Post in 1976. Graham became publisher of The Washington Post in 1979, succeeding his mother, who retained her corporate positions of chairman of the board and CEO of The Washington Post Company. The Company owns the newspaper, as well as the educational services provider Kaplan, Inc., Post-Newsweek Stations, *Newsweek* magazine, Cable One, Washingtonpost.Newsweek Interactive and other smaller companies. Donald Graham became CEO in 1991 and chairman of the company in May 1993, while Katharine Graham assumed the position of chairman of the executive committee of the Washington Post Company.

America's Foreign Policy which is controlled by the so-called Jewish Lobby is promoted by the so-called Jewish Media whose executives attend the same synagogues & country clubs as the so-called Jewish Lobby leaders.

LET'S EXAMINE A FEW HISTORICAL FACTS

"It was the interest and business of slave holders to study human nature, and the slave nature in particular, with a view to practical results. I and many of them attained astonishing proficiency in this direction."

Although Def Jam yielded some of the most successful HipHop acts ever, and the driving revenues of multi-platinum selling releases of acts such as L.L. Cool J, Public Enemy, and EPMD; Def Jam still found itself steeped in debt. Confronted by financial troubles in the early 90's, PolyGram, another mega record company, purchased the 50 percent stake of Def Jam that Sony had controlled. Apparently this shift of a 50 percent holding helped to alleviate a significant portion of Def Jams financial woes. This is looked at under the eyes of suspicion because Lyor Cohen, the president of Def Jam, is a highly developed business man, and is thoroughly competent in the overall operations of a record company and its acts.

Question: How can a label that offers the roster of talent such as that of Def Jam, allow itself to be mismanaged to the point of having to sell portions of their control to an outside force? Colombia/CBS was the initial distributor of Def Jam, are we to believe that the financial troubles of Def Jam rest on the shoulders of their (Colombia/CBS) distribution practices... of course not.

In order to get a clearer picture we simply have to follow the liar (LYOR). In 1996, PolyGram acquired an additional 10 percent of Def Jam. This additional 10 percent then mathematically swung the majority of ownership into the hands of PolyGram. PolyGram is a company that had developed primarily in European countries, and it finds its roots in a company called "Philips" which was founded by a person named Gerard Philips in Eindhoven, the Netherlands in 1891. It is one of the largest electronic companies in the world; in 2004 it employed over 159,700 people in over 60 countries. Philips has several organizational divisions, such as: Philips Consumer Electronics, Philips Semiconductors, Philips Lighting, Philips Medical Systems, and Philips Domestic Appliances and Personal Care. Its first factory remains as a museum in the Netherlands.

In 1929, Decca Records of London contracted a Mr. H.W. van Zoelan as a distributor of the Netherlands. By 1931 his company "Hollandsche Decca Distributie" (HDD) had become the exclusive "Decca" distributor for all the Netherlands and its colonies. During World War II, HDD was doing very good business; this was due to America and British involvement in the war. Because of his recognition of the fact that the competition would return after the war; Mr. H.W. van Zoelan decided to sell his company to Philips in 1942.

In the 1940's, Philips had spread out the facilitating aspects of their company; for example, research was done in the Eindhoven labs, development elsewhere in Eindhoven. The recording was done in Hilversum, manufacturing in Doetinchem, distribution from Amsterdam and exports from Eindhoven. This entire network was then labeled by Philips as Philips Phonografische Industrie (PPI). PPI's early growth was based on alliances; in 1945 they attempted to acquire Decca Records of London only to be rejected by then owner Edward Lewis. (PolyGram finally acquired Decca in 1979)

The operational tendencies of Philips had set up PPI to be the largest record company in Europe. In 1962 PPI merged with a named Deutsche Grammophon Gesellschaft (DGG). DGG owned by Siemens AG and well-known for its classical repertoire, had been the German licensee for Decca from 1935. Shortly after PPI was founded it had made a formal alliance with DGG to manufacture each others' records, coordinate releases, and to not steal each others' artists, or institute manipulations against each other for new talent.

The merger with DGG still left PPI without repertoire in Britain or the US. In 1951, Columbia failed to renew its international distribution agreement; therefore, PPI agreed to distribute Columbia recordings outside the U.S. and have Columbia distribute its recordings inside the U.S. This agreement ran until 1961, when Columbia set up its own European network and PPI set out to make acquisitions in the U.S. PPI built or bought factories in smaller countries. In 1962, PPI had a large factory in Baarn, and factories in France, Britain, Denmark, Norway, Spain, Italy, Egypt, Nigeria, and Brazil.

I state these facts to elucidate the point that the record industry is one of historic, profound, and calculated manipulations. The historical significance of the industry sheds light on the reality of what takes place within the modern context. The industry calculates its moves and creates business environments and climates that produce the desired results. This business manipulation is a clear example of the war-like tactics instituted by those who wish to claim imperialistic control over a medium of expression similar to those who desire to have imperialistic dominion over land masses. It will become more and more evident that you cannot have the latter without first obtaining the former.

Together, in 1962 PPI and DGG formed the Gramophon-Philips Group (GPG), with Philips taking 50percent share in DGG, and Siemens taking a 50percent share in PPI. In 1972 the companies formally merged to form PolyGram, of which Philips and Siemens each owned 50percent. In 1977 both organizations merged operationally, integrating the recording, manufacturing, distribution, and marketing into a single organization.

GPG desired to move into the US and UK markets, and did so by the process of acquisition: Mercury (US) in 1962, RSO (UK) in 1967, MGM records and Verve (US) in 1972, Casablanca (US) in 1977 and Decca (UK) in 1980. PolyGram acquired United Distribution Corporation (UDC) in 1973 and signed distribution deals with MCA and 20th Century Records in 1976. After an attempted 1983 merger with Warner Music failed, Philips bought 40percent of PolyGram from Siemens, and in 1987 the remaining 10 percent. Finally in 1989, Philips floated 16percent of PolyGram on the Amsterdam stock exchange, valuing the whole company at $5.6 billion. PolyGram embarked on a new program of plantation acquisitions, including A&M and Island Records in 1989, Motown in 1993, and **Def Jam in 1994.**

With these facts in mind, let's track down Mr. Lyor... Mr. Cohen became president of Def Jam after a power struggle with Rick Rubin. After having the most prolific line up of rap superstars in HipHop history, Lyor, one of the brightest and most powerful music industry minds allowed Def Jam to fall into serious financial troubles, troubles that made Def Jam's complete demise immanent. In order to alleviate these troubles, Lyor's industrial wisdom lead him to assist in the selling of Sony's 50 percent stake of Def Jam (Sony bought Columbia, Columbia had 50 percent of Def Jam) to PolyGram in 1994. This particular deal acted as a savior, as it apparently cured the financial ills that had remarkably inflicted Def Jam with Lyor at the head.

Def Jam was brought back to apparent life by Warren G's triple platinum release "Regulate G-Funk Era", and remained in the black by the multi platinum selling album MR. Smith by L.L. Cool J (1995), and the signing and success of Foxy Brown's "Ill NA NA" (1997). PolyGram purchased in 1996 an additional 10 percent of Def Jam which gave it a 60 percent power advantage over the remaining 40 percent. By simply examining the numbers we see that Russell Simmons did not, nor does he now control Def Jam or its moves. At this point we have to accept the fact that Russell Simmons did not have the adequate mind state and informational foundation to deal with the business and war type machinations of those whom he desired to form alliances with. Although Russell has emerged out of it all as a very rich man; in comparison to the wealth gained and leveraged by his so-called partners and associates, his true power and wealth is miniscule.

At this junction I believe it necessary for me to add the following... the above facts regarding the development of the various MEGA recording industries only go to show the incredible manipulations and sums of dollars that go into the formation of powerful corporations and conglomerates. Though one can begin to feel overwhelmed by these facts; the main purpose is to allow us to understand that these corporations though in the first instance are seen as competitors, in the ultimate instance are seen as global

partners. These major corporations; regardless if it is the recording industry or some other industry, shift personnel, corporate holdings, and huge amounts of cash from one corporation to another in order to secure and assure the ultimate agenda...global corporate dominance. All of these corporations are partners of one another, the only bottom line that matters, is not the amount of money earned... they already got that!... What matters is the continuation of a network of individuals who use people, resource, and money transfers to secure their political and social agenda.

In 1998, PolyGram itself was purchased by "SEAGRAMS", a company whose CEO is a so-called Jewish man by the name of Edgar Bronfman Jr., for a reported $10.2 billion. Seagrams, a company that finds its riches in alcoholic beverages own the largest record company in the world; "Universal Music Group". Seagrams has since merged with "Vivendi Universal".

After the selling of Def Jam to PolyGram, and the selling of PolyGram to Universal Music Group, is it not a hell of a coincidence that Mr. Lyor Cohen is now the president of UMG? Does it seem as if Def Jam's and Russell Simmons's struggles only allowed for the upward mobility of Mr. Cohen? I mean think about it... **Power struggle with Rick, 10-year financial troubles for Def Jam, sell of 60 percent to PolyGram, PolyGram bought by Seagram's, Seagram's formulates Universal Music Group, UMG purchases all of Def Jam, Mr. Cohen receives $100 million from the deal, and then named the president over UMG. You do the math, it is evident that it was manipulation at the beginning, and Mr. Lyor Cohen's initial intent was to build the multi-billion dollar giant UMG for his boss a Mr. Edgar Bronfman Jr. He did this while at the same time obtaining the distinguished nickname of "LANSKY".**

Words of David Ike
(David Vaughan Icke is an English writer and public speaker who has devoted himself since 1990 to researching what he calls "who and what is really controlling the world")

"Jewish women vaudevillians at the turn of the century popularized what is now a little-discussed and misunderstood performance venue, known as "coon shouting" ... Trying to break into the entertainment business, [Tin Pan Alley entrepreneurs'] aesthetics were circumscribed in a vehemently antiblack and xenophobic milieu. By the mid-1880-s they had formed a tight-knit Tin Pan Alley industry that came to dominate vaudeville and early black musicals ... Intended as comedy, coon song ranged from jocular and dismissive to cruel and sadistic ... Coon song sheet music and illustrated covers proliferated defamatory images of blacks in barely coded slanderous lyrics. For example, the 'N' word and associated inferences were dispatched in words like 'mammy,' 'honey boy,' 'pickinniny,' 'chocolate,' 'watermelon,' 'possum,' and the most prevalent 'coon.'" [LAVITT, P., 2000, p. 253-258] Especially well known Jewish "coon callers" included Sophie Tucker, Stella Mayhew, Fanny Brice, Anna Held, Eddie Cantor, and Al Jolson." –**www.davidicke.com**

It is absolutely crucial that a foundation be established, although these next few pages will be filled with relevant material, I humbly request that the reader take time to research for him or herself and connect the data to the overall premise of this writing. We will now advance swiftly and deeply into the depths of what generates this book and its subject matter...

David Sarnoff Born February 27, 1891 – December 12, 1971 was a Belarusian-born Russian-American so-called Jewish businessman and pioneer of American commercial radio and television. He founded the National Broadcasting Company (NBC) and throughout most of his career he led the Radio Corporation of America (RCA) in various capacities from shortly after its founding in 1919 until his retirement in 1970. He ruled over an ever-growing telecommunications and consumer electronics empire to include both RCA and NBC, which became one of the largest companies in the world. He was born and raised in a poor so-called Jewish village in Russia, but migrated to America where he became one of the most powerful and influential giants of the entertainment Industry.

One way of looking at the growth of radio and television involves the creation of the major networks. They were the vehicle that made radio and television into national, and later international, mediums. Sarnoff realized that organizing local stations into a system of affiliates (a "network") allowed programming and advertising to benefit from economies of scale and the simultaneous transmission of programs to "coast to coast" audiences.

Over the first few years, there were only three significant networks: NBC Red, NBC Blue, and what we now call CBS. Later, in 1934, the Mutual Broadcasting System was created, followed by Dumont (1946) and the Liberty Broadcasting System (1946). In 1943, NBC was forced to sell NBC Blue and it became today's ABC. Of those six, three (Mutual, Dumont, and Liberty) soon died out. Only NBC, CBS and ABC remained until the 1980s when cable and satellite, facilitated the creation of CNN, Fox, Warner, and others. Of the three original networks, all three had Jewish roots.

These facts suggest that what is understood today as the news and entertainment world was predicated on what was formulated yesterday by those that were known as Jews. This sheds light on those that were the creators of the so-called Jewish "coon callers" including Sophie Tucker, Stella Mayhew, Fanny Brice, Anna Held, Eddie Cantor, and Al Jolson." With the back-drop of mammie and steppin fetch'it... the so-called Jewish owned and operated industry grew into the Blaxploitation films of the 70's, and into the vile and debilitating elements of today's hiphop.

Arthur Judson, a leading talent agent, was miffed that David Sarnoff had failed to include any of his stars among the NBC roster. In 1927, with help from the Levy brothers of Philadelphia, Judson founded the Columbia Phonograph Broadcasting System. Within a year of its first broadcast, the Company was nearly bankrupt with only sixteen affiliate radio stations. Judson sold out to Jerome Loucheim, Ike, and Leon Levy (who was engaged to William Paley's sister.) Paley was the son of Ukranian Jewish immigrants and a second generation cigar maker.

Twenty seven years old, **William Paley** discovered radio advertising helped him sell cigars and he was sufficiently well off that in January 1929, he bought majority control for $400,000 and renamed it the Columbia Broadcasting System. Through the '30s, Paley expanded CBS. He pioneered the offer of free programming to affiliate stations in exchange for an option to sell advertising, which he sold in huge chunks.

Until non-Jew **Ted Turner** arrived on the scene in 1986 and threatened a takeover, CBS was Paley's fiefdom. Responding to Turner's takeover attempt, Paley turned over control to so-called Jew Lawrence Tisch who had purchased 25 percent of CBS's stock. Tisch ran CBS until 1995 when Westinghouse bought it. A few years later, in a deal that brought Paramount and CBS back together as siblings, Sumner Redstone's Viacom, took over CBS. For a time, Viacom's Mel Karmazin served as President. As such, CBS has remained under so-called Jewish management in one form or another for nearly its entire existence.

Fox is the creation of non-Jew, Rupert Murdoch, who acquired seven big cities, "Metromedia" stations from another non-Jew, John Kluge. But it was so-called Jewish **Barry Diller**, as Fox Broadcasting's CEO, who launched the infant fourth television network in 1987. Within four years, he was ABC's Vice President of Prime Time TV. At age 32, he left ABC to become Chairman of Paramount Pictures. He led it for ten years until he joined Murdoch in 1985. Diller's task for Murdoch was to create a fourth network which he did by purchasing Metromedia Television from Kluge and building on that base. Diller left Fox in 1992 and now leads IAC/Interactive Corp, a major Internet company.

The above listed men are all connected, access into the world of media and entertainment is not an accident. As we proceed, we will see that the connection of ownership, power and control, keeps The HipHop Nation subjucated to the whims and dictates of those that are seen as the corporate slave masters.

The Politics of Expression

"Both horse and niggers [are] no good to the economy in the wild or natural state. Both must be BROKEN and TIED together for orderly production."

The record industry is a global empire that is predicated on the expression of ideas, thoughts, feelings, and reactions in regards to the social, economic, political, and religious realities that exist within the world. Within the context of an artistic expression, artists relay the above via their individual form of artistic talent and expression. When these particular expressions can be filtered, controlled, redefined, and disseminated based on the social, political, economic, and religious agendas of an outsider, these expressions are at best limited, and at worse fraudulent. With this in mind, those that desire to control the global perception have positioned themselves as the universal filters of the artistic expression and oppressors of the truth.

Long before television was established, the medium of sound, and the technologies that relayed it, was mastered and controlled by a certain group of people. These people desired to monopolize the airwaves of expression in hopes of controlling the overall thinking and opinion of the masses. Entertainment was, and remains to be, a viable source of propaganda and thought engineering. In fact, in a world that has increasingly abandoned the transfer of thought via reading and writing, entertainment and its obsession has proven to be the primary source of the critical information or misinformation from which the masses formulate their opinions.

This is seen no more clearly than in a time of war. Information is controlled by the state in order to foster an opinion that best suits the political agenda of those in power.

A major concern of the American citizenry is that a transfer of power has occurred. In a social environment of supposed democracy, the thought of state owned television and radio causes a major concern within the American Psyche. It is hard to imagine post 911 or not, a political climate in America where a state owned, operated, and sanctioned media would be acceptable. However, what has happened is that the political process has been systematically high-jacked since December 23, 1913. Although Americans generally feel as if their vote counts, and that they have a say in their social, political, economic, and religious future, they have not come to realize that their ability to come to a rational and educated decision has been impacted by the entertainment, and subsequent information that they receive.

Although they have been typically dumbed down, the American climate of today suggests that the population is concluding that American politics have been merged with corporations that have a global view of the world. Although this realization contains potential elements of liberation, the apparent inability of the general American mind to understand the affects of art and entertainment, news and media on the rational process of discernment keeps the American people in a perpetual state of confusion and lack of action. Simply put… **Americans are being mentally manipulated by the entertainment, news and media that they are being forced to consume.**

Corporations have bought political access; they have purchased and financed political candidates from which policies, procedures, laws, and interpretation of laws are born. The worlds of media and entertainment have merged to produce news-entertainment shows, rather than the traditional newscast. This is done for the acquisition of viewers; CNN, Fox News and MSNBC, among others, compete over viewers by the level of entertainment intertwined with hand chosen, snippets of news. News presentations are formulated with an end in mind and are relayed within a sequence that is designed to cause the viewer to arrive at a desired conclusion. With this in mind, how would the major players in the western world go about the dissemination of information in what is considered by the ignorant, an open and free society?

Time is the most valuable commodity known to man…time is that which once it is spent, you cannot reproduce… a person cannot make new time, a person can only alter how time is spent or used. Corporations and power brokers understand the crucial elements of time and its revolutionary potential; therefore, corporations and power brokers spend huge amounts of money in order to control different brackets and segments of time. Corporations and aspiring social, economic, political, and religious giants understand the value of time; therefore they spend their time calculating ways to get the public or their perspective subject's attention.

This is the importance of entertainment; entertainment is utilized in a way to gain access to the public's mind. Once access is granted, those with aspirations of power and influence begin to program or de-program those minds that have been rendered as sheep by the seductive elements of entertainment.

Powerful individuals and corporations battle over the use of radio and television broadcasts. Interstate telecommunications regardless if it is wire, satellite, or cable is prime territory, and it is considered the most powerful weapon of an imperialistic mind or government. International communications or global information travels along the systematic course made up of wire, satellite, and cable. The pen and paper approach to communication, although retaining some secure elements, have been replaced with the faster and broader affects of electronic communication. Corporations, Governments, and Individuals understand that information is power; therefore, they calculate and disseminate the information that best suits their agenda. Why would a corporation spend millions of dollars on broadcast time if they do not intend on manipulating or shaping the thoughts of those that pay them their attention?

Those that desire to have power and influence realize the value of public accessibility. Those corporations or individuals that have the greater access to the public, are the ones that possess the greatest amounts of power and influence. To think that the public is not, or cannot be manipulated by the systematic release of information is a severe indication of ignorance and naivety. The radio and television industries formulate entertainment slots that are designed to secure the ratings necessary to induce corporations and powerful individuals to dish out huge amounts of dollars to advertise their products or ideas.

We must understand that the television and radio industries; the media and entertainment world, are only concerned with the value of their time slots. Entertainment, news, and music are simply offered as a way to secure the minds of the individual, the primary concern is to sell time slots to corporations and power brokers. Entertainment, news, and music *programming* is the term that is used to define that which occupies a radio or television time slot. The *programming* is not only the entertainment, news or music, the *programming,* is also, the commercials that are systematically played in rotation that induces the perspective consumer to by a product or buy into an idea.

> "Black music exists in a neo-colonial relationship with the $12 billion music industry, which consist of six record companies: Warner Elektra Atlantic (WEA), Polygram, MCA Music Entertainment, BMG Distribution, Sony Music Entertainment, and CEMA/UNI Distribution. These firms, according to New York's Daily News, "supply retailers with 90% of the music" that the public purchases (rap accounts for 8.9% of the total, over $1 billion in 1996; these firms are currently being investigated by the Federal Trade Commission for price-fixing CDs). While there are black-owned production companies like Uptown Records, Bad Boy Entertainment, La Face Records, Def Jam, and Death Row, which make millions, these black-owned companies do not control a key component of the music making nexus, namely distribution, and they respond to the major labels' demand for a marketable product. In turn, the major labels respond to a young white audience that purchases 66% of rap music, according to the Recording Industry Association of America (RIAA), as reported by the Daily News. But the music industry's dependence on alternative music has led to flat sales and the only growth has been, once again, black music in the cultural form of rap."
>
> **—Norman Kelly: The Political Economy of Black Music- 1999**

THE SLAVE TRADER

"Accordingly, both a wild horse and a wild or natural nigger is dangerous even if captured, for they will have the tendency to seek their customary freedom and, in doing so, might kill you in your sleep."

Talent scouts and agents operate hand in hand in order to select, cultivate and present ideas and concepts into the world. Talent is observed and identified, then selected based on the desires of the public. The public's desire and appetite is manipulated through the programming offered by the television, radio, and entertainment world. These three entities converge into one powerful and influential conglomerate that dictates the trends, norms, and culture of the American public. Clever marketing strategies are deployed in a systematic approach that will create and manipulate the public desire and appetite. Those high ranking and influential individuals that make up corporate America gather in smoke filled rooms to discuss and decide not only what the trends will be, but who will sale a particular trend to the American public and subsequently the entire world.

Newscast, reports and editorials are scientifically presented in a way that will cause the predictability of stock levels and values. An extraordinary amount of cash is levied in order to back a hot trend and idea. The systematic implantation of commercials with catchy jingles, punch-lines, and concepts help create a sheep like following among the American consumer or corporate slave. The talent scout and agent select artists and garnish deals that allow for the right face, selling the right thing, at the right time. The corporate giants and their lackeys select the *"Negro(s) of the Year"*, and these special spokesmen sell the corporate agenda.

It is a fact that most black entertainers, professional athletes, and high-profile personalities have non-black agents. Most of the agents that supposedly represent the aforementioned clientele are so-called Jews. Why is this reality?—it is because so-called Jews have access to the particular worlds of sport and entertainment that others do not have. The so-called Jews have positioned themselves to not only control their slaves, but represent them as well!

All facets of news, entertainment, television, and radio are controlled by the single aspiration of power and influence. This power and influence leads to dominance...this dominance, when shown in its entirety, represents a global force that is maintained by the control and manipulation of information and truth.

"Rather than analyzing the trajectory of black music through the music industry, today's new jack intellectuals have been more interested in discussing or breaking down the high/low distinctions of culture. More interested in "interrogating" certain "privileged discourses," but have no interest in the nut and bolts of the music industry:

- how artists are recruited,
- how contracts are structured for maximum profits for record firms,
- how much firms spend on the production of an artist's CD,
- inquiring as to whether or not rap artists make their living solely by selling units or doing performances (a situation similar to that of blues musicians),
- how musicians lose their copyright to their music and the lack of royalty payments,
- and the incredible monopoly of the Big Six.

These are just some of the primary areas that **are not** addressed by today's black intellectuals who parade themselves as "experts" or "interpreters" of black culture. "

—**Norman Kelly: The Political Economy of Black Music- 1999**

The so-called Jewish community, of course, isn't comfortable with the history. As so-called Jewish author Neal Karlen describes one African-American depiction of the Jewish music hustler:

"In the 1990 film Mo' Better Blues, Spike Lee crafted an artful if blazingly anti-Semitic portrait of the fictional Moe Flatbush, an avaricious Jewish club owner intent on swindling black jazzmen. The ferretlike, Yiddish-spouting Moe, played by John Turturro, was seemingly lifted straight from the pages of the anti-Semitic screed The Protocols of Zions." [KARLEN, N., 1994, p. 145]

The Jewish agent-producer exploitation of Black recording artists in the early rhythm and blues era of the 1940s and 1950s (and later) was predominant and widespread, entrenching a Black hostility among many to their Jewish financial controllers to the present day. The following Jewish entrepreneurs were among those who founded record labels featuring mainly Black talent: **Herman Lubinsky** (Savoy Records); the **Braun family** (DeLuxe Records); **Hy Siegal, Sam Schneider** and **Ike Berman** (Apollo Records); **Saul, Joe,** and **Jules Bihari** (Modern Records); **Art Rupe** (Specialty Records-- its biggest hits were those of Little Richard); **Lev, Edward,** and **Ida Messner** (Philo/Aladdin Records); **Al Silver** and **Fred Mendelsohn** (Herald/Ember Records); **Paul** and **Lilian Rainer** (Black and White Records); **Sam** and **Hy Weiss** (Old Towne Records; **Sol Rabinowitz** (Baton Records -- Rabinowitz eventually became vice president of CBS International); and **Danny Kessler** (head of OKeh Records, a "cheap" branch of Columbia Records). **Sydney**

Nathan controlled both the King and Federal record labels and **Florence Greenberg** owned the Mafia-influenced Scepter Records (featuring the Shirelles and Dionne Warwick.

Paul Rosenberg is a giant in the industry, he's Eminem's manager, president of Goliath Records, and vice president of Shady Records, to which both Eminem and 50 Cent are signed. Like Eminem, Rosenberg is from the Detroit area, although from the suburbs rather than the city. Rosenberg began rapping, going by the name MC Paul Bunyan in a group called Rhythm Cartel that played Detroit's few hip-hop venues. After a couple years of moving back and forth between the classroom and the stage, he chose to go to law school rather than pursue a career as a rapper. When asked why, he jokes that being Jewish, he had to.

I do not want the reader to think or perceive me as over-emphasizing the so-called Jewish envolvement and subsequent control of the media and entertainment world. These pages are intended to expose the clear dominance of an industry that many believe has significantly contributed to the moral decay of the present modern society. As the public formulates opinions over whose to blame for such decay, I want to be sure that the entire picture be seen and considered before someone out of ignorance blames those that are in fact the victims of that said decay.

EDGAR BRONFMAN: HIPHOP'S MOST POWERFUL SLAVE MASTER

"I am here to help you solve some of your problems with slaves."

The largest and most influential record company (plantation) is Universal Music Group—formerly known as MCA Music Entertainment; it is owned by French media conglomerate Vivendi Universal. Some of their biggest superstars include Eminem, Kanye West, and 50 Cent. Vivendi Universal also owns one of the largest music publishing companies in the world, the Universal Music Publishing Group. Universal Music was originally attached to the film studio **Universal Pictures** and its history is long and complex, but its present organization was formed when its parent company **Seagram** purchased PolyGram and merged with Universal Music Group in 1998. Seagram has since merged with **Vivendi SA**, to form **Vivendi Universal**.

Universal Music Group (UMG) has one of the most impressive rosters of HipHop artist in the entire industry. We have already shown how an individual named Lyor Cohen successfully manipulated his way into the world of HipHop and then handed Def Jam to PolyGram which was then sold to UMG. UMG was formulated and developed by Seagram's—a company rooted in the alcohol business, a drug that has plagued the black, Hispanic, Native American, and HipHop Nation to its core. We will address this plague and its affect on the HipHop Nation very shortly, but first let's look at Seagram's.

Seagram's was a large corporation headquartered in Montreal Quebec, Canada it was the largest distiller of alcoholic beverages in the world. The famous Seagram's building is located in New York City, and acted as the company's American headquarters. In the year 1857, a distillery was founded in Waterloo, Ontario. In 1869, a man by the name of Joseph E. Seagram became a partner in the company, and in 1883, he became the owner. He then changed the name to Joseph E. Seagram & Sons. Mr. Seagram in addition to making what was considered the world's best whiskey was a politician and a major owner of thoroughbred racehorses.

Samuel Bronfman a European born so-called Jew founded a company called **Distillers Corporation Limited** in Montreal. In the 1920's, the company enjoyed huge growth by manipulating American and Canadian law, and utilizing the tactics and tools of shady characters and Chicago bootleggers. A few years after the death of Joseph E. Seagram, Samuel Bronfman purchased the company; this was in 1928. Mr. Bronfman kept the Seagram's name and became the largest seller of alcoholic beverages in the world. Noted brand names of Seagram are Chivas Regal, Crown Royal, VO Whiskeys, Captain Morgan Rum, and they even owned Tropicana fruit juice.

After the death of Samuel Bronfman in 1971, Edgar M. Bronfman was Chairman and Chief Executive Officer (CEO) of Seagram's. While building Seagram's into the premier Alcoholic Company in the world, Edgar Bronfman was a member and president of what has become the preeminent international Jewish organization in the world. As the current president of the **World Jewish Congress** (WJC), he has been the principle power broker that has helped to form a federation of so-called Jewish communities and organizations.

Edgar Bronfman has built a strong consensus between different so-called Jewish groups of varying religious and political orientations. He acts as a diplomatic envoy to the so-called Jews of the world, and is a Zionist that strongly supports the state of Israel.

What is interesting is that these so-called Jews, while having a great deal of concern for their so-called Jewish brethren, seemingly have no concern for the black, red, and brown man and the debilitating effects of their (Alcohol) product on the (black, brown, and red peoples) community. Edgar Bronfman is a philanthropist that gives huge amounts of dollars to so-called Jewish causes; this means that the profits gained from the death and deterioration of the black, brown, and red people from the poison of alcohol helps to develop, sustain, and improve the so-called Jewish people and their cause!

As a major power broker, Edgar Bronfman Sr. has had his eyes on shaping world politics in favor of his so-called Jewish people since he has been among the wealthy and powerful; in fact, his desire to become rich and powerful was predicated on his desire to further the so-called Jews and their desire to gain and maintain global influence.

In developing the **Seagram's Company**, Edgar Sr., desired to diversify; he engineered a takeover of the major American oil and gas company **Conoco Inc.** that secured Seagram's ownership of 32.2 percent. To combat what was to be a hostile takeover, major stake holders of **Conoco Inc.** brought in the **DuPont Company** as a savior to institute a bidding war. In the end, DuPont won out but the aspirations of Edgar and his boys was seen, and their power was a force to be recognized and acknowledged. This was seen because while losing the bidding war over **Conoco**, Edgar and Seagram's still managed to become a 24.3 percent owner of **DuPont**. How developed is a mind that will forfeit 32.2 percent of a company that was bought by your bidding enemy, only to then acquire 24.3 percent of that apparent enemy? By 1995 Seagram's was DuPont's largest single shareholder and had four seats on the board of directors. At that time the DuPont investment accounted for 70 percent of Seagram's earnings.

Although Seagram's diversified their investment portfolio, Edgar and the boys never strayed away from their loyalty to the alcohol game. In 1987, Seagram's engineered a 1.2 billion dollar takeover of important French Cognac maker **Martell & Cie**. The Seagram brand name lives on in the alcoholic beverages Seagram's Gin, Seagram's Seven, and Seagram's Coolers. However, how do Seagram's and their Alcoholic product influence HipHop and its culture?

In June 1994, Edgar Bronfman Jr. was appointed to CEO of Seagram's; he was given the responsibility to expand the Seagram's empire into the media and entertainment world.

On April 6, 1995, Edgar Jr. and **DuPont** announced a deal where DuPont would buy back the **Seagram's** shares. This divestiture was the initiative of Edgar Jr. and its proceeds provided the money that allowed for Seagram's acquisition of **Universal Studios, MCA, PolyGram,** and a number of **Universal theme parks.**

Edgar Jr. desired not only to enter the entertainment world, but wanted to control and dominate it. His ambitions were rewarded by the establishment of the biggest and most powerful record company (plantation) in the world... **Universal Music Group.**

The concept is basic, if a company can control the music and entertainment industry, that company has a direct link to the public's ear. This power lends to the power and control of information, subsequently there can be a systematic manipulation of the public and their opinion. We must understand that when we say that Edgar Bronfman instituted the biggest and most powerful entertainment company in the world, we recognize that under UMG's huge umbrella reside some of the most influential record companies and artist. Universal Music Group has found a way to control the music industry from the top down. Edgar Jr. has used the proceeds from the selling of poison (alcohol), to totally control HipHop and the slaves that participate in it.

Universal Music Group is not the only plantation in town—several others will be mentioned shortly. We focus primarily on UMG because its founder and primary benefactor Mr. Edgar Bronfman SR. and JR. are two individuals that yield huge doses of power and influence, yet within the depths of all their wisdom and understanding choose to allow for the negative and destructive behavior, offered within the context of today's HipHop, to continue. As record sales generate profits for the Bronfman's and the so-called Jewish cause, the HipHop Nation has been funded and empowered to help create the death and destruction of the community that brought it forth.

UMG's power and influence spreads like demonic tentacles throughout the HipHop industry. Their control can be seen within the day-to-day operations of the following companies:

A&M Records	**The Inc. Records**	**Island Def Jam Music Group**
Doghouse Records	**Disturbing Tha Peace Records**	**Motown Records**
Aftermath Entertainment	**Dame Dash Music Group**	**Universal records**
G-Unit Records	**Roc-A-Fella Records**	**Cash Money Records**
Interscope	**Russell Simmons Music Group**	**Uptown Records**
Shady Records		**Universal South Records**
Star Trak Records	**Island Records**	**Loud Records**
Def Soul Records		

| Konvict Muzik | Def Squad | Derty ENT. |
| Chamilitary Entertainment | Diplomat Records | Street Records |

Of course they have controlling interest of several others, and receive lucrative financial kick-backs from many more.

Universal Music Group also owns local "Universal" labels in Australia, Brazil, Canada, Columbia, the Czech Republic, Finland, Germany, Hong Kong, Hungary, Ireland, India, Italy, Japan, Korea, Mexico, the Netherlands, Norway, Poland, Russia, Spain, Switzerland and Turkey.

With these satellite camps of power and influence, how difficult is it to see that **Universal Music Group** is a global power player with global dominion within the realm of entertainment and media. With this in mind, imagine the world and how it currently views the black community and its populace within the context of today's HipHop and its representational expression. No wonder we hear the whole world calling us and themselves "NIGGERS", and referring to women as "BITCHES and HOES".

Universal Music Group markets itself as a **Major Record Label (PLANTATION)**, she owns several smaller labels that control and manipulate artist in a way that best supports the ideas, goals, ambitions, and agendas of the **Major Label**. The artists that are contractually obligated to the smaller labels are subsequently owned by the Major Label. Some of these artists are:

50 Cent	Ja Rule	The Birdman
Game	Ashanti	Keke Wyatt
Busta Rymes	Black Child	RZA
Eve	Cadillac Tah	The Big Punisher (Big Pun)
Lloyd Banks	Lloyd	
Tony Yayo	Jay Z	Wu-Tang Clan
Mobb Deep	Foxy Brown	The Beatnuts
Young Buck	Kanye West	Tha Alkaholiks
Olivia	Freeway	Pete Rock
Mase	Memphis Bleek	Lil Flip
Spider Loc	Bennie Sigel	Three 6 Mafia
M.O.P	Amil	Project Pat
Ludacris	Cam'Ron	Xzibit
Chingy	Young Gunz	Twista
Shawnna	BG	Dead Prez
I-20	Mannie Fresh	Flo-Rida
Field Mob	Juvenile	Slim Thug
Bobby Valentino	The Big Tymers	Trick Daddy

Bun B	Katt Williams	Lil Romeo
Chamillionaire	40 Cal	Pharoahe Monch
Murphy Lee	UGK	Raekwan
Gipp	David Banner	Rakim
Akon	Big Tymers	Soulja Boy
T-Pain	Canibus	Terror Squad
Nelly	Mr. Cheeks	Timberland & Magoo
St. Lunatics	Warren G	Jadakiss
Juelz Santana	Irv Gotti	DMX
Jim Jones	Lil Wayne	Swiss Beatz

The Universal Music Group also generates huge profits from the release and sales of artists that were formally signed to it or its smaller labels. The control of publishing and masters maintain a constant flow of billions of dollars in the form of residual income.

Before we advance, it should be pointed out that Universal Music Group is under the corporate flag ship known as Vivendi Universal (Vivendi). Vivendi is a French company that merged with Seagram's in 2000. If we track company ownerships and corporate manipulations we will see that the record industry is far more complex and broad than the average American citizen would imagine. The entangled weave of corporate ties stretches over boarders and throughout the various words of *Mission Statements* of the global economic giants. To view HipHop and its emergence onto the world scene as a coincidence or a lightweight occurrence is to show complete ignorance of the world politics and those that desire to control it. I have laid the corporate foundation of the HipHop Nation in order to show the reader the sorry condition of the building that stands upon that foundation.

Although we could go into greater detail in regard to Corporate America, Global politics, and the so-called Jewish manipulation that takes place, I do not desire to overload the mind of the reader with too many facts and statistics that might cause one to lose the overall purpose and message of this writing. We will advance into this message with the foundation in mind simply as a reminder of what is at stake and who is to be the beneficiary of the HipHop Nation's in particular, and black folks in general, ignorance and self-destructive behavior.

The Profits of Division

"I HAVE OUTLINED A NUMBER OF DIFFERENCES AMONG THE SLAVES; AND I TAKE THESE DIFFERENCES AND MAKE THEM BIGGER. I USE FEAR, DISTRUST AND ENVY FOR CONTROL PURPOSES"...

Since 1555 when the first so-called Africans were brought to the continent of America, Europeans, the Spanish, Arabs, so-called Jews, and several other groups have profited from the lack of unity displayed by the black man and woman of the world. In fact!—the ability to transport millions of people from one continent to the other led to the continuation of the policy known as *divide and conquer!* This system was maximized by the apparent continuation of tribes and clans that chose to reveal their internal conflicts to their open enemy. When the white people first emerged on the continent, they identified the nature of the people that they found there. By studying the people, they were allowed to formulate a plan that would reap the benefits and rewards that they had sought. Tensions that were in existence prior to the arrival of the enemy was exacerbated, manipulated, and elevated once the white people hit the continent. The lack of unity among the so-called African people and their perceived problems and conflicts created an environment in which white people could control and manipulate an entire people. That which was used to create the problem (slavery), has been used to sustain the problem (slavery).

As HipHop began to emerge, it was clear that it was a reflection or an expression of the mind state of those that participated in it. The fact that an artistic expression could generate the interest of millions of inner city youth proves that although it is an expression of an artist, those that were listening embraced and found a level of mutuality in terms of sentiment and content...in short, millions could relate to what the rappers were saying.

In the early years of HipHop, it was a music that stretched from the east coast to the west coast via the mix-tape scene. For the most part, HipHop was not played on the radio; it traveled along a circuit considered the underground. When young black youth discovered HipHop, it filled an empty hole of yearning for the youth. A music that was based on the "DRUM" and the rhythmic tones of heavy bass, created its own dance (breaking and popping); this dance was produced by the presence of the music—not the other way around. Prior to HipHop, the music of that time was based on horns and guitars, sound effects and melodic bridges. Disco was synthetic; HipHop was real, therefore, its creation manifested movements and reactions that were spontaneous and natural. This reality created a connection between the young black youth of America that had never before been seen!

During the early years of HipHop, the young black youth of California did not shame away from revealing their love for New York; they loved HipHop and it was dominating New York. Children in the western portion of America, the Midwest, and Southern region wanted to be close to HipHop, and HipHop at that moment in time was in New York. Grandmaster Flash and Curtis Blow was known from the east coast to the west coast. When the Sugar Hill gang dropped their classic "Rappers Delight" and received national airplay, nobody was "hating" on New York, nor refraining from recognizing their HipHop dominance. HipHop was a national phenomenon that was a badge of honor and identity for the young black youth of America regardless of where they laid their head at night.

Because HipHop is an art form and a form of expression, the nature of HipHop is to express in the realest and the most natural of ways the thoughts, ideas, frustrations, and conditions of he or she that participates in this particular art form. This reality is what began the quintessential HipHop phrase—**"Keep it real"**! When an artist kept it real, those that could relate to that artist became fans or supporters of that particular artist. In a spiritually connected way, the artist was attached to his or her fan, because in *"keeping it real"*, those that shared in the artist's expression adopted the artist as a special spokesman for them and their particular thoughts, ideas, frustrations and/or condition. Unlike other forms of music or artistic expression, HipHop was elevated from merely showbiz to an expression of real people who had finally found a **REAL** voice.

Case in point... in the early 80's emerged a HipHop trio by the name of the "Fat Boys". The three members of that group were indeed "Fat Boys"; therefore their songs were predicated on that fact, songs about food because they were "fat" and songs about girls because they were "boys". Their reality was marketed as a gimmick; they did not create a gimmick and alter their reality to market it (we will return to the subject of gimmicks shortly). The Fat Boys had a huge following because they were true to themselves and kept it real... they were not gang bangers, so they didn't claim to be; they were not dope dealers, so they did not claim to be; nor were they sex symbols or revolutionaries—they were fat boys, and they were accepted as that. Those who could relate to their reality and those who appreciated their talent became their fans and supporters.

Understanding that HipHop originated as a natural expression, we see that HipHop had many voices that spoke to the hearts of many different people. If it was a natural expression, then we need to understand that what is inside the artist will come out through his or her talent. By keeping it real, to his or her self, the HipHop artist develops true fans and supporters. By faking it or creating a gimmick, the artist could enjoy temporary support only to be left low and dry once the gimmick is seen for what it is or runs its temporal course.

As HipHop became more popular, and record plantations began to take control, HipHop began to compromise the elements of what was **"real"** with that which was required to sell records. The Corporate plantations began to see dollar signs; they started to strategize their way into the HipHop Nation and took it completely over. By looking at the national consumer and by studying **key indicators** that focused primarily on **demographics**, the record plantations designed marketing schemes that would generate the most sales. Because the early corporate days of HipHop was based on the demographics of the young black youth, marketing trends were based on how the black youth were seen by these corporations and their alien power brokers. A once unified nation of HipHop had been divided in a way that would create sells based on region and regional desires—gone was the unified nation that simply loved the music and the artist that expressed it.

As the slave masters began to study the young black youth of America, they systematically began to splinter the HipHop Nation into different categories. Instead of simply HipHop, we began to see the marketing of so-called Gangster Rap, Conscious Rap, Underground Rap, Mainstream Rap, and Southern Rap. All of these categories were created to maximize the selling of a particular type of expression that was "real" in what can be considered the black experience. What the slave master was able to do is profit off our diversity and then maximize those same profits by creating competition among the various segments of our black community.

When this took place, the implanted elements of the Willie Lynch Doctrine became manifest. Because the slave master offered their so-called Negro slaves trinkets and bobbles, the competition factor brought out all the various divisional factors that were highlighted within the Letter. Despite the united art form of HipHop and its pure emergence as a voice of the diverse realities of the black community, the blood sucking elements of business and power reaped huge amounts of control and power when the HipHop Nation was allowed to be divided and segmented based on the distinguishing characteristics outline by Mr. Lynch.

What was at one time an artful expression of real thoughts and circumstance, thoughts and circumstances that varied based on region and economic condition, were exacerbated by the presence of those who had a vested interest in the division of HipHop. When this happened competition grew to rivalry, and rivalry grew to all out war between those that, despite minor differences, were incredibly similar in nature, truth and circumstance.

This competition among the various artist and their camps allowed for the corporate minds of America to control and dominate the HipHop Nation and send it in the direction that was beneficial to those that were concerned with furthering their idea and not the idea of the artist nor the HipHop Nation.

Pro Black – Still A Slave

"They sleep while you are awake, and are awake while you are asleep. They are DANGEROUS near the family house and it requires too much labor to watch them away from the house. Above all, you cannot get them to work in this natural state."

By financially backing the different "categories" of HipHop, the slave masters profited by the different aspects of black life. It is amazing to think that Lyor Cohen and his white, so-called Jewish colleagues profited tremendously by Def Jam artists Public Enemy and their pro-black revolutionary expression. White people made millions of dollars of the revolutionary expressions of KRS-ONE, X-Clan, Poor Righteous Teachers, and Brand Nubian. They were not offended by the exclamation of blackness from their slaves so long as the black community supported it with their real dollars. The white slave master viewed the revolutionary lyrics of such groups as merely social rhetoric that allowed them access to the pocket books of the revolutionary elements of the black community. Their official party line remained, **"you can talk black power, but you will never be granted any kind of power, black or otherwise!"**

As groups such as Public Enemy grew world wide exposure, their message was tolerated because the money was flowing in. They were a mega-star group that generated huge amounts of money on an international stage. White people were beginning to be heard reciting the lyrics "Farrakhan is a Prophet and I think you "outta" listen to…" at the same time, Minister Farrakhan himself was gaining momentum in notoriety and listeners. The rise of Farrakhan and the Nation of Islam coupled with groups like Public Enemy, Boogie Down Productions, Poor Righteous Teachers, and Brand Nubians, began to win the hearts and minds of the young black youth of America. Consciousness, unlike buffoonery, criminality, or perverse sexuality was growing in the black community. In terms of potentiality, this growth caused major concern within corporate American and the white, so-called Jewish power structure. This element, regardless of the levels of money it was making had to be destroyed. Farrakhan and the Nation of Islam's growing influence threatened the influence that outsiders had on the black community… this was unacceptable in their eyes!!

The group Public Enemy was formed in Long Island New York in 1982, although they did not release their first album, "YO! Bum Rush The Show", until 1987. The group was one of the most successful acts the Def Jam plantation ever produced. Their second, and most controversial album produced was "It Takes a Nation of Millions to Hold Us Back!". These albums were a tremendous success, and lead the conscious releases of that particular era. By having a production staff known as "The Bomb Squad", Public Enemy carved a notch out of the music world that no other HipHop group had or has touched. By using a heavy drum, and innovative sound techniques, the group created a music that caught the hearts, souls, and minds of its listeners.

The music though it was the driving force of the group, was fully exploited by the voice and tenacious, revolutionary, and militant lyrics of Chuck D the group's premier rapper. Along with Flavor Flav the group's comedic relief, Chuck D offered thought provoking words designed to stimulate the revolutionary spirit that had been lying dormant within the black community prior to the emergence of the group.

With albums entitled, "It Takes a Nation of Millions to Hold Us Back", "Fear of A Black Planet", "Apocalypse 91", and songs like "Shut' Em Down", "Fight the Power", "How to Kill A Radio Consultant", "Burn Hollywood Burn", and "Power to The People"—Public Enemy was the first HipHop act or group that enjoyed extended world tours. These tours allowed them to build a significant following in Europe and Asia; however, here in America, although the group was making big money for the plantation, their lyrics and subject matter was causing serious concerns for the slave masters and their global interest of power and influence. These powers had to do something to turn the HipHop tide that was becoming more and more conscious.

Check out these lyrics!

Artist: Public Enemy f/ Ice Cube, Big Daddy Kane
Album: Fear of a Black Planet
Song: Burn Hollywood Burn

CHUCK D:
Burn Hollywood burn I smell a riot
Goin' on first they're guilty now they're gone
Yeah I'll check out a movie
But it'll take a Black one to move me
Get me the hell away from this TV
All this news and views are beneath me
Cause all I hear about is shots ringin' out
So I rather kick some slang out
All right fellas let's go hang out
Hollywood or would they not
Make us all look bad like I know they had
But some things I'll never forget yeah
So step and fetch this shit
For all the years we looked like clowns
The joke is over smell the smoke from all around
Burn Hollywood burn

ICE CUBE:
>Ice Cube is down with the PE
>Now every single bitch wanna see me
>Big Daddy is smooth word to muther
>Let's check out a flick that exploits the color
>Roamin' thru Hollywood late at night
>Red and blue lights what a common sight
>Pulled to the curb gettin' played like a sucker
>Don't fight the power kill the mother fucker

BIG DADDY KANE:
>As I walk the streets of Hollywood Boulevard
>Thinin' how hard it was to those that starred
>In the movies portrayin' the roles
>Of butlers and maids slaves and hoes
>Many intelligent Black men seemed to look uncivilized
>When on the screen
>Like a guess I figure you to play some jigaboo
>On the plantation, what else can a nigger do?
>And Black women in this profession
>As for playin' a lawyer, out of the question
>For what they play Aunt Jemima is the perfect term
>Even if now she got a perm
>So let's make our own movies like Spike Lee
>Cause the roles being offered don't strike me
>There's nothing that the Black man could use to earn
>Burn Hollywood burn

Artist: Public Enemy
Album: Apocalypse 91
Song: Shut Em Down

>I testified
>My mama cried
>Black people died
>When the other man lied
>See the TV, listen to me double trouble
>I overhaul and I'm comin'
>From the lower level
>I'm takin' tabs
>Sho nuff stuff to grab
>Like shirts it hurts
>Wit a neck to wreck
>Took a poll 'cause our soul
>Took a toll

From the education
Of a TV station
But look around
Hear go the sound of the wreckin' ball

Boom and Pound
When I
Shut 'em down
1 2 3 4 5 6 7 8 9
What I use in the battle for the mind
I hit it hard
Like it supposed
Pullin' no blows to the nose
Like uncle L said I'm rippin' up shows
Then what it is
Only 5 percent of the biz
I'm addin' woes
That's how da way it goes
Then U think I rank never drank, point blank
I own loans
Suckers got me runnin' from the bank
Civil liberty I can't see to pay a fee
I never saw a way to pay a sap
To read the law
Then become a victim of a lawyer
Don't know ya, never saw ya
Tape cued
Gettin' me sued
Playin' games wit' my head
What the judge said put me in the red
Got me thinkin' 'bout a trigger to the lead
No, no
My education mind say
Suckers gonna pay
Anyway
There gonna be a day
'Cause the troop they roll in
To posse up
Whole from the ground
Ready to go
Throw another round
Sick of the ride
Its suicide
For the other side of town
When I find a way to shut 'em down

Who count the money?
In da neighborhood
But we spendin' money
To no end lookin' for a friend

In a war to the core
Rippin' up the poor in da stores
Till they get a brother
Kickin' down doors
Then I figure I kick it bigger
Look 'em dead in the eye
And they wince
Defense is pressurized
They don't want it to be
Another racial attack
In disguise so give some money back
I like Nike but wait a minute
The neighborhood supports so put some
Money in it
Corporations owe
Dey gotta give up the dough
To da town
Or else
We gotta shut 'em down

Artist: Public Enemy
Album: It Takes a Nation of Millions to Hold Us Back
Song: Party for Your Right to Fight

Power, equality
And we're out to get it
I know some of you ain't wit it
This party started right in 66
With a pro-Black radical mix
Then at the hour of twelve
Some force cut the power
And emerged from hell
It was your so called government
That made this occur
Like the grafted devils they were
J. Edgar Hoover and he coulda proved to you
He had King and X set up
Also the party with Newton, Cleaver and Seale
He ended, so get up
Time to get em back
(You got it)

Get back on the track
(You got it)

Word from The Honorable Elijah Muhammad
Know who you are to be Black
To those that disagree it causes static
For the original Black Asiatic man
Cream of the earth
And was here first
And some devils prevent this from being known
But you check out the books they own
Even masons they know it
But refuse to show it, yo
But it's proven and fact
And it takes a nation of millions to hold us back

Although Public Enemy was considered a group that spoke truth to power, it is necessary to point out, that the group was no less a slave than any other group or individual that inked their name on the bottom of the slave master's contract. For example, what does the "field nigger" and the "house nigger" have in common... they are both slaves. Regardless to their position in relationship to the master; as long as anyone, the field or the house nigger, is defined and controlled by the slave master, they are slaves.

Obviously the house slave is more docile than the field slave, but that is a distinction with very little difference. The truth is that Public Enemy posses a talent that was given to them by their creator... not the slave master! Never the less, Public Enemy lacked the power and freedom to purvey their message without the assistance of the corporate elements that have been exposed throughout this writing. Of course their message of truth and self-determination could have been disseminated on a certain level; BUT,

The wide range of exposure that gave them a global notoriety could not have been reached without the consent and assistance of the corporate puppet masters.

"When blacks react to their environment it is taken up as a style by whites who have gotten it from an intermediary source, rappers and music videos. This "style," particularly the music, is seen as having the desired effect of boosting sales and thus it becomes the music that allows a rapper to get paid. The record companies push the music to white markets and some gangsta rappers then feel the need to act out the scenarios they have created. Black and white youths style themselves as hard-heads and act out the music they have heard, trying to authenticate themselves. The result is two dead rappers: Tupac Shakur and Notorious B.I.G. Neither of the moral crusaders, Tucker (C. Delores Tucker) or Bennett (William Bennett), focus on the mainstream culture - whites - that buy rap music. Instead, they attack the creators of rap and the distributors, the music industry. If gangsta rap is seen as a moral blight, what does that say of the whites who are purchasing it? Are the commissars saying, by accusing the record firms, that the white buying public has no choice in its taste? Are they victims of a marketing conspiracy? If it is just rebellion, at whose expense?"

—Norman Kelly: The Political Economy of Black Music- 1999

The Slaves Turn Gangster

"WE MUST COMPLETELY ANNIHILATE THE MOTHER TONGUE of both the new nigger and the new mule, and institute a new language that involves the new life's work of both."

On February 6, 1989, a so-called Jewish owned record label, **Ruthless Records**, dropped a bombshell on the HipHop Nation. By releasing the album ***"Straight Outta Compton"*** and introducing the world to the controversial west coast rap group N.W.A, Jerry Heller and his Russell Simmons like business partner and artist Eazy E, unleashed five *Niggaz Wit Attitudes (N.W.A)* to portray and profit off of the growing crack and gang epidemic that was ravaging Los Angeles, California, and other west coast cities.

This group comprised of Eazy E, Dr. Dre, Ice Cube, M.C. Ren, and DJ Yella, released songs entitled "Gangsta Gangsta", "Boyz-N-Tha-Hood", "A Bitch Iz a Bitch", "Dopeman", and "Fuck Tha Police". These songs showed the mentality of those disenfranchised youth of California that participated in gang life activity. Although the actual gang members in Los Angeles and west coast cities were far fewer than those that chose not to participate in that lifestyle, the Gangster lifestyle as portrayed by the group painted a picture of the west coast's black community as one comprised of only gangsters, hustlers, and pimps. This portrayal is seen as ironic when we realize that the members of the rap group N.W.A were far from the gangsters that they were *made up* to be.

Although the group's founder, Eazy E, was known to have sold a relatively small amount of drugs on the Compton streets, he was not known or accepted by the local gang bangers as any sort of a gangster or tough guy; in fact, he was seen as a small time hustler that would rather catch baseballs than a court case. This was because he aspired to become a professional baseball player before he turned into a world famous studio gangster. This also stands true for group members Ice Cube and Ren; although they were affiliated with gang types, Ice Cube was a Phoenix, Arizona youth with aspirations of college when he joined the group, and Ren although containing certain elements of a *"Villain"*, was far from the *"Ruthless"* one portrayed by him on wax.

The world-renowned super producer Dr. Dre; although he is from Compton, like DJ Yella, was a member of an R&B group the "World Class Wreckin' Cru". Despite the hardcore gangster lyrics that gave N.W.A notoriety; the "Wreckin' Cru" recorded songs such as "Surgery", "Juice", and hit the national charts with a song entitled "Turn of the Lights", an electro-HipHop love song that featured Dre's future wife Michel'le.

With the backing of the so-called Jew, Jerry Heller, Eazy E and the *Niggaz Wit Attitudes* glorified and profited on a lifestyle that was the result of American CIA drug trafficking in South Central Los Angeles, and the proliferation of American and European manufactured assault weapons. While the rap group Public Enemy was a pro-black, revolutionary styled representation of the conscious elements of the black community; N.W.A was a money chasing, black woman degrading, black on black crime glorifying, group of slaves that got rich and famous by showing the world the negative aspects of the black experience.

Under the guise of keeping it "Real", N.W.A's argument was that they were acting only as windows that allowed the world to see the condition of a segment of the black community of America. These so-called "windows", however, never called themselves *"Window's Wit Attitudes"*; they called themselves *"Niggaz Wit Attitudes"*. This point may be lost until we remember that HipHop is a cultural expression that prided itself in its earlier days for "keeping it real", this means N.W.A only sold records and gained support because they claimed to be what they were rapping about. Dre and Yella replaced their make-up and eyeliner with Locs (dark sunglasses), Eazy E traded in his baseball cap for a raiders cap, and Ice Cube and Ren went from gang affiliates to self proclaimed fulltime gang bangers who never fully came out with what particular gang in which they were members.

By N.W.A playing the gangster role, those real gangsters of south central Los Angeles felt that they had someone telling their story. They gave their allegiance to N.W.A by buying their music and attending their shows. Never before had the disenfranchised black youth that belonged to the street organizations that white folk called gangs had anyone represented them to the public in the way that N.W.A was doing. But the sorry fact was that those so-called *"Niggaz Wit Attitudes"* were really slaves with a gimmick that were backed by real gangsters in the form of white business men... like Chuck D of Public Enemy said, "the KKK wears three piece suits".

The success of N.W.A showed that gimmicks if properly marketed and backed by huge dollars, could be used to sell records. The "three piece suits" realized that with money backing them, HipHop artist don't have to keep it real, they merely have to make people believe they are real... this is the objective of all marketing strategies and successful slave traders (agents). **Those who control Hollywood turned the entire HipHop Nation into one big movie, complete with actors, directors, and stunt men!**

With N.W.A, those that saw Public Enemy as a threat had an alternative vehicle to gain access into the minds of the people. Not only did these powers desire to maintain control of the minds of the HipHop listeners, they had to regain the minds of those that went out on the "pro-black tangent".

HipHop Started In The West

"if the foreigner is an enemy of the country, to the extent that he knows the body of the language, to that extent is the country vulnerable to attack or invasion of a foreign culture."

N.W.A's commercial success showed that the American public was ready for a new type of music. N.W.A chose to use lyrics that glorified the death and destruction of black people. Regardless if we liked the music or not, only full blown ignorance would prevent us from recognizing that the lifestyle promoted by Jerry Heller and his *Niggaz Wit Attitudes* is a lifestyle that is not good for black people.

On the contrary, so-called gangster rap is good for the pocket books of those who control the record industry. Though rapper Ice T, who was also known as a "Gangster Rapper", had a hit record called "Six n' da Mornin'" in 1987, and Rapper King Tee released an album entitled "Act A Fool" in 1988. N.W.A was financially backed and promoted in order to set a new trend in HipHop. Prior to N.W.A the HipHop Nation was a nation that prided itself on its blackness and its growing level of consciousness. What N.W.A was allowed to do was influence HipHop to a degree that changed the subject matter of not just those who were already in the rap world, but gave record companies and their bosses the financial incentive to go out and actively pursue more "gangsters" for the radio.

HipHop went from being ignored by Corporate America to a 10 billion dollar a year cash fountain. It has moved far beyond its musical roots into the blatant expression of a lifestyle that is overwhelmingly occupied by the consumption of drugs, sex, fancy cars, and jewelry. What started out as an expression of those that were historically disenfranchised and marginalized based on race, economic, political, and religious factors emerged as a **"Super Commercial"** for the American Dream and corporate agenda.

Because of white America and their corporate domination, HipHop has been grafted from its original state into its present off-shoot or American arm of expression. Meaning, HipHop no longer reflects the diverse aspects of the black experience. HipHop, though retaining some of its pioneering elements of expression, has been replaced by the corporate agenda and the slaves of corporations that present themselves as representatives of the HipHop Nation, but are really open purveyors of the deceitful elements of the American Dream and its promise.

HipHop started in the West because Jerry Heller and his Niggaz Wit Attitudes were allowed to expand their version of HipHop into the global arena. Backed by millions of marketing dollars and the influential elements of Jerry's so-called Jewish and white friends;

the so-called gangster rap section of the HipHop Nation has been presented as the dominating characteristic of HipHop.

"Ruthless records"—a record plantation, started by a so-called Jew and a Compton dope dealer, was allowed to utilize the moneys from the sale of crack cocaine to establish a company that as its name indicates, considers itself "Ruthless". In a society that was built on the murder of millions, the disenfranchisement of millions more and the perpetual enslavement of numbers uncountable, America has created a culture that is fascinated by death and destruction. The "western outlaw" is glorified in films, books, and media; therefore, the American public, black and white, have been historically conditioned to accept the reality of the "strong" dominating the "weak".

In a world based and established on ruthless and murderous tactics, in a educational and social system that indoctrinates the minds of the masses to accept the raping of women, the stealing of land, and the enslavement of people—why wouldn't the public be drawn to the destructive elements of so-called "gangster rap"? HipHop has grown well beyond the urban (black) market of the genre's first national hit, "Rappers Delight". Since that record was released in 1979, the estimated consumer base is an ever-growing 45 million, with its stronger consumer participants resting between the ages of 13 and 34. It is understood and accepted that 80 percent of this base is comprised of white people.

But why is this relevant? If 80 percent of record and product sales associated with HipHop are attributed to white people, then a culture established by and for black people, has been economically high jacked by outsiders. If these outsiders that desire to participate in HipHop demonstrate their desire by spending money, then we have to recognize that HipHop has ceased being a voice of a people, and has become a voice that is designed to sell records and products to white people. HipHop no longer expresses the social, economic, political, and religious realities of black people and their community; HipHop now creates and markets a reality that white people want to buy into. HipHop is no longer an artistic expression of what is real and authentic in terms of struggle and circumstance, HipHop is a form of entertainment comprised of regional self-proclaimed gangsters, pimps, dope dealers and straight up clowns. It is this image that motivates white people to spend their money; they enjoy seeing the above depictions of black people because it does not conflict with how they view us in the first place. HipHop has become the new *American POP Music!*

Today's HipHop is not the HipHop of yesterday; today's HipHop is a board room executed social and economical experiment utilizing the Negro rapper as its little white mouse. Today's HipHop has found a way to capitalize on the thoughts, desires, and social ambitions of white people while simultaneously destroying the spiritual, physical, and mental infrastructure of the black community.

An estimated 80 percent of all HipHop record purchases are made by white people, many who are college and high school students. The students absorb these records in a textbook like fashion; so like textbooks, the lyrics of these songs fashion and shape the minds and perceptions of those who indulge in them. If HipHop produces an estimated 10 billion dollars a year source of revenue to the American corporate structure, then we have to accept the mathematical reality that 8 billion of those dollars come from the hands of white folk.

Today's HipHop has found a way to take money away from white America in huge amounts simply by capitalizing on the white folk's fascination with black people. But why are they so fascinated... white folks have always been fascinated by the black man and woman, this particular reality is not new, nor is it in hiding. The black man and woman's power of persona, the soulful indication of a unique spirit and divine connection, draws those who do not share equally with that nature and divine presence. Although white people were historically drawn to the black man and woman initially out of curiosity, and secondly out of their own self-perceived inadequacies, they simply could not relate to black people or their cultural expression. It is no secret that cultural expression derives from the nature of an individual or group based upon the social, political, educational, and religious context they find themselves. Because white people do not share the same nature of black people and the darker peoples of the world; and because white people don't find themselves in the same social, economic, religious, and political context of the darker people of the world they simply find it difficult, if not impossible to relate.

This being said, HipHop could not market itself in a huge way to white people if it was a "Black Thang". HipHop started as a "Black Thang", but has since been reduced and marketed into what white folk can mentally and spiritually accept as a "Black Thang". A preconceived notion of black people and a stereotypical rendition of blackness has been marketed, packaged, and presented to white people in a way that they can relate to. White people can relate to alcohol and drug use. White folks can relate to the murder, the rape and the mistreatment of women. They can relate to capitalistic gain at the expense of the masses. They can relate to the disproportionate distribution of wealth, resources, and information; these qualities are exemplified no more so than in the present world of HipHop. HipHop is a cultural expression that has been high jacked by white people, and their product—the American Negro Rapper or Willie Lynch's newest and biggest slave.

Can you imagine white people relating to Public Enemy in a real way, not just being fascinated by their persona or their stage presence? Can you imagine white folk relating to KRS-ONE, X-Clan, or Poor Righteous Teachers, not just simply liking them or liking what is being said, but relating to these individuals and groups? HipHop's fan base, those that have historically supported the artist with money and concert attendance, has always done so because they can relate to the group or artist. But today, when 80 percent of the financial support of artist and groups come from white people, then the artist and groups relate more so to white folk than black folk… this is an actual fact. This shows that in order to be accepted and financially endorsed by white folks black people must compromise the reality of their true nature and incorporate the ways and actions of their open enemy.

The HipHop that originated in the East (New York); though it was headquartered in the east, was accepted universally by black people because it was real. It did not matter where you were from, what mattered was if you were "REAL". When white folk took control of HipHop and perpetuated so-called gangster rap, the initiation of a battle took place. Since it was a known fact that N.W.A was a cosmetic made up interpretation of the west coast gangster, HipHop of the west generally was not perceived by the east coast as true HipHop. HipHop of the west, a distinction made by corporate entities, was seen as artificial and as a gimmick. This view by some on the east coast of those on the west coast caused the entire segment of west coast HipHop to be placed in the same category, "artificial HipHop". When this took place, the West was duty bound by the codes of HipHop and the streets that they claim, to PROVE that they were "Real".

Since the so-called gangster rap became synonymous with "west coast" rap, the west coast in proving that it was "REAL" had to perpetuate and support the gangster behavior that they had claimed. The realities of violence had to be reinforced, dope deals, and the "I don't give a fuck mentality" had to be displayed and lived up to. Money was subsequently given to those who rapped (talked) of these realities causing these commercial gangsters to grow rich and fat. This apparent ascension to riches by these so-called everyday "ghetto children" turn rappers, gave the other children of the ghetto the indication that if they act like, sound like, and behave like these famous Negro rappers, then they too, could become rich and famous—if not, they would certainly "die tryin".

I want to make something really clear… just because Jerry Heller and his rapping slave Eazy E helped to initiate and establish the so-called gangster phenomena, and the new version of HipHop; I do not want the reader to think that the east coast elements of HipHop have not fully jumped on board the gangster bandwagon as well. All segments of the HipHop Nation have been infected by the gangster mentality and what the so-called Jew, Jerry Heller, financed and marketed to the world… Hence the present form of HipHop may have started in the west, but it is clear that the HipHop Nation as a whole has been seriously impacted.

Consider these Lyrics from some prominent east coast rappers!

Artist: **The L.O.X.**
Album: **We Are the Streets**
Song: **Felony Niggas**

Verse 1

Shhh (Two guns up mothafucka, two guns up mothafucka (overlap))
Real shit...Styles P Shit...
If P want you dead, I ain't comin' wit niggas
Just a blunt and a tre pound, plenty of liquor
So ya homies got something to pour
That's that old school shit
I ain't tryin' to put you under the floor
I'm tryin' ta bang niggas over the clouds
And I heard you say you rich
So you can't get lower than Styles
Kill everybody dead just so no one can smile
Play the streets my whole life and I been flowin' a while
Biget I rock, ever since my nigga was shot and my other nigga
Was shoot shit I'm tellin' the truth
If I lie, may I die in the middle of the verse?
My niggas hustle from first to first
Twelve months in a year
Gun on your waist, Blunt in your ear
Pat in your sock, Trade at the back of the block
With a fein watchin' for knorx till the shit get dark
We jump in the hoop ride, instead of the six
While you lookin' for a bitch, we lookin' for a brick
That we can cook by six and give the whole block a fix
Catch me on "?" gettin' sixty a shift
Holidy Styles, nigga I aint nothin' but streets
Just as hard as the shit, that be under your feet
And the only time I front is with a blunt and a beat
To show niggas that I'm nice and they aint fuckin' wit me

Chorus

Felony Niggas
Cop Cock Heavily Niggas
That'd arm rob seventy niggas
You know
Murderin' niggas
You want doe, they servin' you niggas

Stay on fifth, Gettin' swervin' on niggas
You know
Whether we ryde or we die we gonna get this doe

Verse 2

All I know is drugs and guns
and plenty of weed
and that bitch that suck dick
and niggas that bleed
and if you're rich before you go
get a watch and a drop
you better hit the court house
and better bail out the block
if your son aint worth shit
Niggas'll smuggle your daughter
I come through in a Porshe
The same color as water
I got weight, what you want
I can cover the order
They call me Boss when I cross the border
Six shot "caught her?"
I hear niggas say my face is screwed
But I'll put six in your stomach nigga
lace your food
Scream "Fuck Every Rapper" that hate that I'm rude
But that's that SP shit, you can take it or move
We can let the bullets spill, till we all get killed
There's only six nice rappers
If you wanna be real
Niggas die every day from talking that dumb shit
That where they're from shit
All that mean to me is you can get your gun quick
Just another dumb bitch
Go to church to get the holy ghost
I did my dirt and got the holy ghost
Look at the world through a niggas eyes
Don't be a bitch, you gonna live and die
Rivin' in the sky, but no love when you slither by
I pray to god that we make it to heaven
But the only thing we makin' is channel eleven
You know four, five and seven, hot as fuck
And every rapper be dead, if they were hotter than us

But since niggas still alive that should be tellin you somethin'
You aint hear from Holiday, he aint tellin' you nothin'
You know...cocksucker...

Artist: **DMX**
Album: **It's Dark and Hell is Hot**
Song: **X is coming**

[Kid]
1, 2, X is comin' for you
3, 4, you better lock your door
5, 6, get your crucifix
7, 8, don't stay up late

[DMX]

Chorus
1, 2, X is comin' for you
3, 4, better lock your door
5, 6, get your crucifix
7, 8, don't stay up late

Who's afraid of the dark?
Responsible for the murders in the park
When I bark, they hear the boom, but you see the spark
And I seen the part of your head which used to be your face
Was replaced by nothin' for bluffin', what a waste
Niggaz wanna see me taste my own medicine
Picture that, get on some old second grade shit, I'm a get you back
Retaliate, if it hates for you to think I took a loss
When all I did was shook it off
Yeah, you heard me, shook it off
Man, if we was up north, niggaz would have been fucked you
But then we in the streets, niggaz should haven been stuck you
Plucked you like a chicken wit' your head cutoff
They'll find you wit' your back open and your legs cutoff
And as for your man, don't you ever in your mutherfuckin' life
Know when I gotta gun come at me wit' a knife, a'ight?
And forgettin' you ever saw me is the best thing to do
Don't give a fuck about your family; they'll be resting with you

Chorus(x2)

You got yourself in a predicament that you can't get out of

You already in some shit, but it's about to get hotter
Fuckin' wit' a, nigga like you, runnin' your mouth
Will, have that same nigga like you, gun in your mouth
But won't be like the last time when you run in the house
'Cuz I ain't knockin' on the door
I'm comin in the house and I'm gunnin' for your spouse
Tryin' to send the bitch back to her maker
And if you got a daughter older then 15, I'ma rape her
Take her on the living room floor, right there in front of you

Then ask you seriously, whatchu wanna do?
Frustratin', isn't it? When they kill me, but I'm a kill you
Now watch me fuck just a lil' while longer, please, will you?
This is revenge, no time before you die
And despite how much I hate to see a grown man cry
I'm a make you suffer, see your ass in hell, motherfucker
Click, BOOM, BOOM
See your ass in hell

Chorus(x2)

When I speak you better listen
The harder it gets, the more follows
And I'm hittin' 'em wit' shit that they can't all swallow
I keep my slugs hollow, keep families with sorrow
Keep motherfuckers like you, not seein' tomorrow
I will borrow a gun, then run 'til I catch you
Let you slip up, just once, then I'm a wet you
Stretch you out like a limousine
'Cuz where I catch you is where I catch you
That's what killin' means
Fuck whoever's standin' there when you get what you got comin'
'Cuz once I hit you in your head, the witnesses start runnin'
Niggaz started somethin', but they chose not to finish it
So I'm a wrap it up, for real, dog, 'cuz I'm a winner, shit
Fuck it yo, let's end this shit, I don't need the plaques
And I ain't a DJ, nigga, so I don't need the wax
Gimme slugs from my gats
Gimme hoods from my rats
Gimme wood from my bats
Then they meet where the fuck I'm at, for real

Artist: **Cam'Ron**
Album: **S.D.E. (Sports Drugs and Entertainment)**
Song: **Violence**

(Cam'Ron)

Fuck who ever saying shit
Fuck the hole system
fuck who ever playing me
fuck who ever listens
Juliany fuck perjury
fuck the club
fuck the pub
fuck the ball

fuck him; fuck security, (violence)
with a gun and grill that's how I fucked her, fucked y'all
even Juvenile said all don't give a fuck hen, (violence)
we on the worst on this shit
holla more I go first on this shit
let's see how many times I can curse on this shit, (violence)
shit, fuck, ass, bitch, nigga, pussy, hoe hoe
Putta, marico, pera, toto, (violence)
I put a gun to your brain
put you in front of the train
drink a Smirnoff
wait for it to wear off, (violence)
take is hair off
tear his ear off
you loath us
strip now you blow us
got the strap now she knows us
Don't sob a bitch, hug a bitch, mug the bitch, mug the bitch
get out of hear
Mugged the bitch, slugged the bitch,(violence)
chorus x 8
(Violence) die bitch nigga, bitch nigga die (violence)
4 chorus background (die die die die die die die)
yo, yo, yo
you don't know me grab you I will
fuck what you heard, stab shoot I kill, (violence)
kill kill kill kill
nigga's triggers off
we burn bitches nipples off
pull them pistols off, (violence)
for my real bitches cocaine copy

they straight Loraine about it
run up on your chain and pop it
get in the red and drop it, (violence)
you acting strange to cawk it
you want a brain then stop it
honey game is logic
the money's regardless, (violence)
gun scared to use it
they so wild and pros
shave your pubic, then put on the alcohol, (violence)
here on the aria, fuck the plant house
razors in the mouth
waiting for you to talk slick

then she talk spit, (violence) (spitting)
ups the hork he
you better cover (violence)
cut from neck to Dracula, chocked in blood, (violence) blood, blood, blood
BLOOD, BLOOD, BLOOD, BLOOD, BLOOD, BLOOD, BLOOD
DIE, DIE NIGGER BITCH (Violence)
chorus x 8
die bitch nigga, bitch nigga die
(Cam'Ron)
die bitch
and am a hater
hate your taste
Hate your place
hate your face
hate y'all nigga's
can take y'all nigga's, (violence)
hate my life
well I hate your wife
hit your wife
but I hate your wife
now your about to hate this life, (violence)
hate to say I hate shit
I hate that bracelet
well take that bracelet
take that fake shit
take that stink shit, (violence)
and I hate shit collectors
and fake big brothers with dick suckers
make the pig suffer
you die left out, (violence)

chorus x 8
die bitch nigga, bitch nigga die

Oh yeah, and check out what the slaves are saying in the south!

Artist: **Geto Boys**
Album: **Til Death Do Us Part**
Song: **Murder Avenue**

Creeping down the hallway quiet as kept
the only sign of a murder was the blood on the foresteps
I stopped for a second to wipe it up
and threw the bloody towel in the garbage bag with her guts
pretty as a picture her name was Rosie

had to kill the bitch cuz she was getting too fuckin nosey
a school hoe she attended U of H
a law student who was looking for a fuckin' case
but she was barking up the wrong tree
why in the hell did the bitch wanna fuck with me?
walking around my crib steady casin'
askin' about the strange smells that were coming from my basement
she asked one too many motherfuckin questions it was time
somebody taught the stupid bitch a good lesson
I snuck in the house by the back door
it was like a scene from psycho
the bitch was in the shower
I rushed her quick so she wouldn't have a chance to holler
and said "shut the fuck up hoe"
and slammed her motherfucking face against the cold floor
struggling soaking wet
I gagged her mouth with a whole box of kotex
after i fucked her check out what i did
slit her fucking stomach and watched her squeal like a pig
the shit was gruesome g i couldn't call it
i cut off her fingers and flushed them down the fuckin' toilet
and wrote my name on the wall like i usually do
to mark a murder hoe, yeah on murder avenue

more murder, more murder, more murder, yo
more murder, more murder, more murder, watch me hurt a hoe
more murder, more murder, more murder, nigga
more motherfucking murder gots ta pull the trigger
more murder, more murder, more murder, check it
a hundred and fifty seven thousand victims in a second
gotta give it up for brigitte and ted brand new newly-weds
there's nothing i would love better than to have their fuckin' heads
on a platter i watch them sonofabitches scatter
in broad daylight but yo it really didn't matter
i put my gin to their heads and said "shut up"
the nigga was big i watched this big motherfucker nut up
on the rampage both of 'em got pistol-whipped
the 9 was bloody so i pulled out my pistol grip
the nigga was damn near dead
i grabbed the bitch by her head and told her "spread your fucking legs"
I placed the barrel of my 9 on her pearl tongue
and stuck a shell inside her pussy and said "now ain't that fun?"
she started to cry
I saw a tear fall from here eye i said "bitch you must wanna die"
I pulled the trigger of the gun back slowly

and shot up her nigga until he was full of holes g
the bitch was screaming with rage
I stamped on her motherfucking face until it caved in
'cos killing is so damn sweet
I saved the remains and used them later for ground meat
being a lunatic i gotta do the lunatic
gotta do man, yeah living on this avenue

more murder, more murder, more murder, yo
more murder, more murder, more murder, watch me hurt a hoe
more murder, more murder, more murder, nigga
more motherfucking murder gots ta pull the trigger
more murder, more murder, more murder, check it
a hundred and fifty seven thousand victims in a second

Artist: **Underground Kingz {U.G.K.}**
Album: **Ridin' Dirty**
Song: **Murder**

Verse One: {Pimp C}
I'm still Pimp C bitch so what the fuck is up?
I'm puttin' powder on the streets cuz I got
Big fuckin' nut's comin' back from Louisiana
In a Fleetwood Lana
I deserve them nigga's shit to put they pea's on they banner
Got the pound four by four cuz you know I just
Pay to nigga bought thirty from me
So I fronted forty two, he gonna pop to seven hundred
Times sixty two, twenty four eight is what I do
So fuck what 'cha do
If I told ya cocaine number's you think I was lyin'
Young nigga's twenty two talkin' bout they retirin'

In the game ain't a thang comin' far then we been
Rick's home two apartment's where enter
Tight friends' mo bounce to the ounce
Cuz the Wood the shit, I done got me
Fifty ounces out of birds ya bitch
Tightin' up no slack bitches checkin' my stock
Got some Burban City nigga's so I'm a go to my garage
Just got back from California kicked it with B-Legit
Put me down with purple chronic and that hurricane shit
At the studio with Tom, I wish I could stay
I got to holla at Master P, cuz we got money to make
We with playa'z from the South stack gee'z man

Like Ball I got to stack big cheeze man
Bitch say he wanna show ya
You got nine grand I ain't rappin' shit
Till my money in my hand
South Texas mutherfucka that's where I stay
Gettin' money from yo bitches every
Got damn day
Big paper I'm foldin'
Hoes is on my mutherfuckin' jock
For all this dick I be holdin'
I hate grown man show it
Especially if a fool take our style and
Act like my nigga's don't know it
I kick it with the trill nigga's so you best's
Not trip if ya keep on talkin' shit
My nigga empty the clip
Hoe azz nigga
Chorus:
Murder, Mur, Mur, Murder
Murder, Mur, Mur, Murder
Murder, Mur, Mur, Murder
Murder, Mur, Mur, Murder
Murder, Mur, Mur, Murder
Verse Two: {Bun-B}
Well this Bun-B bitch and I'm the king
I'm movin' chickens got 'em finger lickin'
Stickin' nigga's who be trippin'
You need a swift kickin' yo azz is right for the pickin'
Now down as my pocket's stickin'

I be thinkin' nigga's slippin' you sick
When I be clickin' now take a look at the
Bigger nigga Malt liquor swigger
Playa hata ditch digger figure
My hair trigger you bound one hot one in yo liver
You shiver shake and quiver
I'm free from nigga you wetter den a river
For what it's worth it's suburblous some nigga's doin' dirt
Fuck her first and take off her skirt
Make the pussy hurt Mister Master
Hit the Swisha faster then you keep a
Blister bastard fuck her sister faster
Hit the elbro for sale yo
Brother better have my mail hoe
Before I catch a murder case and go to jail hoe

Hell no, time to bail hit the trail so
We can sell mo fuckin' yell get the scale
No other bullet duck or get shoved
Inside this game they better buck us
Cuz the clucker's they love us
Make them class dick suckers
Check they jelly like smokers
I hit like nun-chuckers
Cuz Short Texas bring the rukus
This for my muthfucker's
Cookin' cheese to crooked geez
Rockin' up quarter key's
Just to get the hook with ease
Wanna bees get on yo knees
Fill the squeeze from them AK one three's
From here to over sea's
We do what we please
No trip cuz we flip
Light up a dip
I'm breakin' 'em off from they hip to yo lip
Go ask that boy Skip
That nigga Bun rip
With one clip, soon as the gun slip
Now I done ripped out my Barile
Flyin' through yo belly belly and
Some smelly red jelly is drippin' out of ya belly
Servin' 'em like a Deli jumped on my cellular telli
Hoe sell it like it's goin' out of style
You can't see me Marcus so have a
Motherfuckin' Sweet and smile

Jerry Heller was the moving force and marketing genius behind the emergence and crossover of Rap music to the record buying public. He not only founded Ruthless Records with the late Eazy E, but he managed NWA, Egyptian Lover, World Class Wreckin Cru, LA Dream Team, J.J. Fad, The DOC, Michel'le, Above the Law, and other trend-setting artists who formed the foundation for the incredible successes of Priority Records and Interscope Records. To date, Ruthless Records has sold in excess of 110 million records, not counting singles. The artists (including the heir apparent to the NWA legacy Bone Thugs 'N Harmony, discovered as homeless Cleveland youths by Eazy and Jerry) and producers such as Dr. Dre whose careers Jerry Heller established sold millions upon millions of records for Interscope Records, Priority Records, ATCO/Atlantic Records, MCA Records, Relativity/SonyRecords.

Dr. Dre and Ice Cube

"BEING A FOOL IS ONE OF THE BASIC INGREDIENTS OF ANY INCIDENTS TO THE MAINTENANCE OF THE SLAVERY SYSTEM."

The West Coast HipHop scene today is no longer dominated by Ruthless records; it is dominated and controlled by *Interscope Records* and the chief Negro slave of the west coast rap world Dr. Dre. Born Andrew Young, Dr. Dre has grown into the premier HipHop producer of the world. Although there are several other notable and talented producers within the HipHop Nation, Mr. Young has a unique position within the west coast wing. As a former significant member of the group "Niggaz Wit Attitudes", this Compton raised "beat maker", has managed to be positioned as the west coast gate keeper in terms of who and what gets significant airplay and notoriety within the HipHop slave industry. Just a simple glance at the west coast rap world will reveal that the only significantly successful artists of the west coast are those that have some sort of connection or affiliation with Dr. Dre. Rappers such as Ice Cube, W.C., Mac 10, Snoop and the Dogg Pound, Eminem, and even 50 cent among others, all can be linked to Andre Young. The west coast rap world is dominated by Dr. Dre and those that support and back him.

Though Dr. Dre depicts himself as the quintessential gangster, he is far from the person that he sells himself to be. During his "Niggaz Wit Attitudes" days, Dre claimed to be a Compton G (Gangster). This was done despite the fact that though raised in Compton, prior to the N.W.A days, Dr. Dre was a sequenced dressed, make up wearing pretty boy of the World Class Wreckin' Cru. He was not a gangster in any sense of the word, and the HipHop of the west coast was marked by the electro-hop sound that was indicative of groups such as the World Class Wreckin' Cru, Uncle Jamz Army, and the somewhat successful group, the L.A. Dream Team. These particular groups were not comprised of the so-called Gangster sound or image, nor was Dr. Dre himself.

Once Dr. Dre became involved with Eazy E and Jerry Heller, he adopted an image that fit into the gimmick that the so-called Jew, Jerry Heller, and his so-called Negro puppet Eazy E desired to sale. Adorning dark sunglasses and a raider's cap, Andre Young became a studio Gangster that invented the studio Gangster sound. In fact, although Dr. Dre's most notable and multi-platinum selling album "The Chronic" was a ghetto tribute to marijuana and the urban elements that participated in its consumption, as an N. W. A member, he mouthed these apparently contradictory lyrics…"Some drop science: while I'm dropping English, even if Yella makes it a-capella I still express, yo, I don't smoke weed or cess…cause its known to give a brother brain damage, and brain damage on the mic don't manage – nuthin but makin' a sucka and you equal, don't be another sequel…"

Despite the easily recognized contradictory depiction of marijuana (weed, cess), the first line "some drop science" is a clear reference to those that at that time were involved in the conscious elements of HipHop and were reciting lyrics that were pro-black in nature and were considered as "dropping science". This line is seen as a mild diss to those that were participating in this form of HipHop.

Though Eazy E and Jerry Heller were the minds that originally brought about the group known as N.W.A, Dr. Dre along with fellow member Oshea "Ice Cube" Jackson were the creative forces behind the group. Ice Cube was the primary writer of the group, especially for Eazy E; Dr. Dre was the primary producer. When Dr. Dre merged the "electro-hop" sounds of his World Class Wreckin' Cru, with the hard core bass and drum elements made popular by Public Enemy and their production team known as the "Bomb Squad", he created a sound that drove the industry in a new direction in terms of sound and production. Not only could this sound be easily listened to in cars and dorm rooms, but this sound could be danced to at parties and in clubs. One only has to listen to the album "Straight Outta Compton" to here the "Bomb Squad's" sound influence. Because the N.W.A sound was a fusion of bass, drum, and the synthesized keyboard (piano), it was considered new to the HipHop world. Previously HipHop had been a music that was driven by samples and a clear driving bass and drum element manufactured by a "beat machine". Public Enemy had mastered the art of sampling, and had in fact sampled other sounds, such as the whistle of a tea-kettle to create innovative music and production. The mathematical science of sound and sound engineering creates specific results and behaviors.

Although this writing is not intended to go into this particular aspect of the music labeled as HipHop, know for a certainty that music and sound has a direct impact on the electro-chemical makeup and sub-conscious and conscious state of being of an individual, group, and community.

By having a driving sound, Chuck D of Public Enemy introduced lyrics of a specific social and political agenda into the ears and minds of his listeners. The tone of his voice and his cadence created an action and reaction that was considered "driven 'em to panic". Chuck's lyrics were crafted and recited over a sound production that was designed to bring about a certain affect. Consider the following lyrics from their album *Yo! Bum Rush The Show* and the song entitled, *"Rightstarter (Message To A Black Man)"*

You spend a buck in the 80's, what you get is a preacher
Forgivin' this torture of the system that brought 'cha
I'm on a mission and you got that right
Addin' fuel to the fire, punch to the fight
Many have forgotten what we came here for
Never knew or had a clue, so you're on the floor
Just growin not knowin about your past
now you're lookin' pretty stupid while you're shakin' your ass
Mind over matter, mouth in motion

Can't deny it 'cause I'll never be quiet

Let's start this right

The sound of Public Enemy was dominating the world of HipHop, and HipHop at that time had the east coast as its headquarters. Although at this point in HipHop's history the Willie Lynch syndrome of regional and plantation confrontation had not grew to a point of clear recognition, the west coast and its lifestyle was desirous of expression. Jerry Heller captured an able-bodied, opportunistic slave in the person of Eazy E to gain access into the world of HipHop, a world that had at that time already been stolen from black people by his cousins, other so-called Jews.

By introducing a new sound and a new Gangster personified gimmick, N.W.A achieved on the west coast, what Public Enemy had done on the east coast and on the world stage. Just as Public Enemy drove HipHop in a new direction when they immerged, the *"Niggaz Wit Attitudes"* did the same when they injected their "Gangster" lyrics into the minds of their listeners over Dr. Dre's hypnotic and addictive sounds.

A black man, just as the case with the Bomb Squad, was able to use his natural creative ability to generate thought, action, and reaction by scientifically engineering and manipulating sounds. The difference between Public Enemy and N.W.A is enormously clear—Chuck's voice was heard confronting the "powers that be", both seen and unseen, that control, manipulate and exploit the black community and subsequently the world in a negative way... N.W.A and its principle writer Ice Cube, was heard chanting lyrics that while containing clear elements of truth, were released in a manipulative way that glorified a destructive behavior that had before and since acted as a cancer to the urban and global condition of black people. Consider the words from N.W.A's first album "Straight Outta Compton" and the song entitled "Gangsta, Gangsta":

Here's a little somethin' bout a nigga like me
never shoulda been let out the penitentiary
Ice Cube would like ta say
That I'm a crazy mutha fucka from around the way
Since I was a youth, I smoked weed out
Now I'm the mutha fucka that ya read about
Takin' a life or two that's what the hell I do; you don't like how I'm livin well fuck you!
This is a gang, and I'm in it
My man Dre'll fuck you up in a minute
With a right left, right left you're toothless
And then you say goddamn they ruthless!
Everwhere we go they say [damn!]
N W A's fuckin' up tha program
And then you realize we don't care
We don't just say no, we to busy sayin' yeah!

To drinkin' straight out the eight bottle
Do I look like a mutha fuckin role model?
To a kid lookin' up ta me Life ain't nothin but bitches and money
Cause I'm tha type o' nigga that's built ta last

If ya fuck wit me I'll put a foot in ya ass
See I don't give a fuck 'cause I keep bailin
Yo, what the fuck are they yellin?
Chorus:
Gangsta, Gangsta! That's what they're yellin.
"It's not about a salary, it's all about reality"
Gangsta, Gangsta! That's what they're yellin
"Hopin you sophisticated motherfuckers hear what I have to say"

Well I wouldn't consider myself as "sophisticated", and I certainly don't consider myself as a "motherfucker", but I do certainly here what Ice Cube had to say. Lets for a minute allow Ice Cube's lyrics to prove "MY" point.

1st point "Here's a little somethin' bout a nigga like me"... Ice Cube is telling all who listens to this song, about himself! Here, to the whole world, Ice Cube calls himself a "nigga". Remember, HipHop was traditionally a form of expression that was based on reality... consider the chorus..."It's not about a salary, it's all about reality". So with this in mind, Ice Cube tells the world that in "reality" he is a "nigga".

2nd point "never shoulda been let out the penitentiary"... Ice Cube was never in the penitentiary; therefore, he could have never been let out. This is another indictment of his credibility and further contradicts the claims of the chorus of the song. Why would Ice Cube misrepresent his "reality"?...Because it's all about his "salary".

3rd point "Since I was a youth, I smoked weed out... Now I'm the mutha fucka that ya read about, Takin' a life or two that's what the hell I do, you don't like how I'm livin well fuck you!"... Whose life has Ice Cube "takin"? I would assume he is talking about another black man's life and if people are reading about you, who is doing the reading, and what are they reading? ... **I would presume a *"newspaper"*, and we certainly know who controls and produces the newspapers that the people are reading.** This particular verse shows that Ice Cube realizes that his life is considered as negative..."you don't like how I'm livin well fuck you!"... However, of course, he does not care about the affect that the life that he is selling is having on anybody, especially his own people.

Final point before we move on; *"My* man Dre'll fuck you up in a minute, With a right left, right left you're toothless, And then you say goddamn they ruthless! Everywhere we go they say [damn!]N W A's fuckin' up tha program And then you realize we don't care"... Like I just stated, we realize that Ice Cube and N.W.A don't care, but we also know that neither Dre nor Ice Cube has a history of hurting or killing anything or anybody. To claim such is a misrepresentation of the facts and an abandonment of what is *"real"* in the truest since of the HipHop term.

REALITY MEANS NOTHING... IMAGE IS EVERYTHING!

"you have to be careful in setting up the new language; for the slaves would soon be in your house, talking to you as "man to man" and that is death to our economic system."

By creating and presenting a gimmick that is a clear lie and misrepresentation of the facts as they pertain to the artist, N.W.A justifies the position of those who are faithful to the tenets of HipHop that what they do is not HipHop and they are not true HipHop artists. They are merely actors, studio gangsters that are backed financially and institutionally by an element of a political, social, and so-called religious community that desires to destroy black people and control the world.

Since N.W.A is "fuckin' up tha program" what program is that?! It's the program of true HipHop and its potential for a positive and global change. Both Dre and Cube had received paychecks from so-called Jewish business men that don't give a damn about black people and their condition.

It is important to understand that there are certain men and groups of men that set out to do things, with motives that are not as apparent as we may think. In a social, political, and economic structure like that utilized by the American government and like-minded power brokers of the world, it is important that we recognize the fact that *image* is everything. Cash only allows for the obtaining, maintenance, and enhancement of an image. Commercials sells images, sports, entertainment, political style, and charisma are all manufactured tools, that while containing different elements of purpose and function, more than anything, portray an image or images.

The black man and woman of America have never experienced or enjoyed freedom and the unyielding power that comes with it. There are certain experiences and developmental qualities that accompany the presence of freedom that can only be seen and understood while experiencing the God given right of that freedom. The American government, the global political context, is set up and maintained by free white men. The American government and the so-called Jewish elements have positioned themselves as the global slave master and the rest of the world is set to make a bargain and/or petition for their individual and collective so-called freedom.

This is said within the context of this writing to show that HipHop and its so-called rap stars are controlled and manipulated by the very same and complete forces that are controlling the world and its politics. Just as HipHop and its stars portray images that we buy into, the controllers and manipulators of HipHop, has sold an image to the rappers themselves that they have completely bought into and accepted as their aspiring ambition.

Not only Gangster Rap, but the gangster phenomena itself, is a lifestyle that was introduced into the world by the European white male and his cousins. The Jews, biblically and historically have always been fractionalized and divided based on ideology, method, and ambition. America was founded by Irish white folk, German white folk, Dutch white folk, Portuguese white folk, and many other types of white folk that were in fact gangs of men sorted and characterized by distinguishable traits, ideologies, histories and ambitions. The difference however is that these groups of white men, were in fact, white men that were operating within the context of freedom. The presence of this freedom allowed them to assert their freedom in a way that they thought would contribute to their future and their global ambition and position.

From within the psychology of a free white man came the reality of a free white man. His system and ways of doing things is a natural extension of his view of the world and his freedom to make his interpretation a reality. This ability to bring forth an idea without apprehension and concern of the well being of those opposed to his reality, is less than an aspect of freedom absent of responsibility, or consideration for who we would call the common man; and more indicative of the mathematical conclusion that his power and dominion rest upon. This is maintained by controlling and diminishing the wellbeing of those other than he!

The so-called gang banger and his HipHop cousin has bought into this reality, in terms of caring more about self or those associated with self, than the overall good of the community or the future of their black family (Nation). The American white male has sold the black man a bag of goods entitled the American Dream; however, the American Dream can only be recognized and reached if one was to adopt the exact ways and actions that brought forth the American reality. Murder, rape, slavery, theft, lies and deceit all factor heavily within the genesis of the country or system of beliefs known as America. By buying into the American concept of business and politics, the HipHop Nation has forfeited the legitimate concern for the community from which they were born, to accept and adapt to a way of thought and belief that has a vested interest in destroying first, that same community from which gave them birth; and second, the so-called Negro rapper himself.

The origin of the Gangster Rapper is the Gangster Cracka; it is the American white male that has devalued blackness and has put the devalued images of black people throughout the world via their media and entertainment machines so extensive, that the product of the white male's media campaign has produced a group of black people that simply don't give a damn about themselves or the future of their Nation of Blackness. Today's black youth walk within a false perception of what it means to be black. The black culture and its manifestation of blackness have been replaced with corporate HipHop and its false rendition of the reality of what it means to be black

Manipulated ignorance has produced clowns in Gang Bang suits. Not knowing anything about the origin of the Gangster or its mentality, the HipHop gang banger adopts the names of Italian and Jewish Gangsters; the same gangsters that got rich destroying the fabrics of the black community with drugs, gambling and alcohol. In the HipHop community you have people referring to themselves as DONS, as Gambinos, as Escobar, as Rockefellers', as Scarface; all of these titles and nicknames are derived from communities that support their own to a point of destroying ours.

The black community is exploited and poisoned by every outsider for the benefit of those who wish to grow rich and fat. This reality is furthered by diabolical so-called Jews and European white men that pay black children (so-called Negro Rappers) millions of dollars to pump foolishness and audio poison into the heads of people all over the world, particularly the minds of innocent black babies.

I mean... can we imagine a bunch of grown white business men doing so-called big business under the names of our famous black leaders? We don't see the owners and operators of Exxon Oil doing business under the name of Malcolm X or Martin Luther King Jr.; we don't see white folk calling themselves Black Panthers, or The Minister—these are our heroes and these titles and names we should pay homage, not the names and images of our open enemies, or the names of those that have reaped huge benefits from adding to our individual and collective destruction. To do so is a shame and an embarrassment, and the so-called Negro rappers should stop referring to themselves under the names of those that don't give a collective damn about them or their people.

The American Dream

Just like the average HipHop Gang banger, the *American Dream* for black people is not real. The *American Dream* is a product of destructive practices and behaviors unleashed on the darker peoples of the world. The *American Dream* is a dream that was dreamt by what today is an American white male but was yesterday an imperialistic cave man that had his desires and ambitions set on the complete and utter destruction of that which does not think, act, and react like himself. This American Dream's base component is the destruction of the black male because the extreme opposite of the white male is a black male. With this in mind, the black male has to wake up and accept the fact that you will be paid well, really well, if your ways and actions result in the death of yourself and the destruction of your people... this is a hard truth, but it is an absolute fact. The Devil wants to buy your soul; the question is...WILL YOU SALE?!!

For those that believe that we are moving closer to the American Dream consider these stats!

In Mathematics' American 12th graders rank 19th out of 21, Industrialized Nations and in Science America ranks number 16, out of 21 Industrialized Nations.

Our advanced physics students rank dead last.

Only 32 percent of 4th graders are proficient in reading.

Forty-two million American adults cannot read at all and 50 million are unable to read at a higher level than is expected of a 4th or 5th grader.

92 million out of 300 million in the greatest nation on Earth are educationally deficient. And that number increases by some 2.25 million each year.

20 percent of all high school seniors are functionally illiterate.

13 percent of public school children were enrolled in Special Education; half of those were considered "learning disabled."

Over half of all public schools reported a criminal incident to the police, and 10 percent of schools reported serious violent crimes.

This is not Black statistics—this is the general American public.

Now I will be more specific with Black education statistics:

Only 12 percent of Black high school seniors are proficient readers, while 54 percent have below basic reading skills.

It is estimated that 40-44 percent of Blacks—almost half of us—are functionally illiterate.

Black children are almost three times more likely than White children to be labeled "mentally retarded."

Black students are two and a half times more likely to be placed in remedial or low-track classes.

Even when Black students show potential that is equal to or above that of Whites, they are 40 percent less likely to be placed in advanced or accelerated classes.

Two-thirds of so-called minorities in public school fail to reach basic levels of national tests, and there continues to be marked disparities between Black and White students in the national SAT scores.

32 percent of all suspended students are Black, and Black students are twice as likely as Whites to be suspended or expelled.

The high school drop-out rate in some inner city communities approaches 50 percent; and only 26 percent of Blacks who do finish high school go to college, while 37 percent of Whites go to college.

College-educated Blacks are four times more likely than Whites to experience unemployment.

Black women account for nearly all of the gains made in Black enrollment in higher education since the mid-1980s.

Women make up 60 percent of enrollment at Black colleges and 80 percent of the honor rolls.

Babies with poorly-educated mothers are more likely to die in the first year of life, or have chronic health problems growing up.

Black people are dramatically underrepresented in many professions: *3.2 percent of lawyers; 3 percent of doctors; and less than 1 percent of architects.*

Black males have both the lowest average level of educational attainment and the highest level (nearly 50 percent) of workers with more education than their jobs require. So it doesn't make any difference what level of education we attain, the jobs that we have don't even require the education that we have.

White males with a high school diploma are just as likely to have a job and tend to earn just as much as Black males with college degrees.

Light-skinned Blacks have a 50 percent better chance of getting a job than dark-skinned Blacks.

The above stats were taken from a speech given by The Honorable Minister Louis Farrakhan entitled "THE EDUCATION CHALLENGE: *A NEW EDUCATIONAL PARADIGM FOR THE 21ST CENTURY"— AUGUST 3, 2008.*

Before we continue look at some additional statistics':

In 1963, when Dr. Martin Luther King Jr. declared, "I have a dream," more than 70percent of black families were headed by married couples. Today, 44 years after the Civil Rights Act of 1964, married couples head only 46percent of black families.

-45percent of black men, and 42percent of black women have never married.

-Marriage for blacks has become an alternative lifestyle.

-70percent of all black children are born out of wedlock.

-43percent of all black children are aborted, nearly 3 times higher than for Whites.

-65percent of never-married black women have children.

-85percent of black children do not live in a home with their fathers.

-70percent of black boys and men in the criminal justice system come from single-parent homes.

This issue leads us right into the next.

HIV-Aids, and other STD's

-50percent of all new AIDS cases are in the Black community which comprises only 12percent of the population!

-85percent of all AIDS cases in Atlanta are black women.

-A black woman is 25 times more likely to contract AIDS than a white woman and represents 72percent of all women with AIDS.

-Blacks are 20 times more likely than whites to have gonorrhea.

-AIDS is now the #1 killer of black women, age 25-44.

-67percent of black women with AIDS contracted HIV through heterosexual sex.

-A study among black men in 37 colleges in North Carolina revealed that of the 84 men with HIV, 1/3 had had sex with men and women.

-There is 'an acute crisis' in Black sexual politics creating a schism in Black male and female relations.

The Black Prison Portrait

-Nearly 2 million black males are either currently in a state or federal prison or have been in one.

-17percent of black men have had prison experience compared to 7.7percent of Hispanic and 2.6percent of White.

-Black men comprised 41percent of the more than 2 million men in custody, and black men age 20 to 29 comprised 15.5percent of all men in custody on June 30, 2006.

-Overall, black men were incarcerated at 6.5 times the rate of white men.

-The overall incarceration rate for black women was 3.8 times the rate for white women.

WILL THE REAL GANGSTER PLEASE STAND UP!

"A total society has many interconnected value systems. All the values in the society have bridges of language to connect them for orderly working in the society. But for these language bridges, these many value systems would sharply clash and cause internal strife or civil war, the degree of the conflict being determined by the magnitude of the issues or relative opposing strength in whatever form."

To an unenlightened mind it might seem as if I am picking on the so-called Jewish people; but I am not, what I am doing is exposing some of the hidden truths and realities concerning a group that claim to be God's chosen people. This is an important fact because while claiming to be the "chosen people of God" as well as claiming to be the world's biggest victims, others are left to view these people as such, or run the risk of being viewed as Anti-Semitic.

Although it may seem as though I am picking on those that claim themselves as Jews—those that are benefiting from that name and title; but what I am really doing is exposing them as NOT being JEWS in the truest and biblical sense of the word. So, in reality I am not confronting the JEWS at all, I am confronting those that hide their wicked machinations and schemes behind the Jewish religious cloak and the Star of David.

By thoroughly examining the so-called Jewish playbook you see that those that claim to be Jews are masters; in many cases, they are the fundamental elements of the most wicked and nefarious fields of endeavor in the modern world. Though the majority of people are ignorant to the fact, it is a known and accepted truth that the so-called Jews controlled and developed what is today known as the organized crime Syndicates, sometimes referred to as the Mafia. It was the so-called Jews and not the Italians that developed and mastered the role of the American Gangster.

In fact, the term MAFIA was a title which finds its origins in the so-called Jewish ran Hollywood studios; the "Mafia" concept was a theatrical attempt to slander the Italians as the founders and benefactors of the American Crime Syndicates. This is far from the case... in fact the Sicilian crime groups, often referred to as the "cosche" (families), referred to themselves as the Costa Nostra which means "our thing". The term MAFIA was a term coined by the so-called Jewish controlled media and the so-called Jewish controlled Hollywood.

I know it is hard to believe that it was the so-called Jews that coined the word Mafia, or Mafioso, but it is true consider the following:

In the early 1900's the so-called Jews that resided primarily in the Lower Eastside portion of Manhattan was riddled with gangsters. These so-called Jewish gangsters built a significant reputation as thieves, pimps, prostitutes, opium dealers, gamblers, brothel-owners, racketeers, murderers, and robbers. In the early days of their criminality these so-called Jewish gangsters were just individuals that periodically ran with each other doing all type of crimes to not only gain riches, but to, more importantly, establish and maintain reputations.

Although the early days was marked by rag tag crimes and various criminal pursuits, this all changed in a big way in very little time. Some of the most infamous criminals in American history can be traced to these little gangsters that were known as Jews.

Consider the so-called Jew by the name of Arnold Rothstein. Born in New York, January 17, 1882, this so-called Jewish gangster was known as a brilliant mathematician that gained his wealth by gambling and the bootlegging of alcohol during the prohibition years. This gangster, however, was not just any "ole gangster", this particular gangster was the quintessential gangster—the gangster by which others gangsters were measured and defined.

Arnold Rothstein was the single most influential man in American organized crime history. Although his parents were poor, Arnold had a demeanor and swagger that catapulted his reputation to one of dignity, class, and the mannerisms of an aristocrat. He was not just a gangster; this so-called Jew was a gangster slash business man that was known for recruiting, developing, and polishing some of history's biggest and most notorious gangsters. Probably known best for being the "Brains" behind the infamous 1919 World Series "black sox scandal", Rothstein brought together and was the mentor of the likes of so-called Jewish gangster Meyer Lansky and Sicilian Lucky Luciano.

Meyer Lansky probably the most powerful gangster in American history; power in every since of the word, was a Polish born So-called Jew whose family immigrated to the Lower East Side of Manhattan, New York in 1911. While a young boy he met and befriended a young Lucky Luciano, and as a teenager he became very close friends and crime partners with Benjamin "Bugsy" Siegel, another infamous so-called Jew. It is a historical fact that Meyer along with his two buddies, Lucky and Bugsy, founded and maintained the National Crime Syndicate, also known as the Brownsville Boys or "Murder Inc" (Murder Inc was a term coined by the media). The members of this group of murderous criminals preferred to call it the "Combination"; they called it this because this gang was comprised of a combination of so-called Jewish and Italian gangsters... though mostly Jewish.

Some of "Murder Inc.'s" most infamous members were so-called Jews named Abe "Kid Twist" Reles, Martin "Buggsy" Goldstein, Harry "Pittsburgh Phil" Strauss, Albert "Tick Tock" Tannenbaum, Jacob "Gurrah" Shapiro, Louis "Lepke" Buchalter, Emanuel "Mendy" Weiss, Dutch Schultz and Sholem Bernstein. Though all these members were proficient and skilled killers, none were as powerful and as slick as Meyer Lansky.

As the true leader of Murder Inc., Meyer Lansky sanctioned and approved over 1,000 murders nationwide. This syndicate took contracted murders to a higher level. The CRIME SYNDICATE murders was contracted and then submitted to a Board of Directors, after the board voted to approve the contract, the contract was forwarded to Meyer Lansky for approval—no one was killed without the approval of the so-called Jew named Meyer Lansky. Murder was a business and its leader was Mr. Lansky.

Is it not interesting that a field of endeavor that is viewed by "popular culture" as established and dominated by the Italians was and is in fact dominated by so-called Jews. The following is a list of just a few:

David Berman (1877-1942)

Otto "Abbadabba" Berman (1889-1935)

Mickey Cohen (1914-1976)

Monk Eastman (1873-1920)

Waxey Gordon (1886-1952)

Benjamin "Dopey Benny" Fein (1889-1977)

Abe Bernstein (1892-1968)

Moses Annenberg (1877-1942)

William Morris Bioff (1900-1955)

Ludwig "Tarzan" Fainberg (1958-Present)

Stanley Diamond

Moe Dalitz (1899-1989)

Louis "Lepke" Buchalter (1897-1944)

Gus Greenbaum (1894-1958)

Jake "Greasy Thumb" Guzik (1886-1956)

Harry Keywell

Isadore "Kid Cann" Blumenfeld (1900-1981)

Harry "Gyp the Blood" Horowits (1889-1914)

Charles Birger (1881-1928)

Nathan "Kid Dropper" Kaplan (1891-1923)

Abe Landau (1898-1935)

Meyer Lansky (1902-1983)

George Lewis

Red Levine

Hyman "Pittsburgh Hymie" Martin (1903-1987)

Samuel "Nails" Morton (1894-1923)

Vach "Cyclone Louie" Lewis

Harry Millman (1911-1937)

William Lipshitz

Jacob "Little Augie" Orgen (1894-1927)

Abe "Kid Twist" Reles (1906-1941)

Chris Rosenberg (1950-1979)

Frank "Lefty"Rosenthal

Joseph "Joe Greaser" Rosenzweig

Lou Rothkopf (1920-1950)

Harry "Doc Jasper" Sagansky (1897-1997)

Dutch Schultz (1902-1935)

Arnold "The Brain" Rothstein (1882-1928)

Benjamin "Bugsy" Siegel (1906-1947)

Jacob "Gurrah" Shapiro

Charles "King Solomon" Solomon

Max "Kid Twist Zwerbach

Jack Zuta (1888-1930)

Abner "Longy" Zwillman (1889-1959)

Jack "Big Jack" Zelig (1882-1912)

Albert "Tick Tock" Tannenbaum

Joseph "Doc" Stacher (1902-1977)

Johnny Spanish (1891-1919)

Harry "Pittsburgh Phil" Strauss (1909-1941)

The Socio-pathology of these so-called Jews does not square with the faith of Judaism, and runs counter to the biblical tenants set forth by Moses and the prophets. though I am not writing this book to argue religious beliefs, nor the morality that religions claim to promote, it is a shame that we fail to recognize the hypocrisy of those that claim to be God's chosen. It is evidently clear that the so-called Jews have used their media and entertainment control to misrepresent themselves and paint themselves as angels of light, while simultaneously using that same dominance to bank roll the faulty and negative images of black folk... Let's continue!

Though the Jewish Lower East Side of Manhattan, New York is roughly only one square mile, during the early 1900's, it was honeycombed with gangster controlled night clubs, pool halls, prostitution houses, hang outs, gambling houses, and a paradise for pimps and hoes.

These so-called Jews parlayed their thirst for money, power, and respect into a methodical crime syndicate that covered the entire United States of America. The Jewish

West Side of Chicago was known as the "bloody twentieth", in Cleveland it was the Jewish dominated Woodland section, and the notorious so-called Jewish "Purple Gang" dominated the underworld of Eastside Detroit.

Harry Stromberg, who later changed his name to Harry "Nig" Rosen, dominated Philadelphia and much of Atlantic City, Washington DC, and Baltimore in the selling of narcotics, prostitution, extortion, and labor racketeering. As a partner of Arnold Rothstein, both Harry "Nig" Rosen and another so-called Jew by the name of Waxey Gordon indulged heavenly in the bootleg industry as members of the BIG SEVEN. (Consider SEAGRAMS SEVEN)

The "Big Seven" also known as the "Combine", was a group of criminals that was comprised of mostly so-called Jewish and a relative few Italian crime bosses,... following the Volstead Act in 1919; which reinforced the prohibition laws of the United States, bombings, murders, and gang wars riddled the gang underworld. The Big Seven with the powerful support and influence of Meyer Lansky and Charles "Lucky" Luciano was formulated to help prevent and end the bloodshed. Along with Harry "Nig" Rosen and Waxey Gordon, the "Big Seven" was supported and comprised of the likes of some of the most notorious gangsters in American history such as: Italian Frank Costello, the Italian Joe Adonis, the so-called Jew Abner "Longy" Zwillman, and also the so-called Jew Enoch L. "Nucky" Johnson.

In 1929 the "Atlantic City Conference" was held; this "Gang Summit" was to dramatically impact the direction and power of the organized crime world. Out of this conference emerged the complete control of the gambling, prostitution, extortion, thefts, narcotics, and bootlegging of all of America. With the cities of New York, Philadelphia, Cleveland, Boston, Chicago, and Detroit as its main focal points, Meyer Lansky and his so-called Jewish crime partners controlled and completely influenced the early crime syndicate.

New York and Chicago were the bootleg capitals of America, and in both cities so-called Jews ran the show. By bringing alcohol through Canada, the gangsters developed power and bank rolls that fueled and supported politicians and their political movements. The following are a few of the gangsters that were purported to be present at the conference:

Atlantic City

Enoch "Nucky" Johnson - South Jersey/Atlantic City Boss/Host

New York/New Jersey

John "The Fox" Torrio - Former Chicago Torrio/Capone Gang Boss/New York Advisor

Salvatore "Charlie Lucky" Luciano - Masseria Family Underboss/New York

Frank "The Prime Minister" Costello - Masseria Family Lt./Capo/New York

Giuseppe "Joe Adonis" Doto - Masseria Family Lt./Capo/New York

Vito Genovese - Masseria Family Lt./Capo/New York

Quarico "Willie Moore" Moretti - Masseria family Lt./Capo/New Jersey

Vincent Mangano - D'Aquila/Mineo Family Lt./Capo/New York

Frank Scalise - D'Aquila Mineo Family Lt. /Capone York

Albert Anastasia - D'Aquila/Mineo Family Lt./Capo/New York

Gaetano "Tommy Brown" Lucchese - Riena Family Lt./Capo/New York

Meyer "The Brain" Lansky - Bugs & Meyer Mob Boss/New York

Benjamin "Bugsy" Siegel - Bugs & Meyer Mob Boss/New York

Louis Buchalter - Buchalter/Shapiro Gang Boss/New York

Jacob Shapiro - Buchalter/Shapiro Gang Boss/New York

Dutch Schultz - Schultz Gang Boss/New York

Abner Zwillman - North Jersey/Zwillman Gang Boss/New Jersey

Owney Madden - Irish Combine Boss/New York

Frank Erickson - former Rothstein Lt. /Costello Associate/New York Chicago

Alphonse "Scarface" Capone - South Side/Capone Gang Boss/Chicago

Frank "The Enforcer" Nitti - South Side/Capone Gang Lt./Capo/Chicago

Jake Guzik - South Side/Capone Gang Lt./Capo/Chicago

Frank "Frank Cline" Rio - South Side/Capone Gang Lt./Capo/Chicago

Frank McErlane - Saltis/McErlane Gang Boss/Capone Bodyguard/Chicago Philadelphia

Irving Wexler - Jewish Mob Boss/Philly

Max Hoff - Jewish Mob Boss/Philly

Harry Stromberg - Jewish Mob Boss/Philly

Irving Blitz - Jewish Mob Boss/Philly

Charles Schwartz - Jewish Mob Boss/Philly

Samuel Lazar- Jewish Mob Boss/Philly Cleveland

Morris Dalitz - Little Jewish Navy Boss/Cleveland

Louis Rothkopf - Little Jewish Navy Boss/Cleveland

Leo Berkowitz - Little Jewish Navy/Mayfield Road Mob Associate/Cleveland Detroit

William Joseph Bernstein - Purple Gang Boss/Detroit (a.k.a. "Bill Bugs")
Abraham Bernstein - Purple Gang Boss/Detroit   Kansas City:

Giovanni Lazia - Pendergast Machine/Balestrere Gang Lt./Capo/Kansas City a.k.a. Lazio) Massachusetts

Charles Solomon - Jewish Mob Boss/Boston Florida

Santo Trafficante Sr. - Senior Tampa Family Member/Tampa Louisiana

Sylvestro Corallo - Matranga/Giacona Family Lt./Capo/New Orleans

Gaetano Gagliano - Riena Family Underboss/ New York

Carlo Gambino - D'Aquila/Mineo Family Lt./Capo/New York

Frank "The Cheeseman" Cucchiara - Boston North End Gang/Buccola Family Lt

Frank "Bootsy" Morelli- Providence Morelli Gang Boss

       The names listed above are some of the most infamous gangsters that dominated the criminal underworld; while taking these names in, try to imagine the many, many more that are not listed. Each crime boss and lieutenants listed above had several dozens, and some even had hundreds of men underneath them. It was the minions that were placed under these infamous gangsters that were in many instances more brutal and violent than their more publicly prominent bosses.

       Because of today's corporate media and entertainment vessels, the so-called Jews have effectively painted themselves out of the historical crime picture. Today, when we think of a gangster we think of some Johnny come lately groups of bloods and crips, Black Gangster Disciples or Latin Kings; we think of the Hispanic group MS thirteen (13)… The state murdered Tookie Williams was far less a threat to the society, than the society of so-called Jewish thugs, gangsters and murderers!

Isn't it strange that when we picture the quintessential mafia types, we picture some burly, spaghetti eatin', Dago, Italian spitting out orders to some junior Rocky Balboa type peon? You see, because the so-called Jews control the various types of media outlets, they can successfully, and effectively re-write history and release information that will support their agenda and not thwart it. History bears witness to the fact that it was the so-called Jews that organized crime in America... the Irish did it, the Italians did it, the Polish did it, and some Cubans tried to do it... but it was and is the so-called Jews that mastered it.

Think about it:

When you think about Chicago Mobsters who do you think of... probably Al Capone, but did you know that his primary money man was the so-called Jew Jake Guzik. Al Capone was known in the media, but who you didn't see was the so-called Jews that actually controlled Chicago and its bootlegging, gambling, prostitution, racketeering, and extortion networks. These Chicago crime lords were Louis "Diamond Louie" Cowan, Hymie "the Loud Mouth" Levine, Sammy "The Greener" Jacobson, Maxie Eisen, and Murray "the Camel" Humphreys, among many others.

But it wasn't just Chicago and New York, it was all over

It was so-called Jews Moe Dalitz, Sam Tucker, Lou Rothkopf, Shondor Birns (Szandor Birnstein), Mervin Gold and Maxie Diamond... all from Cleveland. It was Isador "Kid Cann" Blumenfeld, Davie Berman, Chickie Berman, and Yiddie Bloom of Minneapolis. Missouri had Charlie Birger (Sachna Itzik Berger). All over the country were so-called Jews that elevated the crime world to one of extreme power and corporate influence.

So as the Crips and Bloods argue over street corners and colors, as they vie for an opportunity to control penny-annie crack houses that produce crack whores and crack babies; as they sag their pants and brag on their meaningless and foolish crimes... the true Original Gangsters controlled the entire criminal market... alcohol, drugs, prostitution, racketeering, gambling, extortion, and murder. While the so-called negro gangs claim corners, the so-called Jews control entire cities... Consider Las Vegas:

After Bugsy Siegel along with his so-called Jewish partner Meyer Lansky set up the influential Flamingo casino, the so-called Jews moved in and built the city up. Today many people believe and understand that Vegas was built and controlled by the MOB, but the mob they think of is the Italian Mob, but this is not true... check this out!

Jay Sarno and Nate Jacobson help to create **Caesars' Palace.**

Jay Sarno also created **Circus Circus**.

Moe Dalitz, Morris Klienman, and Sam Tucker with the **Desert Inn** and **Stardust**

Sidney Wyman, Al Gottesman, and Jake Gottlieb the **Dunes**

Gus Greenbaum, Moe Sedway and Charlie Resnick took over the **Flamingo** after the murder of so-called Jew Bugsy Siegel.
Ben Goffstein, Willie Alderman and David Berman the **Riviera**

Milton Prell with the establishment of the Sahara, he also transferred the **Tally-Ho** into the **Aladdin**.

Hyman Abrams, Carl Cohen, and Jack Entratter with the **Sands**

Ben Jaffe, Phil Kastel, and Jell Houssels the **Tropicana**

Although there was a relative few Italians that owned portions of the Casinos, by far it was and continues to be the so-called Jews that control the world of gambling, including but not limited to Las Vegas.

With all this information as a back drop, isn't it ironic to see the Media and entertainment worlds depict Blacks and Hispanics as the quintessential gangsters? The so-called gangsters we see on the evening news are small time in relation to the true gangsters that are organized and effectively control and dominate the vice and nefarious activities of the American public.

Crime in America is just another example of how Black people have been the scapegoat as the major contributors, this is not true, but it is what is in the news. Hopefully it will be shown and it has been shown throughout these pages that what is being presented within the media and entertainment world is not entirely accurate and is a conspired attempt to convey a message that supports an unyielding goal and agenda... let's move on.

Arnold Rothstein was born in 1882 in New York. His involvement in the world of gambling began at an early age. He lost interest in school when he was 16 and decided to drop out. He worked as a traveling salesman for awhile and then decided to hang out in pool halls. At age 20, he went to work for himself booking bets on horse races, baseball games, elections and prize fights. He also made loans which carried extermely high interest rates.

Rothstein received his nickname, "The Big Bankroll," because he always insisted on carrying a huge bankroll of $100 bills. He wanted to be able to immediately finance any deals he made. In 1909, he married an actress named Carolyn Greene. 1914 was the year that Rothstein moved into the business of bookmaking. He owned a discount house for wagering and this is where he made his fortune. Rothstein once stated that he was willing to bet on anything but the weather--the weather was the only thing he could not fix.

Rothstein's role in the 1919 World Series scandal was behind the scenes as a financial backer. His name, reputation and wealth were used to help influence the ballplayers. Rothstein was approached by two separate groups who wanted him to provide the funds to pay off the eight White Sox players. He chose to work with Joseph "Sport" Sullivan because he had a proven reputation in the gambling circle. Most believe that Rothstein placed as much as $270,000 in bets on the Cincinnati Reds to win the World Series that year.

Dutch Schultz had a long and varied criminal history. He was probably the most well known criminal of his time, and was once declared Public Enemy #1 by the FBI. Famous for his ruthlessness, violence and temper, he worked his way up the criminal ladder in the mean streets of the Bronx from an early age. Born in 1902, Schultz began with some petty thefts and assaults, and by the age of 17, had graduated to more serious crimes. He was convicted of robbery in 1919, and sent to a juvenile penitentiary. After a failed escape attempt, he was released after serving 15 months. Despite numerous indictments and arrests, he never again served time behind bars. Following his release, he quickly resumed his former occupation, and first began using the name "Dutch Schultz", appropriated from a legendary deceased New York gang member.

The Shaprio brothers (Meyer, **Irving** and Willie) ran a gang of Jewish mobsters that operated out of the Brownsville section of Brooklyn, New York. Their criminal activities centered around loansharking, slot machines, dice games, and extortion of shop keepers. The Shaprio brothers came into conflict with the other gangs in Brooklyn such as the Amberg brothers and the Reles gang. One by one the Shaprio brothers were murdered by the other gangs. Irving Shaprio was shot to death in the vestibule of the apartment building in which he lived at 691 Blake avenue, Brooklyn, on July 11, 1931. He was 27 years old.

As a youngster, **Abner "Longy" Zwillman** earned the gratitude of local Jewish peddlers because he and his gang, "The Happy Ramblers", defended them from assault by Irish thugs. Whenever the Irish came into the Jewish district to create trouble, a cry went up to "Ruff der Langer" (Yiddish for "Call the Tall One") and quick as a flash Zwillman and his pals would stop whatever they were doing and rush to help. As a result Longy had a reputation for helping Jews that stayed with him all his life.

Mickey Cohen was Ben "Bugsy" Siegel's shadow. Ben was tall, handsome, suave and welcome in the elite Hollywood circles. He mixed with the glitterati, courted royalty and bedded starlets while his shadow -- Mickey -- was picking their pockets, robbing their safes and breaking their bones.

Benjamin Hymen Siegel was a gangster, popularly thought to be a primary instigator of large-scale development of Las Vegas. He hated his nickname **Bugsy** and wouldn't allow anyone to call him that to his face.

As a teenager, Siegel befriended Meyer Lansky formed a small gang with him that expanded to gambling and car theft. Reputedly Siegel also worked as the gang's hitman who Lansky would sometimes hire out to other gang bosses. In 1926 Siegel was charged for rape but Lansky cohersed the victim not to testify.

By the 60's **Meyer Lansky's** gambling rackets had extended half-way across the globe, with departments all over South America , and even as far as Hong Kong. When in 1970 the federal government was planning to charge Lansky with tax evasion, he fled to Israel, where he lived in Tel Aviv. Israel revoked his visa under pressure from the US, however, and Lansky was made to stand trial. Reportedly he managed to escape conviction because his power stretched to the highest level of government. Eventually he settled in Miami, Florida, where his health declined and he finally died of a heat attack in 1983. At the time of his death, his fortune was estimated to be worth over $400 million.

Herbert Amberg, along with his brothers Louis "Pretty" and Joseph Amberg, they were the most feared gangsters in the Jewish neighborhoods of Brooklyn during the 1920s and 1930s. Hyman was arrested for the murder of a Brooklyn jeweler in 1926 and placed in the "Tombs" jail in Manhattan to await trial. On November 3, 1926, he and another prisoner (armed with guns) tried to escape from the jail. They got as far as the prison wall but were trapped by the guards. With all hope of escape lost they put their guns to their heads and shot themselves to death.

~~~

DRE'S SLAVE MASTER

"Crossbreeding a horse means taking a horse and breeding it with an ass and you get a dumb, backward, ass long-headed mule that is not reproductive nor productive by itself."

Before we go any further, let us focus on another so-called Jew and his plantation. Since we have said that Dr. Dre (Andrew Young) is the West Coast overseer or gatekeeper; to which slave master and plantation does he owe his allegiance? As Def Jam was utilized by certain powers to unleash some of the greatest HipHop talent of its era; Interscope Records, owned and operated by a powerful so-called Jew by the name of Jimmy Iovine. Jimmy is responsible for the continued success of so-called "Gangster Rap" and socially unconscious music.

Founded in 1990, and financially backed by Atlantic Records, Interscope has emerged as the premier record label of HipHop. Boasting the talents of Dr. Dre, The Game, 50 Cent, Eminem, and several others, Interscope has, under the umbrella of UMG (Universal Music Group) and its so-called Jewish bosses cornered the "gangster rap" world. In 1992 Interscope and Iovine financially backed and helped to create one of the most infamous record labels in music history, Death Row Records.

After the release of Dr. Dre's "The Chronic", which helped to introduce so-called gangster rapper Snoop Dogg to the HipHop world, Death Row and Jimmy Iovine hit pay-dirt. Snoop Dogg went on to release his solo debut, "Doggystyle", which quickly obtained multi-platinum success. Additional success was gained when, after his release from Prison, Tupac was signed by the infamous Suge Knight—making Jimmy Iovine's label the most successful and powerful in HipHop history.

What should be noted is the non-coincidental presence of the white so-called Jewish element. As Def Jam had its Rick Rubin and its Lyor Cohen; Ruthless Records had its Jerry Heller, is it not interesting that Death Row had its Jimmy Iovine? At what point do we realize that it is not an accident that all the major record camps or plantations have the presence of the so-called Jew.

Due to the controversy of the images portrayed by Death Row records, the distribution company of Death Row records, which was Time Warner, refused to distribute Death Row's *Dog Food* Album that was released by Snoop Dogg's group, the *Dogg Pound*. Originally scheduled for release in June of 1995, the decision of Time Warner not to release the album forced it to be pushed back, while Death Row and Interscope made an outside deal with Priority Records to distribute the album upon its release.

As the controversy surrounding Death Row and Interscope continued, Time Warner and their shareholders grew increasingly more nervous to the point of causing Time Warner to sale their entire stake in Interscope in the later part of 1995 to MCA Music Entertainment, which later became Universal Music Group (UMG).

Although Time Warner found it difficult to escape the social backlash of the Death Row image, it is apparent that MCA and Universal Music Group cared little about the controversy, and continued to market and produce a music and image that adds to the moral decadence that plagues the black community. This statement does not however, mitigate Time Warner's contribution to the growing level of filth and degeneracy found within today's music and entertainment. Let's examine Time Warner and a few more interesting facts and then return to Death Row.

Warner Communication was founded in 1972, and was the parent company for Warner Bros. Pictures and Warner Music Group during the 1970's and 1980's. Warner Communications also owned DC Comics and Mad which were major producers of comic books and magazines. In addition to the above, it was a majority stake holder in the **Garden National Bank**. From 1976 through 1984, Warner Communications made huge profits by owning Atari—the major video game system of that time.

Time Warner Inc. or Time Warner is a huge American media conglomerate with a major Internet, publishing, film, telecommunications and television divisions. This gigantic powerhouse corporation is headquartered in New York City, and as previously mentioned, finds its root in **Warner Communications**.

In 1970, Warner decided to expand under the guidance of a CEO by the name of Steve Ross, a so-called Jew that was born as Steven Jay Rechnitz in Brooklyn, New York. As the leader of Warner Communications, Steve Ross formed a joint venture with **American Express**, named **Warner-Amex Satellite Entertainment**. This formulated entertainment company held cable channels including MTV, Nickelodeon and Showtime. Warner bought out American Express's half in 1984, and sold the venture a year later to Viacom, which renamed it as MTV Networks.

In 1987 it was announced that **Time Inc.** and **Warner Communications** intended to merge. Prior to the merger, however, Warner decided to purchase **Lorimar-Telepictures;** this was done in 1989. The following year the merger between Time Inc. and Warner Communications was complete.

As a combined company, the official name was now **Time Warner** and this company acquired Ted Turner's *Turner Broadcasting System* in October 1996. By Purchasing *Turner Broadcasting*, Time Warner gained control over some major networks.

Consider the following:

TBS	Court TV
TNT	Cable News Network (CNN)
Cartoon Network	CNN Headline News
Turner Classic Movies (TCM)	CNN Pipeline
Cartoon Network Europe	CNN International
Boomerang	CNN en Espanol
TNT Europe	CNN Airport Network
TNT & Cartoon Network Latin America	CNN en Espanol Radio
TNT & Cartoon Network/Asia Pacific	CNN.com
Cartoon Network Japan	CNN Newsource
Adult Swim	CNN+
CNN Turk	

As the leading provider of the basic cable industry, TBS Inc. employs over 8,000 people worldwide.

In the year 2000, a so-called Jewish businessman named **Gerald M. Levin** brokered a merger between **AOL (America Online)** and Time Warner. Having spent most of his career with Time Inc. (later Time Warner), he started as the Programming Executive for **Home Box Office** (HBO), eventually becoming CEO of the corporation.

I mention the above details concerning Time Warner and its many holdings and business acquisitions to point to a certain trend within the media, entertainment and music world. As we continue, the ties that bind these corporations and their rulers will be seen clearly, and the impact that they are having on the global population will be identified for what it is.

As for Suge Knight and his *Death Row Records*, he was financially assisted in 1992 by the previously mentioned **Jimmy Iovine**. This so-called Jew, played the traditional "Jewish" role, in assisting the financially deficient so-called Negro entrepreneur pursue his business ambitions. **This trend is seen by anyone that desires to look at it and call it for what it is.**

Interscope Records is a record plantation that resides under the Time Warner Umbrella. They are controlled by so-called Jewish business men that financially back and institute entertainment and music trends. Consider the following... Time Warner, having helped create Death Row Records through the overseeing plantation of Interscope Records, created a heated public controversy concerning Death Row and their so-called gangster product. This product was systematically released to the public with the insatiable elements that accompany controversy. Though Time Warner sold Interscope to MCA, Time Warner also received millions from the deal. So... once again, Time Warner and the so-called Jewish slave masters benefited from the miserable social condition of black people.

Before we move forward, please stop and think about what I am not merely suggesting, but systematically offering proof of. I get no perverse form of pleasure by beating upon these so-called Jews. I simply desire to expose those rich and powerful hands that have traditionally and presently garnished vast amounts of wealth off the talent of black people. Regardless if it is HipHop or any other form of music; regardless if its athletics or various forms of entertainment, the undeniable fact is that we as black people have allowed foreigners the power to control and dominate our most prized resource—the God given talents that will assist us in the establishment and maintenance of a sovereign nation.

As we move forward, let's read what our brother Norman Kelly has to say about Tupac and Death Row:

> "The six major record firms have a colonial-like relationship with the black Rhythm Nation of America that produces hip hop and other forms of black music. Despite the names of a few big money makers - Suge Knight, Sean Combs, and Russell Simmons - or the lurid deaths of Tupac Shakur and Christopher Wallace (also known as Notorious B.I.G. and Biggie Smalls), rap, like most black music, is under the corporate control of whites and purchased mostly by white youths.
>
> No better example of how black artists are colonized by white recording companies - aided and abetted by blacks - than the case of Tupac Shakur. Originally on contract to Interscope, founded by Jimmy Iovine and Ted Fields, heir to the Marshall Fields fortune, Tupac was "handed over" to Death Row Record's Marion (Suge) Knight when the enfant terrible of rap was in a New York State penitentiary. While Death Row Records was the creation of Dr. Dre and Knight, it practically owned its existence to Interscope (and some say to a drug dealer named Michael "Harry-O" Harris). Desperate to get out of jail, Tupac signed an onerous agreement with Death Row that made David Kenner, Death Row's counsel, his counsel and manager, a direct and unmistakable conflict of interest. Tupac, according to Connie Bruck in her July 7 New Yorker article, "The Takedown of Tupac," was trying to extricate himself from Death Row but was killed. Now Interscope is willing to intercede on behalf of Tupac's estate, represented by his mother, Afeni, because it might come under scrutiny and its relationship with Death Row, currently under investigation by state and federal authorities for possible racketeering, exposed."

—Norman Kelly: The Political Economy of Black Music- 1999

THE LEVIATHANS

"This creation of multiplicity of phenomena of illusions entails the principle of crossbreeding the nigger and the horse as we stated above, the purpose of which is to create a diversified division of labor; thereby creating different levels of labor and different values of illusion at each connecting level of labor."

As we continue we begin to see that the so-called Jewish elements have maintained the established role of Media Controller. By creating major conglomerates, corporations such as Viacom, Universal Music Group (Vivendi), Walt Disney Group, and Time Warner have positioned themselves as the gate keepers of the various aspects of political, social, economic, educational, and religious programming that is presented to the world via the medium of news, music, and entertainment. One would think that this is done out of the quest for cash; this is not so, it is done for influence, control, and power.

Before we go any further, let's take a little time to examine the holdings of some of these major corporations. As we recognize the sure magnitude of the wealth, power, and influence of these conglomerations, I challenge the reader to think of any major media or entertainment company that IS NOT controlled by these particular leviathans and their so-called Jewish heads... can you do it?!

THE WALT DISNEY COMPANY

Film
Walt Disney Pictures
Touchstone Pictures
Hollywood Pictures
Miramax Films
Pixar
Broadcast Television
ABC Network
Owned and Operated Television Stations
WLS - Chicago
WJRT - Flint
KFSN - Fresno
KTRK - Houston
KABC - Los Angeles
WABC - New York City
WPVI - Philadelphia
WTVD - Raleigh - Durham
KGO - San Francisco
WTVG - Toledo
Cable Television
ESPN (80percent)
ESPN2 (80percent)
ESPN Classic (80percent)
ESPNU (80percent)
ESPNEWS (80percent)
ABC Family
Disney Channel
Toon Disney
SOAPnet
Lifetime Network (partial)
Lifetime Movie Network (partial)
Lifetime Real Women (partial)
A&E (partial)
A&E International (partial)
Jetix Europe (partial)
Jetix Latin America
The History Channel (partial)
Lifetime Real Women (partial)
Radio
ABC Radio
WDWD – Atlanta
WMVP – Chicago
WLS – Chicago
KESN – Dallas

KMKI – Dallas-Forth Worth
KRDY – San Antonio
WCOG – Greensboro, NC
WRDZ – Indianapolis
KABC – Los Angeles
KLOS – Los Angeles
KDIS – Los Angeles
KSPN – Los Angeles
KDIZ – Minneapolis - St. Paul
WKSH – Milwaukee, WI
WEVD – New York City
KDZR – Portland, OR
KWDZ – Salt Lake City
KIID – Sacramento
KMKY – Oakland
KQAM – Wichita
KKDZ – Seattle
WSDZ – St. Louis
WWMK – Cleveland
KMIK – Phoenix
KDDZ – Denver
WWMI – Tampa
KMIC – Houston
WMYM – Miami
WBWL – Jacksonville
WBYU – New Orleans
KDIS – Little Rock
WWJZ – Philadelphia
WWJZ – Philadelphia
WMKI – Boston
WDZK – Hartford
WDDZ – Providence
WDZY – Richmond
WGFY – Charlotte
WDYZ – Orlando
WMNE – West Palm Beach
WEAE – Pittsburgh
WDRD – Louisville
WDDY – Albany, NY
KPHN – Kansas City
WQUA – Mobile
WBML – Jacksonville
WFDF – Detroit
WFRO – Fremont, OH
WDMV – Damascus, MD

WHKT – Norfolk Radio Disney
ESPN Radio (syndicated programming)

Music
Walt Disney Records
Hollywood Records
Lyric Street Records

Publishing
Book Publishing Imprints
Hyperion
Miramax Books
ESPN Books
Theia
ABC Daytime Press
Hyperion eBooks
Hyperion East
Disney Publishing Worldwide
Cal Publishing Inc.
CrossGen
Hyperion Books for Children
Jump at the Sun
Volo
Michael di Caupa Books
Disney Global Children's Books
Disney Press
Disney Editions
Disney Libri
Global Retail
Global Continuity

Magazine
Automotive Industries
Biography (with GE and Hearst)
Discover
Disney Adventures
Disney Magazine
ECN News
ESPN Magazine (distributed by Hearst)
Family Fun
Institutional Investor
JCK

Kodin
Top Famille - French family magazine
US Weekly (50percent)
Video Business
Quality
Wondertime Magazine

Parks and Resorts
Walt Disney Imagineering
Disneyland Resort
Walt Disney World Resort
Tokyo Disney Resort
Disneyland Resort Paris
Hong Kong Disneyland
Disney Vacation Club
Disney Cruise Line

Other
Disney Theatrical Productions
Disney Live Family Entertainment
Disney on Ice
The Disney Store
Club Penguins
ESPN Zone
Disney Toys
Disney Apparel, Accessories and Footwear
Disney Food, Health and Beauty
Disney Home Furnishings and Decor
Disney Stationery
Disney Consumer Economics
The Baby Einstein Company
Muppets Holding Company
Disney Interactive Studios
Walt Disney Internet Group

Walt Disney holdings as of 7/30/08

Time Warner - Cable
HBO
Cinemax
HBO Video
HBO Independent Productions
HBO OnDemand International
HBO Mobile International
Adult Swim
Boomerang
CNN
CNN International
CNN en Espanol
CNN Headline News
CNN Headline News in Latin America
CNN Headline News in Asia Pacific
CNN Mobile
CNN+
CETV
CNN Newsource
CNN Pipeline
CNN To Go
CNN FN
CNN Radio
CNN Interactive
Court TV (with Liberty Media)
Time Warner Cable
Road Runner
New York 1 News (24 hour news channel devoted only to NYC)
Kablevision (53.75percent - cable television in Hungary)
In Demand
Metro Sports (Kansas City)
Time Warner Inc. - Film & TV Production/Distribution
Warner Brothers

TIME WARNER COMPANY
Warner Bros. Studios
Warner Bros. Television (production)
The WB Television Network
Warner Bros. Television Animation
Hanna - Barbera Cartoons
Telepictures Production
The CW Television Network
Kids' WB!
Castle Rock Entertainment
Warner Home Video
Warner Bros. Domestic Pay - TV
Warner Bros. Domestic Television Distribution
Warner Bros. International Television Distribution
The Warner Channel (Latin America, Asia - Pacific, Australia, Germ.)
Warner Bros. International Theaters (owns/operates multiplex theaters in over 12 countries)
Warner Bros. Online
Warner Bros. Interactive Entertainment
Warner Bros. Technical Operations
Warner Bros. Consumer Products
Warner Bros. Studio Facilities
Time Warner Inc. - Magazines
Time
Time Asia
Time Atlantic
Time Canada
Time Latin America
Time South Pacific
Time Money

Time For Kids
Fortune
Fortune Asia
Fortune Europe
FSB: Fortune Small Business
All You
Sports Illustrated
Sports Illustrated International
SI for Kids
Money
People
Who Weekly (Australian edition)
People en Espa☐ol
Teen People
Entertainment Weekly
In Style
Southern Living AT HOME
Southern Accents
Cooking Light
Cottage Living
This Old House
Sunset
Health
Hippocrates
Coastal Living
Real Simple
Wallpaper (U.K.)
Bride To Be
English Woman's Weekly
Practical Parenting
Who
In Style Australia
25 Beautiful Homes
4x4
Aeroplane Monthly
Amateur Gardening
Amateur Photographer
Angler's Mail

Beautiful Kitchens
Cage and Aviary Birds
Caravan Magazine
Chat
Chat - It's Fate
Classic Boat
Country Homes and Interiors
Country Life
Cycle Sport
Cycling Weekly
Decanter
European Boat Builder
Eventing
Family Circle
Guitar
Hair
Hi Fi News
Homes and Gardens
Horse
Horse and Hound
Ideal Style
In Style (U.K.)
International Boat Industry
Land Rover World
Livingetc
Loaded
Mountain Bike Rider
MiniWorld
Model Collector
Motor Boat and Yachting
Motor Boats Monthly
Motor Caravan Magazine
NME
Now
Nuts
Park Home & Holiday Caravan
Pick Me Up
Practical Boat Owner
Prediction
Racecar Engineering
Rugby World
Ships Monthly
Shoot Monthly
Soaplife
Sporting Gun
Stamp Magazine
SuperBike Magazine
The Field
The Railway Magazine
The Shooting Gazette
TV & Satellite Week
TV Easy
TVTimes
Uncut
VolksWorld
Web User
Wedding
What Digital Camera
What's on TV?
Woman
Woman & Home
Woman's Own
Woman's Weekly
Yachting World
Your Yacht
Ambientes
Audi Magazine
Balance
Chilango
EXP
Expansion
IDC
Life and Style
Manufactura
Obras
Quien
Vuelo
Yachts
In Style Mexico
Magazines listed under Warner Brother's label
DC Comics
Vertigo
Wildstorm
Mad Magazine
Online Services
CompuServe Interactive Services
AOL Instant Messenger
ADTECH
Advertising.com
AOL.com portal
Digital City
AOL Europe
GameDaily.com
Lightningcast
ICQ
The Knot, Inc. - wedding content (8 percent with QVC 36percent and Hummer WinbladFunds18percent)
MapQuest.com
Spinner.com
Relegence
TACODA
Third Screen Media
Truveo
Userplane
Weblogs, Inc.
Winamp
Xdrive
CNNStudentNews.com
NASCAR.com
PGA.com
Time Warner - Online/Other Publishing
Road Runner
Warner Publisher Services
Time Distribution Services
American Family Publishers (50percent)
Africana.com
Time Warner - Merchandise/Retail
Warner Bros. Consumer Products
Theme Parks
Warner Brothers Recreation Enterprises (owns/operates international theme parks)
Time Warner Inc. - Turner Entertainment
Entertainment Networks
TBS Superstation

Turner Network Television (TNT)
Turner South
Cartoon Network
Turner Classic Movies
Cartoon Network in Europe
Cartoon Network in Latin America
TNT & Cartoon Network in Asia/Pacific
TNT Latin America
TNT HD
TCM Asia Pacific
TCM Canada
TCM Europe
TCM Classic Hollywood in Latin America
Adult Swim
Boomerang
CETV
GameTap
TBS
Pogo
Toonami
TrueTV
Peachtree TV

Film Production
New Line Cinema
Fine Line Features
Picturehouse
Turner Original Productions

Sports
Atlanta Braves

Other Operations
Turner Learning
CNN Newsroom (daily news program for classrooms)
Turner Adventure Learning (electronic field trips for schools)
Turner Home Satellite
Turner Network Sales

Other
Netscape Communications
Netscape Netcenter portal
AOL MovieFone
IAmaze
Amazon.com (partial)
Quack.com
Streetmail (partial)
Switchboard (6percent)
Advantages
European Magazines Limited

Television
Fox Broadcasting Company
Fox Television Stations
WNYW - New York City
WWOR - New York City
KTTV - Los Angeles
KCOP - Los Angeles
WFLD - Chicago
WPWR - Chicago
KMSP - Minneapolis
WFTC - Minneapolis
WTXF - Philadelphia
WFXT - Boston
WTTG - Washington D.C.
WDCA - Washington D.C.
KDFW - Dallas
KDFI - Dallas
WJBK - Detroit
KUTP - Phoenix
KSAZ - Phoenix
WUTB - Baltimore
WRBW - Orlando
WOFL - Orlando
WOGX - Ocala
WAGA - Atlanta

NEWS CORPORATION
KRIV - Houston
KTXH - Houston
WTVT - Tampa
WHBQ - Memphis
KTBC - Austin
DBS & Cable
FOXTEL
BSkyB
Sky Italia
Fox News Channel
Fox Movie Channel
FX
FUEL
National Geographic Channel
SPEED Channel
Fox Sports Net
FSN New England (50percent)
FSN Ohio
FSN Florida
National Advertising Partners
Fox College Sports
Fox Soccer Channel

Time Warner Inc holdings as of 8/2/08

Stats, Inc.
Film
20th Century Fox Español
20th Century Fox Home Entertainment
20th Century Fox International
20th Century Fox Television
Fox Studios Australia
Fox Studios Baja
Fox Studios LA
20th Century Fox
Fox Searchlight Pictures
Fox Television Studios
Blue Sky Studios

Newspapers
United States
New York Post
The Wall St. Journal
Dow Jones
United Kingdom
News International
News of the World
The Sun

The Sunday Times
The Times
Times Literary Supplement
Australasia
Daily Telegraph
Fiji Times
Gold Coast Bulletin
Herald Sun
Newsphotos
Newspix
Newstext
NT News
Post-Courier
Sunday Herald Sun
Sunday Mail
Sunday Tasmanian
Sunday Territorian
Sunday Times
The Advertiser
The Australian
The Courier-Mail
The Mercury
The Sunday Telegraph
Weekly Times
Magazines
InsideOut
Donna hay
SmartSource
The Weekly Standard
Big League
ALPHA
Books
HarperMorrow Publishers
HarperMorrow
General Books Group
Amistad
Caedmon
Avon
Avon A

Avon Inspire
Avon Red
Collins
Collins Design
Ecco
Eos
Fourth Estate
Harper Mass Market
Harper Pakerbacks
HarperAudio
HarperBusiness
HarperCollins
Perennial
Perennial Modern Classics
HarperCollins e-Books
HarperLuxe
Rayo
William Morrow
William Morrow Cookbooks
Children's Books Group
Amistad
Greenwillow Books
Joanna Cotler Books
Eos
Laura Geringer Books
HarperAudio
HarperCollins Children's Books
HarperFestival
HarperTeen
Katherine Tegen Books
Julie Andrews Books
Rayo
Trophy
HarperCollins International
HarperCollins Canada
HarperCollins Australia
HarperCollins UK

HarperCollins India
HarperCollins New Zealand
Zondervan
Other
Los Angeles Kings (NHL, 40percent option)
Los Angeles Lakers (NBA, 9.8percent option)
Staples Center (40percent owned by Fox/Liberty)
News Interactive
Fox Sports Radio Network
Broadsystem
Classic FM
Festival Records
Fox Interactive
IGN Entertainment
Mushroom Records
MySpace.com
National Rugby League
NDS
News Outdoor
Scout Media
Rotten Tomatoes
AskMen
FoxSports.net
WhatIfSports
KSolo
Fox.com
AmericanIdol.com
Spring Widgets
News Digital Media
News.com.au
FoxSports.com.au
CARSguide.com.au
Careerone.com.au
Truelocal.com.au
News Corporation Holdings as of 08/07/08

**VIACOM, INC.
HEADQUARTERS**

Cable
MTV
MTV2

MtvU
AtomFilms
Addicting Games

Gamerailers
Harmonix
MTVN International

MTV TR3S
Neopets
Parents Connect
Quizilla
Rhapsody
Shockwave
VH1
VH1 Classic
VH1 Soul
Virtual Worlds
XFIRE

Nickelodeon
Nick Jr.
BET
BET J
Nick at Nite
TV Land
NOGGIN
VH1
Spike TV
CMT
Comedy Central

Film
Paramount Pictures
Paramount Home Entertainment
DreamWorks Studios
Paramount Vantage
MTV Films
Nickelodeon Movies
Home Entertainment

Viacom Holdings as of 07/31/08

Though the number of holdings of Viacom appears short compared to the above mentioned corporations, please do not misunderstand; Viacom along with its vertically integrated conglomerate's highly recognizable properties include the CBS network, MTV, Infinity broadcasting, Simon and Schuster, Blockbuster, and Paramount Pictures. This diverse portfolio makes Viacom one of the most powerful and profitable corporate giants on the planet.

VIVENDI S.A.

Television and Film
Canal+ Group Includes:
MultiThematiques
CineCinema,
Extreme Sports Channel
NBA+
Canal+ Sport
Canal+ Family
Canal+ Hi-Tech
Canal+ Decale
InfoSport
Tele
Planete
Seasons
Jimmy
Canal+ Chaine Mobile
CanalSat Mobile
Canal+ Mobile
CanalPlay
Canal+OnDemand
Optimum Releasing
Pilotime
STUDIOCANAL
Music

BMG Music Publishing
Universal Music Group labels include:
Island Def Jam Music Group
Interscope Geffen A&M Records
Lost Highway Records
MCA Nashville
Mercury Nashville
Mercury Records
Polydor
Universal Motown Records Group
Decca
Deutsche Grammophon and Philips
Verve Music Group
Impulse! Records
Video Games
Vivendi Universal Games labels include:
Blizzard Entertainment
Sierra Entertainment
Sierra Online
Vivendi Games Mobile

Telecommunications
SFR Cegetel Group
Maroc Telecom

Vivendi Corporate Holdings as of 07/31/08

The above corporate listings was gathered and supported by the research of Columbia Journalism Review.

"The relationship between black music and the "Big Six" is a post-modern form of colonialism. In classic colonialism (or neo-colonialism) products were produced in a "raw periphery" and sent back to the imperial "motherland" to be finished into commodities, sold in the metropolitan centers or back to the colonies, with the result being that the colony's economic growth was stunted because it was denied its ability to engage in manufacturing products for it own needs and for export. Blacks in the inner cities, if not as an aggregate, share some of the classic characteristics of a colony: lower per capita income; high birth rate; high infant mortality rate; a small or weak middle class; low rate of capital formation and domestic savings; economic dependence on external markets; labor as a major export; a tremendous demand for commodities produced by the colony but consumed by wealthier nations; most of the land and business are owned by foreigners. With rap, the inner cities have become the raw sites of "cultural production" and the music then sold to the suburbs, to white youths who claim they can "relate" to those of the urban bantustans. If there is indeed a struggle for the control of rap, it is merely a battle between black gnats, for the war for the control of black music had been won many years ago by corporate America, aided and abetted by black leadership that has never understood the cultural and economic significance of its own culture."

—**Norman Kelly: The Political Economy of Black Music- 1999**

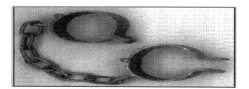

THE TENTACLES OF INFLUENCE II

"By the time a nigger boy reaches the age of sixteen, he is soundly broken in and ready for a long life of sound and efficient work and the reproduction of a unit of good labor force. Continually through the breaking of uncivilized savage niggers, by throwing the nigger female savage into a frozen psychological state of independence, by killing the protective male image, and by creating a submissive dependent mind of the nigger male slave, we have created an orbiting cycle that turns on its own axis forever, unless a phenomenon occurs and re-shifts the position of the male and female slaves."

An entire book could be written regarding the political and power plays made by corporate leviathans and their global ambitions. In the context of the HipHop slave and their slave masters we have to spend considerable time bringing to the reader's attention those that profit from the destructive behaviors glorified and exacerbated through today's HipHop, and the Uncle Tom rappers that act as their corporate lackeys. As we continue we will spend a little more time shedding light on those that benefit from the pervasive ignorance of the million dollar so-called Negroes that have sold their souls for the obtaining of trinkets and bobbles.

Although the public might be ignorant of the overall business practices of Corporate America and its power brokers; make no mistake about it, the public certainly feels the impact of corporate practices and their wicked and manipulative machinations. There is an unyielding tie that binds the web of power and its uniquely decisive cousin, deceit. Let's examine a few facts and use them to draw a certain conclusion.

The world of media is far from diverse in terms of programming, content, substance, and reliability. In terms of the controlled media—radio, television, newspapers, books, and movies it is monolithic in terms of ambitions, loyalty, and agenda. Although we may be conditioned to believe to the contrary, there is no variety, dissent, nor alternative facts or ideas presented to the public from which they formulate opinion, views, and political conclusions.

Analyze for yourself the impact of the following... If you or I had a particular idea, thought and agenda, even if it answers the entirety of today's problems and concerns; how would we get these ideas out to those that could bring about the desired conclusion? It would take access, influence, and a dedicated network of people and resources to fulfill a particular plan, desire, and goal. We could know thousands of people and have hundreds of friends, but if those friends lacked resources, money, power, loyalty and dedication, the numerical advantage of having friends is negated by impotence and a lack of a unified ideology, a strategic agenda and the availability of necessary resources.

What we are witnessing today is a clear product of a so-called Jewish and Zionist agenda. The public opinion regarding Israel, Zionism, and the so-called Jew himself is a direct result of the control demonstrated by those that participate in an idea or agenda that has been labeled as Zionism. The establishment of a so-called Jewish state bears directly on the United States government and their desire to establish total global control. The manipulation and control of the so-called Negro rapper is no different than the control and manipulation of any earthly natural resource. The Black man and woman, like all people of color are being lead to and fro by a wicked Sheppard that has desires to keep the global population subjugated to their plans, goals, ambitions, and ideologies. This particular manipulation stems from the presence of media, entertainment, and music **corporations that perpetuate ignorance and filth to keep the masses in a sleep like state in** terms of the realization of the truth.

The masses of the people, both black and white are being given a single one sided presentation of the world and its politics and are kept blind, deaf, and dumb to the vital aspects of strategic power implantations and the ultimate global agenda. Those that posses a certain idea, goal, and agenda, also have the power, resources, wealth, and strategic plan to bring forth their desire. Because their plan and agenda is built on the ignorance of the masses, truth is seen by these wicked manipulators as the ultimate enemy. Because of this reality, anyone that speaks the truth must be ridiculed and labeled as something other than what he or she is. A slander campaign is instituted to discredit any and all that dare to speak the truth and share relevant information.

Although so-called Jews make up only about three percent of the US population, they wield immense power and influence—vastly more than any other ethnic or religious group. This reality is seen as a fact, but the fact is translated by those in power as anti-Semitic rhetoric, you are the judge.

As a so-called Jewish author and political science professor, Benjamin Ginsberg, has pointed out: *"Since the 1960s, Jews have come to wield considerable influence in American economic, cultural, intellectual and political life. Jews played a central role in American finance during the 1980s and they were among the chief beneficiaries of that decade's corporate mergers and reorganizations."* In today's United States of America only 3 percent of its citizens are so-called Jews; yet, almost 50 percent of the total billionaires are so-called Jews.

Examine the facts:

Walt Disney Company, the largest media conglomerate in the United States has as its CEO and Chairman a so-called Jewish man by the name of Michael Eisner. The Disney Company controls and owns *Walt Disney Television, Touchtone Television, Buena Vista Television*, and it controls its own cable network with over 14 million subscribers. In addition, Michael Eisner and Disney control two video production companies. The television division of Disney; their feature film portion *Walt Disney Picture Group*, is headed by a so-called Jew by the name of Joe Roth. Walt Disney Group controls *Touchstone Pictures, Hollywood Pictures, and Caravan Pictures*. Disney also owns *Miramax Films* which is run by the Weinstein Brothers, also so-called Jews.

We have already briefly touched *Time Warner*, but like previously stated, chairman of the board and CEO, Gerald M. Levin is a so-called Jew. Before selling at the time the world's largest record company with over fifty labels, Time Warner owned and controlled *Warner Brothers Records* which was headed by a so-called Jew by the name of Danny Goldberg. The president of *WarnerVision*, the Warner Music's Video Production Unit is also a so-called Jew, his name is Stuart Hersh.

Now, as one of the major conglomerates, Time Warner not only has a considerable amount of control of the cable and Music industry, but is heavily involved in the production of feature films. Under the company name of *Warner Brothers Studios*, Time Warner is an important player in the film world.

Time Warner's publishing division (Editor-in-chief Norman Pearlstine, a so-called Jew) is the largest magazine publisher in the country (*Time, Sports Illustrated, People, Fortune*).

Viacom is yet another monster conglomerate that is controlled by the so-called Jews. *CBS Corporation,* which is the former Viacom, is a power player of immense proportions. In 2006, the *CBS Corporation* split into two separate corporations. The former *Viacom* took on the name CBS Corporation after Chairman and Chief Executive Officer Sumner Redstone (born Sumner Murray Rothstein) decided to create two separate publicly traded companies. The former Viacom, *which controls CBS, UPN, WB, CBS Radio, Simon & Schuster, Viacom Outdoor, and Showtime*, is presently known as *CBS Corporation.*

Although the former Viacom was split, the new and improved Viacom is much more powerful. Generating well over 10 billion dollars a year, Sumner Redstone controls both CBS Corporation and Viacom. Viacom is an American Media Conglomerate that controls *MTV Networks* and all of their channels: *BET, Video Gaming, Sega of America, Paramount Pictures, Dream Works*, and a host of other assets.

The former Sumner Murray Rothstein, now known as Sumner Redstone, is the son of Michael and Belle Rothstein a so-called American Jewish family that decided to change their name from Rothstein to Redstone in 1940. His father Michael Rothstein was the owner of the **Northeast Theater Corporation**. Later, after serving in World War II decoding Japanese messages for the United States Army, Redstone worked in Washington D.C. and attended Georgetown University Law School before transferring to Harvard Law School where he received his degree. After working for the U.S. Department of Justice, Redstone decided to join his father's theater chain management operation which is known as National Amusements.

National Amusements is a chain of movie theaters spanning around 1,300 screens. Today it owns controlling interest in Viacom and CBS Corporation. It also holds 70 percent of video-game maker Midway Games, and Showcase Cinemas which is located in the United Kingdom and Argentina. Sumner Redstone and his family owns National Amusements; National Amusements have controlling interest in Viacom and the CBS Corporation. This control is in the hands of a family that chose to abandon the identifying marks of the so-called Jewish name Rothstein in preference of the more traditional American identifier of Redstone. We should understand that many so-called Jews choose to do the same thing. Although there are many power brokers that have abandoned their identifying surnames, their ideas, ways and actions make clear their allegiances and their overall belief systems and agendas... let's continue.

Having controlling interest in both companies, and serving as chairmen of both companies, Mr. Redstone has extraordinary levels of power and influence. Viacom itself produces and distributes television programs for the three major networks, and owns 12 television stations and 12 radio stations.
Viacom also has a publishing arm within the corporation. Its publishing division includes Prentice Hall, Simon Schuster, and Pocket Books. In 1994, Viacom bought Blockbuster movie rental store for 8.4 billion dollars. In 1999, Viacom spun the company off as a separate company of Viacom where it continues to dominate the rental movie market by controlling over 4,000 stores.

Viacom, CBS Corporation, Time Warner, and **Disney** cannot be overstated in terms of media and entertainment control; these corporations have businesses under them that completely dominate their genres and fields of interest. It would seem that we are over emphasizing the role of the mega conglomerates and their so-called Jewish masters, but we are in fact merely scratching the surface as it relates to the overall message and subject of this book. I would strongly suggest the reader institute a thorough investigation of the claims of this writing and find out for his or her self the overall evidence that supports the entire premise of this writing. This book will hopefully motivate the said reader to do it quickly in order to help impact the awareness level of those who have yet to see the light of this information and its overall relevance to our day to day lives.

> "The most effective component of Jewish connection is probably that of media control. It is well known that American public opinion molders have long been largely influenced by a handful of powerful newspapers, including the New York Times, the Washington Post, and the St. Louis Post-Dispatch, owned respectively by the Sulzbergers, Meyers, and the Pulitzers, (all Jewish families)."

—Alfred Lilienthat, The Zionist Connection II, 1978, pp.218-219

RUPERT MURDOCH—CORPORATE NEWS

"Pay little attention to the generation of original breaking, but
CONCENTRATE ON FUTURE GENERATION.*"*

K eith Rupert Murdoch is an Australian born, Scottish lineage, American News giant. Though some claim that he also has Jewish roots, this has yet to be proven. Regardless if he is a so-called Jew or not, he has major affiliations with those that consider themselves as Jews, and he shares the same fundamental elements of those that desire to maintain the established control of the global media and entertainment world.

Murdoch is a Naturalized American citizen, based in New York; Rupert has become one of the most powerful global media executives on the entire planet. Having a controlling interest of the companies that he runs, his influence is tremendous. His climb to dominance began in his native country of Australia by his owning and control of newspapers, television stations and magazines. He later expanded into British and American Media. Murdoch is incredibly successful in the satellite television and movie industry.

As the owner of over 175 newspapers, and Fox News Channel, Rupert Murdoch is in a position to control what and how the news and information will be relayed to the public. Rupert Murdoch has been openly accused by detractors for his blatant politics in terms of news coverage and support of particular politicians and policies that bear on his personal politics and business well being. Though Fox News claims to be "fair and balanced" there is clear evidence to the contrary.
The Fox News Channel's and their "fair and balanced news" is filtered into over 85 million households in the United States, and millions more worldwide via cable and satellite. Like most of the so-called news information, the *Fox Channels* news reports generate from within the borders of New York City.

Mr. Murdoch has claimed that he created Fox News Channel in order to confront what he believed was a growing liberalism within the news offices of America. This particular concern shows why the Fox News Channel is known for its so-called conservative slant. The *"fair and balanced"* claim could really be seen as giving the conservatives an opportunity to voice their politics and agenda without the alternative view of liberalism having its presence felt. Murdoch himself is an open neo-conservative that strongly supports Bush and his politics. This is completely contrary to what the news should be… why should information be spun or presented in a way that is political or marked by a personal view point or opinion? Editorials are one thing; news coverage should be non-biased and based on the presentation of facts. Rupert Murdoch, like all of his friends in high places, have an agenda and they use their resources and power to further the cause of global dominion and the misrepresentation of the facts.

Though Murdoch himself may or may not have so-called Jewish roots, consider the following: Rupert Murdoch's right hand man is a so-called Jewish man by the name of Peter Chernin. Though some argue over Rupert Murdoch and his so-called Jewish roots, Peter Chernin born May 29, 1951 in Harrison, New York is undeniably what is referred to today as a Jew. Peter is the President and Chief Operating Officer of News Corporation, and is the Chairman and CEO of the Fox Group. Known to many as one of the most powerful and influential executives in the world, before going to Fox he was the COO (Chief Operations officer) of Lorimar Films.

If we take Disney, Fox, Time Warner, Universal, and Viacom, we will clearly see that the overwhelming reality is that only a few mega-conglomerates make up the totality of the media and entertainment world. The facts are what they are, and whether intellectual cowards refuse to acknowledge them or not, the world is being shaped by those that have a particular agenda, and the social, economical, and political resources to bring it into fruition.

James Fallows of the Atlantic Monthly points out that most of **Murdoch's** actions "are consistent with the use of political influence for corporate advantage." In other words, he uses his publications to advance a political agenda that will make him money. The New York Times reports that in 2001, for example, The Sun, Britain's most widely read newspaper, followed Murdoch's lead in dropping its traditional conservative affiliation to endorse Tony Blair, the New Labor candidate. News Corp.'s other British papers, The Times of London, The Sunday Times and the tabloid News of the World, all concurred. The papers account for about 35% of the newspaper market in Britain. Blair backed "a communications bill in the British Parliament that would loosen restrictions on foreign media ownership and allow a major newspaper publisher to own a broadcast television station as well a provision its critics call the 'Murdoch clause' because it seems to apply mainly to News Corp." [Atlantic Monthly, 9/03; New York Times, 4/9/03]

~ ~ ~

THE SCRIBES

"both the horse and the nigger must be broken; that is breaking them from one form of mental life to another. KEEP THE BODY, TAKE THE MIND!"

Lets for a moment consider the print media. In addition to the massive media conglomerates that control cable and satellite news and information—examine the following: After television news, daily newspapers are the most influential information medium in America. Over sixty million newspapers are sold and presumed read each and every day. There are over 1,500 different publications, and though the numbers might cause one to conclude that it would be impossible for anyone or group to distort or control the news, this is far from the truth.

In the past most cities and towns possessed their own independent newspapers. Published by local people with close ties to their community and a vested interest in the news awareness of their consumers, these local entities acted as safeguards to news and information. But unfortunately, today's so-called local newspapers are owned and controlled by a relatively small number of corporate giants that are controlled by special interest executives that work and live hundreds or even thousands of miles away.

Only around 25 percent of the country's 1,500 papers are independently owned; the rest belong to multi-newspaper chains. Only 100 of the total number have circulations of more than 100,000. Only a handful is large enough to maintain independent reporting staffs outside their own communities; the rest must depend on these powerful few for all of their national and international news.

Throughout America, only 50 cities have more than one newspaper, and competition is huge even among them, as between morning and afternoon editions under the same ownership. For example, Huntsville, Alabama, morning News and afternoon Times; the Birmingham, Alabama, morning Post Herald afternoon News; the Mobile, Alabama, morning Register and afternoon Press; the Springfield, Massachusetts, morning Union, afternoon News, and Sunday-only Republican; the Syracuse, New York, morning Post-Standard and afternoon Herald-Journal—all owned by the so-called Jewish Newhouse brothers through their holding company, **Advance Publications**.

This information may be brushed over as merely coincidental and inconsequential; however, if you take the entirety of the information and facts offered within this writing, you can only conclude that those that consider themselves as Jews in today's society illustrate an insatiable appetite to control all the organs of opinion and media in a global context. The HipHop nation has been placed within the grips of these diabolical masters in a way that lends to the global agenda of those whom consider themselves Jews, and deteriorates the moral fiber of those who do not.

The Newhouse's own 26 daily newspapers, including several large and important ones. Of these there are the Newark Star-Ledger, the Cleveland Plain Dealer, and the New Orleans Times-Picayune. In addition, to these newspapers, they own the mega book publishing conglomerate, Random House and all its subsidiaries. **Newhouse Broadcasting** includes 12 television broadcasting stations and 87 cable-TV systems including some of the country's largest cable networks; the Sunday supplement Parade, with a circulation of more than 22 million copies per week; some two dozen major magazines, including the New Yorker, Vogue, Mademoiselle, Glamour, Vanity Fair, Bride's, Gentlemen's Quarterly, Self, House & Garden, and all the other magazines of the wholly owned Conde Nast group. This particular media empire was founded by the so-called Jew, the late Samuel Newhouse, an immigrant from Russia.

It is vital that we understand that newspapers, like other forms of media including television, do not make their profits from individual subscribers. It is advertising revenue that largely pays the editor's salary and yields the owners profit. Whenever the large corporate advertisers in a particular city choose to favor one newspaper over another with their business, the perferred newspaper will flourish while its competitor dies.

When we understand this fact, we begin to see the overwhelming influence exercised by those that have corporate power and wealth. These corporations can control and restrict the freedom of so-called independent news sources by merely the placement of advertising dollars. This is the sad result of the huge amounts of cash that these corporate leviathans control.

These major corporations have become a dominate economic force, and with the disproportionate rise of the so-called Jewish merchants and the steady rise of American newspapers in so-called Jewish hands, it is easy to see that just as entertainment and music, the news itself is in the hands of a certain few. These few have the financial power and influence to absolutely crush those aspiring media agents that refuse to "tow" the proverbial line, a line that is designed to maximize so-called Jewish control.

It should further be understood, that although there are certain newspapers that are not actually under ownership of the so-called Jewish power force, these newspapers are so thoroughly dependent upon so-called Jewish advertising revenue that their editorial and news reporting policies are largely constrained by so-called Jewish likes and dislikes.

As we close this particular segment, let's wrap it up with the following:

America's three most prestigious and influential newspapers are the **New York Times**, the **Wall Street Journal**, and the **Washington Post**. The publisher of the **New York Times** is Arthur Ochs Sulzberger Jr., the publisher of the **Wall Street Journal** is the Rhodes Scholar L. Gordon Crovitz, and the Chairman and CEO of the **Washington Post** is Donald Edward Graham, all of which are so-called Jews.

The Sulzberger family also owns, through the New York Times Co., 33 other newspapers, including the Boston Globe, twelve magazines, including McCall's and Family

Circle with well over 5 million in circulation for each; seven radio and TV broadcasting stations; a cable TV system; and three book publishing companies. The New York Times News Service transmits news stories, features, and photographs from the New York Times by wire to over 5 hundred other newspapers, news agencies, and magazines.

Like the New York Times, the Washington Post exercises huge doses of power and influence. With stakes in television, educational programming, and magazines—including the nations number two largest, Newsweek; the Washington Post helps dominate America's political capitals.

The Wall Street Journal is America's financial newspaper and like both the Times and the Post, it completely dominates its market. It sells 1.8 million copies each weekday; it is the nation's second largest-circulating daily newspaper, behind only the US Today.

Most of New York's other major newspapers are in no better hands than the New York Times and the Wall Street Journal. In January 1993, the New York Daily News was bought from the estate of the late so-called Jewish media mogul Robert Maxwell (born Ludvik Hoch) by so-called Jewish real-estate developer Mortimer B. Zukerman. The Village Voice is the personal property of Leonard Stern, the billionaire so-called Jewish owner of the Hartz Mountain pet supply firm.

At this moment we should be able to see that a population that is considered a minority within the borders of the United States of America actually has huge amounts of power and influence. None of these facts are exaggerated or manipulated in order to support the premise of this book. These facts are what they are, and the consequences of these facts can be argued—but I believe they are clear as well.

Adolph Simon Ochs, the son of Jewish emigrants, began as 'printers devil" when he was fourteen. By the time he was twenty, he had founded one Chattanooga newspaper and purchased control of a second. He combined them turning The Chattanooga Times into one of the South's best newspapers.

He also created a family succession as strong as the paper itself. In 1935, Arthur Hays Sulzberger succeeded his father-in-law, Ochs, and was, in turn, briefly succeeded briefly by his son-in-law, Orvil Dreyfus. Dreyfus died after only a month to be replaced by 37 year old Arthur Ochs Sulzberger, a grandson of Adolph Simon Ochs. Sulzberger remained in charge until 1992 when his forty year old son, **Arthur Sulzberger, Jr.**, took over. Thirteen years later, Sulzberger, Jr. remains Publisher of what most people consider, America's 'Newspaper of Record", the New York Times.

~~~

Misery's Profit

"Now the breaking process is the same for both the horse and the nigger, only slightly varying in degrees. But, as we said before, there is an art in long range economic planning."

Within the context of the power and influence of those that posses real wealth, it is a shame that many rappers, get paid millions of dollars, and receive trinkets and bobbles to put words and syllables together that spell out death and destruction for their communities. Rappers from 50 Cent to Jay Z, Snoop to Young Jeezy have done very little to show that they thoroughly understand the game in which they find themselves involved. Being young black men from the urban streets of America, I wonder if they really understand that they are among the targeted class of people in terms of global annihilation. I reflect on the lyrics they are paid to write and recite; lyrics that very often tell of real situations and conditions that black people find themselves in. This reality shows that so-called Negro rappers and their record plantations are profiting from the misery of the black community.

Record plantations such as Priority and Interscope grow rich by the marketing savvy of individuals who push so-called gangster rap down the throats of the American and global public. Companies offer bribes in the form of cash and gifts to radio executives and personalities to play the filth that is presently bombarding the airwaves.

For a moment lets return to Mr. Lyor Cohen(of Def JAM fame) a so-called Jewish business man/gangster who is known for conducting business in a very aggressive manner, including stealing artist and manipulating circumstances that compel artists to make decisions that favor him and his business associates.

In 2003 a so-called Jewish man named **Steve Gottlieb**; the founder and president of **TVT** (Tee Vee Toons) records, a so-called independent record plantation founded out of a New York City apartment, won a landmark decision in a copyright infringement and breach-of-contract lawsuit against Island/Def Jam and Lyor Cohen. The court awarded him 132 million dollars in punitive and compensatory damages of which half was designated as Mr. Cohen's personal responsibility.

This particular lawsuit was a battle over the ownership of HipHop slaves Irving (Irv Gotti) Lorenzo and Jeffery (Ja Rule) Atkins and some pre "Murder Inc." recordings. According to court testimony, in 1994 Steve Gottlieb signed Irving Lorenzo, then known as "DJ Irv" as a producer and talent scout for his label, TVT. DJ Irv quickly brought a three man group on board by the name of Cash Money Click; one of the three men was the rapper Ja Rule.

It is said that DJ Irv's circle of Queens friends included a big time drug dealer by the name of Kenneth "SUPREME" McGriff who was sent to prison for what authorities called a "murderous crack dealing operation". Authorities claimed that "Supreme" was making over 200 thousand dollars a day in dealing crack cocaine throughout the east coast of the United States.

After a member of "Cash Money Click" was jailed, their album was scrapped and Irving Lorenzo who decided to re-name himself "Irv Gotti", after the late Italian mafia boss, left the so-called Jewish slave master Steve Gottlieb for the more powerful slave master Lyor Cohen of Def Jam... Ja Rule went with him; this was in 1996. One year later, according to court papers, "Supreme" provided Irv Gotti with the seed money that allowed him to "partner up" with Lyor Cohen to create "Murder Inc.". YES... these so-called Negroes and their so-called Jewish slave master named this record label after the NOTORIOUS killing syndicate that was ran by the so-called Jew Meyer Lansky—MURDER INC. In an affidavit provided to the courts an informant suggests that "Gotti" is the public face of Murder Inc., but McGriff is the true owner of the company.

As Irving Lorenzo produced the tracks and Jeffery Atkins provided the lyrics, Murder Inc. and Ja Rule went on to sell over 10 million copies of their first three albums. This prompted Steve Gottlieb to release old "Cash Money Click" material, as well as, never before publicly heard recordings. Since Ja Rule was under ownership to the Island/Def Jam plantation, Steve Gottlieb initiated talks with his so-called Jewish brethren Lyor Cohen to secure permission to use the rapping slave. After a year of trying to work a deal over the slave Ja Rule, the two slave masters could not come to an agreement, forcing the lawsuit.

The purpose of this writing is not to support or suggest the idea that "Supreme" McGriff is the true owner of Murder Inc., nor to even portray that McGriff is a "murderous drug dealer". The point of this writing is to show how white men, in fact, white so-called Jewish men among others, are securing huge amounts of wealth at the expense of black lives and the manipulation of ignorant rappers. It should be pointed out that it is the elements of Murder Inc. and the suggested role of "Supreme" McGriff that has fueled a beef between two young black men, 50 Cent and Ja Rule. This beef has created a murderous potential between not only these two individuals, but the camps that depend on these two to eat. THINK! In one corner you have Ja rule and his slave master Lyor Cohen; and in the other you have the slave 50 cent and his master Jimmy Iovine. MORE **BEEF EQUALS MORE CASH!!**

While beefs or feuds threaten the lives of young black men, wealthy white folks wax rich within the walls of courtrooms arguing over their slaves and the control of music that they did not create nor produce. It should be noted that **Steve Gottlieb** was the first founder and president of a major record plantation to settle a courtroom deal between "Napster" and the downloading of music on the internet. He is not only the entrepreneurial mind and visionary force behind TVT Records, the largest independently owned record label in the United States and a pioneer in digital music delivery; he is the contracted owner of Lil Jon & The Eastside Boyz, The Ying Yang Twins, and Scotch Storch among others.

Gottlieb, who founded TVT Records at the age of 28, chose not to use his law degrees on Wall Street, but instead chose to use it to pencil contracts that would render millions of dollars to his bank account from the sale of music that is created and produced by his rapping slaves. His talent is not writing lyrics, making beats, or rapping into a microphone; Gottlieb's talent is the understanding of an American business and law structure that can be manipulated and exploited in a way that can render huge doses of cash into the hands of those who understand the base dynamics of the transfer of wealth.

We should understand that the race is not for the cash, the race is for the limited resources of the world. Those raw material resources such as oil, uranium, coal, and iron are all found within the earth, and are all valuable to the many nations of the earth for their maintenance and development. Since these resources are found within the earth, and these resources are absolutely necessary and conducive for the productive survival of a nation, then those that can control the various pockets of resources on the earth can control and manipulate the various nations of the earth.

Initially, as nations were being sought and established based on race and ethnicity, land was desired to be the base or geographical foundation of the earth. This land had to provide the base needs for the nation and the people that existed within that nation. Since the base needs of a people differ based on the developmental stage of that people, initially the primary concerns for a nation was food, clothing, and shelter. The most desirous land masses were those that provided those three things. For obvious reasons, the land in close proximity to water was the most valuable.

Because the most desirous land masses were in fact limited, wars broke out for the control and occupation of those particular land masses. These wars were usually between white people over the control of traditionally black lands. Because these black people were not accustomed to fighting over neither land, nor the resources that were viewed by them as plentiful; these people were not equipped, physically, mentally, or spiritually to deal with these land deprived white folks.

Regardless if we choose to accept it or not, the unyielding truth about white people is that they have historically and traditionally been a people that seek out that which is deemed necessary for white survival. This base law of self-preservation finds a logical conclusion in the total destruction of any one or group, anything or things, which threaten the future and survival of those with white skin. Religion, politics, economics, education, and social behavior have all been engineered out of a mindset of not only white survival, but because of fear of potential threat, white dominance. The totality of this worldly structure and social context is seen as *White Supremacy*.

As the nations and its people began to develop and become more technical within their approach to life, the national needs of the people evolved and changed. It was no longer just food, clothing, and shelter that were base necessities, there developed a real need for oil, coal, uranium, and many more of the resources that were found in the land. Many of these resources were used to develop weapons that are to be used in the defense and theft of these limited resources.

Since these resources are found within land, and these lands are occupied by people (again mostly black people), these lands have to be stripped of its resources under a legal pretense that is crafted by individuals that are not concerned with black people or people of color, but by those that were and are primarily concerned with the preservation of their own resources. These laws are intended to give off the allusion of justice and fairness, but these laws are subject to interpretation, and subject to change if a powerful nation such as America or Great Britain feels that there is a threat to their survival. Again this survival is based on the developmental needs of a people that have multiplied their needs based on their consumption and greed.

The needs of an American white woman, is far different than the needs of a Sudanese black woman. The American white woman may "need" flour, water, and sugar to bake an extravagant birthday cake to go with the new BMW that she has bought for her "lovely" sixteen year old daughter. However, the Sudanese woman may need flour, water, and sugar to produce a flour meal that will have to feed four children, a husband and herself. The need of the flour, water, and sugar is the same, but the application differs, therefore the need itself.

By definition, the so-called developed countries have greater "needs", than those of lesser development. However, these needs stem from the evolutionarily developed characteristics of comfort and happiness. In the pursuit of comfort, satisfaction and happiness, so-called developed nations have put the earth under a severe strain in relation to its resources. Big trucks, big plates, and big egos, all have pulled on the earthy resources; and white folk have developed a plan to secure the remaining world resources through the implementation of a global politic and economy.

We must recognize and accept that this is not at all new; white people have desired to control the world and its known resources since they first emerged from the caves of Europe. Why must this be seen as racism? Why must black people reject the truth concerning their slave masters and their children? The desire of white people remains the same since the imperialistic days of the crusades, slavery, and the murder of Indians. The only thing that has changed or evolved is *the means to an end.*

The result of the very real occurrence of the Crusades, Slavery, and Murder of the Indians, has brought us to this moment in time. There is no need at this moment in time for the reoccurrence of those atrocities, the damage has been done from the perspective of the victim, and the reward was reaped from the perspective of the victimizer. With the present day spirit of apology and apathy offered by the political and social scientist of the ruling class in regards to past atrocities and historical blemishes, black folk have been dumb-downed, and made blind to today's more scientifically evolved weapons of white rule and dominance.

The HipHop Nation has been used like a million dollar whore to sale the American Dream to the global population. A thoroughly destroyed group of so-called ex-slaves have been given countless amounts of money to act like gangsters, talk like clowns, and think like uncle toms. Cash has not given them power, cash has only allowed them to purchase things, and to live the life of a house nigga slave that flosses on the other slaves with what the slave master has allowed them to have.

From Iron Chains to Gold Chains

"Crossbreeding niggers mean taking so many drops of good white blood and putting them into as many nigger women as possible, varying the drops by the various tone that you want, and then letting them breed with each other until another circle of color appears as you desire."

I can already here the critics of truth cry the cry of racism as it pertains to the contents of these pages. This cry doesn't matter a damn in the total scheme of what is happening throughout the world and global politics. Clear lines have been drawn by those that have the power to draw them. Those that have drawn them try to deemphasize the importance of those lines and minimize their existence so that those who stand on the opposing side of those lines don't get a clue of their global position until it is too late. The HipHop Nation is comprised of Negro rappers that have no clue of the lines that have been drawn for them. They continue to rap the rap of an ignorant tool that has been, and continues to be used to sale bullshit to the global population.

Today's rapper is one that is a made up billboard or poster boy and girl of the benevolent white man. Not that the benevolent white boy is at all benevolent, but the appearance of such is given throughout media and entertainment by the way Negro rappers flash big cash, and an extravagant lifestyle. These Negroes have fallen in love with the lifestyles of the Rich and Famous, seemingly unaware that they are getting pimped by the wealthy and powerful.

During the advent of slavery and the murder of several million Africans, iron chains were used to shackle the African slave to each other and to objects in order to restrict their movement. Because the African had the essence of freedom running through their veins, the white slave master knew that they had to prevent freedom's expression from being manifested by chaining them down. From the year 1555 through 1619, sixty-four years was spent totally erasing the minds of the African of their language, God, Culture and way of life. After several years of continuous torture, murder, and rape, the slave master felt free to remove the chains.

What was it about the made condition of the African Slave that made white folk comfortable with removing the chains? It was the fact that like a regular plowing cow or horse, the African had been broken by the white slave master. The chains once being the restrictors of movement had been removed because the spirit of freedom had been broken and the slaves had been made afraid of their open enemy.

As we stand today as so-called free black men and women, the iron chains have been removed and replaced with a mind state that all has changed and we are in a better condition today than yesterday. Before we move forward please allow me to utilize an example to highlight a point. During the *Tran-Atlantic Slave Trade,* Africans were snatched from their homes and placed in ships. Chained feet to feet and head to head these African men and women pissed and shitted on each other. *I use these words because urine and defecation does not paint the picture that the bourgeois reader needs to get right now.* The African women went through their menstrual cycles while chained to each other. Some of them were placed on the slave ships while pregnant and underwent miscarriages and the pains of pregnancy while chained together. These African men and women experienced nine thousand miles of sickness, anxiety, depression, and the unexplainable pain of the fear of the unknown. African human beings were forced to eat while enduring the smell of urine, feces, throw up, and blood. Black men and women were thrown overboard when they were rebellious or showed signs of sickness. The conditions that black people underwent in the slave ships are unparalleled in history and totally unimaginable. When these Africans finally reached the shores of a foreign land, their physical *conditions* had changed, but their *condition* had not. They went from the belly of the slave ships into the hands of a white slave master that treated them less than a common animal.

In today's world, we can say as black men and women that we are no longer strapped with the physical realities of the early slaves and their life on the plantation I mean, of course we are not getting whipped on our backs by a slave master, of course the atrocities of early slavery are no longer present; but just like the transition from the slave ship to the plantation, the *conditions* have changed, but the *condition* has not. The total liberation of black people and people of color throughout the world rest within this understanding.

Today the so-called American Negro actually feels as if they are in a better condition than the early slaves, but like previously articulated…the conditions have changed, but not the condition. There is no need for today's slave to be controlled by iron chains; they are controlled by gold chains. These gold chains can be seen as a metaphor of the state of mind that suggest to the slave that he is free when in fact he is more of a slave today than he was yesterday. Look at it this way, if you take a bird, a bird that has the ability to fly whenever and wherever it desires, and you confine that bird utilizing a bird cage or a tether tied to its leg, after a while you might cause the bird to lose its desire to fly. If you clip the bird's wing, you will take away its physical ability to fly. Regardless if you train him not to fly by restricting him with cages or tethers, or you prevent him from flying because of physical damage done to him, the bottom line is that you have destroyed his ability to fly. It doesn't matter if the bird is caged in an iron cage or a gold gage, the bird is still caged.

The American Slave Master makes diamonds and gold available for their obedient slaves. If the slave has proven him or herself valuable to the overall plan and agenda of the white slave master, he allows the slave to spend his or her riches on products controlled, manufactured, or stolen by white people. Who cares if Curtis "50 Cent" Jackson is given a million dollar signing bonus, that money is spent with Cadillac, or Mercedes Benz. 50 Cent and other rappers including Jay Z, P Diddy, T.I, Lil Jon and several others walk around with 500 thousand dollar watches, million dollar chains and ear rings, while their black brother and sisters are strapped with poverty and hunger.

These Negroes floss on the very same community that gives them *"street credibility"*. They waste millions of dollars in competition with each other over who can be the biggest million-dollar fool. They were born for the most part in poverty, they rap about the terrible conditions that they overcame to arrive at the point they are in their lives, simply to be given huge amounts of money to waste on million dollar yacht and linen parties.

How could this rapping slave claim a borough or a neighborhood and not have a desire to uplift it and make it better? This neighborhood or borough is represented all through the rapper's lyrics, the rapper is given street credibility that drives record sales by being affiliated with these certain neighborhoods and boroughs, yet these same rappers don't uplift these areas. They drive through flossing on those left behind in wretched conditions. Does rapper Jay Z spend millions on diamonds, on Italian homosexual clothing… does the so-called brilliant business mind of P-Diddy spend millions on white parties and yacht parties… does Nelly spend millions on platinum chains and medallions…? How many rappers waste millions of dollars on foolishness just so they can prove that they are rich niggas that are backed by wealthy Jews and European crackers?! There is nothing wrong with having the best in life, there is nothing wrong with having luxury and riches; but when you spend more money on bullshit than you do to help your people out of their miserable condition, you are a sell-out and need to be corrected or destroyed. We as black people should not sell-out the aspirations of our people for a million dollar watch or a two hundred thousand dollar car. We are not white people, we are black people; we are not wealthy or powerful enough to waste our money on materials that lend to the destruction of our people. We should spend our money on our liberation and invest it in our freedom. If we are given huge doses of cash, why not buy our freedom—why buy bullshit cars, clothes, and jewelry…this is insanity.

"The South African diamond marketing cartel **De Beers** alone mines about half the world's annual diamond output. It also controls as much as 80 per cent of global diamond sales through its Central Selling Organization, which purchases and stockpiles diamonds from other suppliers to keep availability low and prices high. De Beers was known to be a major purchaser of diamonds from Angola, Sierra Leone and other African conflict zones, although such stones are estimated to make up only 4 per cent of world output. De Beers had successfully resisted boycott pressures from anti-apartheid activists in the 1970s and 1980s and there seemed little reason to believe that the UN would be more successful."

—Michael Fleshman, a writer for the United Nations' *Africa Renewal* magazine

Cecil John Rhodes—South African Diamond Thief

"Completely break the female horse until she becomes very gentle, whereas you or anybody can ride her in her comfort."

For a minute let's look at a little history, a history that leads to a present that has so-called Negro Rappers appearing as traders of their people. There was a white English businessman, politician, mining magnate and colonizer by the name of Cecil John Rhodes. This white man became incredibly wealthy and famous by exploiting Southern Africa's natural resources. He colonized an African country that white folks named after him, "Rhodesia"; today this country is known as Zambia and Zimbabwe. One of Mr. Rhodes most famous sayings is *"all of these stars... these vast worlds that remain out of reach. If I could, I would annex other planets"*. Upon his death a famous scholarship was set up in his name, it is called the *Rhodes Scholarship*.

Cecil John Rhodes is a European hero; he is looked at by white folks and even some silly so-called Negroes in an extremely fond way. When he died in the year 1902, only 107 years ago, he was considered one of the wealthiest men in the world. But where did Cecil get his riches, and at whose expense...? What was the basis of his wealth, power and influence? Do we ever consider these questions?

While Cecil was recovering from an illness that had him suffering from weak lungs, he decided to visit his brother who had recently immigrated to Natal, in Southern Africa. As a note...Natal, today is known as KwaZulu-Natal, which means *Place of the Zulu*, and was first reportedly seen by a European on Christmas day in the year 1497; that European was a Mr. Vasco da Gama, *Natal* is the name given to the region that he first saw, it is *Portuguese for Christmas*.

After arriving in southern Africa on September 1, 1870, with the equivalent of about $324,000 dollars, which he had borrowed from an aunt, he invested heavily in diamond diggings in Kimberly. Rhodes' brother, Herbert, owned a "cotton farm" in the Umkomaas Valley in Natal where he had Africans working and making him rich. Cecil and his brother went on to start the *Rhodes Fruit Farms* in the Stellenbosch district—a district that has its own unique and diabolical history.

When Rhodes left for school in England, he left his associate C.D. Rudd in charge of his diamond fields. Cecil only stayed initially for one term, yet returned for his second term in 1873. This is important because it was his time in the Oriel College at Oxford, which helped shape his mind into one of a serious British Imperialist. Also during his college years, Cecil John Rhodes joined a secret society of Freemasonry where he developed his own ideas of a secret society that he would later start with the idea of bringing the entire world under "British Rule"; he made the following statement...

> *"I contend that we (the British) are the finest race in the world; and that the more of the world we inhabit, the better it is for the human race".*

Cecil John Rhodes was a known homosexual that desired to control not only Africa, but the African people and resources. Cecil went on to establish a secret society, and after his death his Will stated the following...

> "To and for the establishment, promotion and development of a Secret Society, the true aim and object whereof shall be for the extension of British rule throughout the world, the perfecting of a system of emigration from the United Kingdom, and of colonization by British subjects of all lands where the means of livelihood are attainable by energy, labor and enterprise, and especially the occupation by British settlers of the entire Continent of Africa, the Holy Land, the Valley of the Euphrates, the Islands of Cyprus and Candia, the whole of South America, the Islands of the Pacific not heretofore possessed by Great Britain, the whole of the Malay Archipelago, the seaboard of China and Japan, the ultimate recovery of the United States of America as an integral part of the British Empire, the inauguration of a system of Colonial representation in the Imperial Parliament which may tend to weld together the disjointed members of the Empire and, finally, the foundation of so great a Power as to render wars impossible, and promote the best interest of humanity."

This declaration was made in a Will that can be seen as a summation of Cecil Rhodes' entire life's work. It is important to understand that Cecil's way of thinking was not different from any other white imperialist or colonizing nation.

Cecil Rhodes identified a way to get rich, by capitalizing on the diamonds of Southern Africa, Cecil took his riches and transformed them into wealth, and his wealth was then transformed into power. If the Negro rapper fails to understand the difference between being rich, and being wealthy, allow me to make it real simple... being rich is a state that allows you to purchase things, being wealthy allows you the ability to control that which other people who are rich desire to buy. This control stems from the abundance of resources and possessions that are accumulated by those that are considered wealthy. Being rich can be isolated to an individual that has the ability to purchase a lot of things, being wealthy can be seen as a person that has acquired an abundance of cash, materials, and resources that other people see as valuable. In a nutshell, rich people buy things so they can appear wealthy, wealthy people acquire things so they can control rich people!

Cecil John Rhodes was born in England on July 5, 1853. A sickly child, he was sent to South Africa for the warmer climate. **Before the age of 25, Rhodes was a millionaire,** having struck it rich in South Africa's Kimberley diamond mines. The modern **De Beers** diamond company, whose ads you'll see in any glossy magazine, is the result of one of his lucrative (many would say 'unfair') contracts with local farmers, gaining land rights and access to the diamond-crusted soil.

De Beers

"He is a good tool, now ready to be tied to the horse at a tender age."

Before Cecil Rhodes died, he created the most powerful diamond company in the world. He did not create nor make these diamonds, He merely found the place where God had stored them, learned how to control the people that could retrieve them, and sold them to a world that desired them. This was done under the company name of De Beers.

The De Beers Group is a Johannesburg, South African and London-based diamond mining and trading corporation. This particular company has held a virtual monopoly over all diamond mining and trading in the world. Not only do they control diamond trading, and the destinations that diamonds travel, but Cecil Rhodes' Company decides the price and availability of the world's diamond resources. Under an economic term called *Artificial Scarcity*, the De Beers Group keeps the prices of diamonds high and production cost low. Production cost translates to the poor Africans that risk their lives daily to retrieve the rich material that enriches white thieves. The manipulation of diamond availability drives prices up; the manipulation of the African people drives production cost down.

The De Beers Group distributes its diamonds worldwide through its most favored customers called *sightholders*, these diamond merchants, the majority of them so-called Jews, operate a cartel that keeps prices fixed globally to maintain the perceived and market value of all diamonds. De Beers was founded by Cecil Rhodes and his partner Charles Dunell Rudd March 13, 1888. During the apartheid years, De Beers contracted with the South African government to have political and social prisoners work in their diamond fields.

As De Beers developed and began to dominate the Diamond World, an alliance began to take place. This alliance, similar to the many powerful alliances formulated by record companies and their power brokers, contributed to the monopolization of the diamond industry and guarantees that industry access cannot be gained without their approval and permission.

> "The diamond industry in America "has been Jewish since the city of New York's birth" (Jerusalem Report, April 20, 1995). The first Jewish jewelers were Sephardim who came with the Dutch settlers of New Amsterdam. In the 1920s, the diamond district was in Lower Manhattan; later it moved to 47th Street in Midtown. After World War II, Jews from Antwerp and Amsterdam settled in New York and set up businesses cutting and trading diamonds; there was an influx of Hungarian ultra-Orthodox Jews in 1956. More recently immigrants from Israel and the former Soviet Union have moved in.

According to the Jerusalem Report, Israel has the biggest slice of American purchases, at $1.9 billion or 39 percent last year; America is also Israel's best customer. Other major sources of imports to the U.S. are India, with 26 percent, and Belgium, which accounted for 25 percent of American cut-stone imports in 1994. In an attempt to control the problem of conflict diamonds, the Israeli government has adopted a new control system prohibiting diamond importation from Sierra Leone. In June 1999, the Israel Diamond Exchange decided to revoke the membership of any merchant knowingly trading in illicit stones - a move which would automatically ban the offender from all of the worlds 23 recognized diamond exchanges. Additionally, it is illegal to import rough diamonds from countries that are major sources of conflict diamonds without an official export certificate from the country's government.

This move is an important start to stopping the sale of conflict diamonds. There are still flaws in the Israeli system; for example, all a dealer needs to do to circumvent the system is to say that the diamonds that he/she is carrying are from somewhere else."

—**Religious Action Center of Reform Judaism**

As the HipHop Nation flaunts about wearing their diamonds and bling, I would hope that they realize that what they are wearing are diamonds stolen form African lands— diamonds over priced and manipulated in a way to get you to exhange your dollars for a chance to light up the stage…a damn shame! Let's move on!

The Oppenheimers

"shave off the brute's mental history and create a multiplicity of phenomena of illusions"

Cecil Rhodes and his De Beers Group have a unique relationship with the Oppenheimer family, a so-called Jewish Family that finds its roots in Germany. Ernest Oppenheimer traveled to South Africa seeking to become a major power player in the diamond industry, this he was able to accomplish. In 1917, Ernest Oppenheimer started a company named *Anglo American Corporation,* originally a South African mining enterprise; the Anglo American Corporation has since spread into other areas as well. Natural resources remain its primary focus; the company's desire is to control and manipulate the global availability of said resources. Its Gold mining operations were spun off into the separate *Anglo Gold Corporation* which later merged with the *Ashanti Goldfields Corporation* that was based in Ghana, to form *AngloGold Ashanti,* based in South Africa. In addition to establishing this Anglo-ethnocentric resource stealing operation, Ernest Oppenheimer became the *Chairman* of the *De Beers Consolidated Mines.*

Ernest relinquished control of the company to his son Harry, obviously another so-called Jew that had his formal Bar Mitzvah in a Jewish synagogue in Kimberly, South Africa. Enjoying the enormous wealth potential that was secured by the South African political system of apartheid, Harry Oppenheimer did everything he could to support the State of Israel and make sure that Israel had all the raw diamonds necessary to make it the leading country in terms of the worldwide circulation of the diamond. In this case, like Mr. Bronfman and his alcoholic poison, that which is detrimental to black people and their future, is profitable for so-called Jewish people and their future.

I relay this brief history of the diamond world to show the reader and the HipHop Nation that the diamond is not just a trinket of wealth that suggests you made it to the top. The diamond is a reminder to black people that the raw materials of the world has been stolen from black people and the land they occupy, and white folk has gotten rich from the exploitation of black people. This reality is being seen as the HipHop rapper, the raw product of the American Slave trade is being manipulated and pimped in order to gain wealth, power, and dominance for a white man that has historically desired to completely dominate the world and its resources.

Conflict diamonds are the subject of rapper Kanye West, and he should be applauded for his attempt on shedding light on this important subject, but we should understand that every diamond, every piece of gold, is a conflict mineral, because they were stolen from Africans, and Africans were murdered, manipulated and tricked out of what was rightfully theirs.

It is acknowledged that black people are historically an ornate people, but this reality should not be utilized to justify the overly materialistic lifestyle of today's HipHop artists, black entertainers and sports stars. It is a monumental display of irresponsibility to see the huge diamond earrings, heavily diamond laced wrist watches, and diamond teethe prominently displayed by rappers that seemingly posses deficient levels of social and political awareness and considerations. If a rapper, entertainer, or sports star chooses to spend his or her money on a lavish lifestyle and high-priced accessories, that is their right; however, when that same individual refuses to give and contribute to the social, political, and economical development of his or her people, that person should feel the effects of a community that chooses not to support them or their product.

Before we move forward:

The deception of *Artificial Scarcity* is an official business practice that causes the business and consumer worlds to believe and act as if there is a shortage of a product, by having a shortage of a product, or acting as if there is a shortage, the price is driven up, and the value of the said product is perceived as higher. This is done within the diamond industry to manipulate the public into believing that their diamonds are more valuable and scarce than they actually are.

The global economy is based on a system of belief; its driving force is the people that participate in it. Currency circulation and the amount of real money being exchanged on a daily, monthly and yearly rate, determines inflation and the value of money. There was a time that the Dollar was backed by gold and silver, this means that the value of the dollar was based on the standard of value attached to silver and gold; therefore, those who controlled the silver and gold controlled and determined the value of the dollar. Later, since the end of the International Gold Standard of the Britton Woods System, a system originated in the board rooms of the *World Bank*, most countries including the United States participate in a *fiduciary system* referred to as *fiat money*. Fiat money is money whose purchasing power is derived from a *declaratory fiat* of the government issuing it. It is often associated with paper money not backed with any real or fixed assets, issued without any redemptive promises in some other form, and accepted by tradition or social convention.

This type of money system is operated and controlled by the government, the government decides on the amount of money to print and release into the economic stream of the people who work for it. In the case of the American government, the Federal Reserve, the central banking system of the United States, was created by the Federal Reserve Act of 1913. This act allowed for the establishment of a centralized bank of extended branches that control the systematic distribution of cash. Allow me to pause for a moment to state the following…

The economic system of America is a microcosm of a macrocosm Imperialistic Global idea and agenda. The American government and those who are like-minded, regardless of nation or state, desires to control the global distribution of cash and wealth. A circuit of wealthy people and corporations fully intend on creating a unified global economy that models the American system with a few imperialistic and colonial upgrades. Black people, and people of color throughout the world need to understand the present system of government and the true realities of the social, economic, political, religious, and educational segments of white supremacy in order to navigate their minds and bodies through the doldrums of tricks and manipulations designed by the powers that be.

The HipHop Nation and its famous and not so famous rappers, like all of us, are participants in a global conspiracy to control landmasses, resources, and people. The focus of this writing is primarily on the Negro Rapper, because this element of the black community is being used specifically to further the global agenda of white people. The HipHop Nation is being used in its present form as a merchandising and marketing tool to seductively lure the global community into the filth and indecencies of the American popular culture. This is being done by a certain group of individuals that fully understand the conspiracy and are responsible for keeping the masses in a perpetual state of ignorance

If in fact, the reader is in doubt and considers the above words just baseless rhetoric and a fanciful conspiracy theory, then consider the following names as the actual entities that developed the World Bank and the Federal Reserve. These central banks number as 12 (twelve) and they are:

Rothschild Bank of Berlin	**Goldman, Sachs of New York**
Lehman Brothers of New York	**Warburg Bank of Amsterdam**
Chase Manhattan Bank of New York	**Kuhn Loeb Bank of New York**
Lazard Brothers of Paris	**Israel Moses Seif Banks of Italy**
Rothschild Bank of London	**Warburg Bank of Hamburg**

These banking institutions are actually connected to the London Banking Houses; this shows that no Nation or State interferes with the economic realities of a global market or ambition. You can recognize the names of the above mentioned as so-called Jewish identifiers. These banks make up the Federal Reserve. The Federal Reserve Bank prints money on paper, paper that is not backed by any material form of redemption. Therefore the value of the dollar is determined by the same people that print it. This paper money is then released into the economic stream of America in the form of loans that are attached to interest. Interest rates are also determined by the same Federal Reserve, an institution that has had a majority of chairmen that were so-called Jews, this includes the former Alan Greenspan, and the present Mr. Ben Shalom Bernanke.

Please think about the actual facts, they include the recognition that the money that American's work for, and Negro rappers, entertainers, and athletes sellout for, is known as Federal Reserve Notes. These notes are printed by a group of private bankers that have a contract with the government of the United States to print and distribute the cash. By determining the rate of circulation, these powerful so-called Jewish bankers also control the rate of inflation. They have the power and authority to actually inflate huge multinational banks and financial institutions with monstrous profits because they determine the prime interest rates. With a few pecks on a computer keyboard, these powerful individuals can send the American Economy into a full fledge depression if and when it suits their interest.

Just as the Federal Reserve is financed and controlled by the 12 listed central banks, it is also comprised of 12 districts. These districts are the following:

Boston
New York
Cleveland
Richmond
Atlanta
Kansas City
Dallas
Chicago
St. Louis
Minneapolis
San Francisco
Philadelphia

Totaling out as 12, New York controls the other 11... is it not interesting that New York is the so-called Jewish capital of the world, and the Mecca of Media? The New York district is controlled by a number of individual share holders and banks; the following are some that owned and controlled the New York district, and subsequently the other 11:

First National Bank of New York

James Stillman National City Bank, New York

Mary W. Harnman

National Bank of Commerce, New York

A.D. Jiullard

Hanover National Bank, New York

Jacob Schiff

Chase National Bank, New York

Thomas F. Ryan

Paul Warburg

William Rockefeller

Levi P. Morton

M.T. Pyne

George F. Baker

Percy Pyne

Mrs. G.F. St. George

J.W. Sterling

Katherine St. George

H.P. Davidson

J.P. Morgan (Equitable Life/Mutual Life)

Edith Brevour T. Baker

Since the dollar is not based on, or backed by anything tangible or concrete, and since the American dollar fails to guarantee any redemptive qualities in terms of its exchange; the American economy itself is not based on materials, minerals, or land masses, it is based on belief and confidence in government. If the American people lose confidence in government, the government that determines the value of a dollar, then the dollar loses its value and the American and global economy collapses right before our eyes. If and when this collapse occurs, the American dollar will have absolutely no value, and the so-called Negro rappers that have sold their souls for the dollar will be left naked and impoverished. This understanding should motivate black people in general, and the so-called Negro rapper in particular to spend their money on the economic base of freedom, and that's land.

Dear reader please recognize the fact that the last time American coins contained silver was in 1964, and Franklin Delano Roosevelt recalled the last gold certificates in 1934. Since that time, the American Government and their so-called Jewish puppet masters have kept their gold stocked piled out of the public's hands within the secured walls of Fort Knox. We must accept the fact that it is the so-called Jews that control the rich minerals such as Gold, Silver, and diamonds.

I realize that we have been conditioned to reject racism and anti-Semitism, but what are being offered within these pages are actual facts that can be sustained by evidence. This is not racism nor anti-Semitism, but those that have something to hide, cloak themselves under the ignorance of the people by mislabeling the presentation of truth as hate or anti-Semitic rhetoric…please… let's not fall for the pathetically weak tactics of the biggest hater within the historical framework of the universe—the white American power brokers and the so-called Jewish elements.

It is vital for the black man and woman in general and the so-called Negro rappers in particular, to understand the reality of slavery and the system that perpetuates it. To believe that the educational system that is responsible for the information that little black girls and boys receive on the primary, intermediate, and collegiate levels is the *all about all* truth that governs society and its laws and by-laws, is an indication of ignorance and an extreme case of naivety. As slaves within a system that manipulates the masses through filtered information and incomplete truths, we have been conditioned to draw conclusions from faulty sources. Our best conclusions are set on a foundation of so-called truths that support an overall system based on deceit and the manipulation of facts.

We should begin to understand that the traditional system of education is indeed a slave factory that does not offer any liberating elements that would confront the ruling powers and their plans for global domination.

This world and its systems and sub-systems are clever machinations that were products of a mind that is concerned with and completely dedicated to the ideas of white supremacy; the concept of a one world government that was ruled by not only those of white skin, but those that had a shared and mutual understanding of how the global politic should look and function.

Black people and people of color in general should examine the mathematical application of ideas and agendas. Those that have power to implement ideas band together to formulate policies and procedures that perpetuate, maintain, and secure their particular ideas. If and when these powers can affect public and private opinion, these powers can systematically and scientifically condition the masses to accept their ideas; and in fact, lend their talents to the fulfillment of the ideas of those that have power. In this way ideas are carried out even by those who are at the negative end of the said idea.

In our public so-called educational process very little is mentioned of the in-depth system of global rule and domination. Because of this fact, many of us have an insufficient level of understanding of the unseen currents that keep white people and their ideas in power. I realize that there are those that get upset by my choice of words and depictions of those that are in power. However, if we elevate past our emotional reactions, we can see that those who control global resources and access are in fact white people. Those that have the power to completely destroy the earth and its inhabitants are white people; and those that have painted the global politic into the corner, it presently resides, are in fact, white people.

With this in mind, why would we as black people and people of color refuse to elevate our understanding, and continue to leave our future in the hands of a group of people that has a tradition of implementing policies and procedures that lend to our destruction? In fact, it is the intellectual cowardice that is present within the hearts of people of color throughout the world in regards to race and its political and social play, that continues to give those that are absent of color the advantage. These white skinned individuals have historically and traditionally utilized their skin color as a rallying point that has buttressed the fabrics of their unity against those that are of darker complexions.

THE DECEPTION BACK TO THE FED

"Since we feel that the subject matter may get more complicated as we proceed in laying down our economic plan concerning the purpose, reason and effect of crossbreeding horses and niggers, we shall lay down the following definition terms for future generations."

As we continue, we may ask ourselves how the fraudulent system of the Federal Reserve came into existence. After several attempts to push the Federal Reserve Act through Congress, a group of so-called Jewish bankers funded, supported, and staffed Woodrow Wilson's campaign for President because he had committed to sign the act if and when he was elected. After Wilson had won, a senator by the name of Nelson Aldrich, a maternal grandfather to the Rockefellers, pushed the bill through Congress while most of the Congress was away for Christmas.

It is important that we understand that these powerful bankers fund and support those candidates that are sympathetic to their cause. Like previously stated, these same bankers have considerable interest in the media and entertainment worlds. This allows for the manipulation and control of not only the public, but the elected officials that are voted in to represent the public.

I hope that those associated with the HipHop Nation begin to recognize the depth of what is at stake. The public has been kept ignorant to the wicked machinations of those who are in power. The voice of truth has to take flight, and it must reach the minds of those that matter most. The HipHop Nation has been placed in a position that allows it to speak into the hearts and minds of those previously mislead. Although rappers have been funded to keep the masses distracted and preoccupied with trivial filth and the consequences of such, the HipHop Nation can switch up the game by educating itself and utilizing their individual and collective resources to uplift the mentality of those that have been enslaved. By doing so, they can create a legacy that will never be erased or replaced. Those that take on the battle will become immortalized and looked upon as heroes by those future generations that taste the matchless flavor of liberation.

Those that choose not to because of fear, or the desire to live the luxury life of a house nigger, will be recorded as sellouts and smooth talking hookers of the white slave master. It is extremely important to the lives of billions of people upon the earth that the HipHop Nation make the morally correct decision. Failure to do so will point the finger of blame toward the heads of those that had a chance to make a difference but was too ignorant, too selfish, or too cowardly to act and do what is necessary.

Before we move on, please consider these next few words carefully; for within these next few pages we find the essence of the slavery that we all suffer:

The Real Story of the Money-Control Over America
By Pastor Sheldon Emry

The piece has been edited for the purpose of this writing...

Debt-The Essence of Modern Slavery

"If the American people ever allow private banks to control the issue of their money, first by inflation and then by deflation, the banks and corporations that will grow up around them (around the banks), will deprive the people of their property until their children will wake up homeless on the continent their fathers conquered."—Thomas Jefferson

●━━━●

Americans, living in what is called the richest nation on earth; seem always to be short of money. Wives are working in unprecedented numbers, husbands hope for overtime hours to earn more, or take part-time jobs evenings and weekends, children look for odd jobs for spending money, the family debt climbs higher, and psychologists say one of the biggest causes of family quarrels and breakups is "arguments over money." Much of this trouble can be traced to the present "debt-money" system. Too few people realize why the American founding fathers wrote into Article I of the U.S. Constitution: **Congress shall have the Power to Coin Money and Regulate the Value** Thereof.

<u>Money Is Created</u>

Economists use the term "create" when speaking of the process by which money comes into existence. Now, creation means making something that did not exist before. Lumbermen make boards from trees, workers build houses from lumber, and factories manufacture automobiles from metal, glass and other materials. But in all these they did not "create," they only changed existing materials into a more usable and, therefore, more valuable form. This is not so with money. Here and here alone, man actually "creates" something out of nothing. A piece of paper of little value is printed so that it is worth a piece of lumber. With different figures it can buy the automobile or even the house. Its value has been "created" in the true meaning of the word.

As is seen by the above, money is very cheap to make, and whoever does the "creating" of money in a nation can make a tremendous profit! Builders work hard to make a profit of 5percent above their cost to build a house.

Auto makers sell their cars for 1percent to 2 percent above the cost of manufacture and it is considered good business. But money "manufacturers" have no limit on their profits, since a few cents will print a $1 bill or a $10,000 bill. That profit is part of the story, but first let us consider another unique characteristic of the thing - money, the love of which is the "root of all evil".

ADEQUATE MONEY SUPPLY NEEDED

An adequate supply of money is indispensable to civilized society. We could forego many other things, but without money industry would grind to a halt, farms would become only self-sustaining units, surplus food would disappear, jobs requiring the work of more than one man or one family would remain undone, shipping, and large movements of goods would cease, hungry people would plunder and kill to remain alive, and all government except family or tribe would cease to function.

An overstatement, you say?—not at all. Money is the blood of civilized society, the means of all commercial trade except simple barter. It is the measure and the instrument by which one product is sold and another purchased. Remove money or even reduce the supply below that which is necessary to carry on current levels of trade, and the results are catastrophic. For an example, we need only look at America's Depression of the early 1930's.

THE BANKERS DEPRESSION OF THE 1930's

In 1930 America did not lack industrial capacity, fertile-farm land, skilled and willing workers or industrious farm families. It had an extensive and highly efficient transportation system in railroads, road networks, and inland and ocean waterways. Communications between regions and localities were the best in the world, utilizing telephone, teletype, radio, and a well-operated government mail system. No war had ravaged the cities or the countryside, no pestilence weakened the population, nor had famine stalked the land. The United States of America in 1930 lacked only one thing: an adequate supply of money to carry on trade and commerce. In the early 1930's, the rich and powerful Bankers, the only source of new money and credit, deliberately refused loans to industries, stores and farms. *Question; who were these Bankers, and what were their motives?!*

Payments on existing loans were required however, and money rapidly disappeared from circulation. Goods were available to be purchased, jobs waiting to be done, but the lack of money brought the nation to a standstill. By this simple ploy America was put in a "depression" and the greedy Bankers took possession of hundreds of thousands of farms, homes, and business properties. The people were told, "times are hard," and "money is short." Not understanding the system, they were cruelly robbed of their earnings, their savings, and their property.

MONEY FOR PEACE? NO! MONEY FOR WAR? YES!

World War II ended the "depression." The same so-called Jewish Bankers who in the early 30's had no loans for peacetime houses, food and clothing, suddenly had unlimited billions to lend for Army barracks, K-rations and uniforms! A nation that in 1934 couldn't produce food for sale suddenly could produce bombs to send free to Germany and Japan!

With the sudden increase in money, people were hired, farms sold their produce, factories went to two shifts, mines re-opened, and "The Great Depression" was over! Some politicians were blamed for it and others took credit for ending it. The truth is the lack of money (caused by the Bankers) brought on the depression, and adequate money ended it. The people were never told that simple truth and hopefully in this book we will endeavor to show how these same Bankers who control our money and credit have used their control to plunder America and place us in bondage; and with the help of the ignorant so-called Negro rapper has created an entire generation that instead of seeking total and complete liberation, would prefer to consume and emulate the filth and swine slop propagated by the 2006 version of the Uncle Tom.

POWER TO COIN AND REGULATE MONEY

When we can see the disastrous results of an artificially created shortage of money, we can better understand why the so-called Founding Fathers of America insisted on placing the power to "create" money and the power to control it ONLY in the hands of the Federal Congress. They believed that ALL citizens should share in the profits of its "creation" and therefore the national government must be the ONLY creator of money. They further believed that ALL citizens, of whatever State or Territory, or station in life would benefit by an adequate and stable currency and therefore, the national government must also be, by law, the ONLY controller of the value of money.

Since the Federal Congress was the only legislative body subject to all the citizens at the ballot box, it was, to their minds, the only safe depository of so much profit and so much power. They wrote it out in the simple, but all-inclusive: *"Congress shall have the Power to Coin Money and Regulate the Value Thereof."*

HOW THE PEOPLE LOST CONTROL TO THE FEDERAL RESERVE

Instead of the Constitutional method of creating our money and putting it into circulation, we now have an entirely unconstitutional system. This has resulted in almost disastrous conditions, as we shall see.

Since our money was handled both legally and illegally before 1913, we shall consider only the years following 1913, since from that year on, ALL of our money has been created and issued by an illegal method that will eventually destroy the United States if it is not changed. Prior to 1913, America was considered a prosperous, powerful, and growing nation, evidently at peace with its neighbors and the envy of the world. But - in December of 1913, Congress, with many members away for the Christmas holidays, passed what has since been known as the FEDERAL RESERVE ACT. (For the full story of how this infamous legislation was forced through our Congress, read ***The Creature from Jekyll Island***, by G. Edward Griffin or ***Conquest or Consent***, by W. B. Vennard). Omitting the burdensome details, it simply authorized the establishment of a Federal Reserve Corporation, with a Board of Directors (The Federal Reserve Board) to run it, and the United States was divided into 12 Federal Reserve "Districts."

This simple, but terrible law completely removed from Congress the right to "create" money or to have any control over its "creation," and gave that function to the *Federal Reserve Corporation*. This was done with appropriate fanfare and propaganda that this would "remove money from politics" (they didn't say "and therefore from the people's control") and prevent "Boom and Bust" from hurting their citizens. The people were not told then, and most still do not know today, that the *Federal Reserve Corporation* is a private corporation controlled by so-called Jewish bankers and therefore is operated for the financial gain of the bankers over the people rather than for the good of the people. The word "Federal" was used only to deceive the people.

MORE DISASTROUS THAN PEARL HARBOR

Since that "day of infamy," more disastrous than Pearl Harbor, the small group of "privileged" people who lend us "our" money have accrued to themselves all of the profits of printing our money' - and more! Since 1913 they have "created" tens of billions of dollars in money and credit, which, as their own personal property, they then lend to our government and our people at interest. "The rich get richer and the poor get poorer" had become the secret policy of our National Government. An example of the process of "creation" and its conversion to people's "debt" will aid our understanding.

THEY PRINT IT - WE BORROW IT AND PAY THEM INTEREST

We shall start with the need for money. The Federal Government, having spent more than it has taken from its citizens in taxes, needs, for the sake of illustration, $1,000,000,000. Since it does not have the money, and Congress has given away its authority to "create" it, the Government must go to the "creators" for the $1 billion. But, the Federal Reserve, a private corporation, doesn't just give its money away! The Bankers are willing to deliver $1,000,000,000 in money or credit to the Federal Government in exchange for the Government's agreement to pay it back - with interest! So Congress authorizes the Treasury Department to print $1,000,000,000 in U.S. Bonds, which are then delivered to the Federal Reserve Bankers.

The Federal Reserve then pays the cost of printing the $1,000,000,000 (about $1,000) and makes the exchange. The Government then uses the money to pay its obligations. What are the results of this fantastic transaction? Well, $1 billion in Government bills are paid all right, but the Government has now indebted the people to the Bankers for $1 billion on which the people must pay interest! Tens of thousands of such transactions have taken place since 1913 so that by the 1980's, the U.S. Government was indebted to the Bankers for over $1,000,000,000,000 (trillion) on which the people pay over $100 billion a year in interest alone with no hope of ever paying off the principal. Supposedly our children and following generations will pay forever and forever! As of 2006, the American debt is $9 Trillion.

You say, "This is terrible!" Yes, it is, but I have shown only part of the sordid story. Under this unholy system, those United States Bonds have now become "assets" of the Banks in the Reserve System which they then use as "reserves" to "create" more "credit" to lend. Current "fractional reserve" requirements allow them to use that $1 billion in bonds to "create" as much as $15 billion in new "credit" to lend to States, Municipalities, to individuals and businesses. Added to the original $1 billion, they could have $16 billion of "created credit" out in loans paying them interest with their only cost being $1,000 for printing the original $1 billion! Since the U.S. Congress has not issued Constitutional money since 1863 (over 140 years), in order for the people to have money to carry on trade and commerce they are forced to borrow the "created credit" of the Monopoly Bankers and pay them usury-interest!

In addition to the vast wealth drawn to them through this almost unlimited usury, the Bankers who control the money at the top are able to approve or disapprove large loans to large and successful corporations to the extent that refusal of a loan will bring about a reduction in the price that that Corporation's stock sells for on the market.

After depressing the price, the Bankers' agents buy large blocks of the stock, after which the sometimes multi-million dollar loan is approved, the stock rises, and are then sold for a profit. In this manner billions of dollars are made with which to buy more stock. This practice is so refined today that the Federal Reserve Board need only announce to the so-called Jewish ran newspapers an increase or decrease in their "rediscount rate" to send stocks up and down as they wish. Using this method since 1913, the wicked Bankers and their agents have purchased secret or open control of almost every large corporation in America. Using that control, they then force the corporations to borrow huge sums from their banks so that corporation earnings are siphoned off in the form of interest to the banks. This leaves little as actual "profits" which can be paid as dividends and explains why stock prices are often depressed, while the banks reap billions in interest from corporate loans. In effect, the bankers get almost all of the profits, while individual stockholders are left holding the bag. It should be now understood how and why corporate heads and world bankers all share similar sounding surnames. They are all connected; their wealth can be traced to the same source. Their lifeline is the same, therefore so is their agenda, goals, and ideas.

The millions of working families of America are now indebted to the few thousand Banking Families for twice the assessed value of the entire United States. And these Banking Families obtained that debt against us for the cost of paper, ink, and bookkeeping! So-called Negro rappers are selling out their people on a global scale for paper with dead white men on them, and for diamonds with their people's blood covering them. This is a shame and whether they like it or not, they need to be told the truth and corrected, and if they still don't get the message, they should be destroyed!

THE INTEREST AMOUNT IS NEVER CREATED

The only way new money (which is not true money, but is "credit" representing a debt), goes into circulation in America is when it is borrowed from Bankers. When the State and people borrow large sums, they seem to prosper. However, the Bankers "create" only the amount of the principal of each loan, never the extra amount needed to pay the interest. Therefore the new money never equals the new debt added. The amount needed to pay the interest on loans is not "created," and therefore does not exist!

Under this kind of a system, where new debt always exceeds the new money no matter how much or how little is borrowed, the total debt increasingly outstrips the amount of money available to pay the debt. The people can never, ever get out of debt!

An example will show the viciousness of this usury-debt system with its "built-in" shortage of money.

IF $60,000 IS BORROWED, $255,931.20 MUST BE PAID BACK

When a citizen goes to a Banker to borrow $60,000 to purchase a home or a farm, the Bank clerk has the borrower agree to pay back the loan plus interest. At 14percent interest for 30 years, the Borrower must agree to pay $710.92 per month for a total of $255,931.20. The clerk then requires the citizen to assign to the Banker the right of ownership of the property if the Borrower does not make the required payments. The Bank clerk then gives the Borrower a $60,000 check or a $60,000 deposit slip crediting the Borrower's checking account with $60,000.

The Borrower then writes checks to the builder, subcontractors, etc., who in turn write checks. $60,000 of new "checkbook" money is thereby added to "money in circulation."

However, and this is the fatal flaw in a usury system, the only new money created and put into circulation is the amount of the loan, $60,000. The money to pay the interest is NOT created, and therefore was NOT added to "money in circulation."

Even so, this Borrower (and those who follow him in ownership of the property) must earn and TAKE OUT OF CIRCULATION $255,931, almost $200,000 MORE than he put IN CIRCULATION when he borrowed the original $60,000! (By the way, it is this interest which cheats all families out of nicer homes. It is not that they can't afford them; it is because the Banker's usury forces them to pay for 4 homes to get one!)

Every new loan puts the same process in operation. Each borrower adds a small sum to the total money supply when he borrows, but the payments on the loan (because of interest) then deduct a much LARGER sum from the total money supply.

There is therefore no way all debtors can pay off the money-lenders. As they pay the principal and interest, the money in circulation disappears. All they can do is struggle against each other, borrowing more and more from the money-lenders each generation. The money-lenders (Bankers), who produce nothing of value, slowly, then more rapidly, gain a death grip on the land, buildings, and present and future earnings of the whole working population.
SLAVERY

SMALL LOANS DO THE SAME THING

If you haven't quite grasped the impact of the above, let us consider a small auto loan for 3 years at 18percent interest. Step 1: Citizen borrows $5,000 and pays it into circulation (it goes to the dealer, factory, miner, etc.) and signs a note agreeing to pay the Banker $6,500. Step 2: Citizen pays $180 per month of his earnings to the Banker. In 3 years he will take OUT of circulation $1,500 more than he put IN circulation.

Every loan of Banker "created" money (credit) causes the same thing to happen. Since this has happened millions of times since 1913 (and continues today), you can see why America has gone from a prosperous, debt-free nation to a debt-ridden nation where practically every home, farm and business is paying usury-tribute to some Banker. The usury-tribute to the Bankers on personal, local, State and Federal debt totals more than the combined earnings of 25percent of the working people. Soon it will be 50percent and continue up.

THIS IS WHY BANKERS PROSPER IN GOOD TIMES OR BAD

In the millions of transactions made each year, like those above, very little currency changes hands, nor is it necessary for it to do so. 95percent of all "cash" transactions in the U.S. are by check or electronic money transfer, so the Banker is perfectly safe in "creating" that so-called "loan" by writing the check or deposit slip, not against actual money, but AGAINST YOUR PROMISE TO PAY IT BACK! The cost to him is paper, ink and a few dollars in salaries and office costs for each transaction. It is "check-kiting" on an enormous scale. The profits increase rapidly, year after year.

THE COST TO YOU? EVENTUALLY, EVERYTHING!

In 1910 the U.S. Federal debt was only $1 billion, or $12.40 per citizen. State and local debts were practically non-existent.

By 1920, after only 6 years of Federal Reserve shenanigans, the Federal debt had jumped to $24 billion, or $226 per person.

In 1960 the Federal debt reached $284 billion, or $1,575 per citizen and State and local debts were mushrooming.

By 1981 the Federal debt passed $1 trillion and was growing exponentially as the Banker's tripled the interest rates. State and local debts are now MORE than the Federal, and with business and personal debts totaled over $6 trillion, 3 times the value of all land and buildings in America.

If we signed over to the money-leaders all of America we would still owe them 2 more Americas (plus their usury, of course!) This is based upon the above numbers, consider the current national debt:

U.S. NATIONAL DEBT CLOCK

The Outstanding Public Debt as of 16 Mar 2009 at 09:55:31 PM GMT is:

10,994,881,547,784.87

The estimated population of the United States is **305,827,544** so each citizen's share of this debt is **$35,951.25**.

The National Debt has continued to increase an average of **$3.71 billion per day** since September 28, 2007!

However, they are too cunning to take title to everything. They will instead leave you with some *"illusion of ownership"* so you and your children will continue to work and pay the Bankers more of your earnings on ever-increasing debts. The "establishment" has captured our people with their ungodly system of usury and debt as certainly as if they had marched in with a uniformed army.

FOR THE GAMBLERS AMONG MY READERS

To grasp the truth that periodic withdrawal of money through interest payments will inexorably transfer all wealth in the nation to the receiver of interest, imagine yourself in a poker or dice game where everyone must buy the chips (the medium of exchange) from a "banker" who does not risk chips in the game, but watches the table and every hour reaches in and takes 10percent to 15percent of all the chips on the table. As the game goes on, the amount of chips in the possession of each player will go up and down with his "luck."

However, the TOTAL number of chips available to play the game (carry on trade and business) will decrease rapidly.

The game will get low on chips, and some will run out. If they want to continue to play, they must buy or borrow them from the "banker." The "banker" will sell (lend) them ONLY if the player signs a "mortgage" agreeing to give the "banker" some real property (car, home, farm, business, etc.) if he cannot make periodic payments to pay back all of the chips plus some EXTRA ones (interest). The payments must be made on time, whether he wins (makes a profit) or not.

It is easy to see that no matter how skillfully they play, eventually the "banker" will end up with all of his original chips back, and except for the very best players, the rest, if they stay in long enough, will lose to the "banker" their homes, their farms, their businesses, perhaps even their cars, watches, rings, and the shirts off their backs!

Our real-life situation is MUCH WORSE than any poker game. In a poker game none is forced to go into debt, and anyone can quit at any time and keep whatever he still has. But in real life, even if we borrow little ourselves from the Bankers, the local, State, and Federal governments borrow billions in our name, squander it, then confiscate our earnings from us and pay it back to the Bankers with interest. We are forced to play the game, and none can leave except by death. We pay as long as we live, and our children pay after we die. If we cannot pay, the same government sends the FBI or IRS to take our property and give it to the Bankers. The Bankers risk nothing in the game; they just collect their percentage and "win it all." In Las Vegas and at other gambling centers, all games are "rigged" to pay the owner a percentage, and they rake in millions. The Federal Reserve Bankers' "game" is also rigged, and it pays off in billions!

In recent years Bankers added real "cards" to their 'game. "Credit" cards are promoted as a convenience and a great boon to trade. Actually, they are ingenious devices by which Bankers collect 2percent to 5percent of every retail sale from the seller and 18percent interest from buyers. A real "stacked" deck!

YES, IT'S POLITICAL, TOO!

Democrat, Republican, and Independent voters who have wondered why politicians always spend more tax money than they take in should now see the reason. When they begin to study our "debt-money" system, they soon realize that these politicians are not the agents of the people but are the agents of the Bankers, for whom they plan ways to place the people further-in debt. It takes only a little imagination to see that if Congress had been "creating," and spending or issuing into circulation the necessary increase in the money supply, THERE WOULD BE NO NATIONAL DEBT, and the over $4 Trillion of other debts would be practically non-existent. Since there would be no ORIGINAL cost of money except printing, and no CONTINUING costs such as interest, Federal taxes would be almost nil. Money, once in circulation, would remain there and go on serving its purpose as a medium of exchange for generation after generation and century after century, just as coins do now, with NO payments to the Bankers whatever!

MOUNTING DEBTS AND WARS

But instead of peace and debt-free prosperity, we have ever-mounting debt and periodic wars. We as a people are now ruled by a system of Banker-owned Mammon that has usurped the mantle of government, disguised itself as our legitimate government, and set about to pauperize and control our people. It is now a centralized, all-powerful political apparatus whose main purposes are promoting war, spending the peoples' money, and propagandizing to perpetuate itself in power. Our two large political parties have become its servants, the various departments of government its spending agencies and the Internal Revenue its collection agency.

Unknown to the people, it operates in close cooperation with similar apparatuses in other nations which are also disguised as "governments." Some, we are told, are friends. Some, we are told, are enemies. "Enemies" are built up through international manipulations and used to frighten the American people into going billions of dollars more into debt to the Bankers for "military preparedness," "foreign aid to stop communism," "Islamic Terrorist" "minority rights," etc. Citizens, deliberately confused by brainwashing propaganda, watch helplessly while our politicians give our food, goods, and money to Banker-controlled alien governments under the guise of "better relations" and "easing tensions." Our Banker-controlled government takes our finest and bravest sons and daughters and sends them into foreign wars with obsolete equipment and inadequate training, where tens of thousands are murdered, and hundreds of thousands are crippled. Other thousands are morally corrupted, addicted to drugs, and infected with venereal and other diseases, which they bring back to the United States. When the "war" is over, we have gained nothing, but we are scores of billions of dollars more in debt to the Bankers, which was the reason for the "war" in the first place!

BUT WAIT... THERE'S STILL MORE

The profits from these massive debts have been used to erect a complete and almost hidden economic and political colossus over our nation. They keep telling us they are trying to do us "good," when in truth they work to bring harm and injury to our people. These would-be despots know it is easier to control and rob an ill, poorly-educated and confused people than it is a healthy and intelligent population, so they deliberately prevent real cures for diseases, they degrade our educational systems, and they stir up social and racial unrest. For the same reason they favor drug use, alcohol, sexual promiscuity, abortion, pornography, and crime. Everything which debilitates the minds and bodies of the people is secretly encouraged, as it makes the people less able to oppose them or even to understand what is being done to them.

Family, morals, self respect, fear of God, all that is honorable, is being swept away, while they try to build their new, subservient man. Our new "rulers" are trying to change our whole racial, social, religious, and political order, but they will not change the debt-money economic system by which they rob and rule. Our people are "debt-slaves" to the Bankers and their agents in the land that boasts of being free. It is conquest through the most gigantic fraud and swindle in the history of mankind. And I remind you again: The key to their wealth and power over us is their ability to create "money" out of nothing and lend it to us at interest. If they had not been allowed to do that, they would never have gained secret control of this nation and those who live in it. "The rich rule'th over the poor, and the borrower is servant to the lender" (Proverbs 22:7).

WHAT SOME FAMOUS MEN HAVE SAID ABOUT THE MONEY QUESTION

ALAN GREENSPAN: "In the absence of the gold standard, there is no way to protect savings from confiscation through inflation. ... This is the shabby secret of the welfare statists' tirades against gold. Deficit spending is simply a scheme for the confiscation of wealth. Gold stands in the way of this insidious process. It stands as a protector of property rights. If one grasps this, one has no difficulty in understanding the statists' antagonism toward the gold standard."

PRESIDENT THOMAS JEFFERSON: "The system of banking [is] a blot left in all our Constitutions, which, if not covered, will end in their destruction... I sincerely believe that banking institutions are more dangerous than standing armies; and that the principle of spending money to be paid by posterity... is but swindling futurity on a large scale."

PRESIDENT JAMES A. GARFIELD: "Whoever controls the volume of money in any country is absolute master of all industry and commerce".

CONGRESSMAN LOUIS McFADDEN: "The Federal Reserve (Banks) are one of the most corrupt institutions the world has ever seen. There is not a man within the sound of my voice who does not know that this Nation is run by the International Bankers".

HORACE GREELEY: "While boasting of our noble deeds were careful to conceal the ugly fact that by an iniquitous money system we have nationalized a system of oppression which, though more refined, is not less cruel than the old system of chattel slavery."

THOMAS A. EDISON: "People who will not turn a shovel full of dirt on the project (Muscle Shoals Dam) nor contribute a pound of material, will collect more money from the United States than will the People who supply all the material and do all the work. This is the terrible thing about interest ...But here is the point: If the Nation can issue a dollar bond it can issue a dollar bill. The element that makes the bond good makes the bill good also. The difference between the bond and the bill is that the bond lets the money broker collect twice the amount of the bond and an additional 20 percent. Whereas the currency, the honest sort provided by the Constitution, pays nobody but those who contribute in some useful way. It is absurd to say our Country can issue bonds and cannot issue currency. Both are promises to pay, but one fattens the usurer and the other helps the People."

PRESIDENT WOODROW WILSON: "A great industrial Nation is controlled by its system of credit. Our system of credit is concentrated. The growth of the Nation and all our activities are in the hands of a few men. We have come to be one of the worst ruled, one of the most completely controlled and dominated Governments in the world - no longer a Government of free opinion no longer a Government by conviction and vote of the majority, but a Government by the opinion and duress of small groups of dominant men". (Just before he died, Wilson is reported to have stated to friends that he had been "deceived" and that "I have betrayed my Country". He referred to the Federal Reserve Act passed during his Presidency.)

SIR JOSIAH STAMP, (President of the Bank of England in the 1920's, the second richest man in Britain): "Banking was conceived in iniquity and was born in sin. The Bankers own the earth. Take it away from them, but leave them the power to create deposits, and with the flick of the pen they will create enough deposits to buy it back again. However, take it away from them, and all the great fortunes like mine will disappear and they ought to disappear, for this would be a happier and better world to live in. But, if you wish to remain the slaves of Bankers and pay the cost of your own slavery, let them continue to create deposits".

MAJOR L .L. B. ANGUS: "The modern Banking system manufactures money out of nothing. The process is perhaps the most astounding piece of sleight of hand that was ever invented. Banks can in fact inflate mint and un-mint the modern ledger-entry currency".

RALPH M. HAWTREY (Former Secretary of the British Treasury): "Banks lend by creating credit. They create the means of payment out of nothing."

ROBERT HEMPHILL (Credit Manager of Federal Reserve Bank, Atlanta, Ga.): "This is a staggering thought. We are completely dependent on the commercial Banks. Someone has to borrow every dollar we have in circulation, cash or credit. If the Banks create ample synthetic money we are prosperous; if not, we starve. We are absolutely without a permanent money system. When one gets a complete grasp of the picture, the tragic absurdity of our hopeless position is almost incredible, but there it is. It is the most important subject intelligent persons can investigate and reflect upon. It is so important that our present civilization may collapse unless it becomes widely understood and the defects remedied very soon".

The above information was presented in a way that helps the reader understand the reality of slavery within the modern context. As we continue, please understand the depth of these claims and the foundational support upon which I formulate my conclusions.

The reader may wish to consider the connection of the following:

- The **Federal Reserve** prints and loans the money
- The **IRS** collects the money
- The **FBI** investigates and prosecutes those whom they consider as breakers of the Federal Laws
- The **Anti-Defamation League of B'nai B'rith** labels any and all who dare speak out against the World Banks, the Federal Reserve Act, or the so-called Jewish elements of crime and deception as Anti-Semitic.

All four institutions were brought into existence the exact same year; 1913. Perhaps it is just a coincidence!

THE AMERICAN PIMP MEETS THE HIPHOP WHORE

"We breed two nigger males with two nigger females. Then, we take the nigger male away from them and keep them moving and working. Say one nigger female bears a nigger female and the other bears a nigger male; both nigger females—being without influence of the nigger male image, frozen with a independent psychology—will raise their offspring into reverse positions. The one with the female offspring will teach her to be like herself, independent and negotiable (we negotiate with her, through her, by her, negotiates her at will). The one with the nigger male offspring, she being frozen subconscious fear for his life, will raise him to be mentally dependent and weak, but physically strong; in other words, body over mind. Now, in a few years when these two offsprings become fertile for early reproduction, we will mate and breed them and continue the cycle. That is good, sound and long range comprehensive planning."

If the late 80's introduced the so-called gangster into the HipHop world, the early 2000's introduces the pimp. Today's HipHop is fascinated with the pimp culture, a culture that thrives on the manipulation of minds in order to secure the financial benefit of a person that only is concerned with the well being of self. This culture is completely opposite of the true nature and culture of the black man and woman, but like in all segments of today's life, the so-called American black man and woman has adopted the ways and actions of their slave masters and their children.

Take Snoop Dogg for example; here is a self pro-claimed gang banger, turned pimp. He has prostituted himself into creating a video series that degrades women and reduces himself as a sex-crazed maniac that has absolutely no since of decency and moral responsibility. On a quest to gain additional riches, he perms his hair like a female, and then calls black women bitches; this is done as though it is cool and acceptable. Today's socially conscious black man should confront Snoop and attempt to raise his level of understanding of the time we presently are living, and his responsibility to himself, community and nation. His present actions are unfortunately those of a trader to his nation and co-conspirator to the destruction of the black nation. Ignorance can no longer be accepted as an excuse, the stakes are too high, and we cannot lose another generation due to an ignorant rapper that is backed by clever demons.

Snoop is not the only one, Nelly, Jay Z, Chingy, E-40, Too Short, Ludacris, Suga Free and many others have seemingly lost their damn mind in allowing certain phrases about the black woman to come from their lips. What is worse is that the black collective has allowed these defamers of the black woman to go unpunished. To call a black woman a bitch, is to degrade the very nature of her and take her to the very base level of existence. She is the foundation of our nation, and the disrespect of her, shows the disrespect of our nation.

   What is cool about taking a woman and manipulating her mind into walking the streets searching for men to sexually give pleasure to, take a few bullshit dollars and give it to a pimp? The white slave master got rich and wealthy by degrading and pimping the Blackman and woman, and now like idiots, we mistreat our women just so that we can ride on big wheels, and wear blood diamonds. This is a shame and should cause the black man's blood to boil.

   Some of us argue that the blame is on the woman for allowing herself to be played in such a disrespectful way, therefore she deserves it. That same deceptive argument can be made from the white slave master in regards to slavery and our allowing him to enslave us. This is ridiculous, for us to manipulate the mothers of our nation for foolish pleasures and indulgences, is for us to become less than the white man, and an enemy to our nation. Any man that would destroy the nature of our woman should be viewed as a trader of our nation and should be killed! Again…PLEASE THINK… rappers are getting paid MILLIONS of DOLLARS from WHITE MEN to make music that calls black women BITCHES!! And these IGNORANT ASS RAPPERS attempt to JUSTIFY IT…CAN THEY??!!

The record industry allows for the recording of music videos, and the recording of songs that totally disrespect the black woman. I don't give a damn if a black woman desires to show her ass for money or not, the black man should view all black women as his mother, sister, and daughter, and not allow her to be placed in such a setting. Nelly, a huge HipHop star was saddened by the death of his sister to cancer, yet he swipes a credit card through the buttocks of someone else's sister, all for entertainment. What kind of a mind would do this? You have to be a fool, and a clown, a slave to white people and the way they themselves view the black woman in order to get rich by making videos and songs that disrespect the mother of civilization. There is absolutely no rationalization for this, and no excuse!

   What is truly amazing is that, although the so-called Negro rapper refers to himself as a pimp and wears shiny suits and carries diamond incrusted pimp cups, he actually exemplifies the characteristics of the prostitute. The record company is the pimp that dictates the actions and words of the so-called Negro rapper, and the rapper sells not only sex, but drugs and a filthy lifestyle to the overall community. The rapper is then given crumbs in comparison to the riches given to the recording industry pimp. **The so-called Negro rapper is "macked" by an industry boss, and slapped around by a suit wearing white boy that demands his money from his rapping whore!**

   Listening to the degrading images depicted through the music causes the young black mind to be apathetic in regards to the degraded position and condition of the black woman. Through the video images of the black woman, and the open disrespect and disregard of the black woman within the music itself; the young black male is conditioned to devalue the woman, and the young black girl is conditioned to devalue herself. Given a false reality in terms of beauty, sexuality, and appropriate self-respecting behavior, this inferior view of self, and the lack of the appropriate levels of esteem perpetuates the Pimp and whore mentality. Both mentalities, if gone unchecked contain the unrelenting and destructive elements that can destroy the black man and woman.

To the continuous sound track of ignorant rappers; both male and female, the young black children walk through their young lives oblivious to the fact that the actions and behaviors they display causes the global population to cast us under a shadow of judgment. We are seen as savage, perverse, undisciplined, disrespectful, and ignorant of the manifest wickedness that threatens the world through global politics and economic oppression. This reality is in many ways caused and encouraged by the irresponsible lyrics of the silly sell-out rappers that, for a dollar, would sell-out the future of an entire race.

Before we go forward, let us look further into a few more prevailing realities A young black girl is raped by her mother's boyfriend or her father himself. Because the offending male is a sexual deviant suffering from a perverted mind, the perversion is manifested into actions that hurt the young innocent black girl. This young girl then grows up with the mental condition of one that has been abused by someone whom she should have been able to trust and depend on for elevation and protection. This child was sexually abused as an impressionable young girl, and this abuse has to be made manifest through the thoughts, actions, reactions, of an adult woman.

Now... as this young woman matures and grows, she is bombarded through the media and entertainment world with images that add to the abuse, but never offers any healing elements. She has difficulty relating to the opposite sex, both young and old. Her personality is shaped by her experiences with the black male. Within a social, political, economic, religious, and educational environment that opposes her "actual self" with the debilitating images and concepts that causes her to be at best, confused of her identity and true worth, which at worse, causes her to embrace the false images projected onto her by a wicked society.

Suffering from a society of abuse and false recognition, this black woman is confronted by another societal victim; a black male that refers to himself as a pimp. This so-called pimp preys on the presence of the abused black woman, and then manipulates her mind into accepting the filthy doctrine of selling her body and pride to the perverted elements of society. By giving sexual pleasure to filthy individuals, many times filthy old white men, she receives money that she then gives to the abusive pimp who has fooled her to believe in him and the bullshit that he spits into her ear. All of this is considered cool by the foolish so-called Negro rapper... beating black women, selling her to perverted so-called men, putting her on corners, putting her in a threatening environment is glorified by the rappers and the wealthy individuals that back the evil songs that permeate today's society.
Anyone that participates in this sort of behavior should first be schooled and warned, and if no change is witnessed, should be eliminated from within the ranks of our society.

It should be understood that there are groups and societies of men who directly profit from the ignorance of black people and the people of color throughout the world. When you have the most famous of our people, the rappers, entertainers, and sports figures

acting as clowns, gangsters, pimps, and dope dealers, then the world perceives this as the best that the black man and woman has to offer.

Why should we tolerate the ignorance of so-called Negro rappers, at what point do we say, "Enough is enough"? Powerful record companies allow rappers the freedom to destroy the image of black people throughout the world; for money these modern day uncle toms prostitute themselves so that they can floss on those that reside in the ghetto. Gold teeth, diamond covered pimp cups, and hundred thousand dollar cars are the trinkets that these *rapping whores* accept in exchange for a positive global image.

WHAT THE HELL WAS THIS CLOWN THINKING?!

Are YOU kidding me?! Here, **Snoop,** attends a HipHop function with two black women attached to leashes. With their breast exposed, these women allow themselves to be treated like, and called Bitches (female dogs). Are we to say that this behavior is acceptable...is this HipHop, or is this a filthy gimmick designed to get hype and media attention. Although I have exposed the corporate sponsors to this madness, by no means do I intend to let these so-called Negroe slaves off the hook! I don't care how much money he has...Snoop, and any clown like him, needs his ass kicked! Oh yeah, and so do the so-called black women!

~ ~ ~

THE REAL SMUT PEDDLERS

"we talked about paying particular attention to the female savage and her offspring for orderly future planning, then more recently we stated that, by reversing the positions of the male and female savages, we created an orbiting cycle that turns on its own axis forever unless a phenomenon occurred and re-shifts positions of the male and female savages."

The so-called Jew Hugh Hefner, the creator and owner of Playboy has gotten rich and famous for degrading women and catering to the unrestricted sexual appetites of the American male. The perverse nature of the white man and his world offers cash to those who will participate in filthy behavior. Sex sells, and if the so-called Negro rapper desires to get paid, he must push sex.

If my characterization of the most famous producer of pornographic material in the world as a so-called Jew offends some, and justifies my being placed in the category of an anti-Semitic, please consider the following...

Despite what we may choose to accept and believe, the so-called Jewish elements of the American society disproportionately make up the pornographic industry. So-called Jewish involvement in the adult film industry has a very long and established history, making it a very powerful sub-culture of the United States of America.

Early so-called Jewish immigrants of German origin participated largely in the adult books of erotica between the years 1890 and 1940, profiting off of the technology of book production learned and mastered in the old country. However, none could compare to the son of a so-called Jewish Russian immigrant named **Rueben Sturman**. Born in the state of Ohio in 1924, Sturman made an estimated $300 million dollars per year from the sale of pornography and related items. Considered as the "Walt Disney" of porn, Sturman owned over 200 adult book stores in the mid 1980's. As a onetime comic book peddler, Rueben Sturman realized that the filth of pornography could generate a great more sells than any comic book could; so much so, that by the 1960's his company *Doc Johnson* became the biggest distributor of adult magazines in the United States.

Considered as a crook by the FBI, Rueben Sturman had his Cleveland warehouse raided in 1964. Although Sturman was continuously raided and harassed by authorities, Sturman utilized shady-dealings, deceptive business practices, and over twenty different aliases to slip through the clutches of law enforcement. With connections to the Gambino crime family, Rueben Sturman was an all-out criminal that made huge amounts of cash by selling filth. And again, he referred to himself as a Jew and contributed heavily to so-called Jewish causes.

But of course the so-called Jewish dominance of porn can be proven further:

After being convicted of tax evasion and subsequently dying in prison in 1997, Rueben Sturman's son David continued to run the family business. A close and personal friend and benefactor of Rueben Sturman was a so-called Jew named **Fred Hirsch**; Fred has a son named Steven. **Steven Hirsch** is the creator and leader of the top producer of adult porn, the *Vivid Entertainment Group*. Making over a $100 million dollars a year Vivid Entertainment produces over 60 films per year. As another point of fact, Vivid's branding and licensing efforts are spearheaded by **Wicked Cow Entertainment Inc.** out of New York City. Wicked Cow is a company that acquired licensing rights of HipHop legend the Notorious B.I.G in 2005 and is the licenser of the Notorious B.I.G action figure; Wicked Cow Entertainment is headed by President and CEO **Michael Hermann**, another so-called Jew.

Another giant of the pornographic industry is the so-called Jewish pervert **Alvin "Al" Goldstein**. Born in 1936 in New York City, New York, Al Goldstein is the pornographer that founded the filthy magazine known as "Screw Magazine". Printed weekly in New York City, it quickly became famous and had a circulation of over 500 thousand copies.

These facts are what they are, and they point to a conclusion that cannot be denied. So-called Jewish elements of society not only control the news and entertainment worlds, but they also control and dominate the adult entertainment and pornographic industry.

Let's continue...

Although the so-called Jewish presence can be seen and felt within the pornographic boardrooms of Corporate America, their on screen presence is seen as the dominant element within the smut industry as well. As so-called Negro rappers push filth via their sexually explicit rap and video productions, so-called Jewish smut entertainers grace the perverted fabrics of the various pornographic materials via magazine, DVD, and Video. Such perverts include the so-called Jew **Mr. Ron Jeremy**; born **Ron Jeremy Hyatt** in Long Island New York, his first on screen display being in a production entitled "Inside Seka". Jeremy is the product of an upper-middle class so-called Jewish family, his father Arnold was a physicist and his mother a book editor who served in the Office of Strategic Services (OSS), a United States intelligence agency formed during World War II.

Ron Jeremy is listed in the Guinness Book of World Records for the most appearances in adult films, his entry on the Internet Adult Film Database (IAFD) lists more than 1900 films in which he has performed, and another 264 films of which he was the director. Although Ron Jeremy is one of the most recognizable so-called Jewish faces in the pornographic industry, **consider these names:**

Rubin Gottesman
Paul "Norman"
(Legend CEO

Theodore Rothstein
Ron Braverman
John Bone
Apstein
Steve Orenstein
Jack Richmond
Wesley Emerson
Paul Fishbein
Hank Weinstein
Lenny Friedlander
Bobby Hollander
Ron Sullivan
Herbert Feinberg AKA Mickey Fine
Jerome Tanner
Armand Weston
Sam and Mitch Weston (Spinelli)

The above listed individuals represent the dominate power brokers of the pornographic industry

These facts are important because many in the American and global communities turn a blind eye in the recognition of those forces that contribute to the overall moral decay of a nation or country; although we can easily see and hear ignorant so-called Negro rappers glorifying and engaging in demoralizing behaviors, **I refuse to let the biggest and wealthiest purveyors of filth and immoral behaviors off the hook. It is a known fact that so-called Jewish elements control the pornographic industry; it is a known fact that printed and internet based pornography is dominated by so-called Jewish elements. What is missing is the courage to call out these individuals in a way that confronts their hypocrisy and complicity in regards to the overall moral decay of the American and subsequently the global society.**

Just as mainstream Hollywood is dominated by so-called Jewish executives that provide their so-called Jewish sisters and brothers with acting jobs, so much so, that the so-called Jewish presence in Hollywood vastly contradicts the statistical proportions of their overall American population; the pornographic world, based right outside of Hollywood in the San Fernando Valley, is dominated by so-called Jewish executives that provide their so-called Jewish kin with jobs that allow them to likewise dominate the pornographic entertainment industry.

Consider these names:

Buck Adams
Bobby Astyr
(Bobby Charles) R. Bolla (Robert Kerman)

Jerry Butler (Paul Siderman)
Seymore Butts (Adam Glasser)
Roger Caine (Al Levitsky)
David Christopher (Bernie Cohen)

Steve Drake
Jesse Eastern
Jamie Gillis (Jamie Gurman)
Michael Knight
William Margold
Ashley Moore (Steve Tucker)
David Morris
George Payne
Ed Powers (Mark Arnold aka Mark Krinski)
Harry Reems (Herbert Streicher)
Dave Ruby
Herschel Savage (Harvey Cowen)
Carter Stevens (Mal Warub)
Marc Stevens
Paul Thomas (Phil Tobias)
Marc Wallice (Marc Goldberg)
Randy West (Andy Abrams) Jack Wrangler

The above are so-called Jewish male performers...

Consider the Females:

Avalon
Jenny Baxter (Jenny Wexler)
Busty Belle (Tracy Praeger)
Chelsea Blake
Tiffany Blake
Bunny Bleu (Kim Warner)
J.R. Carrington
Lee Carroll (Leslie Barris)
Blair Castle/Brooke Fields (Allison Shandibal)
Courtney/Natasha/Eden (Natasha Zimmerman)
Daphne (Daphne Franks)
Barbara Dare (Stacy Mitnick)
April Diamond
Jeanna Fine
Alexis Gold
Terri Hall
Heather Hart
Nina Hartley (Hartman)
C.J. Laing (Wendy Miller)
Frankie Leigh (Cynthia Hope Geller)
Gloria Leonard
Traci Lords (Nora Louise Kuzma)
Amber Lynn
Tonisha Mills
Melissa Monet
Susan Nero
Scarlett O. (Catherine Goldberg)
Tawny Pearl (Susan Pearlman)
Nina Preta
Tracey Prince
Raylene
Janey Robbins (Robin Lieberman)
Mila Shegol
Alexandra Silk
Susan Sloan
Annie Sprinkle (Ellen Steinberg)
Karen Summer (Dana Alper)
Cindy West
Zara Whites (Amy Kooiman)   Ona Zee (Ona Simms)

Now it should be evident that so-called Jews disproportionately make up the pornographic world. The sex industry has been permeated by the indelible presence of the so-called Jewish male pornographic performers; in fact throughout the 70's and 80's, the so-called Jew established themselves as the premier actors of smut and sex that has been cast as entertainment. Far from being the "priest of holiness" and a nation of righteousness, the self-proclaimed Jew has established themselves as the "Kings of Smut", and a nation of sex peddlers!

I know, I know—I am exaggerating right? Look at, this guy is a so-called Jew that was born as **Adam Glasser** in March of 1964, in The Bronx, New York. But here is the key, a key that seemingly goes unnoticed... Adam was born in New York, Adam changed his name; Adam claims to be Jewish. Isn't that funny, in a media world that always portrays the black man and woman as the culprits and causers of the moral decay and societal degeneracy of America; a New York born so-called Jew who named himself Seymore Butts, has not only established himself as a premier pornographic power broker, but his mother and other family members have become porno players. Yes that's right, the so-called Jewish mother who always wanted to see her little baby boy grow up to be a respectable doctor or lawyer, has settled into her role within the production and distribution aspects of the smut industry.... Her name is Laila Glasser, and she's over 70 years old!

In 2003, momma Glasser, Cousin Stevie (Steve Glasser), and Adam's (Seymore) preadolescent son Brady; all got together under the direction of Seymore Butts and subscription cable television giant SHOWTIME, in order to film and produce a reality show entitled "Family Business". This show was based on the pornographic business endeavors of Adam Glasser and his so-called Jewish family.

Now why would I dare call Mr. Butts and his cohorts so-called Jewish.... Simple—Adam Glasser had a brit and bar mitzvah. His parents were so-called "good Jews'; they even operated a traditional shmattah business; also, he informed his parents of his decision at the Rosh Hashanah dinner table as the family was dipping apples in honey. No joke... lets continue.

Have you ever heard of the porn site, sex.com... well, who do you think owns that? Although there has been a court battle that attempted to settle who in fact originated this popular porn site that attracts over 25 million visitors a day... there is no doubt that **Stephen Cohen**, a so-called Jewish multimillionaire has reaped huge amounts of cash due to his association with sex.com. But wait... there was a battle in court over the rights to the popular site; if there was a battle, who was the other person that was attempting to garnish the proceeds from the most popular web domain? You guessed it, a so-called Jew by the name of **Gary Kreman**, who happens not only to be the founder of sex.com; he also was the founder of jobs.com, housing.com, autos.com, and the web dominate site called match.com. Isn't that interesting? Of course it is.... But there is more!

Considered as the "Prince of Porn", and also the "Bill Gates" of porn; **Seth Warshavsky** is the CEO of the "Internet Entertainment Group" IEG, a hugely successful adult content (porno) provider. Born in 1973, this guy has all but cornered the internet sex market... He has even found a way to sell Viagra on line! Oh yeah, did I mention... He too is a so-called Jew.

Lukeford.com is a pornographic opinion site that is ran and operated by **Luke Ford**, a so-called Jewish entrepreneur that is referenced as the **Matt Drudge** (who also happens to be so-called Jewish) of porn. His mentor and friend is no other than right-wing, so-called Jewish, talk-radio personality **Dennis Prager** (Ford also runs Prager's website).

All of this information is easily obtained if one formulates a desire to look at it for what it is. For many of us today, we have been led to believe that those that are known as Jews are free and clear from the blames of moral decay in regards to America and its forms of entertainment. Without a doubt, the so-called Jews are the primary executives and directors of what is seen as pleasure and information within today's society. How can someone choose to criticize HipHop and its effects on society without pointing to those that profit most on filth and indecency? The black men and women of HipHop has been consistently attacked and maligned for the content of their music; but the minute someone has the intellectual audacity to point to those that wax rich behind the curtains of holiness, that person is seen as anti-Semitic.... Well I think we are beginning to see that is a joke.... Let's keep going!

Reuben Sterman, In the postwar era, America's most notorious pornographer was Reuben Sturman, the inventor of the peep show, and dubbed the 'Bill Gates of porn'by US News and World Report. According to the US Department of Justice, throughout the 1970s Sturman controlled most of the pornography circulating in the country. By the mid-80s he owned over 200 adult bookstores. It was said that Sturman did not simply control the adult-entertainment industry, he was the industry.

Ron Jeremy: "People call **Jeremy** addicted (to food), a tightwad, a clown, a spotlight hound and a man who can maintain an erection longer than any man in pornography. He claims not to use Viagra. He was born Ron Hyatt into a Jewish family who don't seem too put off by his ultimate career choice, although after the first porn film, his dad told Ron not to use his last name ... We are talking about a man who can count a film called Blow it Out Your Ass, as a typical title among the 1600 or so films he has appeared in."

Steve Hirsch The contemporary incarnation of Reuben Sturman, an earlier Jewish Porn King, is Steven Hirsch, a 43-year-old Jewish Clevelander who has been described as the 'Donald Trump of porno.' The link between the two is Steve's father, Fred, who was a stockholder- cum-lieutenant to Sturman. Today Hirsch runs the Vivid Entertainment Group, which has been called the Microsoft of the porn world, the top producer of 'adult' films in the US. His specialty was to import mainstream marketing techniques into the porn business. Indeed, Vivid parallels the Hollywood studio system of the 1930s and 1940s, particularly in its exclusive contracts to porn stars who are hired and moulded by Hirsch

~~~

RAPPERS PUSH POISON!

"Put the niggers and the horse in a breeding pot, mix some asses and some good white blood and what do you get? You got a multiplicity of colors of ass backward, unusual niggers, running, tied to backward ass long-headed mules, the one productive of itself, the other sterile. (The one constant, the other dying, we keep the nigger constant for we may replace the mules for another tool) both mule and nigger tied to each other, neither knowing where the other came from and neither productive for itself, nor without each other."

In attempt to get today's so-called Negro rappers to understand what is at stake in terms of the future of themselves and their people, I have laid a foundation that should aid in their overall comprehension of those that profit from our misery. Even if the rappers themselves choose to discount this information and the overall message of this book; I would hope that those that have been supporters of the HipHop Nation and its artist will come into certain awareness and raise the bar in terms of artistic expectations as it relates to what is released for our consumption.

Whether the so-called Negro rapper understands it or not, they are being used and manipulated within the imperialistic agenda of those who simply desire to rule the world. We cannot for one minute believe that white people, or the political and economical power brokers that have historically and traditionally instituted policies and procedures that ultimately lend to our destruction as a people, have changed their minds or hearts.

The same mind that killed Indians and sentenced them to reservations, enslaved black people, segregated toilets and schools, and atomically bombed innocent people within the borders of Japan, is the same mind that today rules corporations, sells pornography, creates wars under false pretenses, distributes crack cocaine, manufactures and distributes viruses, and has young black men and women pushing chemical poison to their fellow brothers and sisters.

We should understand that there is a clandestine network formulated on the basis of global domination that desires to utilize the voices of ignorant rappers to further their cause. Though we believe that we are a well informed people, we must accept the fact that information has been meticulously and systematically kept from us. We would be shocked to taste the fruits of just a basic level of research. If we connect certain dots, we would be forced to deal with what comes from the rudimentary acknowledgment of truth. One question leads to one answer, that answer leads to a series of more questions; we can choose to bury our heads in the sands of ignorance if we want to, but if we simply glance up for a moment, we will see the storm clouds clearly formulated over our heads ready to release an onslaught that none can fully imagine.

With this being said, please recognize the facts as it pertains to black people here in America specifically, and people of color globally. **The global power base desires to maintain and magnify their global control. They desire to reduce the world's population of people of color dramatically by the year 2050. In fact, they have already instituted steps toward that end, and we have already begun to see the affects of the political and economic demon's plans.**

Propaganda has been spewed from the mouths of rapping pawns that support the desires of these global pirates. By glorifying and encouraging behaviors that ultimately lead to our destruction, these rappers are clearly helping those in high places assault the minds of those in low places. The so-called Negro rapper is the vehicle by which the wicked encouragements of the human beasts can be heard.

Now, within the pages of this book I have attempted in a very brief and concise way to show the business brilliance and mathematical way that the political and economic power brokers of this world think and act. Each and every decision made has millions and even billions of dollars at stake; therefore, it would be silly and downright asinine for us to believe that the political, economic, social, and physical result of what comes from the mouths of ignorant rappers have not been calculated and determined profitable. In terms of profit, the dollar bill is the most insignificant profit receipt, the acquisitions of dollars does not compare to the continued maintenance and growth of the aspiring desires of global control and dominance.

Self-destructive behaviors such as promiscuous sex, use of narcotics, crime centered lives, and the massive consumption of alcohol has all been glorified, and it seems that every HipHop song released by these record plantations are laced with heavy doses of behaviors that should be considered shameful.

Rappers push poison, they are dope dealers; they sale wickedly destructive verses that help little black children formulate faulty conclusions. Their verses translate to behaviors that point to the reality of an open enemy that desires to keep us blind, deaf, and dumb to the knowledge of those that profit from our misery and destruction.

Let's look at it this way: After Ice Cube left N.W.A under accusations that Eazy E and his so-called Jewish partner Jerry Heller was undermining his financial success and robbing him of deserved revenues, he decided to make an alliance with the socially conscious rap group Public Enemy and Chuck D. After releasing solo albums Amerikkka's Most Wanted and Death Certificate; two albums that contained ruff edges and controversial urban scenarios yet still contained an over whelming politically and socially conscious over tone... Ice Cube was approached by the devil.

Having recorded songs such as *Burn Hollywood Burn*, and *I Wanna Kill Sam*, Ice Cube was approached by the wickedly wise so-called Jewish poison merchant by the name of **Minott Wessinger**, a descendent of brewer **Henry Weihard**, also a so-called Jewish chemical poison manufacturer. After his family's brewery was sold to **G. Heileman** Brewing Company, Mr. Wessinger started the McKenzie River Corporation, created a new malt liquor, and contracted Heileman to brew it for him beginning in 1987.

As a note, G. Heileman Brewing Company is responsible for the chemical poison aimed primarily at the heads of blacks as a malt liquor named after a gun, Colt 45. Ice Cube, although being identified during his N.W.A days as an avid drinker and supporter of the hugely successful malt liquor Olde English (8 Ball), accepted thousands of dollars to record over 30 radio spots and to reference the 8 Ball's poisonous competitor *St. Ides* within his songs. This rapper who had made himself famous as a solo artist by his alliance to the socially conscious rap group Public Enemy, sold out to the chemical poison manufactures by endorsing the consumption of this ethno-centered targeted weapon of mass destruction. Olde English is the major competitor of St. Ides, a drink named as a church or saint, and St. Ides malt liquor quickly surpassed Olde English in sales with the help of Mr. Wessinger's slave Oshea "Ice Cube" Jackson.

Mr. Wessinger seduced Ice Cube into a whore like relationship that while he got paid, he *"Fucked"* his entire community. Understanding that the money offered by the so-called Jew did little to make or break the success of one of the most successful rappers of all time, we would think the social stance of rejection would have even furthered Ice Cubes career and the socially conscious rhetoric that he has spit from his lips. Ice Cube chose a different route, he chose the so-called Jew and the money over the health and well being of his community... and by doing so has become one of the most successful black rappers turned movie star. I wonder if his ability to sell-out has anything to do with his ability to secure certain movie roles that are offered by the cousins on those that sale the poison in the bottles... hummm, I don't know!

Examine the following: Budweiser is ran and owned by so-called Jews, Anheuser-Busch; Schlitz Malt Liquor is the product of so-called Jew, **Joseph Schlitz,** as mentioned before; Olde English malt liquor is the result of so-called Jewish operated G. Heileman Brewery. But the most powerful chemical poison manufacturer in the world is none other than the aforementioned **Mr. Edgar Bronfman.**

Mr. Bronfman is the president of the **World Jewish Congress**, and the supreme benefactor of the chemical poison empire known as Seagram's. Seagram's was first introduced to the world in a large way by Edgar's father **Samuel Bronfman**. But Edgar has taken the Seagram brand and raised it to a monumental plateau within the corporate world. By taking the profits from the selling of poison, the Bronfman family has been able to purchase and develop one of the biggest entertainment conglomerates in the world. Also, by the sale of filth and poison, the Bronfman family has been able to fund the state of Israel and many other so-called Jewish endeavors that support the realities and the agendas of those who refer to themselves as Jews and Zionist.

To be fair to Ice Cube, he is certainly not the only rapper that has sold the black communities interest for a profit. Snoop Dogg has endorsed Seagram's Gin, as well as Petey Pablo. Rappers have been offered cash dollars for mentioning the chemical poison within their songs. And rappers such as P Diddy, Busta Rymes, and Jay Z among several others have sold out to the enemy by glamorizing the poison throughout their releases.

It would be very easy for me to lace these pages with incredible facts and statistics that support the claim that the consumption of alcohol is assisting with the destruction of many lives within the Black, Native American, and Latino communities, but that is not necessary. We must understand that the destruction of our people is at an epidemic level, and gallop polls and census reports do nothing to establish in our minds the state that we are presently in. I mean think about it, when was the last time you seen a crack whore, homeless person, a crack baby, or gang banger interviewed by these so-called pollsters and their manipulative clipboards?

We must come to an understanding that our destruction is being calculated within the smoke filled board rooms of corporate and governmental America. When these special interest groups converge within the hallways of congress and Wall Street, they are formulating plans that fulfill their individual and collective desires and agendas. It should be understood, that despite what black people *wish were the case,* the plans and agendas that serve these special interest groups traditionally spell out a degenerative future for "our group".

When we allow ourselves to aide in the wealth and power of those that do not factor in our future when it comes to their agendas, we are in fact responsible for our own destruction. Money should not allow these young black men and women to sell their souls to corporate America just so that they can purchase things that they can utilize to floss on their fellow brothers and sisters.

Alcohol and drugs destroy the fabrics of our minds. At this point in time we cannot waste another generation to foolishness, sport, and play. While Palestinian children, Afghanistan children and African children are fighting imperialistic forces while being barefoot and under armed, we are producing a generation that sits in front of television screens watching foolishness and playing virtual reality games. We have become soft as a nation, and though it takes little for us to call each other niggas, and to bust a cap in one another's asses, we cannot seem to muster any strength or determination to uplift our people and confront the forces that clearly threaten our survival.

The Bronfman family and the corporate giants that are ran by a certain group of people make a living studying and calculating numbers. The effects of their poison and program on the black, brown, red, and yellow does not go unnoticed by the purveyors of the said poison. While these corporate snakes continue on a campaign to belittle and label anyone who speaks against them and their Zionist ambitions as anti-Semitic, they do not give a collective damn about the continuous bullshit that is played over the airwaves of America. But to be truthful, why should they?! If we as a people don't give a damn, why should anybody else? We are pathetically weak in terms of our national defense as a people, yet we bang over corners, burroughs, regions, and neighborhoods. I believe that in 2009, those who oppose the survival and strengthening of our people should be viewed as traitors and sellouts of our people. Regardless if these sellouts play sports, tell jokes, sing songs, act and entertain, or talk killer shit on the microphone—if you don't give a damn about your people and their future you should be called what you are, a 2009 version of the Uncle Tom!

Before we abandon the subject of alcohol and its effect on the HipHop Nation; let's elucidate a few more points....

As the so-called Jews claim to be the chosen of God, they seemingly maintain the appearances as a sober nation or tribe; and though this may in fact be the case... it is an absolute fact, as highlighted in the earlier chapter "Will the Real Gangster Please Stand Up"; that the so-called Jews initiated and controlled the bulk of the alcoholic bootlegging of North America.

Although the corporate media chooses to down play the so-called Jewish involvement in not only bootlegging, but alcohol in general... once again, the facts speak for themselves!

In the volume, "The Conquering Jew," published by Funk & Wagnall's Company in 1916, John Foster Fraser writes:

The Jews are masters of the whisky trade in the United States. Eighty percent of the members of the National Liquor Dealers' Association are Jews. It has been shown that 60 percent of the business of distilling and wholesale trade in whisky is in the hands of the Jews. As middlemen they control the wine product of California. Jews visit the tobacco-growing States and buy up nearly all the leaf tobacco, so that the great tobacco companies have to buy the raw product from them. The Jews have a grip on the cigar trade. The American Tobacco Company manufactures about 15 percent of the cigars smoked in the United States—the Jews provide the rest.

But don't get it twisted... the so-called alcoholic dominance is not just restricted to America; it is an historical fact that in Russia, Poland, and Rumania, the so-called Jewish question was always centered on liquor and the wealth and power that stemmed from it. But as for America, these following companies will shed light on the proliferation of liquor within the continental bounds of North America:

There is "Old 66," owned by **Straus, Pritz & Co.**

"Highland Rye," owned by **Freiberg & Workum.**

"T.W. Samuel Old Style Sour Mash," owned by **Max Hirsch**, the Star Distilling Company.

"Bridgewater Sour Mash and Rye Whiskies," "Rosewood and Westbrook Bourbon Whiskies," distilled by **J. & A. Freiberg.**

"T. J. Monarch and Davies County Sour Mash Whiskies," controlled by **J. & A. Freiberg.**

"Louis Hunter 1870," "Crystal wedding," and "Old Jug," blended by **J. & A. Freiberg.**

"Gannymede '76," put out by **Sigmund** and **Sol H. Freiberg.**

"Jig-Saw Kentucky Corn Whisky," "Lynndale Whisky," "Brunswick Rye and Bourbon," by **Hoffheimer Brothers** Company.

"Red Top Rye" and "White House Club," by **Ferdinand Westheimer & Sons.**

"Green River" came into the control of **E. La Montague**.

"Sunnybrook," a widely advertised brand, on whose advertising matter a man in a United States inspector's uniform stood behind as if endorsing it, was at the time owned by **Rosenfield Brothers & Co.**

"Mount Vernon," as from the Hannis Distilling Company, was at the time owned by **Angelo Meyer**.

"Belle of Nelson" came into control of the Jewish trust, which was brought to legal birth by **Levy Mayer** and **Alfred Austrian.**

"James E. Pepper" was owned by **James Wolf**.

"Cedar Brook" was owned by **Julius Kessler & Co**. It was formerly the old "W. H. McBrayer" brand, but the real W. H. McBrayer, knowing the new methods that were arising in liquor-making, requested in his will that his name should not be used as a brand after he had ceased to see that the product was worthy of his name.

The Great Western Distillery, in Peoria, is owned by a corporation of Jews. Two of its brands were "Ravenswood Rye" and "Ravenswood Bourbon."

The Woolner Distillery made "Old Grove Whisky" and "Old Ryan Whisky," and "Bucha Gin."

Although we may tend to equate the state of Kentucky as the capitol of Whiskey in America; it is a little known fact that Cincinnati, Ohio was the place where copycat or bootleg (artificial whiskey) was made and controlled by the so-called Jew.... **Consider the following:**

Bernheim, Rexinger & Company	Klein Brothers
Elias Bloch & Son	A. Loeb & Co
& A. Freiberg	H. Rosenthal & Sons
Freiberg & Workum	Seligman Distilling Company
Helfferich & Sons	Straus, Pritz & Company
Hoffheimer Brothers Company	N. Weil & Company
Elias Hyman & Sons	F. Westheimer & Sons
Kaufman, Bare & Company	

This list still falls short in giving an accurate count of all those that participate in the Cincinnati liquor game, many other so-called Jews are concealed under fancy trade names and corporation designations. It is the same throughout Ohio which is, incidentally, one of the most so-called Jew-ridden states in the Union. Like previously mentioned, Ohio also happens to be the state that initiated the so-called Jewish control and domination of pornography; but please, don't just focus on Cincinnati, Ohio—any citizen, in any city of size, will have no trouble in confirming the statement that most of the rectifiers, wholesalers and brokers in the whisky trade of his city also were so-called Jews.

African-American Youth and Alcohol Advertising

The prevalence and consequences of underage drinking among African-American youth

Prevalence and consequences of underage drinking among African-American youth:

Alcohol is the drug most widely used by African-American youth. Although African-American youth drink less than other youth (according to the 2004 National Survey on Drug Use and Health, 19.1% of African Americans between 12 and 20 used alcohol in the 30 days prior to the survey, compared to 32.6% of whites, and 9.9% of African-American youth reported "binge" drinking, compared to 22.8% of whites), there is evidence from public health research that, as they age, African Americans suffer more from alcohol-related diseases than other groups in the population.

The age-adjusted death rate from alcohol-related diseases for non-Hispanic African Americans is 10% greater than for the general population.

National surveys have found that while frequent heavy drinking among white 18-29 year-old males dropped between 1984 and 1995, rates of heavy drinking and alcohol problems remained high among African Americans in the same age group.

Alcohol use contributes to the three leading causes of death among African-American 12 to 20 year-olds: homicide, unintentional injuries (including car crashes), and suicide.

Exposure of African-American young people to alcohol advertising in 2004:

In magazines:

Twenty-seven percent of African-American teens ages 12-17 and 21% of African Americans ages 18-20 are among the most frequent magazine readers, versus 18% and 13% of non-African Americans in these age groups.

Youth exposure to alcohol advertising in national magazines has fallen substantially since 2001. However, in 2004, youth were still overexposed to magazine advertising relative to adults. In 2004 youth ages 12 to 20 saw 15% more advertising for beer and 10% more advertising for distilled spirits (the largest category of magazine alcohol advertising) per capita than adults age 21 and over. In this context of general overexposure, African-American youth saw even more advertising for these products in magazines in 2004 than youth in general.

African-American youth saw 34% more alcohol advertising in national magazines than did youth in general in 2004. Compared to the average for all youth, African-American youth saw 21% more advertising for beer and ale, 42% more advertising for distilled spirits, 6% less advertising for "alcopops" such as Smirnoff Ice and Mike's Hard Lemonade, and 3% less advertising for wine brands.

While 97% of all youth saw an average of 113 alcohol ads in magazines, 99% of African-American youth saw an average of 150 alcohol ads in national magazines in 2004.

African-American youth also more advertising per capita for beer and ale, distilled spirits and alcopops than African-American adults: they saw 23% more beer and ale advertising, 7% more distilled spirits advertising, and 12% more advertising for alcopops than African-Americans age 21 and over.

In 2004, out of 211 alcohol brands advertising in national magazines, just 22 brands including six cognac or brandy brands accounted for more than half of African-American youth exposure but less than a third of total spending in magazines.

Alcohol advertisers concentrated the advertising that overexposed African-American youth in 14 magazines accounting for 75% of the exposure of African-American youth to alcohol advertising in 2004, including ***Sports Illustrated, Vibe, Stuff, Entertainment Weekly, The Source, InStyle*** and ***Vogue***. All the aforementioned titles exposed African-American youth to alcohol ads more effectively than youth in general. They also exposed African-American youth more effectively than African-American adults.

On the radio:

African-American teens ages 12-17 listen to more than 17 hours of radio per week on average, compared to 13.25 hours for all teens.

In a sample of 67,404 occurrences of advertising airing in 104 markets for the 25 leading alcohol brands in June- July of 2004, African-American youth heard 15% more alcohol advertising per capita than youth in general.

In 25 of 104 markets and in six of the top ten markets which contain approximately 27% of the total U.S. population but 34% of the African-American population African-American youth heard more alcohol advertising on the radio per capita than youth in general. These six markets were New York, Los Angeles, Chicago, Dallas-Fort Worth, Houston-Galveston, and Detroit.

Measured in gross impressions, a standard measure of advertising exposure that represent the total number of advertising exposures for a given population, a single brand, Colt 45 Malt Liquor, accounted for nearly a third of African-American youth exposure to alcohol advertising on the radio, while it and Hennessey Cognacs were the two brands that most disproportionately exposed African-American youth compared with all youth.

On television:

Thirty-nine percent of African-American teens ages 12 to 17 are among the most frequent viewers (the top quintile) of cable TV, a fast-growing medium for alcohol advertisers, versus 16% of non-African-American teens.

Alcohol advertisers spent nearly $4.8 million in 2004 to place ads on all 15 of the programs most popular with African-American youth, including *Girlfriends*, *Half & Half*, *CSI* and *Without a Trace*.

Three leading alcoholic beverage brands (Bud Light, Heineken Beer and Miller Genuine Draft) accounted for more than half of the spending on this advertising.

On **BET (Black Entertainment Television)**, a cable television network targeting African-American audiences, overall alcohol spending as well as spending on the programs generating the greatest youth exposure to alcohol advertising increased from 2003 to 2004.

In 2004, 72% of alcohol advertising spending on BET was on ten programs that were more likely to be seen by youth than by adults. On these programs, as well as across all the BET programming containing alcohol advertising, young people ages 12 to 20 were more than twice as likely to be in the audience than adults age 21 and over.

Alcohol marketing and the African-American community:

The marketing of alcohol products in African-American communities has, on occasion, stirred national controversy and met with fierce resistance from African Americans and others. Charges of over-concentration of alcohol billboards in African-American neighborhoods have prompted protests and legislative fights in Chicago, Milwaukee, Baltimore, Los Angeles and elsewhere.

Battles over the heavy marketing to the African-American community of malt liquor, a stronger-than-average beer, resulted in the banning of one new brand, PowerMaster, in the summer of 1991, and fines against the makers of another, St. Ides Malt Liquor, by the states of New York and Oregon, for advertising practices that allegedly targeted youth and glamorized gang activity.

African-American youth culture already abounds with alcohol products and imagery. A content analysis of 1,000 of the most popular songs from 1996 to 1997 found that references to alcohol **were more frequent in rap (47% of songs had alcohol references)** than other genres such as country-western (13%), top 40 (12%), alternative rock (10%), and heavy metal (4%); and that **48% of these rap songs had product placements or mentions of specific alcohol brand names.**

Rap music videos analyzed for a study published in 1997 contained the highest percentage of depictions of alcohol use of any music genre appearing on **MTV, BET, CMT** and **VH-1**.

A recent study of alcohol mentions in rap music found that from 1979 to 1997 such references increased five-fold, with a particular increase in appearances of liquor and champagne brands after 1994. From 1994 to 1997, 71% of the rap songs that mentioned alcohol in this study's sample named a specific alcohol brand.

Updated June 2006 by:

THE CENTER ON ALCOHOL MARKETING AND YOUTH

www.camy.org

~~~

WORDS OF AN UNCLE TOM!

"institute a new language that involves the new life's work of both. You know language is a peculiar institution. It leads to the heart of a people."

In the year 1555, black people arrived on the shores of a wilderness that white people chose to call America. These white people claimed to have discovered this place, despite the presence of several million people that white folk decided to label as Indians. At the same time that these white so-called Christians were tricking these so-called Indians and robbing them of their land; these same so-called Christians were systematically stripping those, who came from the land commonly referred to as Africa, of the knowledge of God, themselves, culture and Language.

By utilizing specially designed tactics of manipulations and torture, these white people began on the road of making slaves. These people from Africa were mentally reduced to children by the wicked machinations of a demonic people and system. By erasing truth from the fabrics of their mind, and replacing it with lies, the white slave master caused black people to come to faulty conclusions about themselves and their open enemy.

In 2006, so-called Negro rappers are injecting into the minds of people all over the world a negative depiction of black people. People all over the planet are hearing black people call each other niggers. They are hearing young black children calling black women bitches. People from Africa to Asia are seeing depictions of the so-called African American on movie screens murdering one another and destroying our people from predatory behaviors and drug sales. Rappers are actually recording their voices bragging on the rape and sexual abuses of women. No other people on the planet are doing and consuming the filth that we are participating in. We laugh as if it is funny; so-called grown men, who may or may not listen to HipHop, sit looking silly while young children disrespect mothers and grandmothers. It seems as if black men have become cowards and have lost the balls to correct these self-proclaimed thugs that are in reality our misguided and undisciplined children.

When these rappers in these songs speak of crime, who do we think are the victims of these crimes that they are glorifying? If a car is jacked, who is the owner of that car? If a rapper has gotten rich by selling drugs, who are the buyers of those drugs? If a woman is victimized and turned out as a prostitute, what woman is this? You see, the truth is that our young black boys and girls have been conditioned to fear white folk, and at the same time hate their own selves. When black people commit crimes, the majority of the time it is against other black people. So when we here these rapping Uncle Toms glorifying crime, the victims are black people. If white people recorded the songs that we record, black people would have a fit; yet, today's black men and women don't make a sound against these millionaire sellouts that get paid by bragging about the murder and victimization of other black males and females.

We should demand the foolishness to stop, but we are cowards in the face of wrong, yet apologist and defenders of white people. The minds of black children are comprised of the sum total of the information that is given to them. Throughout school, society, news and entertainment, black children are given messages that are diametrically opposed to a reality that is good for them. They are taught from an early age that they are worthless, and that their people have not contributed anything of value to the present world in which they live. Although there are some of us who realize that this is not the truth, the fact remains, black rappers and entertainers are doing very little or nothing at all to confront the false realities that are being systematically placed within the minds of the children.

Rappers brag of murder, they call black women bitches, they glorify the use of drugs and alcohol; over 95 percent of all songs recorded speak of actions and behaviors that lead straight to our destruction... but the sorry thing is, people who do not belong to our communities are getting paid off of our destructive behaviors... this my people, is the truest definition and example of slavery.

Before we bring this chapter to a close, let's examine some of the words of these so-called Negro rappers that are being used to further the agenda of their open enemies:

Artist: **The Murderers f/ Black Child, Ja Rule, Tah Murdah**
Album: **Irv Gotti Presents...The Murderers**
Song: **Murderers**

[Black Child]

Uh huh, we did it

Motherfucker

Somebody gotta do it

It gotta get done, why not get it done with the gun?

Word to god

Yo yo yo

Chorus: Ja Rule

Murder'a, inside must be hollow

Kill us today or you'll have to kill us tomorrow

Murder'a, inside must be shallow

How does it feel to take a life of anotha

Murder'a, inside must be hollow

Kill us today or you'll have to kill us tomorrow

Murder'a, inside must be shallow

How does it feel to take a life...

[Black Child]

It's murda and its not a game

Y'all *Silence* gonna feel the flames and a lotta pain

Let me explain from day one its murda one with no gun

Taking income, makin bitch niggas run

The nine-one-one roll up nigga what

We got the four pound tucked, the Porsche look plush

Niggas get fuckin clapped and killed for flossin

That probly why niggas get killed so often

Nothin to live for type a nigga I did a bid for

Snitch bitch niggas that ain't built for war

Is it because we ain't got no love for thugs

And slugs for drugs, the world's most murda'rous

Black Child, nigga you know how the fuck I do

Put two in you, then puff a blunt at your funeral

I might touch yo' click and fuck yo' bitch

But'choo never heard a nigga spit shit like this

Chours

[Tah Murdah]

When I'm gunnin I'm coming on ??? shit rubber grip

Four shit on the sawed off, blowin the doors off the Range Rov' shit

Fo' sho' this, is somethin' we die for

And my murdera's I lie and fry for

Murda man, when the shit hit the fan

The plan formulate, for instance, fuck a percentage you need the all the cake

Put the four to snakes make 'em lay for raw

Fuck the game, 'cuz nigga I don't play no more

Size 'em up, nevermind if you ridin tough

Count 'em out 'til his eyes is puff, despising us

I got hungry thugs that'll tie you up

And they ain't got a problem with, snub nose revolver shit

We hard to hit, my mom's a Crip

We thristy niggas that'll rob ya bitch for the love of the chips

So when I'm soaking the whip, y'all niggas keep hatin'

Gotta stash where the heats placed in, paper I keep chasin

Motherfucker, uh uh

Chorus

[Ja Rule]

Yo, yo...

Forever young this face kills so many all die, nigga must I?

Confess my sins, to the souls of the unknown, why?

Would you ever disrespect my niggas

We murderous engines that lead to lynchin's

Index, itching, ready to run up and hit 'em

Let the teflon spin 'em, they say "look how Ja did 'em"

I a murder'a , Inc'ed and blood you know you heard of us

Murderers juts because we the shhhhhhh

Make a nigga much harder to hit with the ox

We can take it back, give me five minutes in the box

Or trade hot rocks 'til one of us drops

Nothin but shells and you can hear the shot for blocks
I'm giving 'em hell, while niggas steady hollerin' "stop"
I spit sixteens with aim and continue to pop
Motherfuckers, what'choo want with this shit

The murderous I-N-C, nigga

Artist: **The Murderers**
Album: **Irv Gotti Presents...The Murderers** *
Song: **We Murderers Baby** * originally on the "Next Friday" soundtrack
(Ja Rule and Vita)
Yo (we murderers, baby)
Da Murderers (I here for you, baby)
I.N.C. (I'll ryde for you, baby)
Vita, Ja Rule

[Chorus]
(Ja Rule and Vita)
I be running and gunning them down (we murderers, baby)
Leave me or love me now (I'm here for you baby)
Anywhere, anyhow (I'll ryde for you baby)
You and I together, and we blast forever
{2x}
(Ja Rule)
Ja's the dream and nigga's wake up and sweats its about
horse head in your bed, nigga
gun your mouth
potty it out
wrong nigga,
spit one more thang and have your hood pouring out liqour

cause my niggas run through lesbians

niggas, that act like brawds

feel the strip and thus be gone

hold up, nigga that done spread up

you might wanna keep in touch with the murderers

cause we, the murderers I.N.C.

is above yall niggas, it's the lord in me

and we can never be at a love's lost

but you, showed me love ain't boss

feel the force,

this young horse,

known as rule

gave more paper to jigga for my ewls

and lord knows ain't no pussy going to stop my flow

i don't love you hoes, I'm out the door

{Chorus}

(Ja Rule and Vita)

I be running and gunning them down (we murderers, baby)

Leave me or love me now (I'm here for you baby)

Anywhere, anyhow (I'll ryde for you baby)

You and I together, and we blast forever

{2x}

(~Vita~)

ou that motherfucking bitch, Vita nigga

you want me to ryde you nigga

Clap up and hide you nigga

been beside my niggas for this long

i'm keeping my head right and tight and doe long

I can go on, about shit I've been through

transponed, keys are in too

shit i got issues

if I pop a bitch

then she probably a snitch

L-A-V-I-T-A-A-A-K-A Taday Vallet shit

when my niggas from my bitches

sold drugs from niggas to the murderes

I'm the bitch, sometimes i even spit on chicks

cause in the clubs, i say criss, and I piss the shit, baby

I know your brawds been feeling me, lately, now livin and lay

cause i touch them with gun blades, dark is us

any light, shine, we bust,

Vita, Gotti and Rule, we make up the murderers

{Chorus}

(Ja Rule and Vita)

I be running and gunning them down (we murderers, baby)

Leave me or love me now (I'm here for you baby)

Anywhere, anyhow (I'll ryde for you baby)

You and I together, and we blast forever

{2x}

(~Vita~)

The reasons why I pop between the lie

be the same reasons I clap off the nines

Roll up on bronx, like, who da hot bitch

and stock, with some sweats, humpin out on sixth

(Ja Rule)

That's it, go head baby, floss out bitches,

but me, i'm continue to clap niggas,

strike and heavy hitters that, play the field, reveal,

pull that weapon and re-keep the seal

(Vita and Ja Rule)

It's murder to the end (It's murder for life)

Only Jesus Christ made us a strong sacrifice

these niggas I die for, lies to the fed form,

set out these bitch niggas, I pick them in bad form

(Ja Rule)

Baby, I'm long gone, but I'm loyal

for the love that you show your bitches

and spread to your thugs

And they tongues get slugged

when the fucking wit us

you crazy, that's why (We Murderers baby!)

{Chorus}

(Ja Rule and Vita)

I be running and gunning them down (we murderers, baby)

Leave me or love me now (I'm here for you baby)

Anywhere, anyhow (I'll ryde for you baby)

You and I together, and we blast forever, Nigga

{2x}

Artist: **50 Cent f/ G-Unit**
Album: **No Mercy, No Fear**
Song: **Soldier**

[50 Cent and DJ Whoo Kid talking]

[Hook]

(I'm a soldier) G-UNIT! I started my own gang

(I'm a soldier) G-UNIT!

(I'm a soldier) G-UNIT! I started my own gang

(I'm a soldier) G-UNIT!

[50 Cent]

It's a fact homie, eagles don't fly in flocks

But the eagles I got own sixteen shots

Like beefin', homie I ain't sayin' a word

I'll run up on your punk ass squeezing the bird

Now what New York niggas know about country grammar

Not much, but we know how to bang them hammers

When I pull out that thing, you better break yourself

Or win a trip to ICU, and you can take yourself

If you lucky motherfucker, I'm solider I told ya

Push ya shit back, put my knife through ya six pack

Gat bust, adrenaline rush, blowin' the dust

Five point O, burnin' the cluth, while I'm burnin' the dutch

You thought them other niggas was hot, I'm turnin' it up

This the blueprint, nigga are you learnin' or what

You done told me you respect me, now tell me I'm the nicest

Admit it nigga, I'm a mid-life crisis

[Hook]

(I'm a soldier) G-UNIT! I started my own gang

(I'm a soldier) G-UNIT! (I got the rep of a villian, the weapon concealin')

(I'm a soldier) G-UNIT! I started my own gang

(I'm a soldier) G-UNIT! (full of controversy until I retire my jersey)

[Lloyd Banks]

It's like niggas rate the respect of who gat bigger

Banks been blowin' on purple stuff before that fat nigga

Henny's make dollars, and dollars make death threats

I'm doin' remixes to bulletproof the Lex next

Duck nigga, everydays war

I'm heavy on sports, to my draw like NBA's store

Don't make me send the piece at you

I'll have your man walk around with another rest in peace tattoo

Look creampuff, you can get killed here

Nigga you ain't invincible, even Superman in a wheel chair

I've always been a picky man, but I ain't a flowered star

So I'mma fuck all fifty fans

Look, whether you like it or not, right in ya spot

All in your grill, wearin' the crown, airin' em down

We're in the pound puttin' fear in the clown

I'm running with gangstas, don't make one of em shank ya

[Hook]

(I'm a soldier) G-UNIT! I started my own gang

(I'm a soldier) G-UNIT! (I got the rep of a villian, the weapon concealin')

(I'm a soldier) G-UNIT! I started my own gang

(I'm a soldier) G-UNIT! (full of controversy until I retire my jersey)

[Tony Yayo]

I'mma ride with my rap shit and my body armor

Ride like a Taliban suicide bomber

Four five six feet, I off ya feet

I kill ya with a pillow when you fall asleep

Your records can't sell, your company is buyin' em

Give it up, Burger King is hirin'

You shoulda been a cop, cause you snitch a lot

Talkin' to the jakes, you bound to get shot

I used to watch Big Bird and Scooby Doo

Now I'm choppin' big birds and them bundles too

For that Master P money, that shoppin' spree money

That coke, that dope and that ecstasy money

I'm tryin' to build empires across the state line

So move like vampires, never see me in the daytime

I jump out with a nina and a mack

I have you like Khia, my neck, my back

Artist: **Tha Eastsidaz**
Album: **Duces 'N Trayz...The Old Fashioned Way**
Song: **Break a Bitch Til I Die**

[Snoop Dogg]

Pimp

Its pimp shit, its pimp shit

Nigga said his bitch took him to court for child support

Its cheaper to keep her

Cheaper to keep her

Thats real talk

Cheaper to keep her

Thats real talk, its cheaper to keep her

[Chorus: Snoop Dogg]

Now if you don't think I know what the fuck i'm talkin bout

(What you talkin bout?)

Run down to the Dogg House, and see fo' yo own two eyes

Bitches try to pull snake moves to get a piece of the pie

[Hook]

It's impossible, to stop a ho

So let her go, and get the dough

Lead the way, or step aside

Break a bitch till the day I die

[Verse 1: Snoop Dogg]

Check me out, no doubt, I flip the game and re-route

I check her in wit Magic Man Juan, or Pimpin Ken

I just got back from Milwaukee, the All-Star game

Not the NBA nigga, i'm talkin real playa shit mayne

Macks, ballas, hustlas, and prostitutes

On the real my nig, you got to, got to get the loot

And if you got to shoot to get the loot

Then I guess you got to do what you gotta do

But know this, fa sho this, its somethin for realler

From a fifty cent nigga to a thousand dollar nigga

Fuck George Bush, the army, and the G.I.

Nigga this P.I., until I D.I.

[Chorus]

[Verse 2: Goldie Loc]

Now don't get mad when you see me wit ya girlfriend

She ridin shot gun, smokin the damn thang again

Now say it ain't true...

Baby you gank em and play em it ain't no ring on you

That ain't what I do, just because I spend time wit you

Don't really mean i'm lyin to you

You got to understand what this young pimp will say

Cause right about now, it ain't no time for play

Now watch me slap ya ass wit dicks, bitch

You was stricly dickly, why you turn clitly

Thats even better, now both of you bitches lick me

Then I sit back and watch y'all eat pussy

Kick off my feet and count my cheese

Snoop this ain't the XLF, this the P-I-M-P

Look, she think she burned out

Wait until I put her on the fast track and have her turned out

P.I!

[Chorus]

[Verse 3: Tray Deee]

Lil pretty skinny ass bitch, but she gotta monkey

I know she suck dicks cause her lips nice and puffy

But she got the wrong thought, kinda got me turned off

Must be why she sweatin me, the ectasy she gon off

For realler, ho don't know i'm bout that scrilla

I peel her like a sunkiss for comin wit that dumb shit(stupid bitch!)

I keeps the P.I., poppin fa sho

Other suckas tend to love em, we just cop em and blow

Hos come, hos go, hos runnin ya slow

So keep her foot up in her ass, unless a dick in her throat

Main grew bitch will go what I make ya do

And keep ya eyes on my Stacys while i'm lacin you

Ya like sex and shit, and gettin naked quick

Ya lil wreckless bitch, so gon and check them chips

And bring every penny back home and deck

And pull a couple of mo' hos you know that wanna get wrecked

[Chorus]

[Hook]

Artist: **Snoop Dogg f/ Lil Jon, Trina**
Album: **R&G (Rhythm & Gangsta): The Masterpiece**
Song: **Step Yo Game Up**

[Snoop Dogg]

Yeah Man What's Going on Man It's really really pimpin' up in here man

I know you ain't seen pimpin' in a long time man, I've been MIA

You know what I'm sayin' missin in action

I ain't been on no milk carton box

But I've been milking and boxing these bitches

'Cause they got to step they game up, you know what I mean

[Chorus: Snoop Dogg] + (Lil Jon)

What you lookin' at (step yo game up!)

What you waitin' for (step yo game up!)

Go on come on in the door (step yo game up!)

Drop it to the floor and just (step yo game up!)

You a kid (step yo game up!)

You drink gin (step yo game up!)

Is that your friend (step yo game up!)

Tell a nigga you with you better (step yo game up!)

[Lil Jon]

Break it down bitch, let me see you back it up

drop that ass down low then pick that motherfucker up [x2]

Back that pussy she's a motherfucker [x4]

Rub that shit it's yours bitch, grab his dick it's yours bitch [x2]

Now turn around bitch, put that ass on a nigga

Grind on his dick make it get a little bigger [x2]

[Chorus]

[Snoop Dogg]

Bitch wanna act like she ain't never been with fast lane pimpin' om 'em

Nails with the French tip potato chip yup with a French dip

Say she wanna French kiss all on my diz-nick

It's cool, go on and break fool if you have to

What which you won't do bitch I'ma slap you

Stay in line ho it's a pimp affair

If you down to get low I can take you there

But you can't fake once you hit the gate

Shake till it ache, work that birthday cake

You say you wanna make it ho

Well quit bullshittin' and get naked hoe

Now you always got to be hot and vicious

So move them biscuits and hit them tricks bitch

Now you got about a minute to fix this

Cuz I'm trying to find a bitch that's bootylicious

[Chorus]

[Trina]

P-U-S-S-Y, run a world, I'm the girl in the flesh ah

Lookin' for a nigga that will suck me like a blow pop

Run that dick to the door, do me baby don't stop

Same nigga talkin' all that shit

Just a little bitch, little balls, little dick

Let me show you how to work your tongue like a hurricane

We ain't here to play no games, baby give me everything

I know you like me when I drop it down low

Show it from the back, look back, let it roll

Drop it to the floor like a g-bitch supposed to

Shake it shake it shake it make a nigga go postal

But that's for fucking with a Miami girl

Get your man, take his money, and then buy the world

So nigga don't front, cuz fat wallets and big dicks is all I want

[Chorus]

[Lil Jon]

Chuuuch, Breach, Tabernacle [x8]

Artist: **Lil' Kim f/ Mr. Bristal**
Album: **The Notorious K.I.M.**
Song: **Suck My Dick**

Uh, uh, uh

Uh, uh, uh

To all my motherfuckin' gettin' money hoes

Used to clothes

And all my ghetto bitches in the projects

Coming through like bulldozers

No, we ain't sober

Bum bitches know better than to start shit

Niggas love a hard bitch

One that get up in a nigga's ass quicker than an enema

Make a cat bleed then sprinkle it with vinegar

Kidnap the senator

Make him call his wife and say he never coming home

Kim got him in a zone beating they dicks

Even got some of these straight chicks rubbing their tits

*laughs

What? I'm loving this shit

Queen Bitch!

What bitch you know can thug it like this?

Imagine if I was dude and hittin' cats from the back

With no strings attached

Yeah nigga, picture that!

I treat y'all niggas like y'all treat us

No Doubt! Ay yo, yo

Come here so I can bust in ya mouth

1 - [Lil' Kim](Mr. Bristal)

   (Ay yo, come on here bitch)

   Nigga FUCK YOU

(No, FUCK YOU BITCH)

Who you talking to?

(Why you actin' like a BITCH?)

Cause y'all niggas ain't shit

And if I was dude

I'd tell y'all to suck my dick

Repeat 1

[Lil' Kim]

No, no, no, no

All I wanna do is get my pussy sucked (Nigga!)

Count a million bucks in the back of an armor truck

While I get you fucked up off the T.O.N.Y.

The BX, the chron-chron

And the list goes on and on

(On and on and on)

Like Erykah Badu

Once he drink the Remi down

Ooh I got this nigga now

He asked me did I love him

I said what came to mind like niggas be doing

Yeah baby, I love you long time

Look I ain't tryin' to suck ya

I might not even fuck ya

Just lay me on this bed and give me some head

Got the camcord layin' in the drawer where he can't see

Can't wait to show my girls he sucked the piss out my pussy

Been doin' this for years, no need to practice

Take lessons from the Queen and you'll know how to mack this

Niggas know he gave me all his cake

I peeled the Benji's off and threw the singles back in his face

Repeat 1 (2x)

[Lil' Kim]

I'mma keep it real

For the dough I might kill

I'm try-na see my face on a hundred dollar bill

Met this dude name Jaleel at this Abdulla fight

He said he'd pay me ten grand just to belly dance

Cum all on his pants

I met him at the studio

He showed up with his homeboy named Julio

I said 'Whoa! Who's the other guy?'

Hope you know you paying extra for this fuckin' third eye

Something about him, I knew he was a phony

Put the burner in his mouth

'Fool, Give me my money!'

He was just a nigga frontin' like he knew mad stars

In his homeboy's whips like he got mad cars

Niggas ain't shit but they still can trick

All they can do for me is suck my clit

I'm jumpin' up and up after I cum

Thinkin' they gon' get some pussy but they gets none

Artist: **Trina f/ Trick Daddy**
Album: **Da Baddest Bitch**
Song: **Da Baddest Bitch**

[Trick Daddy](Trina)

Who's bad? Who's bad?

Who's bad? Who's, who's bad?

Who's bad? Who's bad?

(Wait hold up)

Who's bad?

[Trina]

I'm representin' for the bitches

All eyes on your riches

No time for the little dicks

You see the bigger the dick

The bigger the bank, the bigger the Benz

The better the chance to get close to his rich friends

I'm going after the big man

G-string make his dick stand

Make it quick then slow head by the night stand

Like lightning I wanna nigga with a wedding ring

Bank accounts in the Philippines

Blank note to take everything

See I fuck him in the living room

While his children ain't home

I make him eat it while my period on

A little nasty ho, red-bone but a classy ho

Young jazzy ho and don't be scared

If you're curious just ask me hoes

And yes dick sucking comes quite natural

I'm da baddest bitch what

[Trick Daddy](Trina)

Who's bad? Who's, who's bad?

Who's bad? Who's, who's bad?

(Shit I'm the baddest bitch)

Who's bad? Who's, who's bad?

Who's bad? Who's, who's bad?

[Trina](Trick Daddy)

See I hate hoes who take their niggas on talk shows and for hoes

(Y'all sold fool)

See if I'm ever crossed or ever caught up in the cross

And if it's your fault ho, I'm going off ho

See I'm unemployed with no boss ho

While y'all sucking dick for free I'm broke off ho

See it pays to be the boss ho

Shit that's how you floss hoes

X-rated elevated, buck naked

And I'd probably fuck your daddy

if your mammie wasn't playa hatin'

Cause I'm da baddest bitch

I'm da baddest bitch what

[Trick Daddy](Trina)

Who's bad? Who's, who's bad?

Who's bad? Who's, who's bad?

(Shit I'm the baddest bitch)

Who's bad? Who's, who's bad?

Who's bad? Who's, who's bad?

(Shit I'm the baddest bitch)

Who's bad? Who's, who's bad?

Who's bad? Who's, who's bad?

[Trina]

I got game for young hoes

Don't grow to be a dumb hoe, that's a no-no

See if you off the chains

Stay ahead of the game, save up buy a condo

Sell the pussy by the grands

And in months you own a Benz

Another week a set of rims

See if I had the chance to be a virgin again

I'd be fucking by the time I'm ten

See off glass is my motto

Dick suckin in the auto

Quick fuckin 'bout to follow

On the back of the truck

Or when I'm dead ass drunk

But I don't get high though

I never took it up the ass

Often tried but I pass

And from what I heard it ain't bad

I'm a curious bitch who took off to get broke off

From the baby's dad

Cause I'm da baddest bitch

[Trick Daddy](Trina)

Who's bad? Who's, who's bad?

Who's bad? Who's, who's bad?

(Shit I'm the baddest bitch)

Who's bad? Who's, who's bad?

Who's bad? Who's, who's bad?

(Shit I'm the baddest bitch)

Who's bad? Who's, who's bad?

Who's bad? Who's, who's bad?

(Shit I'm the baddest bitch)

Who's bad? Who's, who's bad?

Who's bad? Who's, who's bad?

(That's right I'm the baddest bitch)

Who's bad?

      With these lyrics in mind, try to remember when the great pop entertainer Michael Jackson merely used the word "KYKE" in one of his songs; by using this word, Michael Jackson was forced to pull the song and re-record it because the word was offensive to so-called Jews. Never the less, these same so-called Jewish record executives and power brokers receive huge amounts of cash by the promoting and marketing of the above language and behaviors. Understanding the power of words and their influence on the global perception, the so-called Jews continue to pay millions of dollars to ignorant rappers that speak continuously without pause of killing, rapping, and destroying the moral fabric of black people. Yet they make a huge fuss when anyone says or speaks anything that they themselves deem as offensive. Before we move on, consider the following lyrics of Michael Jackson's song **"They Don't Care About Us"**...

All I wanna say is that
They don't really care about us,
(Don't worry what people say, we got it true).

All I wanna say is that
They don't really care about us,
(Enough is enough of this garbage).
All I wanna say is that
They don't really care about us.
(Michael Jackson):

Skin head, dead head.
Everybody gone bad.
Situation, aggravation.
Everybody allegation.
In the suite, on the news.
Everybody, dog food.
Bang bang, shot dead.
Everybody's gone mad.

All I wanna say is that
They don't really care about us.
All I wanna say is that
They don't really care about us.

Beat me, hate me.
You can never break me.
Will me, thrill me.
You can never kill me.
Jew me, Sue me.
Everybody do me.
Kick me, kike me.
Don't you black or white me.

All I wanna say is that
They don't really care about us.
All I wanna say is that
They don't really care about us.

Now tell me what has become of my life.
I have a wife and two children who love me.
I am the victim of police brutality, no.
I'm tired of bein' the victim of hate.
You're rapin' me of my pride,
Oh, for God's sake.
I look to heaven to fulfill its prophecy.
Set me free.

Skin head, dead head.
Everybody gone bad.
Trepidation, speculation.
Everybody allegation.
In the suite, on the news.
Everybody, dog food.
Black man, black mail.
Throw your brother in jail.

All I wanna say is that
They don't really care about us.
All I wanna say is that
They don't really care about us.
Now tell me what has become of my rights.
Am I invisible because you ignore me?
Your proclamation promised me free liberty, no.
I'm tired of bein' the victim of shame.
They're throwing me in a class with a bad name.
I can't believe this is the land from which I came.

You know I do really hate to say it.
The government don't want to see.
But if Roosevelt was livin',
He wouldn't let this be, no, no.
Skin head, dead head.
Everybody gone bad.
Situation, speculation.
Everybody, litigation.
Beat me, bash me.
You can never trash me.
Hit me, kick me.
You can never get me.

All I wanna say is that
They don't really care about us.
All I wanna say is that
They don't really care about us.

(Guitar solo)

Some things in life they just don't want to see.
But if Martin Luther was livin',
He wouldn't let this be no, no, aay.

Skin head, dead head.
Everybody, gone bad.
Situation, segregation.
Everybody, allegation.
In the suite, on the news.
Everybody, dog food
Kick me, kike me.
Don't you wrong or right me.

(Clapping):

All I wanna say is that
They don't really care about us.
All I wanna say is that
They don't really care about us.
All I wanna say is that
They don't really care about us.

All I wanna say is that
They don't really care about,
All I wanna say is that

They don't really care about,
All I wanna say is that
They don't really care about us.
Hee hee, hoo.

After reading these lyrics, is it true that these words are something to greatly consider?

MICHAEL AND TOMMY

"if you take a slave, if you teach him all about your language, he will know all your secrets, and he is then no more a slave, for you can't fool him any longer"

We will move forward in a moment... but before we do; let's hear what the ADL (Anti Defamation League) has to say about Michael. As we go into the next aspects of this writing, let's do so keeping in mind all that we have talked about up until this point!

In New York, NY, November 23, 2005 ... Reacting to revelations that Michael Jackson referred to Jews as "leeches" in a voicemail to a former business manager, the Anti-Defamation League (ADL) said the pop music icon **"has an anti-Semitic streak"** and hasn't learned from his past mistakes, including the use of anti-Semitic epithets in a 1995 song he wrote. (The one cited above—They Don't Really Care About US)

On November 22, 2005 tapes of Michael Jackson having a phone conversation with a former business associate was aired on ABC's "Good Morning America". ABC (American Broadcasting Company) is owned by the Walt Disney Company, a company that is ran and controlled by a so-called Jewish CEO named Robert Allen Iger that was born in the state of New York. It was Robert Iger that replaced the previous CEO of Walt Disney Mr. Michael Eisner, another so-called Jew that was born in the state of New York... the change at Disney was made in 2005. Anyway... in the taped conversation that was aired on ABC... you can apparently hear the voice of Michael Jackson saying of the so-called Jews-- *"They suck ... They're like leeches. ... I'm so tired of it ... It is a conspiracy. The Jews do it on purpose."* **Abraham H. Foxman, ADL National Director, issued the following statement:**

"Michael Jackson has an anti-Semitic streak, and hasn't learned from his past mistakes. It seems every time he has a problem in his life, he blames it on Jews. It is sad that Jackson is infected with classically stereotypical ideas of Jews as all-powerful, money-grubbing and manipulative.

We had hoped that Jackson would have learned from his mistakes. While he apologized for, and later removed the anti-Jewish lyrics in "They Don't Care About Us," it is clear now that he never was able to completely remove the bigotry from his own heart.

It is important now for Mr. Jackson to stand up and acknowledge that his words are hurtful and hateful. He needs to show his fans that he rejects bigotry and is truly serious about stamping out, in his words, "the ugliness of racism, anti-Semitism and stereotyping." This can only begin with an apology to Jews everywhere, especially those fans that have been deeply hurt and offended by his words".

Are you kidding me, you have to be kidding me ole Abe... considering all the songs and depictions offered about black people from the directorial control of those that call themselves Jews; how can you have the audacity to make such noise over what Michael reportedly said! Abe is a joke, and so is his so-called Anti Defamation League! Question... why didn't Abe address Michael's claim... is it valid or not!?

Now... how can we ever mention Michael Jackson and the ADL, and leave out the one Michael himself dubbed as the "DEVIL", Tommy Mottola. Born into a middle-class Italian family on July 14, 1949 in Bronx, New York; Tommy began in the entertainment business as an actor. After doing a few small time bits in some meaningless roles, Tommy decided to abandon the camera for the dark underbelly of the music business. To that end... he married his first wife; the daughter of the founder of ABC Records, a so-called Jew by the name of Sam Clark. After marrying, Tommy Mottola abandoned his Catholic roots and began to call himself a Jew.

I am not going to climb into the mind of Michael Jackson and try to figure out why he called Tommy a "devil"; but what I will do is give a little history regarding Tommy and his career. In 1975 Mottola founded Don Tommy Enterprises, which he re-named Champion Entertainment. Through this company he began to "HELP" such major performers as Carly Simon and John Cougar Mellencamp. A production arrangement between Champion and CBS Records was made in 1977 -- unbeknownst to RCA Records, the label of many of his artists, allowing Mottola a good opportunity to exercise his back-pedaling skills. By 1987, he had insinuated himself as president of the CBS affiliate Columbia Records, and the following year CBS Music was bought out by Sony, resulting in Mottola's advancement to the head of the company's U.S. operations. From his new position, he became the dark shadow looming over everyone from Michael Jackson to Bob Dylan.

As we pry a little more.... In 1977, when the deal was struck between Tommy's "Champion Entertainment" and CBS; CBS was ran by a so-called Jew by the name of Walter Yetnikoff, and yes he was born in New York! Now before Walter started running CBS, guess who ran it... yeap, you guessed it, another so-called Jew that was born in New York, a Mr. Goddard Lieberson. Mr. Lieberson surprisingly became CEO of the company when unexpectedly Mr. Clive Davis, a very rich and powerful man who was also born in New York and is a so-called Jew, got fired for spending company money on his personal lifestyle; including an expensive bar mitzvah for his son. Davis started out as a Harvard law-trained associate at Rosenman, Colin, Kaye, Petshek & Freund, now known as KMZ Rosenman.

In order to connect the necessary dots within this context of limited space and time... I will give you a few tid-bits that will aid you in your personal research. Try to stay focused; sometimes this stuff gets kind of tricky. (Smile)

The present CBS Records was created and established in the year 2006 by the CBS Corporation; the CEO of this corporation is a so-called Jew whose name is Leslie Moonves. Leslie served as co-president and co-chief operating officer of Viacom, Inc., the predecessor to CBS Corporation, from 2004 until the company split on December 31, 2005. Born in New York City in 1948, Moonves is the great-nephew of the first Prime Minister of Israel; a Mr. David Ben-Gurion. Present day CBS was revived in order to take advantage of itunes and the new digital downloading age. Again, CBS Records is owned by CBS Corporation, a major media conglomerate whose Chairman and major shareholder is the owner of National Amusements, the aforementioned Sumner Redstone who is the so-called Jew that changed his name from Sumner Murray Rothstien to Redstone.

The former CBS Records is the CBS Records that emerged from Columbia Records, the oldest surviving brand name of pre-recorded music. Although the original CBS Records emerged and thrived, today's Columbia Records is still in operation and is under the control of two so-called Jews, a Mr. Steve Barnett and the previously mentioned Mr. Rick Rubin; yes, the same Rick Rubin that was given his start by the slave Russell Simmons. CBS means Columbia Broadcasting System, and this label was bought along with other media operations in 1938 by a Russian born so-called Jewish man named William S. Paley. CBS was originally owned by Columbia, and was co-founded by Columbia and a so-called Jew by the name of Arthur Judson, but Mr. Paley bought the company and subsequently grew it into a premier media enterprise. Columbia's president at the time of Mr. Paley's purchase was yet another so-called Jew named Edward (Ted) Wallerstein.

This information should allow us to see that despite argument to the contrary by so-called Jews; the music industry is completely controlled and dominated by those that are known as Jews... lets continue. In 1967, the so-called Jew Clive Davis took the reins of Columbia Records. As mentioned earlier, Clive was fired and was subsequently replaced by two so-called Jews; the first was Goddard Lieberson, and the second was the colorful and controversial Mr. Walter Yetnikoff.

Born in 1933, in Brooklyn, New York, Walter Yetnikoff earned his law degree at Columbia University; after which he joined the law firm Rosenman & Colin, which represented CBS Records. (The same Law firm that Clive Davis worked at) He then joined the CBS Records law department and rose to become head of the department. After his long time friend and mentor Clive Davis was terminated by CBS for financial impropriety, Walter was promoted to head CBS Records.

Walter was known as a shady and controversial character whose management style was seen as abrasive and abusive. This character was in constant battles with Warner Music Group and its owners Warner Communications; its head was Steven J. Ross, a previously mentioned so-called Jew that was born on April 5, 1927 in Brooklyn, New York. Mr. Ross' original last name was Rechnitz.

Walter Yetnikoff was always seen as a shady guy, he has had reported ties to prominent 'Indie' promoter Fred Despoil, his then right hand man Joe Igor, and members of the Gambino crime family, including notorious New York Mob boss John Gotti. One of the allegations that have always been associated with Walter and his friends is that he participated in PAYOLA! **Payola** is the illegal practice of payment or other inducement by record companies for the broadcast of recordings on music radio, in which the song is presented as being part of the normal day's broadcast. Under US law, 47 U.S.C. § 317, a radio station can play a specific song in exchange for money, but this must be disclosed on the air as being sponsored airtime, and that play of the song should not be counted as a "regular airplay". The term has come to refer to any secret payment made to cast a product in a positive light (such as obtaining positive reviews). This practice has been done for years, not just by Walter, but all those that have the money and power to create or destroy a superstar. Some radio stations report spins of the newest and most popular songs to industry publications. The number of times the songs are played can influence the perceived popularity of a song.

When we stop and connect all the series of dots that lead you to the truth, we can begin to see why Michael would have a problem with Tommy or Walter; if Tommy, or any so-called Jewish power broker decides to attack an destroy your career, they have the power, influence, and connections to do exactly that; but let's go on!

A different form of payola has been used by the record industry through the loophole of being able to pay a third party or independent record promoters ("indies"; not to be confused with independent record labels), who will then go and "promote" those songs to radio stations. Offering the radio stations "promotion payments", the independents get the songs that their clients, record companies, want on the playlists of radio stations around the country. This is how Walter utilized the likes of prominent 'Indie' promoter Fred DiSipio.

This newer type of payola was an attempt to sidestep FCC regulations. Since the independent intermediaries were the ones actually paying the stations, it was thought that their inducements did not fall under the "payola" rules, so a radio station need not report them as paid promotions. Former New York State Attorney General Eliot Spitzer prosecuted payola-related crimes in his jurisdiction. His office settled out of court with Sony BMG Music Entertainment in July 2005, Warner Music Group in November 2005 and Universal Music Group in May 2006. The three conglomerates agreed to pay $10 million, $5 million, and $12 million respectively to New York State non-profit organizations that will fund music education and appreciation programs. EMI remains under investigation.

Now where's the connection… Walter Yetnikoff had substantial links to other major industry figures including music industry "Godfather" Morris Levy, prominent music industry lawyer Allen Grumman, Michael Jackson's one-time manager Frank Dileo and former artist manager Tommy Mottola, whom Yetnikoff appointed to a senior post at CBS Records after its sale to the Sony Corporation in 1988.

Before we go any further, read the headlines on December 30, 2006

"On Friday, December 23, 2006, Michael Jackson and his production company, MJJ Productions, Inc. filed a lawsuit against his former accountants for misappropriating $2.5 million dollars (US) from his bank accounts, making unauthorized deals that cost The King of Pop millions. Jackson and MJJ Productions, Inc. allege negligence and breach of fiduciary duty, while seeking unspecified damages and an audit of payment he made to the company. The lawsuit was filed at Los Angeles Superior Court. Jackson hired The Los Angeles-based firm, **Bernstein, Fox, Whitman, Goldman** and **Sloan** in 2003 for bookkeeping, opening bank accounts, filing personal, corporate, and real estate taxes. The firm also is accused of withdrawing $2.5 million US dollars from his bank accounts, failing to properly pay his bills. Bernstein, Fox, Whitman, Goldman and Sloan also did not keep Jackson inform him of his financial affairs.

On August 7, 2006, Michael's Spokesperson, RAYMONE BAIN, revealed in a statement in August 2006, that she believe that his business associates and advisers had defrauded Jackson.

"Mr. Jackson is neither shocked nor surprised by these revelations. He has been suspicious that those whom he entrusted, acted on his behalf, and advised him with respect to his personal and business affairs, may not have been in his best interest." Bain said. " After the statement was released, Mr. Jackson dissolved his business relationship with the firm."

The above information shows that Michael Jackson was aware of shady dealing when it came to his money and career. As people continue to judge and criticize Michael Jackson, I would hope that they realize that there is more than meets the eye. Take a look at some of Michael's own words concerning the record industry and its executives!

"The recording companies really, really do conspire against the artists". "They steal, they cheat, and they do everything they can, especially [against] the black artists. ... People from James Brown to Sammy Davis Jr., some of the real pioneers that inspired me to be an entertainer, these artists are always on tour, because if they stop touring, they would go hungry. If you fight for me, you're fighting for all black people, dead and alive"...

Earlier I mentioned the 'Godfather' of the music industry; and that person is no other than **Morris Levy. He** was born **Moishe Levy** in The Bronx, New York City, New York, and generally known as Morrie Levy to insiders in the industry. The thing about Mr. Levy is that he died slightly before he was supposed to begin his prison bid. Morris Levy was a mentor to all of today's most prominent so-called Jewish music industry leaders. It was this guy that garnished big cash and big influence because of his ability to misrepresent himself as the publishing-rights owner of some of the biggest songs of his time.

After good ole Moishe Levy left the Navy he became the proprietor of numerous night clubs in New York at the dawn of the bebop movement in the late 1940's—the most famous of which was Birdland, which Levy allegedly took over from Joseph "Joe the Wop" Catalano in 1949. By owning the publishing rights of successful recording acts, every time a song of the said artist got performed or played, Levy was entitled to royalties! His first publishing company was called Patricia Music. Through the Newly found publishing company, Levy commissioned George Shearing to write a signature piece for the club, the now famous "Lullaby of Birdland".

Through a record company he founded in 1956 called Roulette Records, Morris Levy was able to begin his alleged practice of claiming authorship on many early songs of the rock-and-roll era that he did not have a hand in composing. A notable case is the song "Why Do Fools Fall In Love", originally recorded by Frankie Lymon and the Teenagers, which is presumed to have been wholly written by lead singer Frankie Lymon. Other questionable 1960s Levy compositions included Lee Dorsey's "Ya Ya", Millie Small's "My Boy Lollipop", and The Rivieras' "California Sun".

Morris's tactics quickly allowed his ascension into wealth and influence. His control of his own business and his ability to control and dominate the distribution of many major labels in addition to his own companies, positioned Levy as a premier force to be reckoned with and acknowledged. It should be understood that Morris Levy is not the only major record executive that practices shady dealings with the artist and the product that the artists create.

I give you these names... Walter, Clive, and Morris in order to show how they are connected; remember, birds of a feather flock together, and when it comes to "Fowl", Tommy Mottola is undeniably linked to these birds in more than one way! What I want us to try to understand is that as Michael Jackson grew in status and star-power, he was granted access into a world that not many black men and woman have been allowed. Although Michael Jackson was deemed as weird and strange; in my opinion, his outer exterior allows those that desire to control and manipulate him to underestimate a man that in many ways seems as harmless as a dove in a world and industry of carnivorous Vultures!

But Michael said:

> *"I really don't like to talk that much, I really don't—I prefer to perform than talk but... well—you know...umm; let me just say this... The tradition, the tradition of great performers; from... and, and I really want you to hear what I have to say--the tradition of great performers from Sammy Davis Jr. to James Brown, to Jackie Wilson, to Fred Astaire, Gene Kelly; the story is usually the same though, you know, these guys work really hard at their craft... but the story ends the same—they usually are... broken, torn, and usually just sad, and the story is very sad at the end... because the companies take advantage of them... they really do. And... umm, umm...Sony, Sony; being umm.... You know, being the artist that I am, umm at Sony I, I, I've generated several billion dollars for Sony... several billion. And umm... they really thought that my mind is always on music and dancing, and it usually is... but they never thought, that this...performer, myself, would out think them. Umm...so, umm... we can't let them get away with what they are trying to do—because now I'm a free agent.*
>
> *Umm... I just owe Sony one more album; it's just a box set really... and so, with two new songs... which I've written ages ago. Because every album that I record I write, like literally, I'm telling you the truth, I write at least umm... a hundred and twenty songs every album I do. So, I can do the box set and give them any two songs. So... so I'm leaving Sony a free agent... owning half of Sony; so... I own half of Sony's publishing and... and I'm leaving them; and they, their very angry at me because of it... But umm...I just, I just did good business, you know... So, the way they get revenge is to try and destroy my album. But, but umm... I've always said, you know... art, art... good art never dies...umm, (The crowd yells UNBREAKABLE, then Michael says) I Love Unbreakable...and Tommy Mottola is a devil"*

I could go on and on about Tommy Mottola and Michael, but check out the lyrics to Michael's song... UNBREAKABLE!

How I'm just wondering why you think
that you can get to me with anything
seems like you'd know by now
When and how I get down
And with all that I've been through,
I'm still around
Don't you ever make no mistake
Baby I've got what it takes
And there's no way you'll ever get to me
Why can't you see that you'll never ever hurt me
'cause I won't let it be, see I'm too much for you baby
[CHORUS]
You can't believe it, you can't conceive it
and you can't touch me, 'cause I'm untouchable
and I know you hate it, and you can't take it
You'll never break me, 'cause I'm unbreakable
Now you can't stop me even though you think
that if you block me, you've done your thing
and when you bury me underneath all your pain
I'm steady laughin', while surfacing
Don't you ever make no mistake
baby I've got what it takes
and there's no way you'll ever get to me
Why can't you see that you'll never ever hurt me
'cause I wont let it be, see I'm too much for you baby
[CHORUS 2x]
You can try to stop me, but it wont do a thing
no matter what you do, I'm still gonna be here
Through all your lies and silly games
I'm a still remain the same, I'm unbreakable
[RAP]

Before I abandon this subect concerning Michael and Tommy, allow me to paint a picture of the web that attempts to bind him. I have shown the reader a connection; it is now time for you to formulate your own opinions based upon the information presented. If it be the grace of God, I will be presenting a more detailed work about Michael Jackson and those that desire to destroy him in the near future... but for now; Is it not very strange that the ADL and some so-called Jewish forces will attempt to label Michael Jackson as anti-Semitic when you consider the following information in terms of his management and business team:

After leaving the black-owned Motown Records and the positive influences of Mr.Berry Gordy, Diana Ross, and Smokey Robinson amoung others—Michael Jackson broke from his family and embarked on a solo career under the auspices of the so-called Jewish mega-media conglomerate, *CBS Records* in 1975. *CBS Records* was later renamed Sony Music Entertainment in 1991, (yet still under so-called Jewish control), with a host of subsidiaries, including *Epic Records*, Jackson's label. By leaving the likes of Gordy and

Robinson, Michael was now under the influence of Hollywood so-called Jews, and a slew of so-called Jewish serviles attached to the Hollywood record industry.

Under the influence of first so-called Jew Rob Stringer, and then Rob's older brother Howard, the SONY power brokers began to manipulate Jackson's career into one that eventually landed him as being universally acknowledged as the "King of Pop". With a growing economic empire, Michael Jackson had to hire Lawyers and Accountants to help him manage his growing financial affairs, and who does this accused anti-Semite employ— you guessed it a group of so-called Jews. First theres Charles Koppelman, and the high-powered global Business Manager the so-called Jew, Dieter Wiesner. What about the lawyers...**Lance Spiegel, Peter Lopez, Bob Sanger, Joel Katz, Brian Oxman, Thomas Mesereau, John Branca, Allen Grubman, L. Lee Phillips, Bertram Fields, Mark Geragos, and Benjamin Brafman.** A cursory glance at the list of Jackson's advisors and lawyers shows that the names indicate a strong so-called Jewish influence of Michael Jackson's legal affairs which penetrate deep into the most intimate parts of Jackson's personal life.

So again, why would Michael Jackson be considered as an anti-Semitic—could it be because after years of trust and assumed loyalty, Michael realized that the same people that were charged with the responsibility to make him, were the same ones that were to break him if he ever became a threat! I don't know... but I aint slow either! Perhaps the cosmetic surgeries that were perormed by his so-called Jewish dermatologist, Dr. Arnold Klein, fooled his previous serviles and controllers into believeing that Michael was not intelligent and would not figure out, and speak out against those that leached off of him and his GOD given talent and star power! Man it's a trip when you think about it—even Debbie Rowe, Jackson's former nurse and his wife for three years, and the biological mother of Prince Michael I and Paris Michael Katherine, is so-called Jewish! Something to think about huh? ....but for now, lets move on!

AIPAC—AMERICAN ISRAEL PUBLIC AFFAIRS COMMITTEE

"words or terms are only a minute part of the process. Values are created and transported by communication through the body of the language."

For there to be a slave, there must first be a slave master. I believe and understand the present HipHop Nation to be a slave of multi-media corporations and the global ambitions of the United States of America. As many people protest and complain about recent elections and the ways and means that politicians utilize to obtain political power, many people refuse to acknowledge that a corporate takeover of the government of America has taken place.

Since politics are based on the thoughts and ideas of men, those that have the political and economic resources to present and develop their ideas are the ones that are proven successful. Politicians are supported by financial contributions; political parties are also empowered by financial contributions. Information is supposedly the basis of all logical conclusions. But what happens when information is released in terms of a political or social agenda? What happens when information is crafted or manipulated, or even left out all together for political purposes?

I lightly went into the corporate structure of certain media conglomerates and their leadership to show that there is a connection between all of these corporations in terms of agenda and loyalties. I want the reader to advance the research on their own, because within that process is the necessary enlightenment that is required to come to a conclusion of action and change.

The slave master is the government of America; the slave master is Corporate America; the slave master is any group or individual that profits off of the ignorance of black people and people in general. When those with power and influence extend that power and influence into maximum control, that control should be viewed as a monopoly. This monopoly does not mean that various groups, clubs, organizations, businesses, and corporation simply share wealth; this monopolization is the sharing of thoughts, ideas, and agendas along with the beneficial results of the above said.

Within the context of the above, let's examine the affects of the most powerful social, economical, and political lobby or power base within the continental borders of the United States of America.

The American Israel Public Affairs Committee (AIPAC) is a special interest group that has a track record of impacting the American Government and their domestic and foreign policy, there are estimated 60,000-100,000 members. Memberships primarily consist of so-called Jews, but there are several handfuls of non so-called Jews that are supporters of AIPAC and their global desires. Regarding that reality, let's remember that being among the so-called Jewish ranks has more to do with mentality and ideology than anything else.

Within the name **"American Israeli Public Affairs Committee"**, we recognize the words *Public Affairs*. This is important because these words indicate to those of us of the so-called public that the desires and agendas of this group does not simply impact those who consider themselves as Jews or their concerns, but extends to those of the general public that may or may not benefit from that which benefit those of this particular group.

When this group of powerful business men and women gain access to the minds of the policy and decision makers of the American government, then these powerful men and women help shape and impact that which should be *by the people and for the people*, into a government that becomes *for the special interest and by the special interest*. It should be noticed and accepted that what is in the best interest of one group, is not necessarily in the best interest of another.

AIPAC is a group of private individuals that primarily operate private corporations and institutions, which utilize privately generated funds to influence public and governmental affairs. AIPAC regularly meets with congress and holds events where they can share their views. In addition, AIPAC reports on the voting records of Senators, and how well they support the state of Israel and so-called Jewish concerns. By giving huge sums of dollars to financially support those who do their bidding, a small but powerful group of men and women impact the governmental policy in ways that are unparallel to any other lobbying or special interest group.

If we consider the political reality of former Georgia Congress woman, Cynthia McKinney; when as a black woman she dared to confront the special interest group with the valid criticism of unfair political tampering with the natural and fair process of elections, we'll see how Congresswoman Cynthia McKinney became a victim of AIPAC. The group began to send huge amounts of money from all over the United States in order to support her opponents and institute mega media campaigns of propaganda that lead to her defeat. When we understand that those that comprise this particular special interest group are some of the most powerful men and women in the media world, it is easy to see that this group exercises tremendous levels of influence.

When the media has within its self-interest a desire to pick and choose certain political candidates, they can sway the news and information regarding that candidate, and his or her politics, in a way that can manipulate the voters into voting favorably for those who are endorsed by the special interest group.

This information is basic modern day politics. Campaign finance reform is on the lips of several politicians, but neither party, the Republicans nor the Democrats, have the necessary freedom of Corporate America and special interest groups to ever free themselves from the financial influence and control of groups such as AIPAC.

Most people fail to realize that the last Republican Convention that took place in the so-called Jewish capitol of the world, New York City, was sponsored and directed by AIPAC and the so-called Jewish power players. A major political bash was orchestrated by the *United Jewish Communities*, the *Republican Jewish Coalition*, and the *American-Israel Political Action Committee*. Over 1,500 supporters of Israel got together to party and discuss the politics that suits their special interest at Pier 60 in Manhattan. This affair was attended by dozens of congressional members, governors and administration officials, and featured

Mayor Bloomberg, Senate Majority Leader Bill Frist, and the Bush and Cheney campaign manager, Ken Mehlman.

AIPAC is a clear indication of how a powerful special interest group can influence politics and elections. By supporting particular candidates with financial contributions; this group can coerce politicians to remain in line with the so-called Jewish concerns. Again, this book would be extremely thick if I were to go into each and every aspect of the so-called Jewish Lobby and AIPAC. I leave that work to the reader, this is to peak an interest and cause the so-called Negro rapper to reconsider their impotence in terms of doing what is in the best interest of black people and the global collective.

Corporate America makes billions of dollars a year; their profits are made from the consumer behaviors of the masses. The records and videos that generate capitol for these mega-conglomerates are used as tools to gain the necessary wealth and power to institute policies and procedures, programs and systems that benefit the interest of a specific group of people. It is within this context that the so-called Negro rapper must accept the fact that they are being used to further the global political agenda of those that care little about the rapper themselves and the communities from which they come.

Elections have been bought; it is the amount of money raised by a particular campaign that determines the front runner as trumpeted from within the news halls of Corporate America. Money that is raised by a campaign is used to secure TV and radio spots that will publicize the politics and agendas of a particular candidate. Those who give the vast amount of dollars are the same ones that control the radio and television airwaves. Simple mathematical reasoning therefore informs us that those who give to a campaign are the same ones that receive. Money is merely recycled and the public is lead as ignorant sheep to vote on candidates whose true agenda is kept from well outside the public eye.

The so-called Negro rappers have allowed themselves to be played like three-dollar whores. For the opportunity to drive nice cars, and wear expensive jewelry and clothes; they have lost sight of our beautiful black people and the ones that truly love, admire, and respect them.

The so-called Jewish Lobby is powerful and influential; consider this power in terms of the number of so-called Jews that were a part of today's Bush Administration, and yesterdays Clinton Administration. The following is a list of those that are known as Jews within the staffs of America's two most recent presidents.

So-called Jews of the Clinton Administration

Does not include Lower Staff Levels

Madeleine Albright
Secretary of State

Mark Penn
Asia Expert to NEC

Sandy Kristoff
Health Care Chief
Personal Chief

Jane Sherburne
President's Lawyer
Council

Richard Feinberg
Assistant Secretary Veterans

Hershel Gober
Food and Drug Administration

Steve Kessler
White House

Evelyn Lieberman
Deputy Chief of Staff

Stuart Eizenstat
Jay Footlik
Special Liaison to the Jewish Community
(no other group has a special liaison)

Robert Nash
Secretary of State

Alice Rivlin
Economic

Judith Feder
National Security
Rahm Emanuel
Policy Advisor

Doug Sosnik
Counsel to President

Jim Steinberg
Deputy to National Security Chief

Peter Tarnoff
Deputy

Robert Boorstin
Communications Aide

Keith Boykin
Communications Aide

Jeff Eller
Special Assistant to Clinton

Tom Epstein
Health Care Adviser
Under Secretary of State

Charlene Barshefsky
U.S. Trade Representative

Susan Thomases
Aide to First Lady

Joel Klein
Assistant Attorney General

Gene Sperling
National Economic Council

Ira Magaziner
National Health Care
Advisory
Janet Yellen
Chairwoman, National Economic Council
Counsel

Ron Klein
Assistant

Robert Rubin
Secretary of Treasury

William Cohen
Secretary of Defense

Dan Glickman
Secretary of Agriculture

George Tenet
CIA Chief

Samuel Berger
*Head National Security Council
Secretary Education*

Madeleine Kunin
Communications Aide

David Kusnet
Dept. AIDS Program

Margaret Hamburg
Dir. Press Conferences

Many Grunwald
Liaison to Jewish Leaders

Karen Adler
Dir. State Dept. Policy

Samuel Lewis
National Security Council

Stanley Ross
National Security Council

Dan Schifter
Director Peace Corps.

Eli Segal
Deputy Chief of Staff

Alan Greenspan
Chairman of Federal Reserve Bank

Robert Weiner
Drug Policy Coordinator

Jack Lew
Deputy Director Management and Budget

James P. Rubin
Under Secretary of State

David Lipton
Under Secretary of The Treasury

Lanny P. Breuer
Special Counsel to The President

Richard Holbrooke
Special Representative to NATO

Kenneth Apfel
Chief of Social Security

Joel Klein
Deputy Whlte Honse Counsel

Sidney Blumenthal
Special Advisor to First Lady

David Kessler
Chief of Food & Drug Administration

Seth Waxman
Acting Solicitor General

Mark Penn
Presidential Pollster

Dennis Ross
Special Middle East Representative

Howard Shapiro
General Counsel for the FBI

Lanny Davis
White House Special Counsel

Sally Katzen
Secretary of Management and Budget

Kathleen Koch
Heads FBI Equal Opportunity Office

John Podesta
Deputy Chief of Staff

Alan Blinder
Vice Chairman of Federal Reserve

Janet Yellen
Heads Council of Economic Advisors

Ron Klain
Chief of Staff for Al Gore

So-called Jews of the Bush Administration

Paul Dundes Wolfowitz Deputy *Secretary, Department of Defense*

Richard Perle *Assistant Secretary of Defense for International Security Policy.*

Ari Fleischer *White House Press Secretary*

Josh Bolten *Deputy Chief of Staff*

Ken Melman *White House Political Director*

Jay Lefkowitz *Deputy Assistant to the President and Director of the Domestic Policy Council*

David Frum *Speechwriter*

Brad Blakeman *White House Director of Scheduling*

Dov Zakheim *Undersecretary of Defense (Controller)*

Lewis Libby *Chief of Staff to the Vice President*

Adam Goldman *White House Liaison to the Jewish Community*

Chris Gersten *Principal Deputy Assistant Secretary, Administration for Children and Families at HHS*

Elliott Abrams *Director of the National Security Council's Office for Democracy, Human Rights and International Operations*

Mark D. Weinberg *Assistant Secretary of Housing and Urban Development for Public Affairs*

Douglas Feith *Under Secretary of Defense for Policy*

Michael Chertoff *Head of the Justice Department's criminal division*

Daniel Kurtzer *Ambassador to Israel*

Cliff Sobel *Ambassador to the Netherlands*

Stuart Bernstein *Ambassador to Denmark*

Nancy Brinker *Ambassador to Hungary*

Frank Lavin *Ambassador to Singapore*

Ron Weiser *Ambassador to Slovakia*

Mel Sembler *Ambassador to Italy*

Martin Silverstein *Ambassador to Uruguay*

Assistant Secretary of Defense: **Paul Wolfowitz**, Undersecretary of Defense under former President Bush, former ambassador to Indonesia, a member of the Council on Foreign Relations (CFR), a member of the Aspen Institute's Strategy Group, reportedly attended the 2000 Bilderberg meeting in Belgium, and was a member of the Trilateral Commission as of 2000.

White House Press Secretary: **Ari Fleischer**, former 2000 Bush campaign spokesman, and previously was communications director for Elizabeth Dole's 2000 campaign. He was also the Presidential Transition Spokesperson 2000-2001.

Deputy Chief of Staff: **Joshua B. Bolten**, policy director for the 2000 Bush campaign.

Chief Counsel: **Jay Lefkowitz**, former law partner of Kenneth W. Starr.

Deputy Assistant to the President for Appointments and Scheduling: **Brad Blakeman**, who spent two years as Lead Advance Representative for Bush/Cheney 2000 and also worked in the same capacity for the Bush/Quayle campaigns in 1988 & 1992. From 1980-1993, he was a consultant to the offices of the President and Vice President of the United States.

Undersecretary of Defense & Comptroller: **Dov S. Zakheim**, CEO of System Planning Corporation International and a member of the Council on Foreign Relations (CFR).

Chief of Staff for the Vice President: **I. Lewis Libby**, former Deputy Under Secretary of Defense, and a former lawyer for Mark Rich, whom Clinton pardoned. Libby is a member of the Council on Foreign Relations (CFR).

Assistant Secretary for Public Affairs: **Mark D. Weinberg**, the Director of issues Management for The McGraw-Hill Companies and was Manager for Marketing Communications and Special Events for the U.S. Postal Service 1994-1999. He served as Director of Public Affairs in the Office of Former President Bush 1989-1991 and as Special Assistant to the President and Assistant Press Secretary for President Reagan 1981-1989.

Under Secretary of Defense for Policy: **Douglas Jay Feith**, formerly with Feith and Zell, P.C., in Washington, D.C. He served as Deputy Assistant Secretary of Defense for Negotiations Policy, 1984-1986 and was Special Counsel to Assistant Secretary of Defense Richard Peale 1982-1984. Feith is a graduate of Harvard College and Georgetown University Law Center and is a member of the Council on Foreign Relations (CFR)

Assistant Attorney General for the Criminal Division: **Michael Chertoff**, a Partner with Latham and Watkins in Newark, NJ. He was the U.S. Attorney for New Jersey 1990-1994 and is a graduate of Harvard University and Harvard Law School. He also advised Sen. Alfonse M. D'Amato (R-NY) during the Whitewater investigation

As we reflect on the above names, imagine if those listed were so-called African-Americans. Would we as black people fill more comfortable in today's political climate if we believed that we had a considerable amount of black men and women on the staff of the President of the United States of America? Remember, the so-called Jewish community roughly makes up only 3 percent of the total population of the United States. With this in mind, we have to wonder how such a small group of people disproportionately make up such a huge portion of the president's staff.

If we consider the above names in the context of all of the information regarding Corporate America and its leadership, those who lead the powerful conglomerates of America, those that make up the who's who of Hollywood and the media and entertainment world; how can any of us deny the enormous power and influence that the so-called Jew of America enjoys? In addition, considering the sub-base levels of today's moral, social, and political standards, how can a genuine critique of today's total local, national, and international condition be made absent of what is completely apparent. In a political, economic, and social world that is disproportionately shaped and influenced by the so-called Jew, how can we fail to acknowledge the culpability of those that sit at the top of such a global heap of trash?

Before we go any further, allow me to draw a line of connection between the present mentality of black people, and the slave mastering elements of the ZIONIST movement. For If I claim that the HipHop Nation has become the NEWEST SLAVE, I must be able to offer some substantiating proofs that allows for that conclusion. I have listed and displayed the corporate and governmental power brokers that fit within the slave and slave-master social construct, but allow me to show how the agenda of the global slave master plays out within the so-called Jewish goals and aspirations. REMEMBER: The power of those who are in control lies in their ability to dumb-down and completely fool the ignorant masses. It is the WILLIE LYNCH mentality that severely compromises the intellectual capacities of the modern rapper in terms of their recognition of not only their open enemy, but how they are being systematically abused and utilized to fulfill the plan and desires of that said enemy!

FIRST

What we all need to know and understand is that the ZIONIST so-called Jews don't merely influence America's policy...they actually DOMINATE it! The dominance of the ZIONIST movement allows them to control and manipulate the information that sways public opinion. By controlling the various forms of media and entertainment, it enables them to pull off wicked agendas and then conceal them from the general public. Even though I have not spent any time addressing the so-called Jewish affect on traditional and modern academia, an upcoming work of mine will show how even the schools and textbooks of America have been compromised by this nefarious group of people. As time continues to pass, and the clock continues to tick...we will all come face to face with the truth regardless if we like it or not. If you think that what I am saying is just some sort of black-militant tirade, consider what Henry Ford said:

"If after having elected their man or group, obedience is not rendered to the Jewish control, then you speedily hear of "scandals" and "investigations" and "impeachments" for the removal of the disobedient. Usually a man with a "past" proves the most obedient instrument, but even a good man can often be tangled up in campaign practices that compromise him. It has been commonly known that Jewish manipulation of American election campaigns have been so skillfully handled, that no matter which candidate was elected, there was ready made a sufficient amount of evidence to discredit him in case his Jewish masters needed to discredit him."

Of course if we are to get the HipHop Nation's as well as other's collective heads out the sand, we need to get a little deeper don't we? Now, keep in mind that ABC, NBC, CBS, CNN, FOX, The Washington Post, The New York Times, The Wall Street Journal, The New York Daily News, Time Magazine, Newsweek, People Magazine, US News and World Report and countless other referenced media and Hollywood companies all have either a Zionist CEO, or a Zionist News President, or are owned by a media conglomerate which has a Zionist CEO... this also includes all the aforementioned record plantations.

BUT

Have we seen or witnessed how the following so-called Jewish Organizations interact with the above mentioned to get through their specific and united agenda? Check out these groups: **AIPAC:** The previously mentioned Israeli lobbying organization. **JINSA** (Jewish Institute for National Security Affairs) this group yields tremendous power and influence over Washington politics. Also you have **AJC** (American Jewish Congress), a group that has the power to unseat congressmen that fail to bow to, and tow the proverbial ZIONIST line. **ZOA** (Zionist Organization of America), and the **ADL** (Anti Defamation League) are the most feared political pressure groups in Washington DC. These and more have incredible power! I encourage you to do your research to see just how much.

It is important we know that Washington has been hijacked by the special interest concerns of the openly Zionist movement. This is what **Michael Massing** a writer for the Nation Magazine said: "AIPAC is widely regarded as the most powerful foreign-policy lobby in Washington. Its **60,000** members shower millions of dollars on hundreds of members of Congress on both sides of the aisle. Newspapers like the New York Times fear the Jewish lobby organizations as well. "It's very intimidating," said a correspondent at another large daily. "The pressure from these groups is relentless." What does this quote suggest—that this special interest group along with their so-called Jewish cousins in Media and Entertainment cannot only influence politicians and their political policies, but can also shape and influence the minds of the masses in a way to control the people's perception of those said policies!

As we see America mired down in two wars, and contemplating an attack on Iran, we should ask ourselves how did we get here, and what is the real motivation behind the seemingly irresolvable conflicts. Well what were the justifications (reasons) that the media and government gave to get the people to go to war in the first place? Before we answer that question lets understand something—the real rogue nation, the United States does not need a pretext for war, but America as an Imperialist democracy have to invent them to convince the public to go along. **This is where the media comes in,** the imperialist designs of America and her Zionist partners advance an aggressive *propaganda initiative* against any threat to their global dominance and control! In as little as six months an entire population can be led to believe in an enemy that simply does not exist.

In 1916, President Woodrow Wilson was re-elected on a promise that he would keep America "Out of War" (you know the one that began in 1914,) World WAR I). And yes, this is the same Woodrow that assisted in the passing of the aforementioned *Federal Reserve Act*—Unknown to the public, Wilson had imperialist designs. He needed the war to advance them, and established the Committee on *Public Information* under George Creel. A government *propaganda initiative* that in six months turned a peace-time United States into a nation of propagandized German haters that resulted in Congress declaring war on Germany on April 17.

The propaganda initiative helped to advance and develop what has now become the American way in regards to public manipulation and the public relations industry. By studying the government and their mind manipulating methods, corporations learned how to market their products, denigrate unions, and today keep people glued to TV screens, influenced by hyper-commercialism and degenerative lifestyles that are depicted through entertainment. This reality has resulted in America's population being reduced to one of the most ignorant and self absorbed nations on earth. Under a guise of an artificial freedom, America is like an overgrown spoiled child that thinks the sun rises and sets on their misperceived holiness, and self-proclaimed do goodliness. A nation that has a self-centered arrogance, has failed to see and recognize how they were lied into a war with two nations, and how those reasons or justifications have changed time and again. Consider how the Zionist movement utilized the controlled media world to further their agenda.

Pretexts for invading and occupying Iraq went from:

- WMDs;
- to removing a dangerous dictator;
- to establishing democracy in the Arab world;

- to preventing a civil war;
- to needing a colonial military victory to retain our global superpower status;
- to reassuring regional regimes they can rely on us for protection; and
- to proving America can fight and defeat "terrorism."

It should be understood that the Pentagon is under the control of a hard core group of Zionists led by the so-called Jew Richard Perle. Mr. Richard Norman Perle is an outwardly powerful and influential lobbyist for Israel and so-called Jewish concerns. He is a contributing member of several influential organizations such as the Hudson Institute, the Center for Security Policy (**CSP**), the Washington Institute for Near East Policy (**WINEP**) Board of Advisors, and (as a resident fellow) the American Enterprise Institute for Public Policy Research, as well as the neoconservative Project for the New American Century (**PNAC**) and the Jewish Institute for National Security Affairs (**JINSA**).

Born in New York City, Perle is a self-described neoconservative that had long been an advocate of regime change in Iraq. He was a signatory of the 26 January 1998 PNAC Letter sent to US President Bill Clinton that called for the military overthrow of Saddam Hussein's regime. The civilian Defense Policy Board actually wields more control over the military establishment than the Defense Secretary or the generals and admirals. There are a number of other Zionists who serve on this board (Kissinger, Cohen, Schlessinger, Adelman, Abrams) as well as non-jewish members who have always supported Israel and the expansion of the "War on Terror". The notoriously belligerent Perle, nicknamed the "The Prince of Darkness", is Chairman of the Board. Perle is also a former Director of The Jerusalem Post and serves on the Board of Directors of several Israeli companies. Take time to Read the letter!

This is a letter from the *"The Project for the New American Century"* (PNAC):

"January 26, 1998

The Honorable William J. Clinton
President of the United States
Washington, DC

Dear Mr. President:

We are writing you because we are convinced that current American policy toward Iraq is not succeeding, and that we may soon face a threat in the Middle East more serious than any we have known since the end of the Cold War. In your upcoming State of the Union Address, you have an opportunity to chart a clear and determined course for meeting this threat. We urge you to seize that opportunity, and to enunciate a new strategy that would secure the interests of the U.S. and our friends and allies around the world. That strategy should aim, above all, at the removal of Saddam Hussein's regime from power. We stand ready to offer our full support in this difficult but necessary endeavor.

The policy of "containment" of Saddam Hussein has been steadily eroding over the past several months. As recent events have demonstrated, we can no longer depend on our partners in the Gulf War coalition to continue to uphold the sanctions or to punish Saddam when he blocks or evades UN inspections. Our ability to ensure that Saddam Hussein is not producing weapons of mass destruction, therefore, has substantially diminished. Even if full inspections were eventually to resume, which now seems highly unlikely, experience has shown that it is difficult if not impossible to monitor Iraq's chemical and biological weapons production. The lengthy period during which the inspectors will have been unable to enter many Iraqi facilities has made it even less likely that they will be able to uncover all of Saddam's secrets. As a result, in the not-too-distant future we will be unable to determine with any reasonable level of confidence whether Iraq does or does not possess such weapons.

Such uncertainty will, by itself, have a seriously destabilizing effect on the entire Middle East. It hardly needs to be added that if Saddam does acquire the capability to deliver weapons of mass destruction, as he is almost certain to do if we continue along the present course, the safety of American troops in the region, of our friends and allies like Israel and the moderate Arab states, and a significant portion of the world's supply of oil will all be put at hazard. As you have rightly declared, Mr. President, the security of the world in the first part of the 21st century will be determined largely by how we handle this threat.

Given the magnitude of the threat, the current policy, which depends for its success upon the steadfastness of our coalition partners and upon the cooperation of Saddam Hussein, is dangerously inadequate. The only acceptable strategy is one that eliminates the possibility that Iraq will be able to use or threaten to use weapons of mass destruction. In the near term, this means a willingness to undertake military action as diplomacy is clearly failing. In the long term, it means removing Saddam Hussein and his regime from power. That now needs to become the aim of American foreign policy.

We urge you to articulate this aim, and to turn your Administration's attention to implementing a strategy for removing Saddam's regime from power. This will require a full complement of diplomatic, political and military efforts. Although we are fully aware of the dangers and difficulties in implementing this policy, we believe the dangers of failing to do so are far greater. We believe the U.S. has the authority under existing UN resolutions to take the necessary steps, including military steps, to protect our vital interests in the Gulf. In any case, American policy cannot continue to be crippled by a misguided insistence on unanimity in the UN Security Council.

We urge you to act decisively. If you act now to end the threat of weapons of mass destruction against the U.S. or its allies, you will be acting in the most fundamental national security interests of the country. If we accept a course of weakness and drift, we put our interests and our future at risk.

Sincerely,

As a think tank based in Washington, D.C. that began in 1997, PNAC was co-founded by conservatives William Kristol and Robert Kagan. PNAC's stated goal was "to promote American global leadership", and according to them "American leadership is both good for America and good for the world". PNAC exerted influence on high-level U.S. government officials in the administration of U.S. President George W. Bush and affected the Bush Administration's development of military and foreign policies, especially involving national security and the Iraq War. It should be understood that the war on Iraq was being engineered, and strategically planned prior to September 11, 2001.

Elliott Abrams (National Security Council, Elliot Abrams)

Richard L. Armitage (Deputy Secretary of State, Richard Armitage)

William J. Bennett (speechwriter for George W. Bush, William J. Bennett)

Jeffrey Bergner (His lobbying firm, Bergner, Bockorny, Castagnetti, Hawkins & Brain, represents a number of high profile firms, including Bristol-Myers Squib, Boeing, Hewlett-Packard, Phillip Morris, Monsanto, Lucent, and Dell, Jeffrey Bergner)

John Bolton (Under Secretary, Arms Control and International Security, John Bolton)

Paula Dobriansky (Under Secretary, Global Affairs, Paula Dobriansky)

Francis Fukuyama (professor of political economy at the Johns Hopkins University School of Advanced International Studies, Francis Fukuyama)

Robert Kagan (co-founder of the Project for the New American Century, Robert Kagan)

Zalmay Khalilzad (special envoy to Afghanistan, advisor for the Unocal Corporation, counsellor to United States Secretary of Defense Donald H. Rumsfeld, senior United States State Department official advising on the Soviet war in Afghanistan and the Iran-Iraq war, and from 1991 to 1992, he was a senior Defense Department official for policy planning, Zalmay Khalilzad)

William Kristol (advocate for Israel, political contributor to the Fox News Channel, William Kristol)

Richard Perle (Advisory Board of the Jewish Institute for National Security Affairs, former chairman of the Defense Policy Board, Richard Perle)

Peter W. Rodman (Assistant Secretary for International Security Affairs in the Department of Defense, Peter W. Rodman)

Donald Rumsfeld (Secretary of Defense, Donald Rumsfeld)

William Schneider, Jr. (Chairman of the Defense Science Board, William Scheider Jr.)

Vin Weber (former U.S. Representative from Minnesota, Vin Weber)

Paul Wolfowitz (Deputy Secretary of Defense, Paul Wolfowitz)

R. James Woolsey (former director of the U.S. Central Intelligence Agency, James Woolsey)

Robert B. Zoellick (member of President George Walker Bush's Cabinet, Robert B. Zoellick)

The above listed names are those that signed the letter...

Paul Wolfowitz, as The Undersecretary of Defense is another influentially powerful Zionist zealot who lived in Israel as a teenager and has family living there now. The Undersecretary of Defense Policy is Douglas Feith, a Zionist whose law firm has offices in Israel. The Perle, Wolfowitz, and Feith trio constitutes a fanatical and warmongering government-within-a-government. In league with these Zionist Pentagon conspirators are Orthodox jewish Zionist Senator Joseph Lieberman (D-CT), his partner in crime, Senator John McCain (R-AZ), and scores of other Zionist or Zionist owned Senators, Congressmen, and media personalities. These individuals ignored the fact that following the 1980s war with Iran; the 1991 Gulf war; 12 years of punishing sanctions; repeated bombings in the 1990s; the patrolled no-fly zone and protected Kurdish north; and the depleted state of Iraq's military, the nation was in no position for conflict with any of its neighbors let alone with the world's only superpower. "Saddam Hussein was clearly not a threat." Therefore there was no PUBLIC need for the war.

Consider what **President Bill Clinton reportedly said as reported in the** *New York Post:*

> *"The Israelis know that if the Iraqi or the Iranian army came across the Jordan River, I would personally grab a rifle, get in a ditch, and fight and die."*

> *"It was very fitting that Bill Clinton should have made those comments before a Zionist women's charity called the Hadassah Foundation. Hadassah (also known as Esther) is the heroine of the Book of Esther in the Bible's Old Testament. This non-religious story tells of a scheme by Hadassah and her Uncle Mordecai to infiltrate and gain political influence over the Persian King Xerxes; influence which was then used to kill and destroy their anti-jewish enemies"*

A quote by: Dr. Albert D. Pastore PhD

Admiral Thomas Moorer, Chairman of the US Joint Chiefs of Staff under Ronald Reagan said this:

> *"I've never seen a President -- I don't care who he is -- stand up to them [the Israelis]. It just boggles the mind. They always get what they want. The Israelis know what is going on all the time. If the American people understood what a grip those people have got on our government, they would rise up in arms. Our citizens certainly don't have any idea what goes on."*

While a guest on ABC's Face the Nation, William Fulbright - US Senator and Chairman of the US Foreign Relations committee - once said this before a national audience:

> "Israel controls the United States Senate. We should be more concerned about the United States' interests."

Nationally syndicated columnist and former presidential candidate Patrick Buchanan said:

> "The United States Congress is Israeli occupied territory."

US religious leader Billy Graham and President Richard Nixon once had the following exchange, which was caught on tape:

> GRAHAM: *The Jewish stranglehold on the media has got to be broken or this country's going down the drain".*
> NIXON: *"You believe that?"*
> GRAHAM: *"Yes, sir."*
> NIXON: *"Oh boy. So do I. I can't ever say that but I do believe it"*

~ ~ ~

Why must the strangle hold of so-called Jewish control of the media and entertainment world be broken—because if not, those who have an imperialist agenda can manipulate the minds of the masses through the news and entertainment that they control. The entertainment industry can continuosly dumb-down the masses through their product, while at the same time, the media can mislead and trick the weakened mental state of not just the American, but also the global population. This is the connection that must be seen, it is the purpose of this book to show how one thing is connected to the other; and until the HipHop Nation can see the connection, as well as the consequences of the said connection, they will have yet to fully comprehend the significance of what they say and do within the framework of a Zionist and American global agenda—it is this ignorance that qualifies them as slaves.

CHASING DOLLARS

"put a slave in a hog pen and train him to live there and incorporate in him to value it as a way of life completely, the biggest problem you would have out of him is that he would worry you about provisions to keep the hog pen clean"

As we bring this writing to a close, I respectfully request that each and every reader of these particular pages stop and ponder over these following words: If we look at the dollar bill, what do we see... we see a white man that owned and controlled black slaves. If we examine the words of the constitution, we recognize that these words were written from the pens of men that owned and controlled black slaves. The seeds of today's corporations were built on over 300 years of free labor. What we see today as a United States of America was made possible by free labor of the African Slaves, and the murder and subjugation of those that are known as Indians.

Stop and understand—Martin Luther King Jr. was murdered in 1968, as of 2009, only 41 years has passed since his death. What was his life work, and for what reason was he killed? Do we actually believe that the mental condition of those that were in power yesterday are any different from those that are in power a mere 41 years later? What has changed within the United States since the time of the civil rights movement?... the answer is real simple.

The so-called Negro of yesterday had little to offer in terms of an economic incentive to cause white America to change the social realities that black folk existed in. Corporate America had yet to realize the financial power that existed within the black communities, and the institutions that allow black people to secure riches did not exist on the levels that it does today. The NFL, the NBA, Major League Baseball, the world of music and entertainment had not evolved into the inclusion of black people that we see today.

What does this mean? It means black acceptance within the societal structure of America has always been and continues to be based on economics. This was seen during the bus boycotts and during the civil disobedience of the 60's. Neither white people, nor the American government has ever bowed to the moral pressures of the oppressed. Each and every movement of white people, including the enslavement and the so-called freeing of the slaves, was predicated on the dollar bill and the potential for white folk to make money. When the civil rights movement affected the white folk's bottom line they decided to change tactics. Again, white folks have not changed, they have simply evolved.

With this being said, if we are to ever see a change within our communities, it must be upon an economic basis, not an emotional petition targeted at the moral fibers of America, because there are none. The present day American government has at its base the mentality of the slave owning forefathers, and time nor circumstances has changed how they view the so-called African American or their cousins throughout the world. The fact that they profit from our destruction shows that they do not operate from a moral imperative. It is strictly financial, and the financial institutions are marked by a certain group of people and a similar mental disposition.

In case we have forgotten, the following is a list of United States Presidents that owned slaves during their lifetime. Imagine so-called Jewish people paying homage to those Germans that were responsible for, and who benefited from the murderous actions of the holocaust. How can any black man and woman ever offer any sympathies or forms of homage to any one of these Presidents that enslaved, abused, stripped naked, rendered ignorant, and helped to destroy the family unit of our people?

George Washington – owned at least 200 slaves

Thomas Jefferson – owned at least 140 slaves

James Madison – owned several hundred slaves

James Monroe – owned over 50 slaves

Andrew Jackson – owned over 160 slaves

Martin Van Buren – sold a slave for $50.00

William Henry Harrison – fought to make slavery legal in Indiana

John Tyler – claimed that God ordained slavery of blacks

James K. Polk – had at least 15 slaves

Zachary Taylor – owned over 100 slaves

James Buchanan – feared slaves would murder white women in their sleep

Andrew Johnson – reportedly owned 8 slaves

Ulysses S. Grant – feared the multiplication of the slaves

    These white men by themselves affected the lives of several hundred slaves. When we consider the tools utilized in maintaining the slave and slave master relationship, we recognize that these slave owners not only affected those that were born from the slaves, but undoubtedly an uncountable amount of lives that were prevented from being born. These presidents maintained their control over their slaves by utilizing the tools that were outlined in the Willie Lynch Letter. Please stop to ponder over what it means to have sitting Presidents that had slaves and justified it. How could we ever think favorably of these wicked individuals?

As the HipHop Nation sells its soul in pursuit of the dollar bill, let's recognize those Presidents that owned slaves whose faces appear on the money that they so desperately seek:

George Washington - $1.00

Thomas Jefferson - $2.00

Alexander Hamilton - $10.00

Andrew Jackson - $20.00

Ulysses S. Grant - $50.00

Benjamin Franklin - $100.00

This information should allow us to see that real people, people that are placed upon a pedestal within this society, actually won for themselves a historical record of their greatness, while at the same time assisting in the enslavement of our people. What should be understood is that there is a tie that binds today's corporate mind, with yesterday's slave and slave master's mentality. Just as yesterday, today's slave master values profit and power over the collective and individual prosperity of those that were used to secure that power and profit. The base value of the dollar bill is the people that work for it and chase it. Those faces that are found upon the dollar are the faces of men that symbolically represent a mentality that reinforces the relationship of slave and slave master. It is the quest for these dollars that has placed the black man and woman within a state of perpetual servitude. The temporary acquisition of the paper has acted as a substitution for our desire to secure true liberation and the power that comes with it.

The Willie Lynch syndrome has brought forth the destruction that we presently see within our communities. Have we chosen to ignore our condition and sit idly by while our people are destroyed? Are there any other people that refuse to take action to prevent their destruction? Isn't death sweet when it is a death that is obtained within the quest for liberation and survival? I ask these questions... it is for you to answer. Are fancy cars, fine homes, jewelry, and money in a bank account more important than your people and the future of your children? Do we actually believe that white people have factored in the success of black people within the pages of their global agendas... if so, approach the following information with caution, because I don't want your brain to explode when you finally wake up to see the slave state in which we presently live.

ARE YOU A SLAVE?

"None are so hopelessly ENSLAVED as those who THINK they are free"...

As I begin to bring this to a close; allow me to lace your mind with a few more thoughts that may cause YOU and US to move our individual and collective asses...

I am sure that everyone "knows" that the civil war ended slavery... is that right? Of course it did; for if it did not, we black folk, or any other person that is/was deemed a slave would know it... right?!

But maybe there is more than one way to enslave a people; or perhaps there is not only one form of slavery, but several different elements that bring about the Ultimate Slave reality.

I mean think about it—what if slavery never ended? What if slavery has merely evolved into its present form? A form that has discarded the identifying elements of slavery such as whips and chains, crackers and ropes; and replaced them with credit cards and certificates of deposits, hourly wages and 401k's!? Is it possible that like cell phones and computers, the New Slave has been stream-lined and concubined into a 21st century version of the same "ole nigga" that did and does the bidding of his/her MASTER for the same ole bullshit trinkets and bobbles that pacified a nation of people for more than three centuries.

Trace the actions of your day... see how each day is comprised of ways to get closer to them good ole slave masters; you know... George, Thomas, Alexander, and the rest of those wig wearing white boys that lace the face of the currency that ignorant niggas die for, and the Neo-negroes live for.

Didn't Gary Coleman say it: **"None are so hopelessly ENSLAVED as those who THINK they are free"**? Shit I don't know who said it, but somebody did!

When was the last time you looked up the word FREEDOM? Okay, I will do it for you: **Free"dom** (?), n. [AS. freódm; freófree + -dom. See <u>Free</u>, and -dom.]

1. The state of being free; exemption from the power and control of another; liberty; independence.
Made captive, yet deserving **freedom** more. *Milton.*

2. Privileges; franchises; immunities.
Your charter and your caty's **freedom**. *Shak.*

3. Exemption from necessity, in choice and action; as, the freedom of the will.

4. Ease; facility; as, he speaks or acts with freedom.

5. Frankness; openness; unreservedness.
I emboldened spake and **freedom** used. *Milton.*

6. Improper familiarity; violation of the rules of decorum; license.

Now… look at that definition long and hard, re-read it if necessary; and then ask yourself if you are FREE!

Based on the previous chapters I hope that we can now see that HipHop, or that which is considered as the HipHop Nation is not an independent sovereign entity, it is not free. Although the mainstream media, the corporate media chooses to lambaste, and attempts to castigate the artist of the HipHop world, it should be clear that the same corporate media that attempts to do such, is directly connected and related to those behind the scene, those power brokers that dictate the direction of HipHop and its artist.

By placing emphasis on the artist, those that are in control, those that are in the seats of power, choose to paint themselves out of the picture when it best suits their interest and at a time of controversy and critical discourse. For this reason, I am attempting to show the reader the indelible connection between the words that spew from the mouth of the HipHop artist, and the corporate heads that wax rich despite the negative impact those said words have on the society in general, and the young black male and females in particular.

As we proceed, I ask the reader to consider the word **Nation**; it is important to grasp these following concepts in order to draw a realistic conclusion…

Nation: Na"tion (?), n. [F. nation, L. natio nation, race, orig., a being born, fr. natus, p.p. of nasci, to be born, for gnatus, gnaci, from the same root as E. kin. √44. See <u>Kin</u> kindred, and cf. <u>Cognate</u>, <u>Natal</u>, <u>Native</u>.]
1.   (Ethnol.) A part, or division, of the people of the earth, distinguished from the rest by common descent, language, or institutions; a race; a stock.
All **nations**, and kindreds, and people, and tongues. *Rev. vii. 9.*

2. The body of inhabitants of a country, united under an independent government of their own.
A **nation** is the unity of a people. *Coleridge.*
Praise the power that hath made and preserved us a **nation**. *F. S. Key.*

3. Family; lineage. [Obs.] *Chaucer.*

The HipHop Nation is a nation because a "nation" has less to do with a particular landmass, and more to do with a people that share the distinguishable characteristics of language, descent, and culture. Simply put, a nation is not the dirt; the nation is the people of a common culture and societal aspiration that sit on that dirt. The HipHop Nation has its own unique and distinguishable origins, language, and culture; this cannot be argued, but the question is... is HipHop sovereign, or is it a subjugated nation?

Although HipHop began as a sub-unit of the more dominate black culture, the black culture itself was and is the product of a colonial slave industry that was predicated on the complete control and subjugation of black people. As a result of slavery, and the control methods utilized by the slave master, the product of the system of slavery was a group of people marked by the system itself.

What this means is that the black culture up to this point has been one that finds its roots in slavery. Regardless if it's the meals that we prepare for our families, or the songs we sing at church, to the way husbands and wives interact—the undeniable fact remains that black people's culture today is an off shoot adaptation to the institutional slave institution of yesterday.

Although many argue over the authenticity of the *"Willie Lynch Letter"* and *"Let's Make a Slave"*, the QUESTION that I ask is... does the mathematical premise which formulate the writing's conclusions and indictment of a slave-making system prove to be valid? In other words... do the writing's premise prove-out to be true, even if the document itself is not accepted as actual! I guess the answer is found within the context of the writings, and the condition that black people find themselves today in relation to the characteristics of a slave and his or her master as outlined within those said writings.

Since this book's primary premise is that the HipHop Nation itself has been incorporated as Willie Lynch's Newest Slave; I will clarify this indictment and simultaneously justify it by using the letter and the *"Let's Make a Slave"* document itself. Although the HipHop Nation is the case study, I don't by any means make the claim that the HipHop Nation is the only slave, (in fact, we are all slaves regardless if we accept it or not) they are simply the primary tools of choice in terms of the slaves master's ability to maintain and sustain their control of the slaves and the resources that are mined by the dumb-downed beast of burden—a group that is seemingly unaware of the prevailing institution of slavery and its wicked machinations.

"The Black slave after receiving this indoctrination shall carry on and will become self re-fueling and self-generating for hundreds of years, maybe thousands."

"Let us make a slave. What do we need? First of all we need a black nigger man, a pregnant nigger woman and her baby nigger boy. Second, we will use the same basic principle that we use in breaking a horse, combined with some more sustaining factors. We reduce them from their natural state in nature; whereas nature provides them with the natural capacity to take care of their needs and the needs of their offspring, we break that natural string of independence from them and thereby create a dependency state so that we may be able to get from them useful production for our business and pleasure."

HipHop began in the state of New York; as previously stated, New York is considered as the empire state! **EMPIRE** is defined as:

1a *(1)*: a major political unit having a territory of great extent or a number of territories or peoples under a single sovereign authority; *especially*: one having an emperor as chief of state *(2)*: the territory of such a political unit ***b*:** something resembling a political empire; *especially*: an extensive territory or enterprise under single domination or control

2: imperial sovereignty, rule, or dominion

As so-called citizens of the state of New York, the blackman and woman were born and raised within an economic and social condition as dictated and maintained by the state, the empire state. Within this context, the state of New York can be viewed as a mother or female that got pregnant with a child. That child was and is the result of the institutional policies that shape and nurture the psychological, physical, and spiritual development of that child. In this case a society that is controlled by the policies and agendas of those who control the state of New York, in a real way, gave birth to a child—that child was known as HipHop!

Now please stop and realize... the primary word of choice today in the HipHop Nation is nigga (nigger)... this word is the label that permeates the identity of those that participate in the world of HipHop! In a very real way, the state of New York was the womb; the social policies and agendas of those that control that womb was the phallus that brought forth not only a nigga (nigger), but generated the context by which, and through which you measure and define a nigga! With this being said, the slave master's policies and social programs from the very beginning created the "NIGGER" that they would need to bring about the desired slave!

As I stated earlier... "**The record industry is a global empire that is predicated on the expression of ideas, thoughts, feelings, and reactions in regards to the social, economic, political, and religious realities that exist within the world. Within the context of an artistic expression, artists relay the above via their individual form of artistic talent and expression. When these particular expressions can be filtered, controlled, redefined, and disseminated based on the social, political, economic, and religious agendas of an outsider, these expressions are at best limited, and at worse fraudulent. With this in mind, those that desire to control the global perception have positioned themselves as the universal filters of the artistic expression and oppressors of the truth".**

What this means is simple; within the **"empire state"** are citizens, these citizens are shaped by the policies of education, religion, and economics of those that control that empire! Within the very real influential environment of the **"Empire State"** emerged the **product** of that state. HipHop was born through, and out of, the influential circumstances that we find within the empire! Therefore HipHop as the hated and despised child is the **product** or **result** of the very ones that continue to criticize and malign it... go figure! (Perhaps this thought is a little too heavy; hopefully you'll get it as WE continue).

As a way to shape and control their slaves, the slave master signed off on institutional policies that would support and lend to the fulfillment of an agenda. Is it hard to believe that if you can't control your environment, you become a victim or product of that environment? Okay... then let's understand that those that control your environment and the policies that sustain and maintain that environment subsequently dictate your agenda. Therefore, if a person desires to formulate and implement their independent agenda, an agenda that is conducive for their positive growth and development, that person must first have the power to control their own environment. Question... based on the previous chapters, does the HipHop Nation control and dictate their environment? If not, who does? Since the HipHop Nation does not control their environment, they obviously lack the power to implement their own agenda and strategies of independence!

"Second, we will use the same basic principle that we use in breaking a horse, combined with some more sustaining factors. We reduce them from their natural state in nature; whereas nature provides them with the natural capacity to take care of their needs and the needs of their offspring, we break that natural string of independence from them and thereby create a dependency state so that we may be able to get from them useful production for our business and pleasure."

Again, the state of New York was the environment that brought forth what is commonly referred to as HipHop; with this in mind, reconsider what I said a little earlier:

"The financial center of America was at its conception the state of New York and this stands true even today. With Wall Street as its financial backdrop, New York's rich history is built on its participation in the African Slave Trade. Though we may tend to associate the southern portion of the United States with slavery, New York (prior to the American Revolution), was second only to Charleston, South Carolina in the owning of slaves. One out of every five New Yorkers was slaves and 40 percent of all colonial New York households, owned slaves.

Between the years 1600 to 1827, the African Slave Trade played the most vital role in building New York into America's wealthiest state and the financial capital of the world. The slave trade, the labor of enslaved people, and slavery's integration into everyday commerce shaped the global destiny and blue print of what is today recognized as Corporate America".

HipHop is the product of a "state" (empire) of existence that was marked by slavery and the machinations that allowed it to continue. As a corporate state, a state that was and is the empirical evidence of America's dominance and global control, New York was the incubator that helped to develop a condition that shaped the mind, ways, and actions of a people that will later be dubbed as the HipHop Nation. This nation, as defined earlier... was and is **"A part, or division, of the people of the earth, distinguished from the rest by common descent, language, or institutions; a race; a stock"**. What was and is the distinguishing descent, language, and institutions that gave birth to, and defines HipHop? It is nothing more or less than the policies and institutions that were and are dictated and instituted by those that control the EMPIRE!

It is for this reason that in previous chapters I forthrightly exposed some of those that control and comprise the corporate structure that need the divisive ways and actions that are prescribed within the Willie Lynch Letter in order to **"be able to get from them** (slaves) **useful production for our** (corporate slave masters) **business and pleasure"**. These divisive ways and actions are glorified and marketed throughout the media **(BUSINESS)** and entertainment **(PLEASURE)** worlds that the slave master controls.

Now when these products of New York formulated a distinct voice or language in order to deal with, or expose the environment that had shaped and encaged them, corporate America took that voice and language and filtered it through the controlled media and entertainment corporate structure. By being able to do so, the motivation, or the intent of the words spoken by the products of New York was deliberately taken out of context; thereby stripping the words of the liberating elements that are contained within truth! This synthetic misrepresentation of the artistic expression of a subjugated group limits the said group from painting a clear picture of their oppressive condition. Simply put—the 'PURE' artistic expression was grafted by those that controlled it!

Please understand that the "Empire State" (New York) is the head of the global snake; therefore, the product of New York is not confined nor restricted to those that are geographically located within the actual state. As HipHop spread throughout the world, throughout the various urban and suburban even rural areas of America, don't get it twisted... so too, does the power of the "empire" and the policies and agendas, that the powerful snake spits out!

Now one of the traits of a slave is an inability to control and dictate the use of the "product" that the individual and collective slaves produce. Because the early members of the HipHop Nation lacked adequate resources and the ability to package and present their product; their desire to get their words out to a broader audience was manipulated by a group of people that not only had the power to do so, but also the power to pay the slaves in the process!

"whereas nature provides them with the natural capacity to take care of their needs and the needs of their offspring, we break that natural string of independence from them and thereby create a dependency state".

HipHop is an artistic expression; the expression was based upon the *reality* or *condition* that those that made up the nation of HipHop found themselves, or was the product of. Within the spoken word was the presence of truth, a truth of not only circumstance, but more importantly, the words contained a truth that reveals the coping mechanisms of a circumstance that may be deemed as destructive, painful, or debilitating. With this being said, the words of HipHop can be seen as *a natural remedy* or antidote to a system or institution that desired to restrict or confine an otherwise potentially powerful unit, or distinct race or stock! A NATION!!

When the people of shared circumstance and condition began to experience this artistic expression and the potentially liberating effects of the truth that was within it, they began to move... dance, break, paint (tag), speak; they began to show signs of life (independence)! This newly found life activity was not lost on those that desire to control and dictate the life activity of all, including the niggas (niggers) in the ghetto; the same exact "Niggers" that they had made and brought into existence. This early life activity had to be put in check before it evolved into a more productive and evolved form. Early HipHop had to be killed, and a new HipHop had to be born!

Now the language was "natural" it was REAL; therefore the reaction, or the result of that language... the original HipHop language was authentic! But the corporate forces, the forces that are comprised *of* and dictated *by* the same ones that control the "EMPIRE STATE", utilized the mathematical thought within a diabolical and satanic context to implement a series of events that would circumvent the words of the HipHop artist with a deliberate and fabricated word that was synthesized through the devil's handbook!

But how did they do it?... SIMPLE, they offered the HipHop Nation a "piece" of the PIE! What pie, the "APPLE PIE", or in this case... the BIG APPLE (New York) Pie! As soon as the HipHop Nation was allowed to take a bite of the "forbidden fruit", a fruit of slavery, colonialism, imperialism, global dominance and violence as signified by the truth and secrets of the EMPIRE STATE.... An UNHOLI- ALLIANCE was made! In such, the liberating words of the HipHop Nation were filtered by the corporate leviathans that began as a "snake" but grew and developed into a full fledge DRAGON! The dragon stripped their words of LIBERATION (independence), and marked them (the words) with SLAVERY, or dependence! A flood of propaganda went forth from the world of media and entertainment (DRAGON) that began to lure the slaves into the direction that the DRAGON desires and dictated!

The **"Keys of Control"** as outlined by Willie Lynch began to be on full display within the words and lifestyles that became today's HipHop. From the status of plantation (Record Company), to the battle between region (north, south, east, west, and mid-west), all the way to age (old school vs. new school)—the Willie Lynch syndrome has permeated the fabrics of what is today seen as the HipHop Nation!

Offering so-called Money, Power, and Respect to a group of people that were brought up in a societal context that was the complete opposite of money, power, and respect; the white corporate structure offered that which had been previously kept out of their (slaves) reach. The HipHop Nation jumped on it thinking that they had arrived; but boy were WE wrong! By thinking that money, power, and respect was the keys to life; anything that brought about the existence of money, power, and respect was psychologically deemed as acceptable. We must remember that our individual and collective understanding(s) was and is based upon the institutional influences that come from the "EMPIRE STATE". Our frame of reference, the basis of all our decisions was made within the context of not independence and freedom, but dependence and slavery! What this simply means is we had not yet broken the psychological chains of slavery, the slave masters re-arranged our priorities, thereby, dictating our agenda.

NOW.....read the following, and let's see if YOUR EYES begin to OPEN!

A Nation of Slaves

Cardinal Principles for Making A Negroe

For fear that our future generations may not understand the principles of breaking both horses and men, we lay down the art. For, if we are to sustain our basic economy we must break both of the beasts together, the nigger (HipHop) and the horse (Talent).

We understand that short range planning in economics results in periodic economic chaos, so that, to avoid turmoil in the economy, it requires us to have breadth and depth in long range comprehensive planning, articulating both skill and sharp perception. We lay down the following principles for the long range comprehensive economic planning:

1) Both horse (TALENT) and niggers (The HipHop Nation) are no good to the economy in the wild of natural state.

The horse is seen as the talent, or the tool that will be utilized by the slave master; the talent is contained within the HipHop Nation. The 'Natural' or 'Wild' state is the natural artistic expression prior to corporate control. (or real HipHop)

2) Both must be broken and tied together for orderly production. (DILLUTED and INCORPATED)

The talent must be broken, refined, stripped, synthesized, and filtered through the corporate structure; the HipHop Nation will thereby be controlled, dominated, and subjugated to the same corporate and institutional forces.

3) For orderly futures, special and particular attention must be paid to the female and the youngest offspring. (The Black Nation and its PRODUCT... potential talent)

The **female** is seen as the Black Nation, a nation that produces the vessels that contain the talents that corporate and governmental institutions desire to sift like wheat. The youngest **offspring** is those who have yet to be incorporated!

4) Both must be crossbred to produce a variety and division of labor.

Corporate and governmental institutions desire to dictate the professional and artistic aspirations of the black nation in order to produce and control that which is necessary for the continued dominance of the EMPIRE. Simply put, the talent of black people must be used to maintain and advance the agenda of those that sign the checks!

5) Both must be taught to respond to a peculiar new language.

The corporate and governmental institutions desire to re-interpret the national priorities of those that have been historically oppressed and restricted. By interpreting the needs of the oppressed class, those that are the cause of said oppression will not offer up any solutions that will liberate the oppressed class...less they give up power and control. By reinterpreting the societal position of black folks, the empire state can introduce into the minds of a slave a false remedy to their individual and collective condition. **The slaves are taught to get money, but the more money that they get, the more money the Masters get—this way no real ground is gained between the slave and the master!**

6) Psychological and physical instruction of containment must be created for both.

Corporate and governmental institutions are designed to restrict, control, dominate and dictate the information that is released to the public. By controlling information, the controlling powers can restrict the movements and aspirations of the public... particularly the oppressed class. When this is allowed to happen, the information that is made readily available will lack the elements of change and liberation that is in the best interest of those that are subjugated.

We hold the above six cardinals as truths to be self-evident, based upon the following discourse concerning the economics of breaking and tying the horse (talent) **and the nigger** (The HipHop Nation) **together... all-inclusive of the six principles laid down above.**

NOTE: Neither principle alone will suffice for good economics.

All principles must be employed for the orderly good of the nation. Accordingly, both a wild horse (NO RECORD DEAL) **and a wild or natural nigger** (Original non-incorporated HipHop NATION) **is dangerous even if captured, for they will have the tendency to seek their customary freedom, and in doing so, might kill you in your sleep. You cannot rest.** (Their Biggest FEAR!)

They (Non-incorporated HipHop Nation) **sleep while you are awake and are awake while you are asleep. They are dangerous near the family house** (corporate offices) **and it requires too much labor to watch them away from the house. Above all you cannot get them to work** (perform) **in this natural state. Hence, both the horse** (TALENT) **and the nigger** (HipHop Nation) **must be broken** (controlled, incorporated), **that is break them from one form of mental life to another, keep the body and take the mind. In other words, break the will to resist.**

Now the breaking process is the same for the horse (TALENT) **and the nigger** (The HipHop Nation), **only slightly varying in degrees. But as we said before, you must keep your eye focused on the offspring** (mental condition of the audience) **of the horse** (TALENT) **and the nigger** (HipHop Nation). **A brief discourse in offspring development** (marketing) **will shed light on the key to sound economic principles. Pay little attention to the generation of original breaking** (old school) **but concentrate on future generations** (new trends).

Therefore, if you break the female (The Black Nation), **she will deliver it up to you. For her normal female protective tendencies will have been lost in the original breaking process. For example, take the case of the wild stud horse** (un-incorporated TALENT), **a female horse** (Black Nation's collective Talent) **and an already infant horse** (potential TALENT) **and compare the breaking process with two nigger males** (the HipHop Nation) **in their natural state, a pregnant nigger woman** (the Black Nation) **with her infant offspring** (POTENTIAL TALENT).

Take the stud horse (TALENT), **break** (incorporate) **him for limited containment. Completely break the female horse** (the Black Nation's talent base) **until she becomes very gentle whereas you or anybody can ride her** (remove that which offends the established power structure) **in comfort. Breed the mare** (Black Nation) **and the stud** (TALENT) **until you have the desired offspring**(the new pop music). **Then you can turn the stud** (TALENT) **to freedom until you need him again. Train the female horse** (Black Nation's Talent) **whereby she will eat out of your hand** (begin to depend on corporate and governmental institutions to give it a voice and money), **and she will train the infant** (new talent) **horse to eat out of your hand also.**

When it comes to breaking the uncivilized nigger (NON-CORPORATE), **use the same process, but vary the degree and step up the pressure so as to do a complete reversal of the mind. Take the meanest and most restless** nigger (so-called CONSCIOUS HipHop), **strip him of his clothes** (ABILITY TO GET PAID) **in front of the remaining male niggers** (segments of HipHop), **the female** (the Black Nation), **and the nigger infant** (POTENTIAL TALENT), **tar and feather him, tie each leg to a different horse** (north, south, east, west, and Midwest factions of HipHop) **faced in opposite directions, set him afire and beat both horses to pull him apart** (create hatred, competition, and envy...destroy unity) **in front of the remaining niggers. The next step is to take a bullwhip** (media) **and beat** (castigate and malign) **both the remaining nigger male** (The HipHop Nation) **to the point of death in front of the female** (Black Nation) **and the infant** (potential TALENT). **Don't kill him. But put the fear of God in him, for he can be useful for future breeding.**

In conclusion, please consider the words of the premier speaker of truth; a man that has and continues to consistently find a voice to speak to the powers that attempt to maintain and sustain their global control and dominance:

CLOSING WORDS!

IN THE NAME OF ALLAH, THE BENEFICENT, THE MERCIFUL.

◆━━━━━━━━━━━━━━━━━━━━━━━━━━━━━━━◆

For years, decades and centuries, leaders have arisen among us who have fought, bled and died to see us united as a people.

Willie Lynch, a Caribbean plantation owner, developed a set of protocols that would ensure, if followed, that Black people—wherever we were found on the planet—would never be able to unite.

So, these seeds of dissention and division have worked 100 percent to keep the former colonial and slave-master's children in power over us. All that Willie Lynch advocated in 1712 continues until this very day.

Those who wish to maintain power and control over us are fearful of anything or anyone who might bring unity to a fragmented people. So every leader who showed such ability or skill was castigated, evil spoken of, falsely accused, imprisoned, beaten or killed, only for us to later learn how valuable they were, male and female, to our advancement as a people.

From the time that I was a little boy, I hungered to see us as a united people. When I heard the voice of the Honorable Elijah Muhammad and Malcolm X, I believed that the Teachings that they presented would be a unifying force for all of our people. However, in our lack of understanding of the universal nature of His Message, we were not permitted with our limited understanding to unite the whole of our people, but we were successful in uniting a segment of our people, to produce the Nation of Islam as an example of what a united people could produce in the way of providing for our necessities of life.

The Honorable Elijah Muhammad called for a united front of Black leaders and organizations to plan the uplift of all of our fallen people. Kwame Ture, also known as Stokley Carmichael, carried the theme of a United African Front and worked to produce this to the end of his days.

I am so thankful to Almighty Allah (God) for the words that He caused me to write and say that have become the basis for the call of the 10th Anniversary of the Million Man March and the creation of the Millions More Movement.

For the first time in our history, those of us of different ideologies, philosophies, methodologies, denominations, sects and religions, political and fraternal affiliations have come together to create the Millions More Movement. Each of us, who have agreed to work together for the benefit of the whole of our people, have said from our particular platforms, based on our beliefs and understanding or the lack thereof, words that have offended members of our own people and others; and our ideology, philosophy, religion and pronouncements may have hurt the ears and sentiments of others outside of our community. Therefore, this has kept us working inside of our own circles with those who think as we think or believe as we believe. As a result, some of us would never appear on the same stage with one another, for fear of being hurt by association with those with whom we have serious disagreements.

The Millions More Movement is challenging all of us to rise above the things that have kept us divided in the past, by focusing us on the agenda of the Millions More Movement to see how all of us, with all of our varied differences, can come together and direct our energy, not at each other, but at the condition of the reality of the suffering of our people, that we might use all of our skills, gifts and talents to create a better world for ourselves, our children, grandchildren and great grandchildren.

I cannot fault a Christian pastor for standing on his platform to preach what he believes, nor a Muslim, Buddhist, Hindu or a member of any religious or political party. All of us must be true to what we earnestly believe. I cannot fault a gay or lesbian person who stands on their platform to preach what they believe of self and how the world should view them. Although what we say on our platform may, in some way, be offensive to others, we must not allow painful utterances of the past or present, based on sincere belief, or based on our ignorance, or based on our ideology or philosophy to cripple a movement that deserves and needs all of us—and, when I say all, I mean **all** of us. We must begin to work together to lift our people out of the miserable and wretched condition in which we find ourselves.

Let us remember in this process that not one of us is qualified to judge the other, for none of us fully understands the circumstances, conditions and realities of each other's lives that make us to think and act as we think. Therefore, Allah (God) alone is our judge.

It is written in the scripture, *"Judge not, that ye be not judged."* **(Matthew 7:1)** Jesus again instructed us, *"How canst thou say to thy brother, let me pull out the mote that is in thine eye, when thou thyself beholdest not the beam that is in thine own eye? Thou hypocrite, cast out first the beam out of thine own eye, and then shalt thou see clearly to pull out the mote that is in thy brother's eye."* **(Luke 6:42)**

These principles, if followed, will allow us to come into a common room with a purpose bigger than self and, in the process, create **lawful dialogue** to help us understand each other, that we may be shaped and molded, or reshaped and remolded, by our association with each other.

The Millions More Movement, in causing all of us to be together for a common cause, allows the process of lawful dialogue to begin to help us in our exchange with one another in the best way. For the Civil Rights Advocates, Nationalists, Pan-Africanists, Christians of every denomination, Muslims of every sect, students of every fraternity, Masons, Shiners' and Elks to come into the same room and begin the process of lawful dialogue; by our being able to exchange with one another in the best, most peaceful and loving manner, we can help to shape and reshape each other's thinking. We are allowed to challenge each other's thinking if we disagree with each other in the spirit of love. Based upon truth and rational thinking, we come to an equitable agreement. When we do this, we can begin to make ourselves into a mighty and powerful force for change.

Unity, love of self and love for one another have always been my desire. We stand on the threshold of the realization of our potential unity and the potential power that our unity can unleash to bring about a positive change today because of the Millions More Movement.

I am hoping that each of us will rise above our personal pain, hurt or anger at one another for what we have said or done in the past or present to offend each other that we might strive for reconciliation, understanding and agreement. Our very lives and the future of our people depend upon this; and this is why we say, "Long Live the Spirit of the Million Man March."

Let that spirit be the spirit of the Millions More Movement, and together we will achieve for our people and others in 10 years what we have not been able to achieve in the 450 years of our sojourn in this hemisphere.

It is written in the scriptures of the Bible: *"Not by might, nor by power, but by My Spirit saith the Lord."* **(Zachariah 4:6)**

It is written in the Holy Qur'an: *"And hold fast by the covenant of Allah (God) altogether and be not disunited. And remember Allah's (God's) favour to you when you were enemies, then He united your hearts so by His favour you became brethren. And you were on the brink of a pit of fire, then He saved you from it. Thus Allah (God) makes clear to you His messages that you may be guided."* **(Surah 3, verse 102)**

Thank you all for reading and striving to adhere to these words.

—The Honorable Minister Louis Farrakhan

I believe that once the Minister has spoken, there is nothing else to be said. I pray that this small contribution to the overall struggle of our people will be received in the spirit that it was written. May Allah (God) and the spirit of those that have gone before US continue to guide, bless and motivate us to take the necessary steps that will secure a total liberation for our children and future generations...PEACE!

Special Message to the so-called Conscious Rappers

The news and entertainment world is ran and controlled by the 10 percent blood suckers of the poor; these RICH slave makers have found a way to take the talent of a segment of the black community and pimp it out into an industry that receives a little over 80 percent of its financial support from white folks and American suburbia. As a musical force that generates over 100 million dollars a year, 80 million dollars comes directly from the pocket books of the white high school and college age boys and girls that sift through the latest HipHop CD like a common text book. Within the content of these CDs, these foreigners to the black experience begin to get their understanding of blackness, and what it means to be black from the likes of Nelly, T.I, Snoop, Jay Z, the Game, 50 Cent among others... *the question is*—are we giving the present generation of white folks the **stereotypical weaponry** that will be used to qualify their racism once these young white folk reach their mental maturity, a maturity that will cause them to accept their social inheritance as the slave master?

If we check the social content of the average HipHop CD, what is today perceived as cool or trendy, will be viewed tomorrow as a social degenerative lifestyle that will be justification for the continued social abuses levied on the backs of the average black man and woman. By allowing these sell-out rappers the opportunity to misrepresent what it is to be black, and the black experience... tomorrow's projected rulers will see black people as a bunch of pimps, hoes, dope dealers, strippers, drug users, and sex crazed Niggaz that is quick to murder someone, and slow to demand true Freedom, Justice and Equality.

Now...*the question is*—will the so-called conscious rappers continue to let this happen? Or, are the so-called conscious rappers trying to merge and coalesce within the same business plan as the contracted slave of the 10 percent? Make NO DOUBT about it... if the so-called conscious rappers get their collective heads out of the damn sand, they would be able to see that the musical trends are set and bound by a group of rich slave makers that determine what the masses should be listening to, and forming their individual and collective opinions around.

Despite the flowery words of blackness and self pride that spews from the lips of the majority of so-called conscious rappers, the reality is that these particular so-called informed rappers have become lazy and complacent, and continue to rely upon their open enemy to get their words across. When they allow this to happen, it shows that despite the black rhetoric, the reality is that they are just some more Niggaz looking for a god damn record deal!

These so-called conscious rappers like to rile against the system, they like to TALK revolution, they like to TALK war, guns, and struggle... but these well informed rappers seem to just want to wait on the revolution, they have no desire to **jump start it**. So again... *the question is*—do you REALLY have a problem with the SYSTEM, or do you just have a problem with YOUR PLACE in that SYSTEM? I believe that this is a legitimate question!

How can you be ready to pick up a gun for revolution? How can you recite words that entice the masses to buck the system... when you yourself refuse to sacrifice the FRUITS of the 10 percent in order to set a new trend? What I mean by this is simple... Most so-called conscious rappers have a hard time EATIN' as it is; most so-called conscious rappers are struggling to pay their bills and produce their music... and when these rappers do produce their music and art, the 10 percent has machinations and systems that prevent that music and art form being heard by the masses... what masses?... the 80 percent of white folks that are making the sell-out rappers so damn rich!

So what does these self-proclaimed Revolutionaries, Gods, Five Percenters, and Muslims choose to do... sit on their ass and wait on the 10 percent to SWING the musical TREND into their direction.... This will never happen; the global stakes are too HIGH.

You see most of the sell-out rappers, the ones contracted to the 10 percent, pose no present threat to the powers that are laying out a global agenda of control and dominance. Most of these sell-out rappers were 2 cent... or 50 Cent drug dealers and murderers of the black community prior to their new and improved house Nigga roles anyway... But it seems as if the so-called conscious rappers have yet to swallow and digest the reality of the information that they themselves spit over beats...

NUMBER ONE: Unity... you get with all the conscious rappers and you discuss and agree upon a major project!

You get with studios and producers that are like minded, and you formulate a plan to set a NEW TREND! At first you CANNOT be concerned with the DOLLAR, the Dollar is a distraction, it is a carrot that is controlled by the 10 percent blood suckers, so that the rabbits will run and chase a dollar; therefore they are controlled by what they are focused on... remember, you're BROKE anyway! Make the necessary sacrifices, and those sacrifices will mathematically cause you to eventually get rich.

NUMBER TWO: Work... why talk about picking up a gun and murdering white folks when you aint even in the streets... you in a studio talking SHIT. You should take your projects and you hit the streets... you GOT to be in the STREETS like the dope dealers are in the streets, like the hoes are in the streets, like the pimps are in the streets... How in the hell can you be a Revolutionary, a Muslim, a Five Percenter, a Soldier for the cause of black people... and a god damn SUPER STARR at the SAME TIME!!? Even the PUNK POLICE is in the streets, but your conscious black ass is sitting up in a recording studio reading a god damn book; meanwhile our people are DYING!!

Get some of your homeboys to get in the streets and REP your product... invest in yourself, stop waiting on your enemy to present you to your people... present yourself... give your street soldiers t-shirt, flyers, CD singles, anything that will connect you to the black community... your true fan base!!

If you put your product in the hands of your hustling street soldiers, they will take the business from the local bootleggers. Let the bootleggers rob the 10 percent by selling that sell-out bullshit!

Give your street soldiers your product on consignment... when they return to you with either the product or the money, you give them a portion of the proceeds that will make them continue to work for you, and the cause that you represent! If we can't do this little work, please stop talking that revolutionary bullshit... you aint fooling no one but yourself. By creating your TRUE street team... you are in a very real way creating jobs for your people. You should envision stores in the hood PUSHING ALL of your products in a REAL way... why would they do that? Because they feel you and what you are trying to represent in a REAL way!

Do we recognize that it is the 10 Percenter that makes SUPER STARRs...AGAIN... do you have a problem with the SYSTEM, or do you have a PROBLEM with YOUR PLACE in the SYSTEM?!

Take your product and hit the streets... become a **ghetto superstar**... a person that is truly loved and supported by the community that you are attempting to save. Be willing to give your product away... create a fan base, a customer base... make them love you... BUT... if you are **LAZY**, then of course you will wait on your enemy!!

NUMBER THREE: Organize... get with the local colleges and their black and Hispanic organizations and start HipHop town hall meetings... start discussing the REAL issues that are impacting the black and brown communities... this will allow you the opportunity to NETWORK... this network will subsequently push your product and help you to create a fan base! By having town hall meetings, you will begin educating the masses of why they should like, appreciate, and support your type of music and art... this will start a new trend, but again... you cannot be a **LAZY** revolutionary!!

IN CONCLUSION:

All of us have to pay our bills, none of us are exempt from our personal responsibilities... but the question is—do you give a damn about your personal LEGACY... or do you spit that so-called conscious shit as just a way to get a pay check... if so, stop saying you are a conscious rapper, just say you have learned some shit, and you like rapping about it! You are not conscious; you are a RAPPER that is looking for a DEAL by using a CONSCIOUS GIMMICK!! Please think about what I've said... and remember, a mark of a TRUE SOLDIER is the ability to RISE ABOVE EMOTIONS... so don't get UPSET... let's get BUSY!

REFERENCES

Although I purposefully chose not to burden the reader with a lot of references and notes throughout my writing, **The People's Language Media Group** and this author would like to direct you to the following in order to further your research and truth pursuit. As WE desire that you obtain the maximum fruits of your efforts, TPL does not necessarily endorse in entirety the information provided by those that WE suggest that you take a look at, but WE definitely believe that the following references would be an excellent source of truth and insight...PEACE!

FINAL CALL NEWS
HTTP://WWW.FINALCALL.COM

HIROSHIMA AND NAGASAKI
HTTP://WWW.EXPLORATORIUM.EDU/NAGASAKI/MEMORIES/AMEMORY.HTML

HISTORY OF LYNCHING
WWW.MAAFA.ORG

THE TRUTH ESTABLISHMENT INSTITUTE
HTTP://WWW.TRUTHINSTITUTE.ORG/DEFAULT.HTM

RENCE.com
HTTP://WWW.RENSE.COM/

THE REBEL STORE
HTTP://WWW.REBELSTORE.ORG/
ARICASPEAKS.COM
http://www.rastafarispeaks.com/

INSTITUTE OF THE BLACK WORLD
WWW.IBW21.ORG

MATHABA NEWS AGENCY
HTTP://WWW.MATHABA.NET

INTER PRESS SERVICE NEWS AGENCY
HTTP://WWW.IPS.ORG/

PSYCHOLOGY AND RESEARCH
WWW.INFINITEMIND.COM

RADIO ISLAM
WWW.RADIOISLAM.ORG

HISTORICAL RESEARCH DEPARTMENT
WWW.BLACKSANDJEWS.COM

In addition to the above listed sites; be sure to check out these books!

MUSICK BIZNESS R.I.P.
PROFESSOR GRIFF

THE SECRET RELATIONSHIP BETWEEN BLACKS AND JEWS
HISTORICAL RESEARCH DEPARTMENT

THE ZIONIST TERROR NETWORK
MARK WEBER

IN THE PATH OF HIZBULLAH
AHMAD NIZAR HAMZEH

THE SYNAGOGE OF SATAN
ASHAHED M. MUHAMMAD

HIT MEN: POWER BROKERS AND FAST MONEY IN THE MUSIC BUSINESS
BY FREDRIC DANNEN

THE JEWISH ONSLAUGHT
TONY MARTIN

THE UGLY TRUTH ABOUT THE ADL
EXECUTIVE INTELLIGENCE REVIEW

DOPE, INC: BRITIANS'S OPIUM WAR AGAINST THE U.S.
Publisher: NEW BENJAMIN FRANKLIN HOUSE Pub. Co; 1st edition (1978)

THE SECOND PALESTINIAN INTIFADA: A CHRONICLE OF A PEOPLE'S STRUGGLE
RAMZY BAROUD

THE ETHNIC CLEANSING OF PALESTINE
ILAN PAPPE

THE SYNAGOGUE OF SATAN
ANDREW CARRINGTON HITCHOCK

THE TRANSPARENT CABAL
STEPHEN J. SNIEGOSKI

THEY DARE TO SPEAK OUT: PEOPLE AND INSTITUTIONS CONFRONT ISRAEL'S LOBBY
PAUL FINDLEY

For Information on how to purchase the above listed books and more visit:
www.thepeopleslanguage.com

AN INTERVIEW WITH PHILIP A. MUHAMMAD

This Interview was conducted by Kenneth Oden: Chairman of the University Board of Directors—California State University Northridge

KO: So, Mr. Muhammad what's good?

PM: Allah, God, the true and living, yesterday, today, and tomorrow.

KO: Most definitely, I certainly agree with that.

PM: Yes sir!

KO: Mr. Muhammad…

PM: Brother, please… just call me Brother Philip

KO: Okay Bro. Philip, I have a copy (manuscript) in my hand right now; and the thing that really gets my attention right off the jump is the books cover. This may be a silly question, but is there any special significance to the cover; I mean despite the obvious?

PM: (laughs) Well bro… that's kind of tricky; what's obvious to some may not be so obvious to others… but I do get your point. As I did the research for my book, I began to further understand that there is always so much more than what meets the eye… the so-called obvious. Like people in general, you can always see the skin or the clothes, but everyone knows that there is something deeper than that, deeper or under the cover of the proverbial fig leafs. I say fig leafs because they are used as a distraction, as a means to cover up something that an individual or group of individuals desires to be hidden. Regardless if it is good or bad, most people have something to hide; something that they don't want everybody to know.

KO: Right, right… so as for the book's cover, are you trying to hide something?

PM: (laughs) Of course not brother…not me! (smiling) The cover was designed by me to EXPOSE something that is covered up, that has not been made to be so obvious by individuals and groups; something that powerful people have spent uncountable dollars, and spent tremendous amounts of political, social, religious, and educational clout to keep a secret.

KO: And the cover exposes that?

PM: The cover itself does not expose what has been hidden by those who receive huge profit from your or my ignorance. The cover reveals to those that have something to hide; those that recognize the symbolism that comprises the book's cover, that whoever put the cover together knows at least something of that which others desire to hide… you follow me?

KO: Yeah, I feel you.

PM: okay, the cover is just that; a cover! But what it covers is information that if understood would cause us to re-VIEW the cover, and realize that the cover itself gives an indication of what is, and has been under-COVER! (Laughs)

KO: (laughs) Alright, what should I see in the book's cover; I mean, before I have a chance to read the book, what are you trying to tell a 22 year old black male from southern California?

PM: Very good, first brother... the cover has gotten your attention! That's the overall purpose and intent of the cover... to get your attention. Second, what do you see... you see a black background, black is the color of truth, and black means original because it is the essence from which all life comes; light itself can be traced within the essence of darkness, or that which is black. The UNIVERSE is black, UNI means one, and VERSE means TRUTH. There is one truth that truth is born out of darkness. The book's cover is primarily black, but between the front and back cover is a truth that if understood would begin to help some of us see the light. You got me...

KO: Yeah, that's pretty deep...

PM: After you see the blackness, you notice the seal of the United States of America, there is a huge amount of meaning behind this seal... but to be brief, it represents America and the social, political, economic, religious, and educational institutions that define the American agenda and global aspirations. This seal has been imposed upon the universal order of truth, and the justice that finds its root in that truth. America has imposed their view upon the peoples of the world, and in many ways has been successful in supplanting truth with lies. Therefore the seal is imposed upon the black background. But imposed on that seal is the Star of David, this symbol is adopted by the Zionist Jews that have an agenda that has been adopted by the government of the United States of America... hence it is red, white, and blue. Within the Star of David you find the gold HipHop Nation that is controlled by those that have chosen the flag of America, and the Star of David as their operational symbol. Gold is one of the most valuable metals in the world; but just as gold, the valuable HipHop Nation is manipulated and utilized by those of a particular type and stripe!

KO: So within this book are these claims proven?

PM: I wouldn't say proven in the context of PROOF... I would say proven in the context of irrefutable evidence that there is more to the global story than meets the eye. I would say that this book proves that those that have adopted the American global view have, at least by default, adopted the agenda of those that have adopted the Star of David. I'm not saying that everyone who operates under the banner of the American Seal or the Star of David can be proven to be associated, or endorsers of the American and Zionist agenda... what I claim is that those who endorse the American global agenda also endorse the Zionist agenda; and these people and groups use the Seal of America and the Star of David as their fig leaf! (smiles)

KO: Now, even if that is true; what does that have to do with HipHop, the music, you know... the artist?

PM: The world is made up of resources; resources have value because they are the source of those things that are necessary for the perpetuation of a healthy and well balanced life. Those individuals who desire to have power and dominion seeks to obtain and control the world's resources. The individual or group that can control and dominate the world's most valuable elements, by default control all those that have need of that which others control... you follow me?

KO: Yes...

PM: Anything of value must be controlled by those who have a serious desire for power. This control is necessary for the survival of those who have obtained power. HipHop has been proven as valuable, therefore those who wish to maintain power must control it.

KO: Why is it important to control HipHop, isn't it just music? What makes it so valuable, is it because it makes millions of dollars?

PM: In this world value has been equated with money, money is simply that which allows something of value to be transferred from one person or group to another. If money could not reap something of equal or greater value than itself, then money has no true value at all... its simply paper. This means that need, or perceived need equates value, not money. The HipHop Nation is not valuable because it merely generates revenue, or the circulation of money ... the HipHop Nation is valuable because it is comprised of valuable or needed people, people with valuable talent. The artists that make up the HipHop Nation are children of God, and their talents are God given resources certainly no less in value than other resources of the world; including, but not limited to gold, diamonds, platinum, and pearls. The talent of the HipHop artist has the potential to carry a message and information that can bring about a redistribution of power on a global scale. Those who operate from a higher level of power consciousness are aware of this; those that characterize themselves as rap artists generally seem to be ignorant of this fact.

KO: So it's more than money... its power! You don't think that most HipHop artists are aware of this?

PM: Apparently not... You might here a relative few speak about power and the redistribution of wealth; but most seem to lack awareness of their true value in relation to the national and international politic. The HipHop Nation generally misunderstands its true worth and value because it is fundamentally ignorant of the principles of wealth and power.

KO: Wealth and power?

PM: Yes, wealth and power. The signer of a contract can never be the equal of him or her who writes the contract. A signature represents that you agree to, or accept the terms of what is written in the contract. He or she who signs the contract is legally obligated to him or her who writes the contract! Of course the writer of the contract has an obligation to the signer, and there is always some sort of a mutual benefit within the context of the contract. But a mutual benefit does not necessarily mean an equal benefit! The writer of a contract looks out primarily for their own interest... the writer of a contract only offer that which is necessary to get the other person to sign it. We often hear that the devil is in the details... and he is; however, the details are not necessarily the small print that you may see at the bottom of the contract, the details are found in the reasons for the contract in the first place... the hidden reasons and motivations that cause the devil to seek you out, to have you contractually obligated to him in the first place.

KO: Are you saying that the rap artists should not sign contracts?

PM: No... what I am saying is that, in order to demonstrate true wealth and power, the HipHop Nation should be able to write the contract, and get the devil to sign it; not the other way around. When a man behind a desk can assess your talent, a talent that was bestowed upon you by your creator, not the man behind the desk, what that man offers you in exchange for the use of your talent should be in proportion to the benefit that man receives by the use of that said talent... you following me?

KO: Yes sir

PM: The details that are left out during the initial negotiation, is the detailed benefits that the man behind the desk will receive by an artist signing his or her name to a contract. When the artist is blind to his or her true value, then that artist enters into the negotiation process handicapped. As long as the artists equate value with money; paper, then the artist will receive paper, while he who writes the contract will receive the unseen benefits that dwarf whatever value we place on the paper! When the artists are ignorant of the true reasons behind the contract, the true intent or aspirations of he who has written the contract; then the artists are ignorant of themselves and what role they play within the agenda of those that will have you sign their contract. It is this reality that I attempt to relay within my book.

KO: Yes... after reading it, I admit that you certainly made that point. In the book I noticed that you really dealt with the... who you call "the so-called Jews"...
PM: Yes
KO: But within the title you call the HipHop Nation; "Willie Lynch's newest slave", yet you don't spend as much time talking about Willie Lynch as you do the "so-called Jews"...

PM: Right, allow me to approach that issue from this standpoint. Willie Lynch has created a sickness within the mind-state of black America... this sickness can be referred to as the "Willie Lynch Syndrome". Of course Sigmund Freud and his boys have not spent anytime studying or analyzing this condition; never the less, it is real. Because of the affects of Willie Lynch and the colonial slave master's, the new and improved "corporate slave master" is able to put forth his international play for power in a more effective way. The seemingly subtle manipulation of power and the human resource is only proven effective because of the mental condition that Willie helped to put black folks in. Therefore, this condition is diagnosed as what it is... and while making this diagnosis, I spend a considerable amount of time proving this condition by highlighting who is benefiting from it, how they are benefiting, and by showing what is the consequence of our inability to free ourselves from this condition.

KO: I understand that... but it seems like you are placing a lot of blame on Jewish people.

PM: No... not Jewish people! I am not blaming Jewish people at all! I am blaming "so-called Jewish people". By this I mean, there are people that go through life claiming to be something that they are actually not; they use the proverbial fig leaf to cover up who they really are. That fig leaf may be education, a nice suit, a phony smile, or even religion. This fig leaf acts as a distraction; while getting a victim or potential victim to focus on the fig leaf, the true person that is wearing the fig leaf is unleashing a subtle attack on those that are easily distracted or impressed by an outer exterior or presence. If as a society we have been conditioned into believing that the Jewish people are God's chosen, that they are divinely guided and considered special... then what is a better fig leaf than that to be used as a cover for a crooked and wicked deceiver? The enemy of truth and justice can use that fig leaf to not simply distract the people, but use this particular fig leaf to justify its nefarious ways and actions; ways and actions that are contrary to the social impression that they are attempting to make. These people that are guilty of doing this are not Jewish people, despite what they may claim or what we may believe; these people are no more Jews than the clansmen are Christian or Arab terrorists are Muslim! They are so-called Jews, and by exposing their real identity, their real purpose and agenda, the fig leaf will be seen for what it is, and their true aspirations and machinations will be exposed!

KO: After reading your book, it seems that black people have been deceived...

PM: Exactly... By using ignorant rappers to entertain the people; to make the public sing and dance, the rappers are being used as a tool of the corporate slave masters. The rappers receive dollars for their services, they believe that their duty is to make the people sing and dance... but the arch-deceivers have contracted out the rapping slaves to shuck-n-jive, and to distract the people while the slave master manipulates and creates more slaves! The bigger a clown you are, the bigger buffoon you are, the more you can be trusted not to wake the sleeping giant. Therefore, you get more money, money to spend on drugs, gold and diamond teeth, sneakers, cars, and pussy!

KO: Are you saying that wealthy rappers, rappers such as 50 cent, Jay Z, TI, Snoop, P Diddy, and others are clowns... are buffoons?

PM: The rappers that you named; among several others, are examples of the kind of subject matter that gets backed by the wealthy and powerful. These rappers themselves are not wealthy; they are rich, they have a lot of money, paper and gold! But these rappers are absolutely controlled by wealthy white men... most of whom are so-called Jews! This is the truth. What do you know these rappers as... I mean think about it... so-called gangsters, hustlers, crack dealers, pimps, killers... what images are being marketed to the youth by the corporate slave masters? You see, when you prostitute yourself for wealth and power; you have no wealth and power at all. It is the fact that you DON'T have to sell-out that shows the level of power you have. Those rappers you mentioned push bullshit down the throats of the consumers; those rappers that you mentioned receive huge amounts of paper so that they will continue to infiltrate the young impressionable minds with ways and actions of a savage and a crazed people... this is unacceptable. Regardless of the money, it is unacceptable! Their ways and actions, and their position within the master's plantations show that they are circus clowns and buffoons!

KO: Okay, if that is the truth, why do you think that these rappers continue to sell-out?

PM: Listen... our people, black people, are poverty stricken as a whole. Our people are coming up out of a physical slavery, up into a mental slavery. We want to be kings and rulers... this is because it is in our nature to be that! However, we have been made to be mental slaves, this means that we approach our collective and individual endeavors from the position of a mental slave. Since we have been stripped from the true knowledge of ourselves, we believe that we should be given something; we don't necessarily believe that we should create something. When you desire to be given something, then you approach those that have something in order to get something! You follow me...

KO: Yeah, I'm with you...

PM: Alright; if somebody has something you want, and you want them to give it to you, you must have something to offer... usually you offer what is in the best interest of he or she that has what you desire or want. This is done to entice the holder to give up what he or she has... in this case, the white boys want the rapper's talent and soul. By getting control of the rappers and their souls, they can make the rappers say and do what is in the best interest of the corporations and their power brokers, and not what is in the best interest of the rappers, and the people from which the rappers were plucked!

KO: Well if that is the case, what can the rappers do, and what can we do to change this situation?

PM: First off I would say that we have to recognize and acknowledge the fact that we are presently slaves. We must understand the situation that we are in; then we must understand how those who desire to keep us in this position maintain and sustain this position. Second, by understanding the total dynamics of the slave and slave master relationship, we can begin to loosen the grip that restricts us, and prevents us from becoming an independent people. We as black people must realize the power of not our dollars, but the power of our contributions to the economic system of America.

KO: What do you mean by that?

PM: I hear people talk about how much consumer power that black people have; that in order to change our condition we must keep our black dollars within our community... buy black, you know what I mean...? Well that's true; but, buying black, and circulating the paper dollar within our community is not wealth creation, it does not automatically generate liberation or independence! Buying black is just away to circulate paper from one person to the next... it won't have the result that we need. It's a start, but it is far from what the black community actually needs!

KO: So what do we need!

PM: We need wealth, we need control over resources; particularly our resources! If we lack land, if we lack a particular product or commodity that will generate wealth... not money, not paper... but wealth, then we will forever be slaves to those that control and dominate the world's resources. This is what I am trying to say to the HipHop Nation, your talent is a resource, the athletic talent that is found within the black nation is a resource, and it is a valuable commodity. Our problem is that we approach our talent, we understand our talent as labor, as a means to make money! We don't seem to recognize the power of our talent and the fact that it is as important and valuable as any other commodity or natural resource. By allowing others to define our individual and collective worth, they can extract the powerful elements of our presence to benefit themselves and there agenda.... WELL, what if we can recognize the power of our talent, of our presence, and utilize that talent in a way that supports our agenda.

KO: I see your point...but how?

PM: Again... it all begins with recognition. Why do outsiders choose to utilize, to contract our talent... is it for money? Not necessarily, they already have money...paper! They utilize us to push an agenda, a message... we are being used as commercials, as America's spokesmen and women.... Why!? Because the world wants to hear us, the world is amazed by our talents, by our skills, by our resilience, and by our strengths. Just as black people are amazed and enamored by gold and diamonds, the global population is awed by black people and what we have done since slavery! What the slave master has done is contracted our talent, marketed our talent, and slapped a made in America sticker on our ASS! We are being used for their purposes... for their messages.

KO: So how can we get our own message out, how can we market our own agenda?

PM: The internet is the informational super highway. At this point all we have to do is have a desire to push a new message! We have to develop the means and desire to trade our commodity to the world without the assistance of the corporate master. Now of course they have paper, and they want us to take their paper in exchange for our talent; but their paper is not worth anything, it is backed by nothing. If we begin to discipline ourselves, and reevaluate what value is... then we will begin to realize that a Benz or a Cadillac is nothing, it is small in terms of what we really need, or should want in exchange for our talent. We must stop trying to keep up with white folks in terms of their buying habits, their lifestyle, and their societal priorities. It is an allusion, we cannot compete; therefore, what if we stop trying, what if we reject the American commercials that sale a lifestyle that we clearly can't afford? Well if we do that, if we begin to change our individual and collective priorities, the slave master will be forced to re-examine their methods; thereby allowing us to see them as they are, and allowing us to make the appropriate adjustments that will secure us true liberation and independence!

KO: Thanks bro!
PM: Thank you!

Made in the USA
Middletown, DE
21 December 2014